Estanislao Severo Zeballos

Argument for the Argentine Republic

Estanislao Severo Zeballos

Argument for the Argentine Republic

ISBN/EAN: 9783337379025

Printed in Europe, USA, Canada, Australia, Japan

Cover: Foto ©ninafisch / pixelio.de

More available books at **www.hansebooks.com**

ARGUMENT

FOR THE

ARGENTINE REPUBLIC

Upon the Question with Brazil in regard to the

TERRITORY OF MISIONES,

SUBMITTED TO THE

ARBITRATION OF THE PRESIDENT OF THE UNITED STATES.

IN ACCORDANCE WITH THE TREATY OF SEPTEMBER 7, 1889.

PRESENTED BY

ESTANISLAO S. ZEBALLOS,
Envoy Extraordinary and Minister Plenipotentiary of the Argentine Republic.

ACCOMPANIED BY DOCUMENTS AND MAPS
UNDER THE TITLE OF "ARGENTINE EVIDENCE."

WASHINGTON, D. C.
1894.

GIBSON BROTHERS,
PRINTERS AND BOOKBINDERS.
WASHINGTON D. C.

PART FIRST.

IMPORTANCE OF THIS INTERNATIONAL DISPUTE.

GEOGRAPHICAL VIEW OF THE DISPUTED TERRITORY.

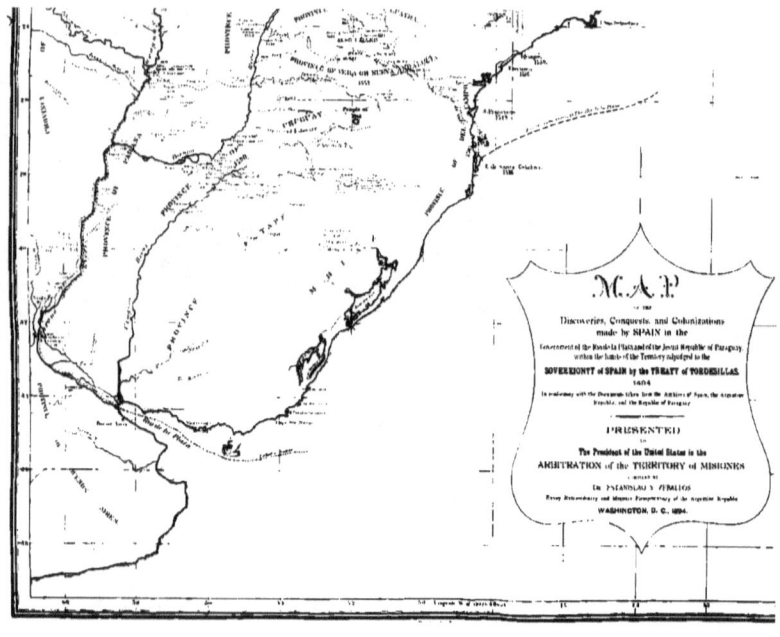

PART FIRST.

IMPORTANCE OF THIS INTERNATIONAL DISPUTE—GEOGRAPHICAL VIEW OF THE DISPUTED TERRITORY.

Mr. PRESIDENT:

The Territory which is the subject of this Arbitration is situated between 25° 35′ 17″ and 27° 09′ 37″ south latitude, and 53° 50′ 13″ and 51° 18′ 25″ longitude west of Greenwich.

Its boundaries are as follows: On the East the rivers "*San An-* Geographical situation. *tonio Guazú*" and "*Pepiry*" or "*Pequiry-Guazú*," according to the documents upon which the Argentine Republic claim is based. Brazil gives other names to these rivers: the San Antonio *Guazú* it calls "Yangada," and the Pepiry or Pequiry-*Guazú* the "Chapecó." On the West the rivers "*San Antonio Mini*" and "*Pepiry*" or "*Pequiry-Mini*," according to the same Argentine title-deeds; to which streams Brazil gives the names "*San Antonio-Guazú*" and "*Pepiry-Guazú*." The treaties of 1750 and 1777, between Spain and Portugal, referring to these boundaries, use the name "Pepiry" or "Pequiry," both applying to the same river. The map herewith gives the position of these rivers, with their double names.[1] On the North the river "*Yguazú*,"[2] an important affluent of the River Paraná; and on the South the River Uruguay.

The Argentine Republic maintains that according to these treaties Argentine rights. the boundaries are the rivers called by it "*San Antonio-Guazú*" of Oyarvide, and "*Pepiry*" or "*Pequiry-Guazú*." The Empire of Brazil recently changed these official names of the Eighteenth Century to the names "Yangada" and "Chapecó," as I have said; but the Arbitrator will note that in no document of the Sixteenth, Seventeenth or Eighteenth centuries is any mention made of these names, which

---

[1] "Mini" and "Guazú" are words of the *Guaraní* language, the native tongue of the Territory, and are adjectives qualifying the name Pepiry or Pequiry: "*Mini*" meaning "*small*," and "*Guazú*" signifying "*big*."

[2] From "Y" meaning "water," and "Guazú" "big," hence "big river," or "Rio Grande de Curitiva," as it is now called.

are arbitrarily introduced into the discussion. The claim of the Argentine Republic is based upon its written title-deeds and a possession of nearly four centuries, as I shall briefly set forth to the Arbitrator.

Territory in dispute. The Territory in dispute is called "MISIONES," and it has an area of 31,000 square kilometres, equivalent to 1,240 square leagues. Its tropical climate and the rugged nature of its surface render difficult and sometimes impossible all efforts in the way of colonization. The *Roads.* roads that unite this Territory with the more populous parts of the Argentine Republic and Brazil are still in a primitive condition, being *Cultivation.* long, difficult, and not always without danger. Agriculture and cattle raising are, under such conditions, of little importance in this Territory, and the few countrymen who work in or frequent it lead a miserable existence.

Importance of the case. The importance of the question which the President of the United States is to settle does not depend upon the present or future economic or strategic value of the Territory. Its material worth is certainly insignificant to Brazil, for that nation possesses more than 3,200,000 square miles of land, the whole or even the greater part of which it will not be able to occupy or civilize for many centuries.

Statement of the dispute. This quarrel about boundaries originated in the antagonistic relations of Spain and Portugal. The situation of this Territory, in the heart of an unknown country, gave it an undeserved importance, and it was made use of as a pretext to keep alive the rivalries growing out of questions as to the preponderance of power and frontier lines on the Map of Europe. The difference of opinion regarding it being inherited by the Argentine Republic and Brazil, the latter has always considered it more as a political than a territorial dispute. The position of the former can be stated as follows: The policy of territorial usurpation, followed with tenacity during four centuries by the Crown of Portugal against Spain, and continued by the Empire of Brazil after the Emancipation against the Republics of Argentina, Uruguay, Bolivia, Paraguay and others, should be definitively restrained within the limits fixed by solemn treaties, thus eliminating all reasons for uncertainty or alarm that might paralyze the progress of Civilization in that part of the New World.

Means of solution. There were three ways of settling this question: war, direct negotiation and arbitration. All of these three methods have, in less than a century, been put into practice.

War of 1825. The Argentine Republic was obliged in 1825, soon after South-American Independence became a fact and the Empire of Brazil was established, to oppose by its arms Brazilian aggressions, when that country attempted to take possession of a part of the territory belonging to the Vice-Royalty of Buenos Ayres, situated on the eastern shore of the mouth of the Rio de la Plata, in order to divide with the growing Argentine Republic the control of that immense estuary, just as the King of Portugal had fruitlessly attempted to do from the time of Charles V.

This aggression by the Brazilian Empire was defeated at the battle of *Ytuzaingo* on the 20th of February, 1827, and the country invaded by its arms was evacuated. This territory was an old Spanish Province, under the jurisdiction of Buenos Ayres; but as a consequence of this war, and under the generous protection of the victorious Argentine armies, it became the new Republic which took the name of the "Oriental del Uruguay."

After this unsuccessful military attempt, Brazil was occupied in discussing its assertions in regard to the frontiers of Venezuela, Colombia, Ecuador, Peru, Bolivia, Paraguay and the Republic of Uruguay itself, all along the immense arc described by its possessions, from the Orinoco to the Rio de la Plata; but it did not attempt to again advance into the Argentine territory. Recent pretensions of Brazil.

The Argentine Republic from 1862 to 1880 passed through one of the most acute political crises of its History, being divided during this period into two parties. The powerful, wealthy and leading state of Buenos Ayres made sometimes armed and sometimes pacific opposition to the influences directing national politics which prevailed in the thirteen other provinces of the littoral and interior of the Republic. For some time the national sovereignty was divided by the separation of the state of Buenos Ayres from the Nation. This long and painful struggle, which was aggravated in every presidential campaign, came to an end in 1880 by Buenos Ayres being chosen as the permanent capital of the Republic. During the dark days of this period of anarchy the Empire of Brazil attempted to secure advantages and to advance its military lines nearer the limits of the region now in dispute. The Argentine government protested against these proceedings, and, as will be shown in the proper place, took active measures to protect its interests. In reply to its protests Brazil answered *that it had not intended to occupy the Territory in dispute, adding that its newly decreed settlements were situated outside of this Territory.* Argentine claims and acts Brazil makes satisfactory explanations.

The policy of the Empire was always distrustful and sometimes hostile in its relations with the neighboring republics of the Rio de Hostility of the Brazilian monarchy against the republics of the Rio de la Plata.

la Plata. The most eminent statesmen of the Empire were anxious to extend its frontiers into the republics of Uruguay and Paraguay, and they attained their object by means of arrangements in regard to boundaries, to which these countries always submitted, notwithstanding the clearness of their rights, on account of their deplorable internal situation, arising in the case of the former from successive dictatorships, and in that of the latter out of its civil wars. The advance of the Empire towards the South and West had for its object to get nearer the control of the Rio de la Plata and its great affluents the Paraná and the Uruguay, which Portugal had not succeeded during the past centuries in separating from the possessions of Spain, notwithstanding her constant desire and attempts to do so.

The Empire advances upon Uruguay and Paraguay.

This policy was based upon the fact that Brazil had inland provinces whose communications with the Atlantic Ocean by means of overland roads were long, difficult and sometimes impracticable, while the only relatively convenient outlets were the Argentine rivers, the Paraná, Uruguay, Rio de la Plata and Paraguay.

Free navigation of the rivers.

The dictatorship of Rozas, which dominated the Argentine Republic for twenty years, down to 1852, had closed those rivers to general free navigation, and this precedent was seized upon as a pretext by the politicians of the Empire; but the Argentine people struggled during this bloody period of their history to overthrow the Dictator, in the name of those guiding principles which govern their destinies to this day. They sought the alliance of the Republic of Uruguay, and even of the Empire, in order to hasten the downfall of the Dictatorship, and after accomplishing this at the battle of Caseros, on the third of February, 1852, the free navigation of these rivers was proclaimed by the Argentine Congress, and set forth in the treaty of July 10, 1853, entered into between the Argentine Republic and the United States of America. The Brazilian policy could not thenceforth, with any reason, devote its attention to this important interest.

Fugitive slaves.

Finally, slavery was always a cause for suspicion and discussion between these adjoining countries. The slaves that escaped from Brazil and took refuge either in the Argentine Republic or Uruguay were *ipso facto* free, being protected by the respective constitutions of those countries. The politicians of the Empire often endeavored to negotiate their surrender, and urged by the leaders of the nobility and the planters even endeavored to wrest from the republics of the Rio de la Plata treaties providing for the imprisonment and extradition of such slaves, although contrary to their Constitutions and to the principles of Liberty and Humanity which they had proclaimed with their Independence.

The imperial policy was therefore a constant source of apprehension, sometimes exaggerated, along the Rio de la Plata, where the Emperor, Dom Pedro II, was looked upon with favor, although his most eminent counsellors were, and sometimes with very good reasons, regarded with positive distrust. The downfall of the Empire and the proclamation of the Republic, which occurred on the 15th of November, 1889, in the city of Rio de Janeiro, were greeted by the neighboring countries bordering on the Rio de la Plata as the advent of a new era of peace and international fraternity. These anticipations were confirmed a few days after that memorable date, for the first important act of the Brazilian Republic was to extend to its sister republics of the Rio de la Plata a solemn assurance of its political sincerity and its eagerness to close the era of distrust and international armaments. This initiatory movement, conceived and unanimously carried out by the body of notables who were then at the head of the first republican government, to proclaim the new purposes of Brazil's frank and friendly foreign policy, had in view the settlement of one of the oldest and most vexed questions,—the boundary dispute with the Argentine Republic. Downfall of the Empire.
The Brazilian Republic repudiates the foreign policy of the Monarchy

This contest concerning part of the Territory of Misiones not only disturbed the pacific relations between Argentines and Brazilians, but also, in an indirect way, the tranquillity and future of the republics of Uruguay, Paraguay, and Bolivia, united in a common destiny with the welfare of the countries engaged in this dispute. In order to bring about international harmony and incorporate the Republic of Brazil in the family of its neighboring sister countries, under the sacred auspices of political fraternity and humanity, the Government of Brazil proposed to that of Argentine that the Misiones question should be settled by the division of that Territory in an equitable manner. This was the origin of the treaty of Montevideo, signed on the thirtieth day of January, 1890, which I present to the Arbitrator, together with the map upon which the military engineers of both nations traced the boundary agreed upon in that very document by which the Plenipotentiaries sealed the arrangement. The Republican Government proposes to fraternally settle the boundary question with the Argentine Republic.
Equitable division of the Territory.

The Argentine Republic based its right to and its possession of the disputed Territory upon decisive documents and on unquestionable possessory acts. It however took into consideration the basis of settlement proposed by the republican government of Brazil, because Reasons for the attitude of the Argentine Republic in this case

<small>Argentine foreign policy.</small> this spontaneous initiative of that country eloquently condemned the traditional policy of the Empire, preferring a noble and stable peace to the small territorial advantages of the past. The Argentine Republic, although well armed and powerful, with an energetic and warlike character that distinguishes it in South America, has always directed its foreign relations towards the beneficent paths of conciliation and good faith, honoring thus the sacred interests of Civilization and Humanity, as far as this policy was consistent with its national dignity and the integrity of its territory. The agreement with the Republic of Brazil was in perfect harmony with these antecedents, and in giving up a few square kilometres of territory, the title to which was perfectly assured, the Argentine Republic made a sacrifice which confirmed the good faith of its foreign policy, in homage to Peace, which is so essential for the consolidation of the nations of South America, in order that they may perfect their institutions and attract European immigration.[1]

<small>Solemnities attending the Treaty of 1890.</small> To give to this conciliatory course the solemnity which was due to its hoped-for civilizing influence upon the destinies of South America, the State Departments of both countries arranged for the following formalities. The Ministers of Foreign Affairs of the Argentine and Brazilian Republics respectively, Doctor Don Estanislao S. Zeballos for the former, and Don Quintino Bocayuva for the latter, agreed to meet on neutral soil in order to negotiate and sign the treaty by which the Territory of Misiones was to be divided, and chose for <small>Meeting of the Foreign Ministers of both nations in a Neutral country.</small> this purpose the City of Montevideo, the Capital of the Republic of Uruguay. They arrived there escorted by the naval squadrons that had been purchased during the period of mutual distrust which the imperial policy excited, and which was now to be dissipated by this arrangement.

<small>The treaty is signed in the Government Mansion, Uruguay.</small> The treaty and the map showing the division of the Territory were signed in the Government Mansion of the Republic of Uruguay on the 30th of January, 1890. The President of the Republic of Uruguay <small>The government of Uruguay celebrates the event with public formalities.</small> awaited the plenipotentiaries in a hall adjacent to the place where their sessions were held, welcomed them in the presence of his entire Cabinet, and invited them to an official banquet to be given by him, in the name of his country, to commemorate this happy international event. The banquet took place at the Government Mansion at Monte-

---

[1] The Argentine Republic, next to the United States, receives the greatest number of immigrants of any country. In the year 1889 they aggregated 295,000 persons.

video, the representatives of foreign countries being present, among them the Minister of the United States. The Government of Uruguay signified by these acts that the policy followed by the two great Republics of Argentine and Brazil was deemed an augury of confidence and peace for its own country.

The Minister of Foreign Affairs of Brazil immediately afterwards visited the Argentine Republic in order to proclaim the lasting friendship of these two nations, that had so long been embroiled in unreasonable quarrels. The Argentine people, represented by honorable Commissioners, coined medals in commemoration of the proclamation of the Republic in Brazil and of the frank friendship now sealed with Argentine. The Minister of Brazil visits the Argentine Republic. A medal coined in his honor.

The Brazilian Minister returned to his country and explained the treaty to the Government Council which had sent him to negotiate it, and his acts and the document itself received unanimous approval at a full session of the Council, as will be shown in due time. The Brazilian Government approves the treaty of Montevideo.

Thus was adopted a new policy between the ardent nations of South America, of which the Plenipotentiary who subscribes this paper can speak with propriety, for he had the honor to contribute to its initiation and its support, in his double character as the Argentine Minister of Foreign Affairs during the boundary dispute with Brazil and also with Chile, and as one of the signers of the treaty of Montevideo. This treaty declared that a frank and fraternal negotiation was the best means of adjusting differences between countries united in the past, possessing identical institutions and the same humane ideals of Peace, Liberty and Labor. This was a policy even more advanced than that of Arbitration itself for the solution of international questions, since, being founded on the reciprocal sympathy of nations, it avoided the resentments which naturally follow the decision of another Power, where there must always be a victorious and a vanquished party. New South American policy thus initiated. Negotiation as a solution for international questions.

Unfortunately the Republic of Brazil could not overcome the difficulties attending this period of transition, and the government which had been formed in the first days of spontaneous, sincere and patriotic enthusiasm, was overthrown by the effervescence of personal ambitions and irreconcilable interests, and by reason of the lack of preparation of the masses for free government, misled by new politicians and the preponderant influence of the military class, which absorbed and dominated the situation. The Republic soon degenerated into a Military Dictatorship, and the republicans who had overthrown the Empire after thirty years of a glorious written and verbal propaganda, being Disturbances in Brazil. Overthrow of the first Government. Military Dictatorship.

divided and undisciplined, were unable to re-establish institutional system, and also incapable of avoiding a new rising by the powerful imperialist party. Favored by the condition of anarchy which existed, this party gained a majority in the Congress called by the first free government after the expulsion of Dom Pedro II.

Monarchists attack the treaty with Argentine and allege the republicans are responsible for its signature.
Scarcely had this Congress assembled when all the ex-ministers of the Empire appeared simultaneously in the Brazilian Press, unfurling as a flag of war against the Republic the fraternal treaty of Montevideo. Their most eloquent argument was: " The Republic did this wrong in the most flagrant manner. It shall never be overlooked or extenuated. History will severely condemn it." [1] But the Empire had also proposed, as will be seen further on, a similar arrangement, which, however, was not carried out by the Imperial statesmen, because they often changed the course of their foreign policy, subordinating international questions to the tactics required in their internal struggles. On the other hand, the traditional tendencies of the Empire were incompatible with the republican institutions set up in Rio de Janeiro by the Government of November, 1889, whose brief foreign policy was high-minded without petulance, and honest without weakness.

The Monarchical majority of the House of Deputies rejects the Treaty with Argentine.
The ex-servants of the Empire having attracted to their ranks some prominent military men, always ready to foment international difficulties, the imperialist majority of the House of Deputies rejected the solemn Treaty of Montevideo. But this very important event only indicated the course of affairs, and this blow given to the most noble and humane act of the republicans was followed by other domestic events which alarmed the dictatorship. Fearing that the Congress would drag it over too dangerous roads, that body was dissolved by a *Coup d'état.*

Dictatorship dissolves the Congress.

Republican opinion favorable to the Treaty.
When I visited Rio de Janeiro on my way to Washington, I had occasion to notice that the republicans of most influence in Brazil were still convinced that the Treaty of Montevideo was for Brazil the best solution of the existing difficulties, because it established a permanent policy of peace and progress between the two Nations. But the Dictatorship has not had the necessary moral support to negotiate a new arrangement, although it desired to do so and its Plenipotentiary in the Argentine Republic attempted to raise the

Moral weakness of the Dictatorship. Its attempt to arrange the question.

---

[1] Barão de Ladario, ex-Minister of Marine under the Empire. "Argentine Evidence," work entitled, "A Questão de Missões," p. vii.

question in 1891. The Government of my country, however, naturally received this proposition with some reserve, declaring that it preferred to submit the case to Arbitration, on account of confidence in its rights and also of the uncertain condition of internal affairs in Brazil.

Therefore the question which comes before the Arbitrator is in its nature an eminently political one, between the irreconcilable tendencies of traditional imperialists and modern republicans. The Dictatorship itself has twice been obliged to accredit before the Arbitrator representatives chosen from among prominent persons of the *Imperialist Party*, who still remained faithful to their political traditions after the downfall of the Empire.[1]

<small>Precedent for the Arbitrator.</small>

The arrangement, therefore, initiated and signed by the first republican Government, condemns the policy followed by the Empire in this boundary question, and corroborates, as a precedent of capital importance, this statement which I have the honor to submit to the Arbitrator, as an introduction to my Argument, to show the true significance of the dispute submitted to his decision.

[1] Baron Aguiar d'Andrada, who unfortunately died last year in the United States, was the Minister sent by Brazil to Buenos Aires in 1879, in order to sustain the policy of the Brazilian Empire against Argentine territory. The Baron de Rio Branco, the present representative of Brazil, is the son of the most celebrated diplomat of the Empire, and has himself served for many years in the imperial diplomatic corps.

PART SECOND.

I.

POSSESSION AND JURISDICTION OF SPAIN IN THE TERRITORY SUBMITTED TO THE ARBITRATOR.
1500—1810.

II.

POSSESSION AND JURISDICTION OF THE ARGENTINE REPUBLIC IN THE TERRITORY SUBMITTED TO THE ARBITRATOR.
1810- 1893.

PART SECOND.

I.

POSSESSION AND JURISDICTION OF SPAIN IN THE TERRITORY SUBMITTED TO THE ARBITRATOR.

1500–1810.

The Discovery of America gave a definite form to the rivalry between the two great discovering countries of the fifteenth century, whose navigators heroically explored the *Mare Tenebrosum* of the tragedy of Seneca and the legends of *Thule*. The great geographical problem at the end of that century was the exploration of the routes to the Indies and the countries there. Spaniards and Portuguese undertook this object simultaneously, and thus conflicts of sovereignty originated which disturbed the relations between the two Crowns. The Pope acted as mediator between the Christian Powers in that age, especially in quarrels arising out of the boundaries of their discoveries. This feature of the Public Law of that epoch rested upon the supreme authority of the papal decisions or arbitrations; and from 1454 down the Pope had delivered opinions concerning the special matter of the discoveries and conquests made on the coasts of Africa and the islands of the Ocean. *Rivalry between Spain and Portugal. Intervention of the Pope.*

In conformity with these international precedents, Pope Alexander VI intervened in the dissatisfaction shown by Portugal after America was discovered by Spain. The former country alleged that the latter was invading regions subject to its sovereignty by previous discoveries. Alexander VI, in the Papal Bull of May 3, 1493, confirmed the possessions taken in America by Christopher Columbus in the name of the Sovereigns of Spain, authorizing them to continue their discoveries and conquests in the Islands and on *Terra Firma*. But the Bull of May 3d was a mere declaration of rights in favor of Spain. Analogous pontifical documents, previously promulgated, favored the Crown of Portugal over the immense and unknown field of the seas and lands which were the object of these discoveries and rivalries. It was there- *Bull of Alexander VI May 3, 1493. Bull of May 4th, 1493, tracing the boundaries of the sovereignties of the two Crowns.*

fore necessary to trace a positive boundary of the authority of both sovereignties, and Alexander VI put forth on the 4th of May of the same year one of the most noteworthy political documents in the annals of International Law and Geography. This was the Papal Bull dividing the dominion of the Globe between the Crowns of Spain and Portugal by means of an arc of a great circle, which was from that time called the "*Meridian of Demarcation.*"[1]

The Meridian traced on the "Mapa Mundi" This line was for a long time the subject of controversy, because the Pope had not given exact references by which to locate it, and also because the geodetical skill of that period did not afford the greatest precision in tracing its course. In later times this operation has been attended with no difficulties. The *Meridian of Demarcation* has in fact been studied and traced by many modern scientific authorities, but I will only mention two, who by reason of their high character and independence in regard to American questions deserve entire confidence. I refer to "*The Academy of Sciences*" *of France* and to the celebrated English historical institution, "*The Hakluyt Society.*" In volume LXXXI of its library, entitled "*Works issued by the Hakluyt Society,*" and devoted to the "*Conquest of the River Plate,*"[2] there is a historical map of South America that contains a most scrupulous delineation of the celebrated line of division. The lack of technical clearness in the Papal Bull was the origin of the first boundary question between Spain and Portugal. It was, in fact, necessary to determine the exact situation of the point in the Azores Islands through which the Meridian should pass. It was not even known which one of this group of Islands, extending over a large region in the Atlantic Ocean,

Insufficiency of the Bull.

Treaty of Tordesillas, June 7, 1494. ought to be selected in order to locate the point of reference. But the difficulty was amicably settled by the two Crowns by means of a treaty, no less memorable and important to Hispano-Portuguese America than the Papal Bull. This Treaty was signed at *Tordesillas* on the 7th of June, 1494. The document[3] furnished the geographical data prerequisite to tracing the line of demarcation and augmented

---

[1] In "*Argentine Evidence*" I have the honor to present to the Arbitrator a translation of the Papal Bull of May 4, 1493, although it is a very well-known document. (See Vol. I, p. 9.)

[2] I have the honor to present to the Arbitrator among the books of the "Argentine Evidence" a copy of this work, entitled: "Works issued by the Hakluyt Society. The Conquest of the River Plate. No. LXXXI. London. Printed for the Hakluyt Society, 1891."

[3] I present to the Arbitrator in the "Argentine Evidence," a translation of the Treaty of Tordesillas, Vol. I, page 13.

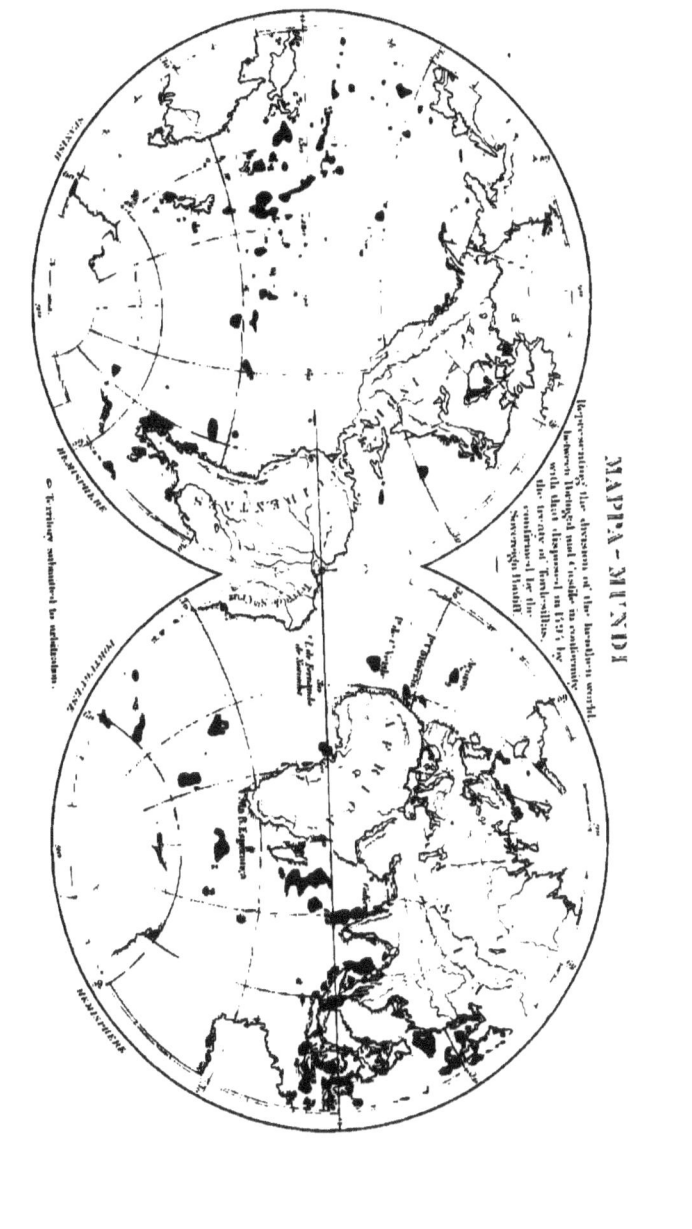

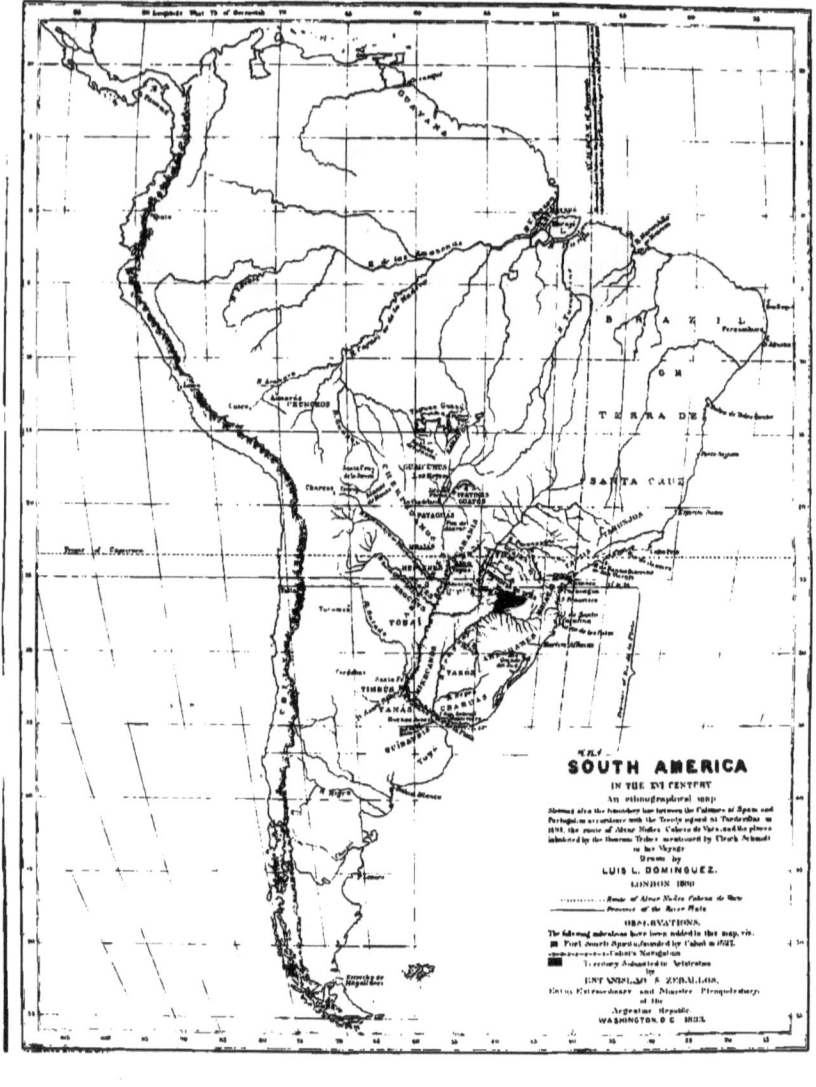

the area of the territory granted to Portugal by Pope Alexander VI. In the book published by the *Hakluyt Society*, which I have the honor to present, may be read the following commentary upon the Bull and regarding the Treaty of *Tordesillas*, page XXI:

<small>Modifications of the Bull of May 4, 1493, by Treaty of Tordesillas.</small>

When speaking or writing of the conquest of America, it is generally believed that the only title upon which were based the conquests of Spain and Portugal was the famous Papal Bull of Partition of the Ocean, of 1493. Few modern authors take into consideration that this Bull was amended, upon the petition of the King of Portugal, by the above-mentioned Treaty, signed by both Powers in 1494, augmenting the portion assigned to the Portuguese in the partition made between them of the Continent of America. The arc of meridian fixed by this treaty as a dividing line, which gave rise, owing to the ignorance of that age, to so many diplomatic Congresses and interminable controversies, may now be traced by any student of elementary mathematics. This line is shown on the accompanying map, and runs along the meridian of 47° 32′ 56″ west of Greenwich. The coast of the South American Continent between the equator and the vicinity of the Tropic of Capricorn describes a great curve, closed on the west by the aforesaid dividing line, which enters the sea a little south of San Vicente, or Santos. *West of this line were the Spanish possessions.*

The diplomatic and official historian of Brazil, A. de Varnhagen, Visconde do Porto Seguro, confirms this explanation in his work which I present to the Arbitrator. He has published the accompanying map of the division of the World between the two Crowns, which I reproduce, putting in English the annotations.[1] He also comments upon the Treaty of Tordesillas, saying that Portugal gained a zone 270 leagues wide in addition to the dominions conceded to that country by the Bull of Alexander VI. These are his own words:

<small>Brazil officially recognizes these facts.</small>

The meridian of demarcation was carried much further to the west. It was agreed that it should pass 370 leagues to the eastward of the Cape Verde Archipelago, and not, as had been proclaimed by the Papal Bull of the previous year, at a distance of 100 leagues from this Archipelago and from the Azores, so that this latter was situated, as compared with the former, in longitude much further west.

The same map of the *Hakluyt Society*, already presented, shows the position of the Territory submitted to this Arbitration. It was part

<small>The Territory submitted to Arbitration</small>

---

[1] *La Historia Geral do Brazil*, volume I, page 68.

<small>The Bull and the Treaty of Tordesillas.</small> of the unexplored central region, which, according to the Bull of May 4, 1493, and the Treaty of Tordesillas, belonged to Spain.

<small>Juridical character of this demarcation, according to official Brazilian publications.</small> Brazilian statesmen have affirmed with entire unanimity, the juridical character of the pontifical demarcation, confirmed by the Treaty of Tordesillas. I will quote, in corroboration of this fact, only one of the highest Brazilian authorities, who stands, in the opinion of contemporaneous critics, the first of all. I allude to the writings of the celebrated Statesman, Diplomat and Historian, the above named Visconde do Porto Seguro, commissioned by the government under the Brazilian Empire to study in European archives the questions relating to Brazilian boundaries with the Republics of Uruguay, Argentine, Paraguay, Bolivia, Peru, Ecuador, Colombia, Venezuela and French Guiana.

<small>Occupation subordinate to Right.</small> According to his language the fact of conquest remained subordinate to the Rights recognized by solemn treaties. The lands that Spain and Portugal subdued by their arms, amidst unknown regions and between uncertain limits, did not belong to either of these countries by the mere fact of occupation. They must also be located in that part of the World which belonged to them respectively according to the dividing line of the Treaty of Tordesillas. Even the fact of the discovery and conquest of desert regions, situated in the interior of the already existing Spanish sovereignties, could not modify the Treaty of Tordesillas, for that was the supreme law governing Spain and Portugal in these matters. This is the Brazilian doctrine, stated by the aforesaid Diplomat, in an official publication of the Brazilian Empire:

> Thus this legacy, that embraced a great part of the territory of the present Empire of Brazil, still unknown to Europeans, belonged to Portugal, *not by virtue of what is called the right of conquest or of discovery, equivalent to that of the first occupant, but by virtue of a solemn treaty, made with the nation that discovered the West Indies, and sanctioned by the Pope, who settled all differences between the Christian Powers of Europe, not yet divided by schisms and heresies.*[1]

<small>Modern principles of International Public Law.</small> This is also the modern doctrine of International Public Law, universally accepted and obeyed. The circumstance that a territory

---

[1] *General History of Brazil before its Independence and Separation from Portugal;* by the Visconde de Porto Seguro, of Sorocaba. 2d edition, greatly augmented and improved by the Author. Volume I, page 69 (Rio de Janerio, E. & H. Laemmert, 66 rue d'Ouvidor). Presented to the Arbitrator among the books of the "Argentine Evidence." Two volumes in Portuguese.

remains unknown or uninhabited within one sovereignty, does not authorize its occupation by another.

Portugal obtained by the Treaty of Tordesillas part of the American coast situated upon the Atlantic and cut by the Equator; but it was at first ignorant of this, and its vessels did not sail towards the New World until the year 1500, when one of the discoverers on his way to India was accidentally driven by irresistible currents to the Main Land, now the Brazilian coast. Spain, on the contrary, occupied a part of this territory, and instead of taking advantage of the ignorance of Portugal, receded towards Panama in order to confine itself strictly within the agreed limits. The Visconde de Porto Seguro, cited above, recognized the integrity with which Spain respected the Treaty of Tordesillas. These are his words, referring to the ignorance of Portugal as to American matters, and the casual discovery of Brazil: *Spain gives the first example of obedience.* *Brazilian statesman recognize this integrity.*

How and when Portugal was informed of the existence of the legacy to which, a few years before, it became entitled by the testamentary treaty of Tordesillas; how Portugal paid no attention to this at first nor to the benefit it obtained through it, and finally how, amidst many vicissitudes (including wars with the countries that, like itself, were most occupied in colonization since the 16th Century and later, *ie.* Spain, France, England and Holland), Portugal saw a new empire, whose destiny was to figure among the nations of the world under the government of one of the most important dynasties of our times, arise in the extensive territory embraced by this legacy—such is the purpose of the present history.

Portugal only knew of the existence of the great territory it was entitled to according to the Treaty of Tordesillas, in 1500, six years after the treaty. Continuing its efforts to find a route to India by doubling the southern extremity of Africa, it at last saw the solution of this problem when Vasco da Gama arrived at Calecut, in 1498. Thus was proved the possibility of carrying on the spice trade from the Indian Ocean by another route than that of Egypt. In order to secure this trade in favor of Portugal, by establishing factories, a squadron of 13 ships, commissioned by private merchants, but all under the command of Don Pedro Alvares Cabral, a man of illustrious birth, although not yet famous for anything which he had done, sailed from the Tagus on the 9th of March, 1500. In the written instructions which he received, some of the most important fragments of which have fortunately come to our hands, it was recommended that they should get as far away as possible from the coast of Africa, in the latitude of Guinea, in order to avoid there the most tedious and wearisome calms. Obeying these instructions, which had been inserted under the advice of Vasco da Gama, they deviated from the African coast and naturally impelled by the ocean or pelagic currents, after sailing for more than forty days, on the 22d of April sighted in the West an unknown land.[1]

Origin of the possession and jurisdiction of Spain.

The Treaty of Tordesillas cleared the way for Spanish and Portuguese discoverers and conquerors; and South America was at once overrun by officials of the former Nation by way of the Isthmus of Panama, along the coasts of the North and South Atlantic, as well as of the Pacific Ocean. Portugal never made any opposition to this enclosing movement of the Spanish conquests, which was soon to subject to the arms of Spain and open to its colonizers the greater part of South America.

Discovery of the Rio de la Plata in 1516.

The Chief Pilot of Spain, Juan Dias de Solis, discovered the Rio de la Plata in 1516, and was killed by the Indians on its bank after taking possession of that country. His companions brought news of this event to the Metropolis, and in 1528 the Emperor Charles V. dispatched one of his navigators, named Diego Garcia, to confirm the possession taken by Solis and proceed with the conquest of this new land. When Garcia reached the place where Solis had died he was informed that a year before, in 1527, Sebastian Cabot, another of Spain's royal pilots, who had been commissioned to seek a route to India, had altered his course and penetrated into the Rio de la Plata. And in fact Cabot navigated that great estuary, sailing up its principal tributary called the Paraná as far as its junction with the river Paraguay, which he explored as far up as *Angostura*, a place near the present city of Asuncion, the capital of Paraguay.[2]

Occupation of its Territory in 1527.

First occupation of what is now the Argentine Republic.

Cabot sailed back to Europe after having solemnly confirmed, in the name of the King and in accordance with the Treaty of Tordesillas, the occupation by Spain of the country now covered by the Republics of Argentine, Uruguay and Paraguay. In order to maintain this jurisdiction and extend it, he established on the Rio Paraná the fort of *Sancti Spiritus*, near the present city of Rosario.[3] But this locality was too far from the sea-coast and it was necessary to get nearer the natural route of communication with Europe. Consequently the Spaniards decided to abandon this fort for a time and to proceed to the

Abandonment of "Sancti Spiritus" and foundation of the fort of "Ygnay."

---

[1] Work cited above, volume 1, pages 70 and 71. Presented among the books of "Argentine Evidence."

[2] See accompanying map of the "Hakluyt Society," page 18 of this Argument. Cabot's voyage in the interior of America is marked with a line of red crosses.

[3] See same map, marked in red.

Atlantic coast, in order to found there a city that might serve as a port of refuge for trans-oceanic navigation, as well as a base from which to undertake the conquest and colonization of the Rio de la Plata. This was the origin of the fort of "*Yguapé*," situated on the coast, which now belongs to Brazil, owing to a generous cession made by Spain to Portugal.[1] In the erudite *Introduction* to the work of the "*Hakluyt Society*," presented to the Arbitrator, we read:

When Cabot returned to Spain in 1530, and told of the pieces of silver he had seen among the Indians of the Chaco, the King of Portugal sent Martin Affonso de Souza to establish himself in the extreme south of his possessions in Brazil; and this Portuguese captain, after examining the coast of the ocean as far as the entrance of the Rio de la Plata, founded at the close of the year 1531, in the island of San Vicente, the first regular colony on that coast, where now stands the little city of Santos.

The vicinity of these two rival colonies — the much smaller Spanish one of *Yguapé*,[2] and the stronger Portuguese one in *San Vicente*—endangered the peaceful and tranquil possession of those lands; and for this reason the Spanish Government resolved on sending immediately a formal expedition which should permanently occupy the north of the territory belonging to it, according to the above-mentioned treaty, on that coast. This expedition was placed under the orders of the first Adelantado and Captain-General of the province of Rio de la Plata, Don Pedro de Mendoza.[3]

The Portuguese Governor of the colony of San Vicente, the most southern possession of Portugal in South America, made the first attempt at usurpation in the valley of the Rio de la Plata, crossing the meridian of demarcation according to the Papal Bull and the line of the Treaty of Tordesillas. He in fact reached that river and pretended to found a Portuguese settlement in the very heart of the territorial sovereignty of Spain. The Emperor Charles V. had ordered his Embassador in Lisbon to ask for an explanation concerning the object of the expedition which had left Portugal for Brazil under the orders of the Governor, Martin Affonso de Souza, and the King of Portugal answered that this Armada should respect the Meridian of Demarcation in America. When the Emperor was informed, however, that notwithstanding this previous explanation, the Portuguese navigator had

Violation of the line of Alexander VI, and the Treaty of Tordesillas by the Portuguese.

Intimation by Emperor Charles V to the King of Portugal.

---
[1] See map of the *Hakluyt Society*, page 18, Atlantic coast.
[2] The same map.
[3] *Conquest of the River Plate*, Introduction, page XV to XVIII, work of the *Hakluyt Society* presented in the Argentine Evidence.

pretended to occupy the valley of the Rio de la Plata in the name of his Government, he directed his Minister in Lisbon, Don Lope Hurtado de Mendoza, to require of his most serene Majesty, the King of Portugal, that none "*of his armadas or captains should enter the rivers de Solis or la Plata, Paraná, or Uruguay, nor go inland, . . . and that if any of them had entered the aforesaid rivers or lands, or were they actually there, he should immediately send orders and provide for their leaving without excuse or delay.*" [1]

<small>Foundation of Buenos Ayres and first Government of the Rio de la Plata.</small> The Emperor Charles V being resolved to hasten the settlement of the Rio de la Plata country, and to oppose his forces to those of the Portuguese Governors of Brazil, entered into an agreement with Don Pedro de Mendoza on the 21st of May, 1534, appointing him "Adelantado" and Captain-General of the Rio de la Plata, and charged him with the discovery of new lands and the establishment of colonies in this temperate region of South America, from the coast of the Atlantic to the Pacific Ocean, or Southern Sea, as it was then called. The boundaries given in this contract have been traced in red by the "Hakluyt Society" upon its map, which is universally accepted as authoritative. Don Pedro de Mendoza arrived in the Rio de la Plata with a fleet of sixteen vessels and one thousand persons at the end of the summer of 1536, and founded the city of Buenos Ayres on the right bank of the great estuary, under the jurisdiction of which were immense regions of South America, and in the interior of which is situated the Territory in dispute. Mendoza immediately dispatched an expedition under the orders of <small>Mendoza occupies South America from the Plata to 20° south latitude.</small> Captain Juan de Ayolas, with the object of navigating up the rivers Paraná and Paraguay, and it went as far as 20° of south latitude; that is to say, North of the limits fixed in the contract with the Adelantado, but still within the sovereignty of Spain. All the way up he proclaimed the authority of the Emperor Charles V until he reached the line of demarcation on the East, and he also penetrated into the immense tropical deserts of the West, in compliance with the orders of the Adelantado, who had instructed him to communicate with the Spaniards of Peru, on the other side of the Continent.

The Territory now submitted to the Arbitrator was thus incorporated by Ayolas under the jurisdiction of the Adelantado and Captain-General of the Rio de la Plata, established in Buenos Ayres, where it rightly belonged according to the Bull of 1493 and

---

[1] "*Historia del Puerto de Buenos Ayres,*" by Eduardo Madero, etc., Buenos Ayres, 1892, page 89. This book is one of the printed works collected in the "Argentine Evidence," and presented to the Arbitrator.

the treaty of 1494, by which it became subject to the Crown of Spain. The historical map of the *Hakluyt Society* demonstrates that this Territory was in fact situated within the boundaries traced by the Emperor in his agreement with Mendoza. The latter, being seriously ill, delegated his command in 1537 to Ayolas, the valiant chief of his vanguard, and went back to Spain. But Ayolas did not reappear after he had penetrated into the immense solitudes of the central portion of the Continent,[1] and it was only years afterward that the news was received of the fatal end of himself and his companions in arms. _{Mendoza delegates his command to Ayolas.}

While Mendoza's soldiers were laying the foundations of civilization in the basin of the Rio de la Plata and in the vast territory which was afterwards divided between the republics of Argentine, Brazil, Uruguay, Paraguay, Bolivia, Chile, and part of Peru, the Emperor Charles V made a new contract ["*Capitulacion*"] with Don Gregorio de Pesquera Rosa, by which he was to go forth and occupy the country situated North of Mendoza's possessions on the Atlantic coast, bounded on the East by the line of demarcation of the Treaty of Tordesillas, and one hundred leagues in width. This document, signed on the 21st of August, 1526, said: _{Agreement with Pesquera Rosa in 1537}

> Firstly: We grant you permission and authority, to you, the said Gregorio de Pesquera Rosa, or whoever may hold your power of attorney, to produce the said spices within fifty leagues from the said coast of the Rio de la Plata and one hundred leagues inland, beginning at the place known as *La Cananea* towards the river Santa Catalina.[2]

The consequence of this act was that Charles V strengthened the forts of *Cananea* and *Yguapé*, founded some years before, and advanced his possessions as far as the very confines of the Portuguese Government of San Vicente.[3] _{Charles V strengthens his possessions on the Brazilian coast.}

The death of the first Adelantado of the Rio de la Plata, and the fear that Ayolas and his companions would never return alive from their enterprise, impelled Charles V to secure the dominion of these _{Capitulation with Cabeza de Vaca in 1542.}

---

[1] I present the Arbitrator with the Agreement between Charles V and the Adelantado, Don Pedro de Mendoza, and also the order of the latter naming Juan de Ayolas as Lieutenant Governor. See "Argentine Evidence," Vol. I, pages 129 and 143, and Group A of certified manuscripts and original documents. Nos. 19 and 21.

[2] See translation of this document, Vol. I, page 135, of "Argentine Evidence." The certified Spanish text will be found in the Group A of Manuscripts, Document No. 20.

[3] See map of the Hakluyt Society, etc., cited.

countries by succoring the unfortunate first colonizers. Alvar Nuñez
Cabeza de Vaca, one of the glorious conquerors of Florida in North
America, on his return to Spain received the Emperor's confidence
as a person capable of carrying out his political projects in regard to
the southern regions of the New World.[1] He was accordingly appointed
Adelantado, or Governor-General, of Rio de la Plata, by a royal
decree on March 18, 1540, which confirmed the limits of Mendoza's
jurisdiction.[2]

Possessory acts of the Adelantado over the Territory submitted to Arbitration. The voyage of Alvar Nuñez Cabeza de Vaca was signalized by some important judicial acts of an international character. On his arrival at Santa Catalina on the coast of Brazil he issued a proclamation taking possession of the territory in the name of the Emperor Charles V on the 8th of April, 1541.[3] Pero Hernandez was the Notary Public of the Government of the Adelantado, Alvar Nuñez Cabeza de Vaca, and in the celebrated book published by him in Valladolid in 1555, called "*Comentarios*" (Commentaries), a translation of which is to be found printed in the work of the "*Hakluyt Society*" presented to the Arbitrator,[4] he says:

> And he gave the Indians to understand that he was sent by His Majesty to bring help, and he took possession of the land in the name and on behalf of His Majesty, and also of the harbour called Cananea, which is on the coast of Brazil, in twenty-five degrees, more or less. This harbour is fifty leagues from the island of Santa Catalina, and during all the time that the governor remained in that island he treated all the Indians, natives of that and other parts of the coast of Brazil,[5] (vassals of His Majesty) with great kindness.

[1] An account of Alvar Nuñez Cabeza de Vaca's journeys in Florida has been translated into English by Buckingham Smith and published in Washington, in 1851, as well as by the Hakluyt Society, in the copy presented to the Arbitrator with "Argentine Evidence."

[2] A translation of this act of jurisdiction is presented to the Arbitrator in Vol. I, page 115 of the "Argentine Evidence," and the certified document in the Group A, of Manuscripts, No. 22.

[3] A translation of this document is presented to the Arbitrator in the "Argentine Evidence," Vol. I, page 109, and the certified Spanish copy in Group A of Manuscripts, No. 25.

[4] Works issued by the Hakluyt Society No. LXXXI " *The Conquest of the River Plate* (1525 1555)," page 100.

[5] All of the American coast of the Atlantic Ocean that produced the "*Brazil*" wood bore this name, and the line of demarcation divided this territory between Spain and Portugal.

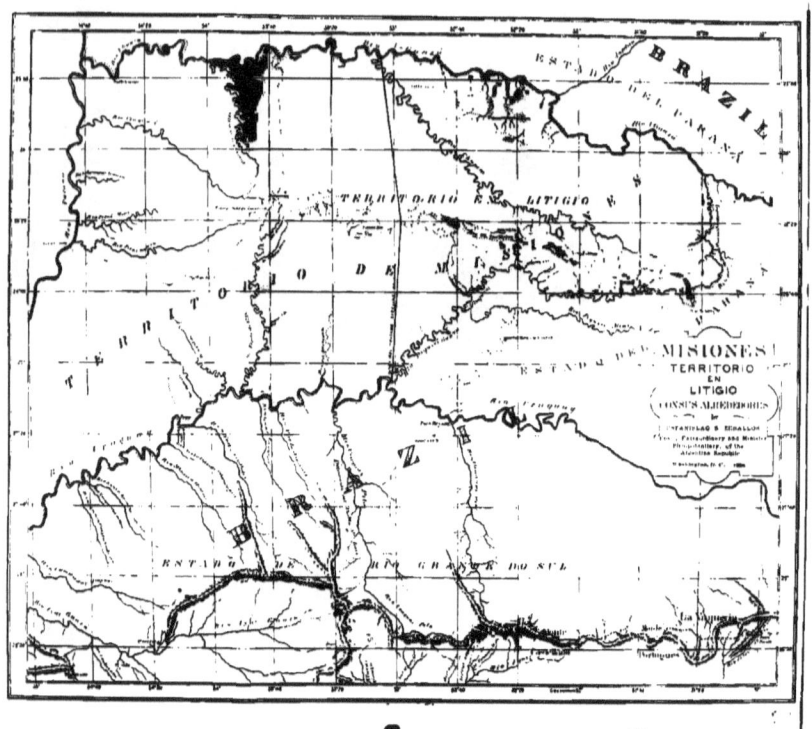

Chapters V and VI of these "Commentaries" contain an interesting relation of the jurisdictional acts performed by the Adelantado over the vast region that extends west of the *Yguapé* and of *Santa Catalina*. The Adelantado, indeed, left Santa Catalina with the object of making an over-land road to facilitate communication between Buenos Ayres and Asuncion and Spain. After a march of ninety days he found himself in the central regions of South America, where the Territory which is submitted to Arbitration is located, and he made a halt there to proclaim the sovereignty of Spain.[1] In chapter VI of the same work (pp. 107 and 108), we learn that the Adelantado was then in the Indian village called *Tocanguazú* :

The Adelantado in the Territory submitted to Arbitration.

Of this people and their territory the Governor took possession, in the name of His Majesty, as newly discovered land, and called it the *Province of Vera*, as it appears from the deeds of possession that were drafted by Juan de Araoz, notary royal. And this being done on the 29th of November, the Governor and his people left Tocanguazú. And after two days' march, on the 1st of December, they arrived at a river called by the Indians "Yguazu," which means "big water."

The document alluded to was dated November 28, 1541, and runs as follows :[2]

Formation of the Province of Vera, of which the Territory in controversy was a part.

At the Village and Camp of Tocanguazú, belonging to the Province of Vera, on the twenty-eighth day of the month of November, the year of Our Saviour Jesus Christ, one thousand five hundred and forty-one, the illustrious Señor Alvar Nuñez Cabeza de Vaca, Adelantado, Governor and Captain-General of the Province of Rio de la Plata, appeared before me, Juan de Araoz, notary royal for their Majesties, and the witnesses mentioned below, and presented a Royal Charter granted in his favor by reason of the conquest of said province, and of the discoveries and settlements to arise from said conquest, as it is further explained in said capitulations, in which the said two chapters were contained of which he wished to avail himself presently, these two articles by him exhibited, being the one after the other as follows : * * *

Accordingly, said Governor stated that in virtue of the authorization granted to him by said Charter, he has taken royal and actual possession of the land and its regions and all their belongings, from the Island of Santa Catalina, from where he departed, to this pueblo and camp, where he is at present with the army at his

---

[1] See map of "Discoveries and Conquests," etc., in this Argument.
[2] See translation of this document, "Argentine Evidence," page 170, and the certified Spanish document in Group A of Manuscripts, No. 26.

command, breaking and opening routes, and mastering, conquering and pacifying said land: said possession to extend over all that he may gain, conquer or discover, or might therefrom gain, conquer and discover, in accordance with both said chapters; and for the greater firmness and strength of said possession, and as evidence of it, he had that land marked out and its boundaries set, and commanded to have it marked out and bounded as said appointed Province of Vera, to which effect he marked along his route by crosses and posts, here in said town and camp. * * *

This was an actual possession of the Territory now submitted to the Arbitrator, for the village of *Tocanguazu* was situated North of the river *Yguazú*, which is one of the boundaries of this Territory, at a distance of two days' walk; that is to say, about thirty kilometres, as is stated in the preceding text. Besides the documents authorized by the Adelantado and his royal notaries, I also lay before the Arbitrator an original statement, presented to his Sovereign by the Governor, in which he gives an account of his discoveries and the possessions occupied West of the Line of Demarcation, on the coast and in the interior of the Territory, as well as the seaport of Cananea.[1]

Appointment of Juan de Sanabria, 1547.

The Governor, Alvar Nuñez Cabeza de Vaca, was overthrown by a military mutiny, and was sent to Spain as a prisoner, after the chief of the mutineers, Captain Domingo Martinez de Yrala, had been put in his place. Meanwhile the Court of Madrid appointed a third Adelantado and Governor of the Rio de la Plata, extending his jurisdiction according to the terms of the following "Capitulacion," or royal appointment:[2]

First, I give permission and authority to you, the said Juan de Sanabria, so that by his Majesty and in his name, and in the name of the Royal Crown of Castile and Leon, that you shall discover and settle, by virtue of your contract, two hundred leagues of coast from the mouth of the Rio de la Plata, and the coast of Brazil, beginning in latitude thirty-one degrees South and from there towards the equinoctial line, and also that you may settle a piece of land from the mouth of the entrance of said river on the right-hand side at the said thirty-one degrees latitude, to which you shall have access through said river, for you and all those with whom His Majesty made

---

[1] See "Argentine Evidence," Vol. I, page 173. Group A of manuscripts, No. 27. Also see Map of "Discoveries," in this *Argument*, upon which the journey of Alvar Nuñez Cabeza de Vaca has been traced by a red line, with the possessions which he took.

[2] Presented in the same volume I, page 151, and Spanish version in the same Group, numbered 23.

contracts for the discovery of all that remains undiscovered in the thirty-one degrees, as well as everything lying on the left-hand side to the point which is contracted with the Bishop of Placencia, which said two hundred leagues is to extend in width to the South Sea....

Sanabria died before accomplishing this voyage, but his wife, Doña Mencia Calderón, and his son Diego de Sanabria, obtained from the King the same favor granted to the father. Don Diego set out from Spain as the Adelantado of the Rio de la Plata, but was wrecked at the mouth of that river. In the meantime Sanabria's widow traversed the country from *San Francisco*, on the coast of Brazil, to the south of *Yguapé* to *Asuncion del Paraguay*, confirming the Spanish jurisdiction on her way across the vast extent of the interior district, within which is situated the Territory now in controversy. _{Acts of jurisdiction in the region now in controversy.}

Antonio Herrera, the celebrated Royal Chronicler of the Indies, appointed in 1596 by Philip II to write the "History of the Discovery and Conquest of Spanish America," in his notable and well-known official work, which was approved by the King under the title of "General History of the Western Islands," [*Historia General de las Islas Occidentales*] says that this Monarch ordered Sanabria to settle [*poblar*] the port of San Francisco near Santa Catalina.[1]

Charles the V persisted in the far-sighted political idea of concentrating a Spanish population near the boundary between the possessions of Spain and those of Portugal, within the maritime district of Brazil, and after the unsuccessful expeditions of the two Sanabrias he signed, on the 30th of December, 1557, and on the 13th of January, 1558, two decrees appointing Jaime Rasquin Governor of the Rio de la Plata, with the obligation of establishing "*a town on the coast of Brazil, within the demarcation of Castile, called San Vicente, and another in 'Viaça,' also called 'Puerto de los Patos*.'"[2] _{Charles V increases the population on the coast of Brazil in 1557.}

The "*Capitulations*" or decrees which have been referred to, and the acts of jurisdiction exercised by Spanish officials over that portion of the Brazilian coast which according to the meridian of the Treaty _{Good faith of Spain in these discoveries}

---

[1] Decade 8, Book 4, Chap. 12, of this book, Congressional Library.
[2] The circumstances of the Voyage by Rasquin were published in the well-known collection of "Documents concerning the Indies," issued officially in Spain. See also the work cited and presented to the Arbitrator upon the Port of Buenos Ayres, by Don Eduardo Madero, page 168.

"*Viaça*" is an incorrect form of the *Guaraní* name "*Mbiaça*," a place located in what is now the Brazilian province of Rio Grande do Sul, near the lake of *Los Patos*.

of Tordesillas was situated within the sovereignty of Spain, were strictly legal and in conformity with the text of that treaty. When the Spanish sovereigns ordered the *occupation of the coast of Brazil within the zone extending between Yguapé and the Island of Santa Catalina*, as well as in the instructions given to their royal pilots and Adelantados, they forbade any landing, under pain of death, upon the lands that belonged to the King of Portugal, according to the Treaty of Tordesillas. In the Royal Cédula [warrant or letters patent] of November 24, 1574, by which Juan Dias de Solis was ordered to discover and occupy the coast of Brazil, we read as follows:

Item. That thou, the said Juan de Solis, art obliged to go to the other side of the earth, where now is Pedro Arias, my Captain-General or Governor of *Castilla del Oro*, and from thence thou shalt make further discoveries, beyond the aforesaid *Castilla del Oro*, one thousand seven hundred leagues and more, if thou canst, counting from the line of demarcation which runs from the extremity of the aforesaid *Castilla del Oro* onward towards the regions that have not yet been discovered, *provided thou touchest not any coast of the lands that belong to the Royal Crown of Portugal, under pain of death or loss of property by our Council, for our will is that what has been adjusted and agreed upon between this Kingdom and that of Portugal shall be wholly observed and accomplished.*[1]

In another Royal Cédula, of March 14, 1525, issued to Sebastian Cabot, the first colonizer of the Rio de la Plata, a similar prohibition will be found. Besides all this, the King of Portugal never disputed these Spanish settlements upon the coast of Brazil, for they were not situated within his dominions.

The Government of the Rio de la Plata in the middle of the 15th century. The failure of the expeditions of the Sanabrias and of Rasquin left the growing colonies of the Rio de la Plata without any legal government, and subject to the arbitrary rule of the famous Captain Domingo Martinez de Yrala, who was, however, confirmed by Charles V as the Adelantado and Governor of the Rio de la Plata, toward the end of 1552. *Yrala's expedition to the region of the Territory in controversy.* In that year Yrala organized an expedition against the *Tupi* Indians of the Province of *Vera*, in order to punish them for interfering with communications between the Spanish colonists along the coast of Brazil and those of Buenos Ayres and Asuncion del Para-

---

[1] This document is in the General Archives of the Indies at Seville.—Case I, drawer No. 1, group No. 1- 26; Ro. 6 ; and has also been printed in the " History of the Port of Buenos Ayres," by Don Eduardo Madero, page 314, which is presented to the Arbitrator.

guay. The first historian of the Rio de la Plata, Rui Dias de Guzman, who was Governor of the Province of Vera, gives an account of this expedition in the eighteenth chapter of his valuable and well-known work, entitled: *Historia Argentina del Descubrimiento, Poblacion y Conquista de las Provincias del Rio de la Plata, escrita por Rui Dias de Guzman en el año* 1612 (Argentine History of the Discovery, Population and Conquest of the provinces of the Rio de la Plata, written by Rui Dias de Guzman in 1612).[1] After explaining the events that took place up to the time of Yrala's arrival at the river *Yguazú*, which is the northern bonudary of the Territory submitted to the Arbitrator, he says, on page 88:

——— and dispatching by that Brazilian road[2] to Juan de Molina, who was the "*Procurador*" of the Province at the Court,[3] he set sail with his armada, and arriving with good fortune at the river *Pequiry* he treated with its natives.

In chapter XIV, page 89, of his History, Rui Dias de Guzman refers to the new expedition sent by Yrala in 1554, two years after he entered the Province of Vera, under the command of Captain Garcia Rodriguez de Vergara, who founded the city of *Ontiveros* in the region to which the disputed Territory belongs. He says:

_{Foundation of the city of Ontiveros in the disputed region in 1554.}

It seemed then to Garcia Rodriguez that this location was the best and most suitable for his purpose, being on the proper course of the river and road from Brazil, as well as by reason of the great number of native Indians there.

[1] I present to the Arbitrator the first edition of this work, which is well known and respected by the Brazilian historians of most credit. It is contained in Volume I of the "*Coleccion de Obras y Documentos Relativos a la Historia Antigua y Moderna de la Provincia del Rio de la Plata; Ilustrada con notas y disertaciones por Pedro de Angelis* (Collection of works and documents relating to the ancient and modern history of the Provinces of the Rio de la Plata; illustrated with notes and dissertations by Pedro de Angelis [an Italian]). The authority of Rui Dias de Guzman is unquestionable among modern historians. He was one of the first conquerors born on the Rio de la Plata; the son of Captain Alonso de Riquelme and grandson of the Adelantado Yrala. Riquelme was a Hidalgo of the great house of the Dukes of Medina Sidonia of Spain, and was the first Governor of the provinces of Vera and Guayra, and consequently of the Territory now submitted to Arbitration. The historian Rui Dias de Guzman was himself Governor of these provinces after the death of his father. The translation of chapters III of Book I, and chapters XIII, XIV, and XV, of Book II, of this valuable work, and of chapters III, IX, X and XVII of Book III, is included in the "Argentine Evidence," Vol. 1, page 209 et seq.
[2] Ports occupied by the Spaniards on the Atlantic coast.
[3] Court of Madrid.

<small>Third expedition to the territory in controversy in 1556.</small>
The Indians were very hostile towards the city of *Ontiveros* and Governor Yrala sent Captain Pedro de Segura, in 1556, with able soldiers from Asuncion, to punish the savages.[1]

<small>Road between the coast of Brazil and Asuncion.</small>
Ever since 1541 a regular service of communication had been established by the Spaniards *between Europe and Asuncion*, the capital of the Province of the Rio de la Plata, by way of the ports of *Cananea*, *Yguapé* and *San Francisco* on the coast of Brazil.

Yrala himself received a messenger from the Court of Spain by this highway, who brought him the title of "Adelantado and Governor of the Rio de la Plata," according to the statement of the celebrated first historian of these regions.[2] Hernando de Trejo, Governor of the port of *San Francisco*, abandoned it and entered the district of which the boundaries are now controverted. From thence he went to Asuncion, where, says Rui Dias, "*General Yrala asked him why he had abandoned the Port of San Francisco*, and as he gave no sufficient reason therefor, he arrested him and kept him always a prisoner."[3] This fact confirms the interest with which Spain cared for its possessions along the coast of Brazil.

<small>The first cows are brought to the Rio de la Plata by this road.</small>
Trade between the Portuguese and the neighboring Spanish colonies on the Atlantic had already commenced, and had even extended into the interior as far as the capital of the Government of the Rio de la Plata by way of the highway opened in 1541 by the Adelantado Cabeza de Vaca.

The great value of the herds now existing within the valley of the Rio de la Plata comes from seven cows and one bull, which were imported from Holland and taken to Asuncion by the honorable Portuguese merchants Xipion and Vicente de Goes[4] over this road which ran overland from *Santa Catalina* as far as *Ontiveros*, and from there were taken to Asuncion by the rivers Paraná and Paraguay.

<small>First Portuguese hostilities against the Spanish colonies, 1552 to 1554.</small>
The course pursued by the Spanish Conquistadores and their priests had resulted in attracting to the Christian faith and to the

---
[1] Rui Dias de Guzman.—Work cited, page 90, chapter XVI translated and presented to the Arbitrator in Vol. I of the "Argentine Evidence," page 209 and following.
[2] Work cited, Chapter XV, page 91, translation attached to the "Argentine Evidence," Vol. I.
[3] Chapter XV, same page.
[4] This interesting event was also related by an eye-witness, Rui Dias de Guzman. It is proper to mention here that Somthey, the English author of the best history of Brazil, translated into Portuguese in 1862 at Rio de Janeiro, frequently follows with the greatest respect the testimony of Rui Dias de Guzman.

See road traced on "Map of Discoveries and Conquests," of this Argument.

places where it was preached, between the coast of Brazil and Asuncion, thousands of Indians, while the neighboring Portuguese colonies could not obtain the same result and therefore lacked the basis of progress—an industrious population. Rui Dias Melgarejo advanced the conquests of Spain towards the north, into latitudes not far distant from the *Amazon River*, and founded at the sources of the *Paraná* the city of *Villa Rica del Espiritu Santo*, in the centre of a region having mines of gold, silver and copper which he had discovered.[1]

<small>New conquests by Melgarejo North of Ciudad Real.</small>

Some Portuguese, settled in the Captaincy-General of San Vicente on the Atlantic, began towards 1552 and 1554 to undertake expeditions into the interior, either alone or in company with the savages, attacking the Spanish settlements and making their Indian subjects prisoners, for the latter were active laborers in the cultivation of the soil, in mining and other industries. These prisoners were sold as slaves in the Portuguese colonies of the Government of San Vicente.

<small>Traffic in white slaves.</small>

The matter could not have been more odious. Many of these prisoners were *Mestizos* [of mixed blood], for ever since the beginning of their great conquests the Spaniards had a clear foresight of the advantages to be derived from a fusion of the races, as the only humane means of colonizing the New World. These abominable acts were repeated until it became a regular trade, and the Adelantado Yrala dispatched, in 1553, the well-known Captain Ñuflo de Chaves with a powerful force, in order to defend the settlements of the Province of Vera against the vandal aggressions of the Portuguese. This important expedition, which extended the Spanish discoveries nearly as far as the basin of the Amazon, is well known in the history of the Rio de la Plata and can be read particularly in the account by the writer Rui Dias de Guzman, cited in the work presented to the Arbitrator.[2] After the triumphs of Ñuflo Chaves throughout these immense regions, Yrala resolved to increase the Spanish population that occupied them. He therefore appointed Captain Rui Dias Melgarejo, one of the most valiant conquerors of the Rio de la Plata, as Governor of the Province of Vera, within which was located the

<small>Expedition of Ñuflo Chaves against the Portuguese. 1553.</small>

<small>Foundation of Ciudad Real near the Territory submitted to the Arbitrator. 1554.</small>

---

[1] I present the Arbitrator with an official document that proves these facts, copied from the original in the *General Archives of the Indies*, Seville. See "Argentine Evidence," Group A of manuscripts, document No. 30, and its translation in volume I, page 183 *et seq.* of the same.

[2] Page 100, chapter II, part III.

district called *La Guayra*[1] by the Indians. Rui Dias de Guzman, in the book presented, chapter III, book III, page 101, says:

> With this resolution he also indicated that a settlement should be made in the Province of La Guayra, to serve as *a stepping-stone and passage-way for the road to Brazil.*

Consequently when Melgarejo arrived at *Ontireros* he incorporated its inhabitants with the colony he commanded, depopulated that place and went and founded another city nine miles further North, upon a better ground, with the name of *"Ciudad Real,"* in 1554.[2] The first census of the population of the region showed sixty Spanish families and forty thousand Indian fires; by a "fire" being understood an Indian with his wife and children. Therefore this Spanish colony could not have had less than one hundred and fifty thousand inhabitants, a great part of whom lived within the Territory now submitted to Arbitration. The same historian adds, on page 100, cited, that—

First census of the Territory submitted to Arbitration.

Prosperity of this Colony.

> ... for some years they lived in great repose and quiet, being very much respected and kindly served by all the Indians of that Province, and so well provided with the products of the earth, such as wine, sugar, cotton, and linen that the Indians wove, that they were considered the most well-to-do of that government.

These facts are officially confirmed by the document entitled, *"Petition of Captain Don Manuel de Frias, citizen of Santa Fé, wherein he gives an account of the services of Captain Rui Dias Melgarejo, grandfather of his wife Doña Leonor Ortega de Guzman, dated 9th of January,* 1603." The original document is preserved in the *General Archives of the Indies,* Seville, and a copy is presented to the Arbitrator.[3] These are solemn proofs that Spain fully civilized this Territory, and these facts have never been denied nor even questioned by either Portuguese or Brazilian statesmen. On the contrary, they have frankly admitted them, as the books show which I have the honor to present to the Arbitrator. To corroborate this I will simply cite

---

[1] The Adelantado, Alvar Nuñez Cabeza de Vaca, had called "*Provincia de Vera,*" as above stated, the immense country *of which he took possession, extending from the Atlantic to the Paraguay,* within which were comprised the territories that the Indians called *de los Tapes, de la Guayra,* etc.

[2] See Map of the Discoveries, etc., banks of the upper Paraná, this Argument.

[3] "Argentine Evidence," Vol. 1, page 183 and following.

"*La Historia del Brasil*," (History of Brazil) written by an impartial person, Sir Robert Southey, already referred to on page 32 of this Argument, which was translated into Portuguese and annotated in 1862, by two Brazilian literary authorities, who in the preface wrote as follows:

> The work now translated into the national language is considered the best History of Brazil.[1]

Southey narrates the facts I have briefly set forth, and in harmony with the present statement. In volume I, chapter XI, page 347, in referring to the disputes about the Brazilian frontiers, he writes, in the English edition of his History of Brazil, as follows:

> The progress of Paraguay did not keep pace with that of Brazil; but it is rather to be wondered at that this colony should have continued to exist, than that it did not flourish, remote as it was from the sea and from every other Spanish settlement. *Happy would it have been for Paraguay had it been equally remote from the Portuguese. The Guaranies on the Parana were infested by the Tapuyas of the Brazilian frontier, whom the slave-hunters headed in their expeditions. They called upon Yrala for protection; he went to their assistance, drove back the assailants, and made them promise to leave the subjects of the King of Spain in peace. He judged it, however, expedient to found a town there, for the purpose of securing the frontier, and opening a readier communication with the sea;* and as soon as he returned to Asumpcion he dispatched Garcia Rodriguez de Vergara, with eighty men, upon this service. The site chosen for the new settlement was on the Paraná, above the great falls. Vergara called it Ontiveros, after his own birthplace in Castille; but it obtained the name of Guayra, from the province in which it stood. After a few years Ruy Diaz Melgarejo removed it three leagues higher, and to the opposite beach, near the place where the Pequeri falls into the Paraná, and from that time it was called Ciudad Real.

The Adelantado Domingo Martinez de Yrala, who had advanced the population of the Territory now in controversy, and consolidated its colonization, died on the 3d of October, 1556. He was replaced the same year by Juan Hortiz de Zárate, a nobleman from Peru, who went

_{Death of Yrala. His successor 1556.}

---

[1] There is presented to the Arbitrator among the books of the "Argentine Evidence" the first Portuguese edition of this work, in six volumes, published at Rio de Janeiro in 1862, by the most celebrated publishing house in Brazil, B. L. Garnier, Rua D'Ouvidor 69; Paris, Garnier Frères, editeurs, Rue des Saints Pères. The English edition of Southey's work is in the Congressional Library of the United States, in 3 vols., 8vo, entitled, "History of Brazil, by Robert Southey, London, 1822."

to Spain in order to arrange the affairs of his government, leaving a governor *ad interim*. Yrala had come to the Rio de la Plata with the first Adelantado, Mendoza. Having therefore been associated with all the events of the time, he was known and feared by the native tribes. His death and the fact that the government was without a head while the King of Spain was taking the necessary measures, led to disturbances among the Indians, so that the settlers in Ciudad Real, in the Province of Vera, who were the furthest from the centre of the government, asked for help in 1561, being fearful of an uprising among the aborigines. The Governor *ad interim* of the Rio de la Plata then sent the nobleman Captain Alonzo de Riquelme, who was the father, as I have said, of the first historian of these regions, who reached *La Guayra* with seventy Castilians and re-established confidence.[1] In 1563 Rui Dias Melgarejo, Governor of the province of La Guayra, was sent on a mission to Spain, and Captain Alonzo de Riquelme was appointed Governor of these colonies and of these immense territories.[2] Coleman, an English adventurer, who had come to the Rio de la Plata with one of the Adelantados, instigated a revolution against Governor Riquelme, in 1569, at Ciudad Real, and the latter was compelled to retreat to Asuncion with a few faithful soldiers.[3] He returned with reinforcements in order to re-establish his government, but was made prisoner by the rebels and imprisoned in a fortress which they had built in the territory of La Guayra, forty leagues north of Ciudad Real, where he remained one year.[4] In 1573 his authority was re-established by another popular uprising, when the city in which he was imprisoned was attacked and he was set free. Alonzo de Riquelme pacified the Province of La Guayra, and governed it with justice, to the satisfaction of the people.[5] Meanwhile the new Adelantado, Juan Hortiz de Zárate, had arrived from Spain. His orders read as follows:

First. We grant you the government of the Rio de la Plata, of that which is now discovered and settled, as well as of all which you may hereafter discover and settle in the provinces of Paraguay and Paraná, as well as in the other American provinces, by you and by your captains and lieutenants whom you may appoint for

---

[1] Rui Dias de Guzman, work cited, Book III, chapter IX, page 115.
[2] Same author, same book, chapter X, page 117.
[3] Same author, Book III, chapter 17, page 131. "Argentine Evidence," Vol. I, page 209 *et seq*.
[4] *Idem*.
[5] *Idem*.

the coast of the Northern Sea, and for that of the South in the district of demarcation which His Majesty, my father, the Emperor, gave and granted to Governor D. Pedro de Mendoza, and after him to Alvar Nuñez Cabeza de Vaca, and to Domingo de Yrala,[1] etc.

The Adelantado immediately showed that he came with special instructions to consolidate the royal possessions and stimulate the progress of the provinces that extended from the sources of the Paraná and the Uruguay to the sea. His acts in the Territory.

Captain Rui Dias Melgarejo, the lieutenant to the Governor of these provinces, had sailed for Spain in a caravel, as I have already said. But while on the coast of Brazil he was informed that the Adelantado, Don Hortiz de Zárate, had passed there, on his way to the Rio de la Plata; so he immediately sailed back to that estuary, in order to present himself to his superior and offer his services. The latter received him gratefully and named him as his Lieutenant-Governor and Chief Justice of the aforesaid provinces of the upper Paraná and the Uruguay, as far as the Atlantic. He gave him titles, provisions and instructions to carry on the work of colonization as far as the port of San Francisco on the coast of Brazil, and granted to him the ownership of great landed possessions and Indians in "*encomiendas*."[2] These facts are judicially confirmed in an interesting document of that period which has been cited several times. It records the merits of Rui Dias Melgarejo and justifies the grants in the following language:

> So also in one of the places where the said metals were discovered on your coast is ordered to be built and peopled a village and fort named "*Espiritu Santo*," where I have now been informed that mines of lead have been found, and God will be served if silver be discovered, for all redounds to His holy service and that of his Majesty, and to the use and well-being of all the neighbor-

---

[1] A translation of this document is presented to the Arbitrator in the "Argentine Evidence," Vol. I, page 157, and the Spanish text is contained in the Group A of Manuscripts of the same, No. 24.

[2] The Instructions of Captain Manuel Frias, cited, sheet 27 of the Spanish copy in Group A of Manuscripts, No. 30, and in the "Argentine Evidence," Vol. I, page 183 *et seq*.

"Encomiendas" means a system of vassalage, by which a right or authority was granted by the Sovereign to certain individuals, extending over a certain number of Indians. It was the intention of the Council of the Indies that these natives should be rather serfs than slaves, but they were bound to labor, and in return they were to be maintained and taught the Christian religion and habits of civilization. The grant was for two lives, as it was then thought the natives would be sufficiently advanced to become free.

ing inhabitants in that Government and the provinces, thus being
founded that village of "*Espiritu Santo*" on the road to the Port
of San Francisco, which with the help of God our Sovereign designs
to people.

<small>Remarkable case of criminal justice in the territory submitted to the Arbitrator, 1577.</small> In 1577 there was begun in the disputed Territory the first criminal process of extraordinary importance, on account of the high position of the persons who took part in it, one being the daughter of a ruler and chieftain of the native soldiers and the other an officer of the royal troops who were the founders of the city of Buenos Ayres. The event occurred on the river Pequiry, and the lawsuit lasted until 1582, when the judgment was rendered. The original document is to be found in the archives of Asuncion, in Paraguay, where I personally took the copy that I now present to the Arbitrator, certified by the Consul-General of the United States in that Republic.[1] On the back of folio 68 of the process is found the following:

> . . . And thereafter, on the said day, month, and year, the neighbor Juan de Ruiz was called as a witness, and taking the oath before God and Santa Cruz as well as the Cross, which he took in his right hand, said, as stated in the conclusion of said oath, yes, I swear and Amen, and being inquired of concerning the nature of this action said that he knew it, and saw and heard—that is to say, that this witness came by *land with the horses to this Villa Rica del Espiritu Santo*, and that after our Captain arrived he heard all that which is stated at the head of this process, saying that the said Antonio de Arbildo *committed in the coast of the Yguatú with the said Indian girl* Maria, and which is public and notorious all that which is therein contained. . . .

This document is of the greatest interest, as well as the document of Captain Manuel Frias

<small>Acts of the Adelantado Vera y Aragon, in 1583</small> A new Adelantado and Governor had been appointed to the Rio de la Plata, Don Juan de Vera y Aragon, who, like his predecessors, gave great importance to the maintenance of communication between the interior colonies and the port of San Francisco on the coast of Brazil. He therefore commissioned his Lieutenant-Governor, Captain Don Alonso de Vera y Aragon, to undertake an expedition against the

---

[1] The original process in Spanish is contained in the Group A of Documents No. 29 of the "Argentine Evidence," and an extract in English of the same in Vol. I, p. 177, of the said Evidence.

Mbiaçá Indians of the Province of Tape.[1] On his return from the country of those savages he happily proceeded on his victorious march until he came to the aforesaid port of San Francisco, which remained thenceforth free from neighboring enemies.[2] At the same time he appointed as Governor, Justice, and Constable [Alguazil] of the Provinces of *La Guayra*, *Coracivera* and *los Tapes*, according to the Map of "*Discoveries and Conquests*," herewith presented, the historian, Captain Rui Dias de Guzman. By the document which conferred upon him his titles and commissions in charge of this government, (to which reference is made in the preceding footnote) it is proved in the solemn form of a state paper that this warrior and historian did not only consolidate the conquests of his predecessors, but that he also extended them, founding to the northwest of these the new Province of Xéres. Rui Dias de Guzman will always be remembered as the most progressive Governor of the vast region we are now considering. The old towns had not been located with the necessary care and study, so Rui Dias de Guzman ordered the removal of *Villa Rica del Espiritu Santo* and *Ciudad Real* to places near by and much more convenient, somewhat to the *eastward* of their first locations. He founded the City of *Xéres* on the West of the Paraná, and that of *La Guayra* to the *east* of the Paraná, at the junction of this river with the Paraná Panema. This vast Government extended from the Cordilleras of the Paraguay to the Atlantic Ocean, and from the Rio de la Plata to the sources of the Amazon, so that any regular government was impossible. Therefore Rui Dias de Guzman subdivided his immense dominion, called by Cabeza de Vaca the "*Province of Vera*" in 1541, and by the Adelantado Hortiz de Zárate, "*Nueva Andalusia*" in 1583. Of these two combined he formed five Provinces, in the following order: On the North, the *Province of Coracivera*; on the West, that of *Xéres*; on the South, that of *Tape*; in the Centre, that of *La Guayra*, and on the East, extending

<small>Progress of colonization under his Government.</small>

<small>New Cities, 1588.</small>

<small>Division of the territory into provinces.</small>

---

[1] See the "Map of the Discoveries and Conquests of Spain," this Argument.

[2] As a proof of this fact and what follows, I have the honor to present the Arbitrator with the document copied from the "*General Archives of the Indies*" in Seville, entitled "1588. Title and Commission in favor of Rui Dias de Guzman, given to the Governor's lieutenant, Alonso de Vera y Aragon, in virtue of powers granted to him by the Adelantado of the Rio de la Plata, Licenciado Juan de Vera y Aragon, for the conquest of the Provinces of Miarús, in the Paraná, 1593. The aforesaid territory and the asiento de San Salvador taken possession of, and the city of Santiago de Xeres founded." "Argentine Evidence," Vol. I, page 225 and following; Group A of Manuscripts, document No. 31.

as far as the Atlantic, the Province of *del Campo*, with San Francisco as its capital and port.[1]

<small>First map of this government.</small> Rui Dias de Guzman then began to prepare, in 1593, the first map of this government, and the copy of this precious document which accompanies this work was taken from the original that exists in the General Archives of the Indies at Seville, bearing on its back the signature of the celebrated warrior and historian, and the date 1612.[2]

<small>Its probatory value in this dispute.</small> This ancient map is of an extraordinary value as evidence, and contains the following data: 1. Boundaries between the dominions of Spain and Portugal, according to the Treaty of Tordesillas in 1494. The line is traced without scientific exactness, but the Territory now submitted to the Arbitrator remains situated within the jurisdiction it assigns to Spain. 2. All the cities, Indian villages and forts that Spain possessed in 1593 on the West of this line of Demarcation. 3. The possessions of Spain in the Provinces of *Tape* and of *La Guayra*, which bound on the North and on the South the Territory submitted to the Arbitrator, and also in the Provinces of *Xéres* and *del Campo*, which enclose it on the West and on the East. 4. The course of the river *Pepiry* or *Pequiry*, a tributary of the Uruguay. 5. A *Colony of Indians*, formed by Spain in the centre of the Territory submitted to the Arbitrator, near the sources of the *Pepiry* or *Pequiry*.

<small>The Rio Pepiry or Pequiry in 1593.</small> The Brazilian writers have argued that the Rio Pepiry, the *quid* of the question under debate, was not known before the foundation of the vast Jesuit Republic in these regions; but the error of that view is clearly demonstrated by this map, the notes upon which show that in the first century of the discovery and conquest of the Government of the Rio de la Plata, from 1527 to 1593, the river Pepiry or Pequiry was known and frequented for its gold-mines. This is the reason why we read on this map at the junction of the Uruguay and Pepiry: "*El Rio de Pepiri dónde hay oro*" (The river of Pepiry where there is gold); and not far from its mouth, in the centre of the region also appears the Spanish settlement or colony of aborigines, with this legend: "*Pueblo de Indios llamados Tobacos*" (Village of Indians called Tobacos). The engraving herewith is a faithful reproduction of this part of the original map.

---

[1] See map of "Discoveries and Conquests of Spain to the East of the Paraná," presented to the Arbitrator; and the document of Rui Diaz de Guzman, cited, page 39 of this Argument.

[2] Portfolio of original or authenticated maps of "Argentine Evidence," map No. 1, seventeenth century.

Map of Ruy Diaz de Guzman.
1612.

This map shows that the position of the *Pepiry* or *Pequiry* was further East than the Brazilians have pretended to locate it, and also shows that it is a river of large volume, the greatest of the tributaries of the Uruguay on its right bank, instead of the short, shallow and narrow river, or mere brook, which Portugal and Brazil alleged it to be. This observation is of capital importance, and I shall recur to it at the proper place.

Besides the former possessions which have been referred to, the Adelantado Hórtiz de Zárate had founded the *City of Vera*, at a point on the river Paraná called "*las Siete Corrientes*" (the seven currents), with the object of providing a port and place of refuge for navigation between the mouth of the Rio de la Plata and Paraguay and the central provinces governed by Rui Diaz de Guzman. The foundation deed, dated April 5, 1588, shows that the Adelantado Vera y Aragon personally took part in the ceremony, and that on this occasion he asserted his rights over all these countries, from the Paraná towards the East as far as the Atlantic. He says, in fact:

_{Foundation of the City of Vera de las Siete Corrientes in 1588.}

> I, ... found, set and settle the city of Vera, on the place called '*de las Siete Corrientes*,' Province of Paraná and the Tape, with the boundaries and the lordships of the cities of La Asuncion, Concepcion de Buena Esperanza,[1] Santa Fe,[2] and San Salvador,[3] Ciudad Real, Villa Rica de Espiritu Santo, San Francisco and Veazá,[4] on the coast of the Northern Sea, for the present and forever. . . .
> Signed April 3, 1588.

This valuable document, which proves once more that the jurisdiction of the government of the Rio de la Plata extended as far as the Atlantic, on the coast of Brazil, has been published, with those cited hereafter, in the official work of the Argentine Republic attached to this Argument, under the title of: *Coleccion de Datos y Documentos referentes á Misiones, como parte integrante del Territorio de la Provincia de Corrientes, hecha por una Comision nombrada por el Gobierno de ella. Primera parte. Corrientes,* 1877, *Imprenta de la Verdad.*[5] ("Collec-

---
[1] Now a town of the Argentine Chaco.
[2] Now the Argentine Federal State of Santa Fé.
[3] City of the province of Xeres, near the Paraná. See "Map of Discoveries and Conquests of Spain," etc.
[4] *Veazá* is bad spelling for *Mbiaza*, in the *Provincc del Campo*, upon the Atlantic. See "Map of the Discoveries and Conquests."
[5] Corrientes, a Federal State of the Argentine Republic. The translation of this document and those following (Vera y Aragon, will be found in Vol. I, page 201, of the Argentine Evidence; and in the "Collection of Data and Documents," etc., page 1 *et seq.*, presented to the Arbitrator.

tion of Data and Documents referring to Misiones, as an integral part of the Territory of the Province of Corrientes, made by a Commission named by the Government of the latter. (Part 1. Corrientes, 1877, Printing office of La Verdad.")

The Adelantado Vera y Aragon, and his jurisdiction over the disputed ground. Just as in the case of the foundation of Corrientes, so in all the documents issued by his government, the Adelantado Vera y Aragon asserted his jurisdiction over these territories.

Distribution of Indians in "encomiendas." In various documents about the distribution of Indians in "*encomiendas,*" practised in the city of *Vera de las Siete Corrientes,* from 1588 to 1593 we find the same heading at different dates, as follows:

In the city of Vera, on the second day of the month of November, 1588: Alonzo de Vera y Aragon, Captain General and High Justice of Paraná, Uruguay and Tapé to the North Sea,[1] San Francisco and Viaça and Guayra for the Adelantado Juan de Torres de Vera y Aragon, Governor, Captain General, High Justice and Officer in all these provinces of the Rio de la Plata for His Majesty, etc.[2]

New provinces of Paraná and Uruguay. 1593. The Adelantado Alonzo de Vera y Aragon completed Rui Dias de Guzman's administrative and geographical work by dividing the vast territory enclosed within the Rio de la Plata, the Province of Tape and the rivers Paraná and Uruguay, into two new Provinces, which he called *Paraná* and *Uruguay.* The map of " Discoveries and Conquests of Spain" shows these divisions geographically. The *Province of Uruguay* consisted of the territories situated between the rivers Paraná and Uruguay, as far East as the Province of del Campo; and the *Province of Paraná* included the territories situated on both margins of the river of that name, to the South of the *Provinces of Xéres* and *Uruguay.*[3]

The Territory submitted to the Arbitrator in the XVIth century. These solemn documents, the greater part of which are new to the History of America, definitively demonstrate that at the end of the sixteenth century the Territory submitted to the Arbitrator remained under the Government of Spain and under the jurisdiction of the city of *Vera de las Siete Corrientes.* This possession was sanctioned by the Treaty of Tordesillas, and never disturbed the harmony that existed between the two Crowns. Spain exercised its full power on the West of the Line of Demarcation of 1494, and Portugal did the same on the East. The events during the seventeenth century were not less favorable, as I am about to show, for the origin of the Right and Title of the Argentine Republic to this Territory.

[1] The Northern Sea was the Atlantic; the Southern Sea, the Pacific.
[2] See *Collection of Data and Documents* quoted, pages 5 and 6, and "Argentine Evidence," Vol. I, pages 202 and 206.
[3] See also documents added to the " Argentine Evidence," Vol. I, pp. 239, 241, and Group 1 of Manuscripts, No. 18.

Spain obtained these extraordinary results in the colonization of these central territories without the help of funds from the treasury and without reinforcements of men or additional materials. The Adelantados had orders to people the lands they discovered, and they did so at the expense of the conquered country, out of their own resources and those of the *conquistadores*. The Adelantado Yrala was the author of this system, founding it upon the cupidity of his officers and soldiers to whom he entrusted the subjection of these territories, giving them as a reward the Indians they subdued in "*encomiendas*." But the Indians suffered exceedingly from this method, and at the beginning of the sixteenth century Spain modified her colonization policy so as to make it more humane toward the natives, and suppressed the system of "*encomiendas*." Personal interest disappeared as an element of colonization and the progress realized in the preceding century was retarded for want of European settlers, and on account of the Indians reconquering their independence, notwithstanding their indolent temperament.

<small>Spain's system of colonization in the XVIth century.</small>

The Jesuits had explored the Rio de la Plata during the last years of the sixteenth century, and, attracted by the importance of this region, from 1610 they concentrated their greatest efforts upon South America.

<small>The Jesuits. Their action and system, 1596-1610.</small>

The Indians had been treated by the Spaniards as machines for producing wealth, and by the Portuguese as slaves and wild beasts. The Jesuits treated them paternally and the tribes took refuge under their kind protection. Upon this principle rested the foundation of the celebrated Spanish Jesuit Republic of South America, in the centre of which was situated the Territory in controversy.

King Philip III gave it his solemn authorization in his Royal Cédula or Letters Patent of January 30, 1609, by which he provided that the Indians should be subdued by evangelical means. Another Royal Cédula of 1634 approved the occupation of the interior provinces, where the Territory submitted to the Arbitrator is located; that is to say, the provinces of Coracivera, La Guayra, Tapes, Paraná, Xéres, Uruguay and del Campo. The veracity of the historical account thus far made is solemnly and in detail recognized by an official publication of Brazil, which I have the honor to present to the Arbitrator among the printed works of the "Argentine Evidence." It is entitled:

<small>Proof of these facts by official Brazilian testimony.</small>

Historia da Republica Jesuitica do Paraguay, desde o descobrimiento do Rio da Prata até nossos dias, anno 1861, *pelo Conego Joao Pedro Gay, Vicario de San Borga nas Missoes Brazileiras.* (History of the Jesuit Republic of Paraguay, since the discovery of the Rio de la Plata, until our days. Anno 1861. By the Canon, John Peter Gay, Vicar of San Borgia in the Brazilian Misiones.)[1]

This work was received and approved by the illustrious and erudite Emperor of Brazil, Dom Pedro II, who authorized its publication in volume XXVI of the annals of the official geographical society, over which he presided, which were entitled: "*Revista Trimestral do Instituto Historico Geographico é Etnographico do Brazil, fundado no Rio de Janeiro, debaixo da immediata proteccao de S. M. I. o Senhor Dom Pedro II.*"[2] (Quarterly Review of the Historical, Geographical and Ethnographical Institute of Brazil, founded in Rio de Janeiro under the immediate protection of H. I. M. Dom Pedro II.)

The history of the *Jesuit Republic*, which may also be called the history of Spain's permanent jurisdiction over the Territory submitted to the Arbitrator, from 1600 to 1768, that is to say nearly down to the time of the Independence of South America, was written with accuracy and a high-minded spirit by Father Gay, a Frenchman in the Brazilian service. His work was admitted under the Empire to be the most important upon this subject and it was officially published as above stated. Its presentation to the Arbitrator, which I have the honor to make, saves me the task of setting forth the historical and jurisdictional facts that it recognizes in favor of Spain. I will, therefore, merely call the attention of the Honorable President of the United States to this decisive book and only quote in this Argument some paragraphs of vital importance.

Boundaries of the Jesuit Republic, accepted by Brazil.

On page 51 we read:

It is known that the Jesuits exercised their ecclesiastic functions in the three provinces of Paraguay, Buenos Ayres and Tucuman, which they called, as I have said, the *Province of the Company of Jesus of Paraguay*, and which formed at first but a single Province, being for the most part in the Province of *Guayra, between the river Yguassu and the river Tieté, extending over an area of three degrees of latitude and two of longitude, from 21° to 24° South and from 54° to 56° longitude West of Paris, where, as we have seen, the Spaniards had already founded the cities of Ontiveros, Villa Rica, Ciudad Real, Xéres*, etc., and

---

[1] On the East Bank of the Uruguay, ceded by Spain to Portugal in 1750.

[2] The Royal *Cédulas* or Letters Patent of Philip III, of 1609 and 1634, cited, are published in Portuguese in Vol. XXVI, page 244, of the above-mentioned *Review*, which is presented to the Arbitrator.

thirteen settlements on the coast of the great river Paraná and to the North of Salto Grande (Great Fall) of this river and of Vera, where below the Falls the Spaniards had already founded nine settlements in which these first Missionaries showed their apostolic zeal. At the same time, according to the destination assigned to them, the first seven Jesuits evangelized and established settlements between 23° and 30° of South latitude and between 56° and 60° of longitude West of Paris; Belem being the most northern settlement, situated in 23° 26' 17" South latitude and 59° 28' 00" of longitude West of Paris; and the settlement of Yapeyú, the most southern of all and nearest to the river Merinhay, that divides this region from the rest of *Entre Rios*, situated in 29° 31' 47" South latitude and 58° 38' 28" of longitude West; the boundaries of this Jesuit Republic being:—on the North the river Tebicuary, which flows into the Paraguay, the farthest ramifications of the Cordillera of this country and the thick forests that covered it as far as Belem; on the West the Lake Ibera and the Rio Merinhay; on the South the eastern bank of the Uruguay or river Ubicuy; on the East the mountains of the Tapes and of Herval, and the ravine of San Martino; and on the North-east the virgin forests of Uruguay as far as *Mato Castilhano*, and the virgin forest of this territory as far as the Yguassu; an immense land, watered by three of the most important rivers in the world and their innumerable tributaries, picturesque in its mountainous portions and virgin forest regions, extremely fertile and with a climate perfectly mild and healthy.

This description of boundaries, officially detailed by the first geographical institution of Brazil, under the direct authority of the Emperor, proves that until 1768[1] the Jesuits held for the King of Spain the territory submitted to the Arbitrator, exercising in these Provinces a Supreme Authority, in accordance with the new colonization policy initiated by Philip III. For a better understanding of these boundaries see "Map of *Discoveries and Conquests of Spain*," already presented.[2] In volume XXVI, page 362, and following, of the aforesaid "*Revista del Instituto Historico del Brazil*," etc., is found an exact and minute account of the settlements by the Jesuits, founded in the name of the King of Spain, from 1610 to 1768, which ends as follows, on page 363:

Villages of the Jesuit Republic during more than a century and a half. 1610 to 1768.

The aggregate of the population governed by the Jesuits in the Province of the Company of Jesus of Paraguay amounted to thirty-three villages (*pueblos*), four of which were of Spanish

[1] The year of the banishment of the Jesuits from the dominions of Spain.
[2] The rivers of the great forest of Mato Castilhano have been drawn in accordance with the work of the Argentine-Brazilian mixed commission which examined the territory in 1885-1890.

origin, the remaining twenty-nine being purely of Jesuit creation. These thirty-three settlements or *pueblos* formed the celebrated Christian Republic of the Jesuits of Paraguay.[1]

The Arbitrator will find in this volume an accurate narration of the settlements made and the jurisdiction exercised by Spain in the Territory in dispute, from 1527 to 1810, and by the Argentine Republic from 1810 to 1860, when the work was written. Father Gay frequently denies with energy that Portugal ever exercised any control over the territory situated West of the Uruguay; and hereafter I will refer when necessary to his statements. A careful analysis of this official work of Brazil will be sufficient to produce the conviction that the land in controversy belongs to the Argentine Republic.

Definite judicial acts.

It is unnecessary to farther consider the events of the seventeenth century in order to strengthen the evidence of the possession by Spain of the Territory submitted to the Arbitrator. The Jesuits maintained its sovereignty by means of their political, ecclesiastical, judicial, administrative, and military jurisdiction, and this antecedent fact alone is conclusive. Notwithstanding the fact that the history of the delegation of these powers by the King of Spain to the Jesuits is universally known, I will quote some vital and positive acts done by this Monarch, which are of evident judicial value.

Treaties of the XVIIth century.

During the seventeenth century Spain and Portugal, constantly impelled by the interests and agitations of European politics, entered into various treaties, which will be considered in the chapter relating thereto, in which they provided for their relations and interests in the New World. These treaties, however, did not alter the judicial and international facts that have been stated, for they did not comprehend the Territory submitted to the Arbitrator. In fact the King of Spain continued legislating in regard to the Territory which is to-day in dispute, and he issued his celebrated *Cédula*, or Royal Decree, dividing the largest of his governments in the Indies, that of the Rio de la Plata, into two parts. One was to have its head in Buenos Ayres and the other in Paraguay.[2] This division had been requested by the *Cabildo* (City Council) of Buenos Ayres in 1612, in order to give more effi-

Other judicial acts of the King of Spain, 1617.

---

[1] Paraguay, as stated, was one of the provinces of the government of the Rio de la Plata, and the Jesuits gave the name of Paraguay to their central missions in order to distinguish them from those which they possessed West of the river Paraguay in the Argentine territory of El Chaco, as well as in Bolivia and in Brazil.

[2] See translation of this document in the "Argentine Evidence," Vol. I, page 245, and certified Spanish copy in the Group A of Manuscripts, Document No. 1.

ciency to the Government, and the King answered with the Royal Cédula of December 16, 1617. Referring to the limits of the Government of Buenos Ayres, this document said: *Division of the "Gigantic Province of the Indies," as the Historians of that epoch called it. 1617.*

"I have resolved that said Government of the Provinces of the Rio de la Plata be divided into two parts, one to be the Government of the Rio de la Plata, embracing the cities of Trinidad, Puerto de Santa Maria de Buenos Aires, the city of Santa Fe, the city of San Juan de Vera de las Corrientes, and the city of Concepcion del Rio Bermejo."

On page 41 I have proved that the foundation deed of the city of Corrientes gave it jurisdiction over the disputed Territory submitted to the Arbitrator. However, in order to avoid doubts and conflicts of jurisdiction between his Lieutenants, the King made clear this point in his Royal Cédula of November 6, 1726, in which he said:[1]

"Therefore, I order the Vice-Roy of Peru and the Audiencia de Charcas, that as soon as this Royal Letter be shown to them, they shall give positive orders to have it executed, seeing that the separation from the Government of Paraguay of the thirty Indian pueblos of the Company of Jesus is fulfilled, and that the said reductions are placed under the control of the government of Buenos Ayres, taking care also that the Governor and officers of Justice of Paraguay restore to the Fathers of the Company of Jesus the College of La Asumpcion; said Vice-Roy of Peru and Audiencia de Charcas being charged to inform me of the execution of this Royal letter patent at the first opportunity.

Given at San Lorenzo, on the sixth day of November, in the year one thousand seven hundred and twenty six.—THE KING.

These thirty *pueblos*, or villages, included, beside those situated between the rivers Paraná and Uruguay, in what is now the Argentine Republic according to the boundaries now claimed in this proceeding, the *Misiones* on the right bank of the river Paraná (now belonging to the Republic of Paraguay) and the *Misiones* situated on the left bank of the river *Uruguay*, now belonging to Brazil, in the State of Rio Grande do Sul, for reasons which will be explained in another chapter.

The seventeenth century ended leaving Spain the mistress and civilizer of the immense central regions of South America, of which the Territory in controversy was an integral part. It should be *The disputed Territory in the XVIIIth century.*

[1] "Argentine Evidence," Vol. I, page 261, Group A of Manuscripts, Document No. 3.

noted here that this possession, extensive as it is shown to have been by the maps of the "*Discoveries and Conquests*," had been respected by Portugal during the sixteenth and seventeenth centuries, in conformity with the fundamental Treaty of Tordesillas; and if some of the acts of Portugal seem to have violated these boundaries, they were contested on the part of Spain, as has been shown, and were properly accounted for by the government at Lisbon.

<small>Spanish colonization during the XVIIth century, according to the Portuguese authorities.</small> Portuguese colonization advanced very slowly from the coast of the Atlantic towards the region of its boundary with territory of the Crown of Spain. Father Gay in his official Brazilian work, cited, devotes chapter VII to a description of the sources of the Rio de la Plata,[1] and chapter VIII to explaining what were at that time (seventeenth century) the Provinces of Rio Grande do Sul, Santa Catalina, Matto Grosso, etc.

These are his clear and positive words:

> I am going to treat in this book of the discovery and settlement of the Provinces of the Rio de la Plata; nor will it be out of place to describe them in all their parts and conditions, to specify how far they extend in latitude and longitude, to treat of the rivers of great volume that unite with the principal one, and to enumerate the multitude of Indians of different races, customs and languages who live within their confines.
>
> Consequently it is well to know that this government is one of the largest possessed by *His Catholic Majesty* in the Indies, because although His Majesty calculates it to extend over four hundred leagues of south latitude on the coast of the Atlantic Ocean, it extends in reality over eight hundred, from this same Ocean to the confines of the government of Serpa and Silva. . . .
>
> From Cape Santa Maria on the north, on the side of Brazil, this government extends nearly two hundred leagues, *as far as Cananea, where the Adelanto Alvaro Nuñez Cabeza de Vaca placed an army in order to determine the boundaries of the lands under his jurisdiction.*
>
> The coast of the Rio de la Plata and of Cape Santa Maria towards the north is low and without shelter as far as the Island of Santa Catharina, which has three ports for small vessels. . . .
>
> From here to the north the entire coast is rugged and mountainous, with large trees and many fruits of the earth. Every four or five leagues there is found a river and a harbor for ships, particularly at San Francisco, which is so deep and so safe that the largest craft can come alongside the shore.

---

[1] "*Revista do Instituto Historico*," etc., "*do Brazil*," Vol. 26, page 762 and following.

From San Francisco to Cananea, it is a distance of thirty-two leagues. Here are the boundaries of Paraguay.

The eighteenth century offers more of interest, for during its course there were profound agitations in Europe, which disturbed the progress of the World and naturally influenced the South American colonies, which had been founded and which had received such an extraordinary impetus. Ever since the seventeenth century the Jesuit colonies on the North of the Rio Yguazú had suffered from the hostilities of the hordes of semi-savages from the country under the Captaincy-General of San Vicente, in Brazil. These crowds of natives and *mestizos*, subject to the King of Portugal, lived by plundering the neighboring countries settled by Spain, and had their headquarters in the town called "*Villa de San Pablo*," for which reason history also calls them "*Paulistas*." Their most important and wicked occupation was that of hunting the Indians who had submitted to the rule of the Spanish, in order to sell them afterwards as slaves in the Portuguese colonies situated on the Atlantic, as far North as Rio de Janeiro. The prosperity of these colonies was retarded by the want of laborers, for they lacked the tact necessary to induce the native tribes to mingle with them, and therefore bought these native slaves in order to remedy this situation. The Jesuits resisted the invasions of those engaged in this traffic; but the latter formed bodies of cavalry, of the Bedouin type, audacious and irresistible, which overran immense deserts and sometimes even went so far as to threaten the very city of Asuncion. The Jesuit Republic, being immense, could not be defended without dividing its forces. The resistance to these "*Mamelukes*," as they were called, was everywhere weak for that reason, and more than sixty thousand of its subjects had been captured and sold in the slave-market of San Pablo. The Jesuits then decided to concentrate their establishments between the rivers Uruguay and Paraná, abandoning the thirteen towns they possessed on the North of the river Yguazú. The "*Mamelukes*" destroyed this cultivated country, with its industries fostered during an existence of over two centuries, and burned the towns and slaughtered or reduced to captivity the few Indians who did not follow the Jesuits into the Territory protected by the two large rivers Paraná and Uruguay, and which was therefore easier to defend.

Then took place a memorable and solemn emigration of several hundred thousand souls, *mestizos* and persons belonging to the *Guarani* tribes, commanded by the Jesuits, fighting day and night against the

slave-robbers, with a spirit of abnegation and sacrifice which brings to
mind the people of Israel. The acts of these "*Mamelukes*" of San Pablo
were solemnly condemned by the Kings of Portugal and by the whole
World, moved by the martyrdom of hundreds of thousands of peaceful
and laborious creatures, and the modern Brazilian historians honestly
repeat this condemnation. This Territory, abandoned for a time, continued however under the legal dominion of Spain, according to the
solemn Treaty of Tordesillas, and Portugal did not pretend to base any
possessory rights upon the crimes narrated, which it repudiated. Farther
on, in a special chapter, will appear the documents that refer to the
vandalism of the "*Mamelukes*," and these, in connection with this
brief historical résumé, will judicially prove the following fact: That
the depopulation of the territory situated between the rivers $Yguazú$
and *Tieté*, far from prejudicing the exercise of Spanish sovereignty
over the Territory submitted to this Arbitration, between the rivers
Paraná and Uruguay, only affirmed it, for the Jesuits took refuge in its
heart, and there they victoriously resisted, for more than fifty years,
the attacks of the savage hordes of slave-hunters.

These extraordinary events took place from the middle of the seventeenth to the middle of the eighteenth century and they coincide with the
perspective, each year becoming more definite, of a new policy on the
part of Spain concerning the territory she had possessed ever since
1516 on the coast of Brazil. She had occupied and developed these
possessions during two centuries simply as a means of communication with *Asuncion del Paraguay*, in which city the government of the
Rio de la Plata was concentrated by Yrala in the middle of the sixteenth century. The Historian Southey, cited, recognizes this with
entire frankness, in the following terms:[1]

> These measures show an intention on the part of the Spaniards to keep up a communication with Europe through Brazil; an
> object of great importance before they had succeeded in establishing a settlement at Buenos Ayres; for it must very rarely
> have happened that a vessel proper for crossing the Atlantic sailed
> from Asumpcion.

But the foundation of the city of *Santa Fé* in 1573, the second
foundation of *Buenos Ayres* in 1580 and that of *Corrientes* in 1581,
constituted, together with the Fort of *San Salvador* on the eastern
shore of the Rio de la Plata, a chain of flourishing ports along the

---
[1] English text, Vol. I, page 348; Portuguese text, page 470.

rivers of La Plata, Paraná and Paraguay that attracted direct navigation from Spain. It was easier and quicker to communicate with the Government of the Rio de la Plata by water, after the foundation of these cities, than by the long and difficult overland road of Alvar Nuñez Cabeza de Vaca, so that this road fell into disuse, being only casually frequented for local matters and by the Indians. In 1726, when the King ordered that the *Misiones* should be added to the Government of Buenos Ayres, the Governors of the Rio de la Plata abandoned the overland route, devoting themselves to building up the international and interfluvial navigation from Buenos Ayres to the *Yguazú*, to the sources of the Uruguay, and as far as the upper Paraguay. <small>Spanish colonies of the coast of Brazil.</small> This explains the fact that the largest river system in the World [the Plata, Uruguay, Paraná and Paraguay], being open to coasting trade as well as to seagoing vessels, the Court of Spain preferred to concentrate its material, still scarce for such an extensive government, on the margins of these water-courses, in preference to undertaking inland colonies, distant, difficult of access, and complicated in administration. They were not, however, altogether abandoned, as is <small>The King of Spain protects his dominions in South America.</small> proven by the *Royal Cédula* already quoted,[1] incorporating the Jesuit *Misiones* under the jurisdiction of Buenos Ayres, the most powerful of the southern governments of Spain.

In 1727 a question of ecclesiastical jurisdiction was resolved by the King, establishing the boundaries to the authority of the Bishoprics of Paraguay and of Buenos Ayres. This decision placed all the territories on the sources of the Rivers Paraná and Uruguay, East of the Paraná, under the jurisdiction of the Prelate of Buenos Ayres.[2] Another *Royal Cédula*, dated December 28, 1743, and published in the same book cited, gave the names of the thirty *pueblos* or settlements of *Misiones*, directed by the Jesuits, including among them the Territory now in controversy, and ordering how these settlements were to be governed.

Portugal did not advance into this region upon the dominions of <small>International difficulties.</small> Spain, and the international difficulties that arose, and were settled

---

[1] Page 47 of this Argument.
[2] The extensive papers in this case have been officially published by the Argentine Republic, in the book presented to the Arbitrator in the "Argentine Evidence," under the title of "Annex to the Memoir on the Boundary Question between the Argentine Republic and Uruguay: by Manuel Ricardo Trelles. Official publication. Buenos Ayres, 1867."—Page 140 and following. —Documents No. 38 39 40 and 41.

in Europe during more than a century, only affected in the Rio de la Plata the *Colony of Sacramento*, to which I will further refer, but never caused any trouble in *Misiones*.

Nevertheless the frequent conflicts between the irresponsible hordes of the "*Mamelukes*" and the peaceful Spanish colonists occasioned diplomatic claims and bad feeling which demanded a definitive solution. Both Courts did, in fact, come to a boundary agreement. This was a secret transaction. Spain ceded to Portugal some of its central territories, on the East of the Paraná and Northeast of the Yguazú; and the Crown of Portugal renounced any pretension to possess ports on the banks of the Rio de la Plata, where it had several times during two centuries endeavored to secure a foothold by force, but always being defeated by the Spanish arms. This transaction was traced by both governments on a map, officially prepared by the Government of Portugal before reducing the treaty to writing;[1] and the boundary agreed upon was delineated by means of a *red line*. Thereupon the Plenipotentiaries of both Crowns signed and sealed two copies of this map one in Portuguese, the other in Spanish, in order that the treaty should be drawn up in conformity with the line thus agreed upon, and this was done.

_{Boundary Treaty of 1750.}

This map, Mr. President, is another indestructible judicial foundation for Argentine Right, for the *red boundary line* runs by the point that Spain maintained during the last century and which the Argentine Government is now defending. In the special chapter on treaties I shall present this map, the existence of which Portuguese and Brazilian writers have denied during a century and a half, or alleged that it was a fabrication, the Argentine Government having discovered it in 1892, under the triple authority of the Governments of France, Spain and even Portugal itself, in the archives of which are preserved the originals and authorized copies.

In order to maintain the logical order of my discussion of the acts of jurisdiction that protect the Argentine Right, I leave till later on the examination of this Treaty of 1750, the fruitless demarcations it occasioned and its annullment by another treaty, which, however, declared the permanent validity of the map of 1749, known in the history of these negotiations by the name of "*Mapa de las Cortes*" (Map of the Courts).

Acts of the City of Corrientes, 1751.

In 1751 the city of Corrientes had doubts as to the exact extent of

[1] See this Argument, chapter referring to the Demarcation of the Boundaries.

its boundaries, and the "Cabildo" (City Council) assembled on the 26th of April of the same year. After comparing the ancient titles the following was declared in the document then issued :[1]

. . . that the jurisdiction of this city for the part of the river downward begins from the mouth of the great marshes that are between the river Corrientes and Santa Lucia, which is the place where at present we have the sign that divides this jurisdiction from that of *Santa Fé; and the part of the river above to the sources of the Uruguay river, Tape, Mbiasa, and San Francisco*,[2] as is more fully expressed in an agreed chapter made in the past year, 1673, the 15th of June, when was presented the book cited of the foundation that was made of this city the 3d day of April, 1588, as the licentiate Juan de Torres de Vera y Aragon, Governor and Captain-General, who was of this Province of Paraná. . . .

The treaty of 1751 met with opposition among all the Pueblos of the Governments of Buenos Ayres and Paraguay. This opposition has been attributed to the Jesuits, of whom, on this account, History has spoken very severely, in ignorance of the diplomatic secret connected with this affair. The Jesuits were in harmony with the public opinion of the country, and they were right. The King of Spain, in fact, neither sufficiently knew his dominions in America, nor did he give them the importance they deserved. Therefore, in the secret treaty of 1750, he gave up to Portugal the immense lands of La Guayra, and others situated on the East of the Government of the Rio de la Plata, which were far from being wild lands, as the agents of Portugal made the Councillors of the Spanish monarch believe, but on the contrary were well-populated countries, with cities, industries and hundreds of thousands of subjects. How could these consent to change their King, their jurisdictions and their laws? The inhabitants therefore resisted this treaty that enlarged the Kingdom of Portugal by the gift of lands rich, valuable and thickly settled, which Spain relinquished through carelessness and ignorance. But however things may have been, the truth is that the Territory now submitted to the Arbitrator remained within the dominions of Spain.

Agitation caused by the treaty of 1751.

The Jesuits continued the administration of the *Misiones*, in the name of the Crown of Spain, until the year 1768, when they were expelled by the *Royal Cédula* of February 27, 1767.[3] The documents

Banishment of the Jesuits, 1767.

[1] Collection of "Data and Documents," etc., page 26 (No. 13.)
[2] Coast of Brazil, Province of *del Campo*.
[3] See work of Brabo, pages 37 *et seq.*, cited later.

and history of the banishment of the Jesuits by the King of Spain from his dominions in Europe and America, have been published in a book of European celebrity, which I present to the Arbitrator, and which makes any further discussion of this matter in this Argument unnecessary. It is entitled :

> *Coleccion de Documentos Relativos á la Expulsion de los Jesuitas de la República Argentina y del Paraguay, en el reinado de Carlos III ; con introduccion y notas por Don Francisco Javier Brabo, Comendador de numero de la Real Orden Americana de Isabel la Católica. Va precedida de la Autobiografía y retrato del Colector. [Madrid. Establecimiento tipográfico de José Maria Perez. Corredera baja de San Pablo No. 27. 1872.]*
> [Collection of Documents relating to the expulsion of the Jesuits from the Republics of Argentine and Paraguay, in the Reign of Charles the III ; with an introduction and notes by Don Francisco Javier Brabo, etc., etc., preceded by an autobiography and portrait of the author, etc., etc.]

New government of Misiones The territories of the Jesuit Republic were not for this reason abandoned. The instructions issued by Count Aranda, Minister of State of Spain, dated March 1, 1767, established the fact that the King had delegated his entire authority and powers to the Viceroys, Presidents and Governors of the Indies and the Philippines. Articles V and XII of these instructions read as follows :[1]

> V. In all the *Misiones* administered by the Company of Jesus in America and the Philippines a Governor shall be placed in each province, *ad interim*, who shall be a person of recognized probity and who shall reside at the chief city of the *Misiones* and attend to the government in conformity with the people in the laws of the Indies. It will be well to establish therein some Spaniards, opening and facilitating reciprocal commerce, it being understood that he shall look after the welfare of each one particularly, according as he shall see the occasion therefor.
> . . . .
> XII. As the distance does not allow consultation in their proceedings, and as the Viceroys, Presidents or Governors respectively shall be arbitrators, without failing to regard the spirit of the laws over the whole extent of their command, they shall employ to this end the needful means or add any precautions they may think necessary, behaving themselves with firmness and integrity in case the offences should be of gravity in the execution of the Royal service.

[1] Work by Brabo, page 13 *et seq.*

Brabo also publishes in the same book, page 101, the document by which the Mayors and Caciques of the thirty *pueblos* of *Misiones* governed by the Jesuits accepted the authority of the King, directly exercised by his Lieutenants or Governors. This precious document is written in the *Guaraní* language and has a Spanish parallel translation.

At page 199 of the same work is found the official list signed by the Viceroy of Buenos Ayres, Bucarelli, of the *Pueblos* of the *Misiones* of Uruguay, which were confided to the government of Don Juan Francisco de la Riva Herrera, and of the Paraná *Misiones*, confided to General Francisco Bruno de Zavala. Among the former was San Xavier, the capital city of the Territory submitted to the Arbitrator, as will be demonstrated by means of documents, which will also show clearly its geographical situation, and *Corpus*, the capital and port of the same Territory, on the river Paraná.[1]

At page 255 and following Brabo publishes the official documents concerning the submission of the *Guaraní* Indians, who occupied the precise Territory now in controversy, to the authorities of *Corpus*. Regarding the exact location of the *Guaraní* Indians, the official Brazilian work, by Gay, says:

> The second is the tribe of the Guanases (singular Guaná), which occupies the region on *the left bank of the Paraná*, and of the *Yguazú* to the South, having for its centre the lands called *Nhuguassú* or *Campo Grande*.

Having expelled the Jesuits and consolidated the royal government in its ancient dominions, the Court of Madrid created the Viceroyalty of Buenos Ayres, in order to centralize and strengthen in these distant and immense regions the authority delegated by the King and to more effectually oppose its arms to those of Portugal, which had already attempted to extend its dominions West of the celebrated line of the Treaty of Tordesillas. Portugal had in fact taken forcible possession of the Spanish ports founded in the Sixteenth century on the coast of Brazil and the Island of Santa Catalina. *Creation of the Viceroyalty of the Rio de la Plata. 1776.*

The celebrated Royal Cédulas of August 1, 1776, creating the Viceroyalty of the Rio de la Plata, and appointing General Don Pedro de Ceballos Commander-in-chief of the expedition sent by Spain to expel the Portuguese from the old colonies on the coast of Brazil which they had usurped, are documents of universal celebrity. The Royal Cédula of August 1, 1776, reads as follows in its vital part:

---

[1] This *Argument*, chapter referring to the Argentine Jurisdiction over the Territory.

THE KING, to Don Pedro de Ceballos, Lieutenant-General of my
Royal troops. Being satisfied with the repeated proofs you have
given of your love and zeal for my royal service, and having appointed you to the command of the expedition that is being prepared at Cadiz and bound to South America, with directions to
*obtain satisfaction from the Portuguese for the wrongs they have com-
mitted in the Rio de la Plata, I have decided to appoint you my
Viceroy, Governor and Captain-General of the Provinces of Buenos
Ayres, Paraguay, Tucuman, Potosi, Santa Cruz de la Sierra,
Charcas*, and of all the districts in my provinces, Pueblos and Territories, to which the jurisdiction of that *Audiencia* extends, over
which you may preside in the case of going thereto, with the same
powers and authority which the other viceroys of my dominions
in the Indies enjoy, according to the laws thereof.

The disputed Territory in the Viceroyalty.

As clearly appears by the Royal Cédula of 1726, the Jesuit *Misiones*, in the centre of which was situated the Territory submitted to the Arbi-
trator, belonged to the Government of Buenos Ayres. Therefore that
Territory remained in 1776 subject to the Viceroyalty of the Rio de la
Plata, the capital of which was Buenos Ayres.

War of Spain against Portugal in America.

Thus the first Viceroy of Buenos Ayres was the above-named Governor of Madrid, General Don Pedro de Ceballos, who left Spain in 1776
at the head of a powerful military expedition to attack the Portuguese
and re-establish the rights and dominion of Spain, in conformity with
the Line of Demarcation of the Treaty of Tordesillas, the validity of
which had once more been recognized by both Crowns in the Treaty of
1768, to which I will refer later on. The Royal Cédula for the
Ceballos expedition further said :

Don Pedro de Ceballos, Caballero of the Royal Order of San
Genaro, Commander of Signo y Senet in that of Santiago, Special
Private Counsellor of the Supreme Council of War, Lieutenant-
General of my armies and Governor and Commander-General of
Madrid and its districts; You are authorized to organize an expedition for Buenos Ayres composed of 8,000 men of infantry in
one complete regiment, and ten second-class battalions, including
one of light troops, each battalion with a strength of 688 men,
and more than 600 dismounted dragoons who are to be mounted
on their arrival there, and 400 artillery-men, all with their competent officers; a detachment of artificers, a body of ten engineers
and two trains of artillery, one of siege and the other of field
guns, with gunpowder, munitions of war and other like materials,
a detailed list of which you will receive; *all for the purpose of
recovering the ports that the troops of the King of Portugal have
lately taken within my dominions of Rio Grande, San Pedro, and*

elsewhere which they may have invaded in those countries, as well as also to conquer from them others if possible, especially the Island of Santa Catalina and the Colony of Sacramento. I have decided to select and send you upon this very important enterprise, expecting from your proven zeal and good conduct the best discharge of this trust, to which end the present instructions are directed.

The *Royal Cédulas* referring to the creation of the Viceroyalty of the Rio de la Plata and the Campaign of General Ceballos are documents of universal celebrity and for this reason do not accompany the text, but remain in the Archives of the Argentine Legation at the disposition of the Arbitrator. Besides, they have been officially published by the Argentine Republic in the work of Dr. Don Vicente Quesada, presented to the Arbitrator among the books of the "Argentine Evidence," with the title of "*Virreynato del Rio de la Plata,*" [Viceroyalty of the Rio de la Plata,] Buenos Aires, 1881. pp. 42 and 46.

This campaign was a rapid and successful one and the Portuguese were everywhere defeated. The absolute dominion of the Viceroy of Buenos Ayres in conformity with the title deeds of three centuries, which have been set forth in this Argument was fully re-established from the Cordillera of the Andes on the West to the Atlantic Ocean on the East, and from the sources of the Amazon on the North to the Polar Sea on the South, in accordance with the "Map of Discoveries and Conquests." [Defeat of the Portuguese. Limits of the Vice-Royalty.]

After this victory the Viceroy Ceballos dedicated himself to the organization and administration of his extensive government, and ordered a general census to be taken. I have the honor to present to the Arbitrator the original Census of the Pueblos of Corpus, on the Paraná, and San Xavier, on the Uruguay, kept in the Archives of the Argentine Republic, which, as I have already said, exercised municipal jurisdiction over the disputed Territory.[1] [Census of 1776 and 1777.]

To complete the sketch of the jurisdiction of Spain over the disputed Territory down to the opening of the nineteenth century, I will only present some of the numerous undisputed and indisputable official documents that my country possesses. [Treaty of 1777.]

The difficulties that arose between the Crowns of Spain and Portugal in tracing upon the ground the boundaries of the Treaty of 1750, the abrogation of this Treaty, and the attempt at demarcation in 1759

---

[1] "Argentine Evidence," volume I, page 289, and Group A of Manuscripts, Nos. 6 and 8.

according to the new Treaty of 1761, had left the situation insecure for the authorities of both Monarchies in America. Being aware of this they hastened to sign a new preliminary boundary treaty, a celebrated document which affected all South America and is known as the Treaty of San Ildefonso, dated October 1, 1777.

This treaty strengthens the Argentine title. As I will demonstrate in the proper place, the failure of the demarcation of boundaries by reference to the Treaty of 1750, occurred because the Demarcators made a mistake, taking a small stream for the boundary instead of the river *Pepiry* or *Pequiry*, which was clearly indicated on the official map (*Map of the Courts*) prepared by Portugal and accepted by Spain to guide the demarcation. To avoid further mistakes the treaty of 1777 added to the name of the river *Pepiry* or *Pequiry* the qualifying word *Guazú*, meaning "*large*," in order to distinguish it from the small stream which the Demarcators of 1759 had called by mistake *Pepiry* or *Pequiry*, considering it as the boundary river.

This adjective cleared away all doubts, showed the error of the Demarcators of 1759, already annulled by the solemn pact of 1761, and once more settled the quarrel on the basis which the Argentine Republic has asserted since 1810.

New demarcation. 1783-1791. After this treaty the Monarchs sent new Commissions of Engineers to locate the boundaries in South America, from the Rio de la Plata to the Orinoco, but, as we will see further on, this survey was unsuccessful in the Rio de la Plata, because the Portuguese Engineers refused to recognize the boundaries of the Treaty of 1777, and their Government, taking advantage of the internal difficulties that the French revolution created in Europe, and especially in Spain, whose American colonies were excited, being already threatened by Napoleon, claimed more territory than belonged to it. The boundary commissioners of both countries suspended their work in 1791, after ascertaining the *true river of the treaty of* 1777, and awaited orders from their Governments. These never came, because Spain and Portugal, as is well known, continued involved in the Napoleonic wars, and Spanish America shortly afterwards rose, proclaiming its Independence.

The disputed Territory at the end of the XVIIIth century. During the period that elapsed from 1777 to 1800, the Territory submitted to the Arbitrator remained under the jurisdiction of Spain and was directly governed by the Viceroy of Buenos Ayres. This has never been denied by Brazil, which from 1516 to 1800 neither coveted nor explored it, neither drove a stake in it nor in its neighborhood, and neither exercised, directly or indirectly, any acts of jurisdiction there, nor indeed even pretended to discuss the matter until 1857. Besides the legal proof I have presented, the fact was officially established in the Arbitration between the Republics of Argentine and Paraguay, decided in 1878 by President Hayes, the papers of which are preserved at the State Department. These papers show that the Provinces of *Paraguay* and *Buenos Ayres*, which were integral *parts of the Viceroyalty of the Rio de la Plata*, alternately governed [1] the Territory in dispute, in the name of the Viceroy of Buenos Ayres and for the King of Spain, until 1803.

Abundant proofs of this jurisdiction can be given and I will refer to the documents I have the honor to present to the Arbitrator, in the form of copies authenticated by the American Consuls, taken from the public archives where the originals are kept.[2] These are:—

> 1803. Royal *Cédula* (Letters Patent) concerning the resolution for the arrangement of a new plan of Government for the *Guarani* and *Tape* Indians.

This Royal Cédula says:

> The above-mentioned Viceroy, concluding the report that had been asked for, in his letter of March 8, 1800, after proposing the means which seemed to him the most convenient and best suited to the natural civil constitution of these natives, proposes they should be allowed the same liberty as the Spaniards, restoring to them their individual properties and their conquered country, so that they might live with the security established by laws, governing themselves according thereto and observing the ordinances of the country as far as they were adapted to them, as well as those of the Captain-General, Bucarelli, as far as these were proper to the critical circumstances of passing from a state of ignorance and rudeness to one of enlightenment and liberty; thus suppressing the "*encomiendas*" of Paraguay, of the *Mitayo* Pueblos, in the *Misiones* of Paraná and Uruguay. My Viceroy has taken this resolution in consequence of my Royal Order of November 30, 1798, giving liberty to three hundred fathers of families, to whom lands and cattle have been awarded, with only the moderate charge of one dollar, which had been fixed some time before.

---

[1] See the official document issued by the Viceroy of Buenos Ayres, in the "Argentine Evidence," Vol. 1, page 297 *et seq.*, and in Group A of Manuscripts, No. 9.

[2] Argentine Evidence *ibidem*, Group A of Manuscripts, documents Nos. 9, 10, 11, 12, 13, 14.

1805. Title of Governor of the province of Paraguay, with the additional command of the thirty *pueblos* (settlements) of *Misiones*, in favor of Don Bernardo de Velasco.

1806. Concerning the necessary expenses for the new settlement ordered to be established at the junction of the rivers *Uruguay* and *Ybicuy*.

1806—Concerning the new plan of defence of the thirty *pueblos* of *Misiones* and others: Report of the Bureau of Fortifications of Spain.

I will still further mention, in addition to these important documents, a table, the original of which is kept in the archives of Buenos Ayres, containing the latitude and longitude of the most important Pueblos, and those which served as Department capitals in the "*Misiones*."[1]

In 1856 Paraguay recognized the *Misiones* and the Territories situated to the *East of the river Paraná*, among which is the disputed Territory, as belonging to the Argentine Republic by right and by its lawful acts of material occupation. It was afterwards conclusively established that the boundary between Paraguay and the Argentine Republic on the East was the river Paraná, according to the treaties of the Triple Alliance between Brazil, Uruguay and the Argentine Republic, signed May 1, 1865, and the Boundary Treaty between the Republics of Argentine and Paraguay, signed on February 3, 1876.[2]

This latter treaty says:

ART. I. The Republic of Paraguay is separated on the Eastern and Southern parts from the Argentine Republic by the middle of the current of the principal channel of the river Paraná, from its confluence with the river Paraguay until its left bank becomes one of the boundaries of the Empire of Brazil, the Island of Apipé belonging to the Argentine Republic, and the Island of Yacireta to the Republic of Paraguay, as was declared by the treaty of 1856.[3]

---

[1] It is a translation of the original document existing in the Archives of the Royal Academy of History, a copy of which, duly certified by the United States Consul at Madrid, forms part of Group A, No. 13, of manuscript documents, "Argentine Evidence," Vol. I, page 319.

[2] See Memoirs of the Argentine and Paraguayan Plenipotentiaries, presented to President R. B. Hayes in the Arbitration concerning the Chaco Territory, which was decided in Washington on the 12th of November, 1878. The treaties and documents to which I refer in this part of my Argument were printed among the papers of the Chaco Arbitration.

[3] See *Chaco Arbitration*, cited, held during the Administration of President Hayes (Appendix and Document annexed to the Memoir filed by the Minister of Paraguay, on the question submitted to arbitration, New York, etc., 1878. Pages 53 and 179. This work, authenticated by the Government and American Consul at Asuncion del Paraguay, is among the books of the "Argentine Evidence." It is also in the library of the State Department.

The Treaty of the Triple Alliance, signed by the Plenipotentiaries of Brazil, Argentine Republic and Uruguay, had made the following declarations in 1865:

> ART. IX. The independence, sovereignty and territorial integrity of the Republic of Paraguay will be guaranteed collectively in conformity with the foregoing article, by the high contracting parties, for the term of five years.
> ART. XVI. The Argentine Republic will be divided from the Republic of Paraguay by the Paraná and Paraguay rivers, until reaching the boundaries of the Empire of Brazil, these being, on the right bank of the Paraguay river, the Bahia Negra.

In consequence of the acts of jurisdiction exercised by Paraguay over the Territory submitted to the Arbitrator, in the name of the Viceroy of Buenos Ayres, it was subject to Spain until 1810, and after that year to the Argentine Government.

Amid the military troubles of the time, the Spanish Monarch did not lose sight of the Territory of *Misiones*, the importance of which had been disclosed to the world by the noisy expulsion of the Jesuits, who had governed it ever since 1610, that is to say, during not less than two centuries. This Territory was at the time thickly settled, and according to the census then taken, its industrial wealth furnished the following descriptive information: *The Territory in question during the XIXth century.*

> They excel in music, in sculpture, and in making statuary, as well as in casting metals, ironwork, and as locksmiths. From the cotton which they cultivate there they make very fine textures, and dye them beautifully with brilliant colors. They also make from the cotton plant linens so fine that they surpass the very finest Hollands and even silk. There is also in this province an innumerable number of domestic animals. As elsewhere stated, at the time of the banishment of the Jesuits there were 769,859 head of cattle, 81,078 horses, 13,905 mules, 221,537 hogs, 7,493 donkeys, and 596 goats. These are the ones that belong to the thirty *pueblos*.[1]

The unjust attempts made by Portugal during the unsuccessful demarcations of 1759 and 1793 to extend its territories as far as the mouth *New Province of Misiones, 1803.*

---

[1] "*Descripción de los Obispados de Sud America por Don José Maria Suarez de Valdes.*" [Description of the Bishoprics of South America, by Don José Maria Suarez de Valdes.] Printed during the last century and presented to the Arbitrator in Spanish among the books of the "Argentine Evidence," page 6, a little before the end of the book, and manuscript page 110.

of the Rio de la Plata, show us that the King of Spain proceeded deliberately and with foresight, binding together and giving administrative importance to his central territories of *Misiones*. On the 17th of May, 1803, he dictated the well-known *Cédula* creating the Province of that name in the Viceroyalty of Buenos Ayres. That same year he appointed as Governor of the *Nueva Provincia de Misiones* [New Province of Misiones] Don Antonio de Velasco, who was to be placed in possession of his new command by the Viceroy of Buenos Ayres.

Finally, these undisputed and indisputable facts of national sovereignty were followed during the same year by two Royal *Cédulas*, setting forth a new plan of government for the indigenous populations that hitherto had obeyed the Jesuits and now recovered their municipal independence, within the Viceroyalty of Buenos Ayres.[1]

RECOGNITION OF THE SOVEREIGNTY OF SPAIN BY BRAZIL.

Confirmation of the preceding chapter by Brazilian authorities.

I have frequently stated that Portugal, during the four centuries studied, recognized the sovereignty of Spain over the Territory in controversy. Some official Brazilian opinions will be given to strengthen this argument. The Visconde de Porto Seguro is, as I have said, the highest and most indisputable authority in Brazil in the matter of international boundaries. In volume I of his "*Historia Geral do Brazil*," (General History of Brazil), presented to the Arbitrator on page 20 of this Argument, he constantly recognizes the truth of the facts I have narrated, but not to burden this Argument with too many analogous citations, I will confine myself to translating some of his fundamental conclusions. At page 122 of that volume, when relating the events of the first Portuguese expedition to the coasts of Brazil and the Rio de la Plata, in 1531, he says:

Declarations of the Visconde de Porto Seguro in his *General History of Brazil*.

1531.

> Once on shore they were to take occasion to make frequent astronomical observations,[2] in order to establish the exact latitude and longitude of the place. *Thus they were convinced, as also their Captain, that this coast, and with more reason the entire Rio de la Plata, was situated beyond and further west than the line to which the dominions of Portugal extended in those regions, according to the Treaty of Tordesillas.*

---

[1] Although these facts were recognized by both parties, the Argentine Republic and Paraguay, in the Chaco Arbitration, the documents concerning the new province of *Misiones* can be referred to in Vol. 1, page 287, of the "Argentine Evidence," and in Group A of Manuscripts, document No. 5.

[2] Note: This is confirmed by the mathematician Don Pedro Nuñez in one of his works.

After categorically stating that the Treaty of Tordesillas was the 1557.
supreme law of both crowns touching their boundaries in America, he
also declares that the good faith of Spain went so far as to order its
troops of the Rio de la Plata to defend the city of Rio de Janeiro, the
Capital of the Portuguese Colonies, against the attacks of the French.
He says on pages 279 and 280, volume I:

> When the news which the colonies had communicated from
> Asuncion by the river San Francisco do Sul, that Rio de Janeiro
> had been occupied by the French, reached the Court of Castille,
> the order was immediately sent from there, in the month of Feb-
> ruary, 1557, to the governor of the Rio de la Plata, to establish a
> settlement on the Rio San Francisco; and in May he was ordered
> to dislodge the French, also establishing some settlements wherever
> it might be most convenient, in case he found it necessary.

At pages 487 and 488 he considers the Jesuit *Misiones*, situated on 1628
the river *Tieté* and the regions that extend from the Paraná to the
Atlantic Ocean, acknowledging that they belong to Spain. Referring
to the Portuguese attempts at usurpation I will quote later on some
very eloquent words by this illustrious author.

At page 690, of which a translation will be given at the right place, 1654.
he condemns the invasions made by the Portuguese of San Pablo into
the Spanish colonies of La Guayra.

All of Section XLIV, from pages 933 to 962, is devoted to the nar- 1777.
ration of the campaigns of the Spanish generals to maintain and confirm the authority of their king on the Brazilian coast of the Rio
Grande and Island of Santa Catalina.

Southey is the Brazilian Historian who has the greatest prestige, as Testimony of
a foreign author, among the Brazilians themselves. The Visconde 1600
de Porto Seguro has taken him for a guide, as is stated in the " Introduction " to the "*Historia Geral*" referred to. I have already recorded
in this Argument the words of Southey fully recognizing the discoveries and colonizations by the Spaniards of the territories that
extend from the sources of the rivers Paraná and Paraguay to the
Atlantic.[1]

Chapter XXIII, Vol. III, of Southey's work,[2] which contains one hun- 1586 and 1670.

---

[1] Page 35 of this Argument.
[2] "*Historia Geral do Brazil*," already presented to the Arbitrator in its Brazilian
edition. The quotations herewith are taken from the Portuguese edition and compared
with the English text in the Congressional Library of the United States.

dred and eight pages in the Portuguese translation presented to the Arbitrator, is entirely devoted to the account of the conquest and settlement of that territory, bordering upon those of Portugal along the Captaincy of San Vicente, according to the "*Map of Discoveries*," etc., and does entire justice to Spain in its pages, while at the same time energetically condemning the attempts at usurpation made by Portugal. This work has been translated with the official authorization of Brazil, as I have already said.

At page 343 he says:

> While the northern provinces were engaged in this long struggle against the Dutch, the Jesuits established that dominion in Paraguay,[1] of which the rise, progress and overthrow are inseparably connected with the history of Brazil.

1610.

At page 361, Vol. III, he gives the boundaries of the Spanish Jesuit colonies, in conformity with the "*Map of Discoveries and Conquests*," etc., attached to this Argument, and says:

> Guayra was the scene to which these missionaries were destined. Under this name was comprehended a large tract of country, of which the Uruguay formed the Southern and the Paragnay the Western boundary; ....

1627.

Just in the centre of this region is situated the Territory submitted to the Arbitrator. Southey relates in Vol. III, page 391, the colonization of the interior lands where the Brazilian Province of Rio Grande is now located, and says:

> Gonzalez now entered the Serra de Tape, a mountainous district which bounds the province of Paraguay on the East, and extends about two hundred leagues East and West. The numerous streams that form the Ybicuy, which fall into the Uruguay, rise on the western side of this district, and on the eastward are the sources of the Yacuy, which forms the Laguna Grande de los Patos, called at its mouth the Rio Grande de San Pedro.

1750.

At page 155, Vol. VI, Southey explains the reasons and the practical commercial interests which induced the Portuguese to forget the treaties and take possession of the Spanish and Jesuit territories of the Province of Tape. He says with effect:

---

[1] A province of the government of Buenos Ayres.

It was of great importance to the Portuguese to possess this country on account of its port, its adaptability for the culture of the cereals and its abundant pastures, covered with cattle and horses.

He then narrates the occupation of this Province in 1737 by order of the Portuguese Governor Vasconcellos; and afterwards how the usurpers were attacked and defeated by the Spanish General Don Pedro de Ceballos in 1763 and the following year, which are facts within the domain of universal history.

I have already presented among the books of the "Argentine Evidence," that of Father Gay, published under the direct authority of the Emperor of Brazil, Dom Pedro II, in volume XXVI of the "*Revista do Instituto Historico, Geographico e Ethnographico do Brazil*."[1] I here repeat what was there said, that this Brazilian publication is the most complete defence of the Argentine Right. In the preface to Volume XXVI of this Review we find at page 5 the following paragraphs, which are the first of the book: Testimony of Gay in his "*Historia da Republica Jesuitica do Paraguay, 1896-1861.*

It was scarcely three hundred and fifty years since the first Europeans had reached the territory of the Rio de la Plata. From that time the sources of the majestic Paraguay, the great Paraná and the superb Uruguay, which covered the territory, were occupied by a multitude of savage tribes, which were usually called Guaranis.

The first discoverers and Spanish Conquistadores who founded the immense Province of Paraguay, subjected and enslaved all the persons they could secure, or compelled them to seek refuge in the dense and extensive forests. The Missionaries of the celebrated Company of Jesus, charged with assisting the Spanish colonization and above all with reducing the aboriginal peoples to Christianity, more humane than the Conquistadores, sought by mild means to civilize hundreds of thousands of Indians, with whom they settled the thirty-three villages, which composed precisely the now extinct Jesuit Republic of Paraguay.

This was written in 1861. In the centre of this country of the *Guaranis* is also found the Territory submitted to the Arbitrator. According to Gay ("*Revista do Instituto*," etc., Volume XXVI, page 51), the boundaries of the Jesuit *Misiones* are those already set forth in the translation at pages 44 and 45 of this Argument. 1610-1768.

This passage is of vital importance and I ask the serious attention

---
[1] See page 43 of this Argument.

of the Arbitrator to it. When studied with the maps it is seen that the "*Matto Castelhano,*" or "*Monte Castellano,*" is situated to the North, opposite the rivers San Antonio Guazú, of Oyarvide, and the Pequiry or Pepiry-Guazú, claimed as their boundaries by the Argentines.[1] Father Gay, without raising any questions, traces the boundaries of both countries along these rivers. His words refer to the possessions of the Jesuits until 1768, when they were banished, according to the boundaries agreed upon in the treaty of 1750, which the Portuguese in bad faith claim to trace more to the South than the true line described in the trustworthy data given by Gay, the French Priest in the service of Brazil.

At page 726, and following, is found the date of the foundation of the first Portuguese settlements on Spanish territory, San Pedro, Alegrete, Rio Grande, Santa Victoria, all between 1755 and 1822, that is to say, the period within which Spain attacked and subdued these possessions during the last century, as we have already seen, and within which, in this century, the Argentine Republic, already independent, opposed itself to Brazil, and paved the way for the events which resulted in the defeat of the latter at the battle of Ytuzaingo.

But these advances took place upon the sea-coast; there was not a single act, exploration, colonization, or individual settlement by Portuguese upon the Territory submitted to the Arbitrator during those centuries, nor during the nineteenth century until a very recent date, and that I shall discuss further on. No one can deny the affirmation that according to the documents presented the question of boundaries must be decided in favor of the Argentine Republic.

Father Gay says, at page 730, that Brazil had not settled even the territories that it occupied in this century upon the coast of the Atlantic Ocean and the confines of the Republic of Uruguay. These are his words:

> According to the brief chronological sketch I have just given it is clear that the first settlements in the Province of *San Pedro do Rio Grande do Sul* were the villages founded by the Jesuits on the eastern bank of the River Uruguay.

Testimony of Fernandez Barros, 1877.

In a discussion about boundaries between the Brazilian States of Paraná and Santa Catalina, the following official report was made, which I have the honor to present to the Arbitrator among the books of the "Argentine Evidence":

> ";Map of the Discoveries and Conquests," etc.

Discussão da Questão de limites entre o Paraná e Santa Catharina, por Bento Fernandez de Barros. Publicação do Club Literario Curitybano.—Rio de Janeiro, 1877. (Discussion of the boundary question between Paraná and Santa Catalina, by Benito Fernandez de Barros, etc., etc.)

At pages 14 and 15 it is admitted that during the centuries from 1500 to 1738 Portugal officially kept herself quiet within her possessions, according to the Treaty of Tordesillas, but that afterwards, in 1738, she founded the Captaincy of Santa Catalina and San Pedro, advancing upon the lands of Spain, later reconquered by the Spanish army of the Viceroy Ceballos, as I have shown.

The provinces of Paraná, Santa Catalina and Rio Grande are precisely those that are contiguous to the Territory submitted to the Arbitrator, but the official geographer of their internal boundary debate agrees with the Visconde de Porto Seguro, Southey and Gay in recognizing that the field of their actions was the sea-coast, and that Portugal never did absolutely never—in any way advance upon the Territory now in question.

In the next chapter I will prove that the Governments of Portugal and Brazil have acknowledged through their diplomats that they never possessed the disputed territory; and I will also demonstrate this by an examination of the treaties between the two Crowns. Direct testimony by the Government of Brazil.

Even at the risk of a superfluity of reasons I will present at the end of this Argument the most authentic map of the last century, in order to prove on the authority of universal geography that the Portuguese never laid any claim to the Territory now submitted to the Arbitrator, nor did they advance upon it during the centuries in which Spain maintained her power there until the Independence of South America, thus faithfully observing the Treaty of Tordesillas. Universal testimony.

PART SECOND.

II.

POSSESSION AND JURISDICTION OF THE ARGENTINE REPUBLIC IN THE TER-
RITORY SUBMITTED TO THE ARBITRATOR.

1810-1893.

Independence of South America, 1810.   Such was the legal condition of the Territory submitted to the Arbitrator when the city of Buenos Ayres declared at an end the authority of the King of Spain in South America, on the memorable days of May 23, 24, and 25, 1810, and its "*Cabildo*" or Council, assuming all the powers of the state, began the heroic struggle for the Independence of South America. The Argentine armies, composed of volunteer patriots, attacking the regular garrisons of the King of Spain, conquered them and secured the liberty of the immense region where to-day prosper the Republics of Argentine, Uruguay, Paraguay, Bolivia, Chile and Peru, and allied with the forces which Bolivar commanded they aided in securing the independence of the northern extremity of South America on the battle-fields of Rio Bamba, Junin and Ayacucho, in 1824.

Free government and the disputed Territory.   From the very first the popular government of Buenos Ayres was intent upon controlling the territories most distant from the capital which belonged to it as the successor of the immediate authority of the Viceroys and of the supreme authority of the King. In fact, the "*Cabildo*" of Buenos Ayres turned out the Royalist Governor of *Misiones*, Velasco, who had been appointed in 1803, as already stated, and appointed in his place Colonel Don Tomas de Rocamora, on the 26th of May, 1810, that is to say, the day after this new American Government had been proclaimed. Colonel Rocamora was then living in the Territory of *Misiones*, in the city of *Yapeyú*.[1]

[1] On the bank of the Uruguay, *vide* Map of the Discoveries and Conquests.

In the plea presented by Paraguay in the Chaco Arbitration case these facts were clearly recognized and related in the following terms:[1]

Subsequently the same *Junta*, on the 27th of May, 1810, addressed officially Col. Rocamora, and sent to him some printed papers setting forth the reasons why a Provisional Executive Junta had been established, and what were their purposes and intents, adding that no doubt was entertained about the patriotic way in which he would assist the Junta to remove and overcome the obstacles which might possibly embarrass the uniformity of action *within his district.*

As soon as Rocamora received this communication he sent a circular to the different sub-delegates of the Departments to which the *thirty pueblos of Misiones* belonged, and directed them to celebrate the installation of the said Junta. He also directed them to forward a list of the names of all persons fit for military service, specifying those most fitted for it, and make a statement of the Spaniards living in each Department, of the armament therein existing, of the troops in actual service, and of the amount of money kept in the Treasury.

Rocamora obtained favorable responses, and communicated them to the Provisional Government of Buenos Ayres, in these terms:[2]

<small>The Pueblos of Misiones recognize the New Government.</small>

. . . .
. . . I also, inspired with the same zeal, solemnized my recognition of your Excellency, and will contribute in everything within my power to propagate and maintain the uniformity of the same sentiments, *as it is at present what upholds our territorial safety,* and for the future will be the fundamental basis for the great work of sovereign representation to which your Excellency directs and consecrates all efforts.
. . . .

The Royalist Governor, Velasco, made an attempt to resist the orders of the "*Junta Revolucionaria*" (Revolutionary Council) of Buenos Ayres and took refuge in Paraguay. The Junta answered by reenforcing the authority of its Governor, Colonel Rocamora, declaring besides that the Royal *Cédula* of 1805 was repealed, by which the

<small>Separation of the Misiones from Paraguay.</small>

---

[1] See the cited work "Appendix and Documents annexed to the Memoir filed by the Minister of Paraguay," etc., etc., presented to the Arbitrator, page 20 in English and 205 in Spanish.
[2] See this document and the decree separating the *Pueblos of Misiones* from Paraguay in the "Argentine Evidence," Vol. I, page 451, and Spanish text in Group G of Manuscripts No. 1.

Province of Paraguay had been authorized to intervene in the Government of *Misiones* as the representative of the Viceroy of Buenos Ayres.[1] Another decree, of August 13, 1810, strengthened the preceding resolution, declaring all communication at an end between the *Misiones* and Paraguay and Montevideo, where the Royalist supporters were engaged in their preparations for resistance, taking advantage of the unsuspecting character, want of discipline, and anarchical spirit of the creoles.[2]

In 1811 the Government of Buenos Ayres sent an expedition to Paraguay to combat all royalist tendencies, and Colonel Rocamora took part in this, with four hundred soldiers from the *Misiones*. Paraguay abandoned the plan of settling matters by arms, and came to an agreement with the Government of Buenos Ayres, in order to maintain an indissoluble alliance in the common interest.[3]

The unfavorable position in which Spain was placed by the Argentine revolution against that country, led Portugal to attempt a new occupation of the territories contiguous to the mouth of the Rio de la Plata and upon the Uruguay from which it had been dislodged ever since 1762 by the successful campaign of the Viceroy Ceballos. Thereupon a Portuguese army violated the frontiers and the agreements established and guaranteed by the treaties of 1777 and 1778, and occupied the left bank of the Rio de la Plata, which now belongs to the Republic of Uruguay.

The pretext of this invasion was to assist the King of Spain, allied with Portugal in Europe against Napoleon I. So they supported the royalists of the Province of Montevideo and the Viceroyalty of the Rio de La Plata, and also communicated with the Spanish Generals in Peru, exhorting them to march against the Argentine armies and place them between two fires, one on the North and one on the South. They also fomented and offered to support a conspiracy of Spaniards that was being prepared in the city of Buenos Ayres, but which was discovered

---

[1] See translation of this document in the "Argentine Evidence," volume I, pages 451 and 452, Spanish text, Group G of Manuscripts, No. 2.

[2] This document has been published in the Official Register of the Argentine Republic, volume I, page 67. It is at the Argentine Legation in Washington, at the Arbitrator's disposal.

[3] These facts have been narrated in documents published by General Bartolmé Mitre, ex-President of the Argentine Republic, in his "*Historia de la Independencia*" (History of Argentine Independence), which is in the Archives of the Legation, at the disposal of the Arbitrator. The Agreement with Paraguay is published in the "Collection of Treaties of the Argentine Republic," presented to the Arbitrator.

and its leaders shot. But, as I have said, these were simply *pretexts*. What the Portuguese armies intended to do was to occupy the Spanish Province of Montevideo and stay there, thus realizing, under cover of the disorders produced by the first stages of the revolution, the old dream of their country of sharing with Spain the control of the course of the great rivers of the basin of the Rio de la Plata.

But the popular Government of Buenos Ayres determined to resist this invasion, and early and prudently negotiated in the capital of Brazil for the retreat of the invading army. Don Juan, the Prince Regent of Portugal, saw the impossibility of carrying out this enterprise, and therefore appointed a special commissioner to proceed to Buenos Ayres and come to an arrangement with the revolutionary Junta. This Commissioner, Lieut.-Colonel Don Juan Rademaker, signed in the capital of the newly born Argentine nation, on the 12th of May, 1812, an Armistice, entering into an obligation to respect the sovereignty of Spain. Article third said:

<blockquote>
ART. III. As soon as the Most Excellent Generals of the two armies shall have received the notice of this convention, *they will give the necessary orders not only to avoid all warlike engagements, but also to retire as soon as possible the troops under them within the limits of the territory of the two respective States; these boundaries being understood to be the same as those acknowledged as such before the Portuguese army commenced its marches towards the Spanish territory;*[1] *and in testimony and faith that these territories remain inviolable while this convention lasts and that everything therein stipulated will be exactly fulfilled,* we sign this document for its due proof, in Buenos Ayres, on the twenty-sixth of May, one thousand eight hundred and twelve.[2]
</blockquote>

The Minister of Foreign Affairs of the Prince Regent of Portugal addressed the revolutionary Junta of Buenos Ayres a significant note to inform it that this army had evacuated the Spanish territory. It reads as follows:

<blockquote>
Your Excellencies: A few days ago I received by transmission of a British man-of-war the answer of Your Excellencies, dated the 17th of July last, concerning the result of the Commission of Lieut.-Colonel Juan Rademaker; and having presented to His Royal Highness, the Prince Regent of Portugal, the Convention for an
</blockquote>

---
[1] The boundaries according to the treaties of 1777 and 1778.
[2] See Vol. I of the "Argentine Evidence," pages 105, 107, and 452. The Spanish text is in the Group A of Manuscripts No. 15.

Armistice, which was there arranged between that Government and the Portuguese negotiator, His Royal Highness was pleased to approve the terms of said Convention, the salutary provisions of which should at once be carried into effect; and then, the hostilities between the two armies having ceased, the Portuguese troops will, without the loss of time, *begin their retirement within their respective boundaries* in such manner as the rigor of the season and the condition of the transportation will permit. Hoping, therefore, that from this step will flow, as a consequence of the good faith with which it is taken, all the advantages which in this way can be secured for both countries, renewing those friendly relations and good intentions which so much tend to the reciprocal interests of two nations united by such sacred ties, His Royal Highness has determined to recall the Portuguese negotiator, as his stay there is now no longer necessary, and directs me to so inform your Excellencies. I have the honor on this happy occasion to renew the assurances of my most distinguished consideration, with which I have the honor to serve you as your most faithful servant.

CONDE DAS CALVEAS.

To the President and members of the Junta of Buenos Ayres.
Palace at Rio de Janeiro, Sept. 13, 1812.

First National Congress, 1812.
On the fourth of April, at 1 P. M., the first free congress in South America, composed of the deputies of the Spanish provinces that formed the Viceroyalty of the Rio de la Plata, was opened in Buenos Ayres. The Territory evacuated by the Portuguese troops on the eastern bank of that river sent its representatives, who were Don Valentin Gomez and Don Francisco Bruno Rivarola.[1]

Assistance to the Misiones, 1812
During the occupation of the Province of Montevideo by the Portuguese the Government of Buenos Ayres took steps to defend the Territory of *Misiones*. The invasion did in fact take place and four hundred Portuguese soldiers took possession of the central and strategical position of *Yapeyú*. The *Pueblos* of *Misiones*, situated to the West and North, immediately organized a contingent of three hundred volunteers, who descended the river Paraná and joined themselves to the Argentine army that was already marching against the invaders. In conformity with the Armistice of Rademaker, the *Misiones* were evacuated. The proof of the preceding facts is found in the book presented to the Arbitrator, on page 41 of this Argument, under the

---

[1] The document is published in the "*Registro Oficial*" of the Argentine Republic, 1812, Vol. I, page 161, and is at the Argentine Legation in Washington, at the disposal of the Arbitrator.

title of "*Coleccion de Datos y Documentos referentes á Misiones,*" (Collection of Data and Documents referring to *Misiones*,) Argentine official publication, Part III, pages 519 to 524, Documents No. 250 to 256.[1]

In 1813 the seeds of the Argentine Nation were planted at the meeting in Buenos Ayres of the first Constituent Assembly, for the Congress of 1812 had only been a provisional body.

The new Nation. 1813.

This Assembly enacted the political constitution, provided for a national coat-of-arms and coinage, and gave the name of *Provincias Unidas del Rio de la Plata* (United Provinces of the Rio de la Plata) to the new Nation; and among the other measures designed to cement a free Government approved the national anthem, which ends thus:

> And the free people of the World respond,
> To the great Argentine people, welcome!

On the second of February the National Assembly passed one of its first laws, declaring the existence of slavery to be outrageous and dishonoring to Humanity; and this glorious measure not only protected the negroes but also the Indians, and especially those of *Misiones*, for the Spanish and Jesuit *regime* had created in South America a system of slavery for whites as well as the blacks. These laws were published in the native languages, *Quichua* and *Guarani*, the latter being spoken in the *Misiones*, so that the natives might take suitable action in defence of their liberty.[2]

Freedom of slaves 1813.

This Assembly, famous in the History of America, reconstructed the immense Spanish Viceroyalty of the Rio de la Plata, for the territories of Paraguay, Upper Peru, the Banda Oriental of Uruguay and the Jesuit *Misiones* insisted upon being represented in it and elected deputies.[3]

Reconstruction of the Viceroyalty of Buenos Ayres. 1813.

It was necessary to concentrate the political, military and administrative functions of the United Provinces of the Rio de la Plata, then at war with Spain for their independence and with Portugal for their rightful boundaries. This great assembly, therefore, substituted for the collective form of the executive power an individual one, by creating the office of Chief of the State, with the name of "*Director Supremo.*" At the same time it asserted its sovereignty over the territories adjoining those

---

[1] Some of the official reports of the chiefs of the Argentine army are found in English in the "Argentine Evidence," Vol. I. page 153 *et seq.*

[2] Official Register of the Argentine Republic, 1812, Vol. I. pages 194, 203 and 205.

[3] Official Register of the Argentine Republic, Vol. I. page 265, at the Argentine Legation.

of Brazil, in accordance with the treaty of 1777, and created the *Provincia Oriental del Uruguay* [Eastern Province of Uruguay], in the capital of which, Montevideo, the last army of the King of Spain in the Rio de la Plata had taken refuge and had remained besieged by the patriots of Buenos Ayres.

The decree said:

> It has been declared, and it is declared by the present decree, that all the towns in our territories, with their respective jurisdictions, which are situated in the Banda Oriental of Uruguay and the eastern and southern districts of the Rio de la Plata, shall henceforth form part of the United Provinces, and shall be called the "*Oriental del Rio de la Plata*," and governed by a "*Gobernador Intendente*" with the powers granted to those of his class. The residence of the "Intendant Governor" shall be for the present at the place which may be most convenient to best attend to the duties of his government, until such time as the capital of the "*Intendencia*" may be selected.

New Provinces that included Misiones.

After securing the Portuguese frontier on the Rio de la Plata, the Government of Buenos Ayres took similar measures to confirm its sovereignty on its northeastern frontier and in *Misiones*. The decree of December 10, 1814, reads as follows:

> 2. The city of Corrientes and the *Pueblos* of *Misiones*, with their respective jurisdictions, will, from this time forward, form a Province of the State, with the name of the "Province of Corrientes." Its boundaries will be on the North and West the River Paraná, *as far as the dividing line with the Portuguese dominions*, on the East the River Uruguay, and on the South the same line which has been designated as the boundary of the northern portion of the Province of Entre Rios.

The line of division from the Portuguese dominions is that of the *Mapa de las Cortes* (Map of the Courts) of 1749, followed by the boundary treaties of 1750 and 1777, and guaranteed by that of 1778.

Military operations, 1816.

During this year the forces from Buenos Ayres operated in the Territory of *Misiones* against the Portuguese of Uruguay, the revolted Indians, and the smugglers. The reports of the military chiefs are included in the aforesaid "*Coleccion de Datos y Documentos*," pages 525 to 528, papers Nos. 258 to 265, in which these facts are related.

On the 9th of July, 1816, the General Constituent Congress of the *Argentine Independence July 9, 1816.* United Provinces of the Rio de la Plata assembled in the city of Tucuman and proclaimed the Independence of the Argentine Nation, thus fixing a new starting point in International Law and with the other states of the World. In this Congress were represented the *Provincia Oriental*, the old Spanish country of *Los Tapes* and the *Misiones*, as integral parts of the new Nation.[1]

Meanwhile the Government of Portugal, persuaded of the inability *Portuguese invasion. 1816.* of Spain to rule South America, undertook to secure some advantages from the situation and to extend its dominions. In 1816 it iniquitously violated the Armistice signed by Rademaker in 1812, and occupied the city of Montevideo with a squadron and an army under the orders of General Lecor. The Argentine government asked that officer for an explanation before he carried out his design, but receiving none prepared for the struggle.

At the beginning of the following year, 1817, the Government of *Protest and armed resistance of 1817.* Buenos Ayres issued a protest, asking the Portuguese invader to conform to the existing treaties, and evacuate the territory of the *Provincia Oriental* To support this protest it armed the said Province and also the other Provinces of the Nation in order to repel the invasion. This movement by Portugal was confined to the sea-coast, its design being to control the mouth of the great rivers which rise in the interior of the continent; but it in no way affected the Territory of *Misiones* now in dispute. The Portuguese General issued a proclamation declaring *Declarations of Portugal. 1817.* that the invasion would not extend to the *western bank of the Rio Uruguay, which the Portuguese Government considered an integral part of the Argentine territory.*[1]

The Portuguese invasion was stopped in the *Banda Oriental* of *Treaty of 1818, fixing the boundaries between the two sovereignties* Uruguay, while the Argentine Plenipotentiary in Rio Janeiro sought a peaceful solution of this state of war, and he did, in fact, secure this in 1818 by negotiating a treaty, the second article of which provided—

> That the *course of the Uruguay shall be the provisional Line of Demarcation between Brazil and the United Provinces*, according to the Armistice of 1812, it being expressly understood that within the latter remain, as belonging to Argentine, the *Territories of Paraguay, Corrientes,* and *Entre Rios.*[2]

[1] These facts are a part of the general history of that period, and can be verified in the Archives of the Argentine Legation in Washington, in the Official Register of 1817 and in the history by General Mitre; also in the notable work by Dr. Don Vicente Fidel Lopez, "*Historia de la Republica Argentina*," cited.

[2] See Official Register of the Argentine Republic, Vol. I, pages 569 and 570.

This important treaty ceded to the Crown of Portugal the immense
territories situated on the East of the river Uruguay, and which had
always formed a Spanish Province down to the end of the Eighteenth
century, but saved to the Argentine Republic the Territory now in controversy.

*Portugal re-
cognizes Argen-
tine indepen-
dency. 1821.*

In September, 1821, there arrived at Buenos Ayres a diplomatic
agent of the Portuguese government, who made frank declarations of
friendship and supported them by recognizing, in the name of his
sovereign, the independence of Argentine, with the same boundaries
as the Viceroyalty of Buenos Ayres.[1] In 1821 the first Provincial
Legislature of Corrientes assembled, and passed an act, of which the
following article refers to the matter of boundaries:

*The province
of Corrientes in
the nation. 1821*

ART. 2. That the Province is composed of all the Pueblos included within the territory which *have been in its uninterrupted
possession from time immemorial;* without being obstructed by
any new change without lawful title. . . .
Corrientes, November 25, 1821.

DN. JUAN FRANCISCO CABRAL,
President.

BALTAZAR ACOSTA,
Secretary.

This *immemorial and uninterrupted possession* of Corrientes extended as far as the Atlantic Ocean on the East, as the documents
commented upon in this Argument prove. [See page 41 *et seq.*] After
1750 these possessions were limited to those agreed upon between
Spain and Portugal, and this agreement left within the jurisdiction of
Corrientes the entire Territory now submitted to the Arbitrator.[2]

*Military re-
ports on Mis-
iones. 1821.*

A military report dated September 5, 1821, made to the Commander
who occupied *Misiones*, has the following:

As to the affairs of Misiones, it is necessary that you should
adopt conciliatory measures towards the Indians. Present emer-
gencies require it. Commander Esquivel will speak with you on
this subject.

*The savant
Bompland in
Misiones. 1821*

The same Argentine General who signed this report recommends the
celebrated French traveller M. de Bompland, a companion of Hum-
boldt in his American explorations, who, attracted by the wonderful

[1] See Official Register of the Argentine Republic, Vol. I. pages 569 570.
[2] See "Argentine Evidence," Vol. I. page 451 *et seq.*; and the official book, entitled
"Coleccion de Datos y Documentos," etc., pages 229 230.

natural wealth of *Misiones*, had resolved to remain there until his death. This document, dated November 11, 1821, says:

> No doubt you have some *yerba* which you can send me for the use of the troops, which *yerba* you will please to remit immediately, and I also need all you can get from *Misiones*.
> Please send a Priest to *Misiones* with Don Amadeo Bompland. The services of the priest are needed there under the present circumstances. Bompland writes me that he has decided to make another trip, and that he will try to calm the feelings of the inhabitants. I think the idea is a good one, and you will please to consult with him in regard to this important subject. Health and Liberty. General Headquarters, Paraná, September eleventh, one thousand eight hundred and twenty-one.—Ricardo Lopez Jordan.—To Señor Evaristo Carriego, Military Commander of Corrientes.[1]

Several native chiefs of the *Misiones* assembled in 1822 and agreed to submit to the Government of the Province of Corrientes. I present the documents to the Arbitrator in Volume 1, page 458, of the "Argentine Evidence."[2] At the same time the Governor of the Argentine State of Santa Fé appears to have been commissioned to protect the Indians of *Misiones*, for reasons of interior policy, and with this in view he addressed a letter to the Governor of Corrientes saying:

Acts of jurisdiction in 1822.

> Santa Fé, *November* 17, 1822.
> It being indispensable that this Government, as the protector of the *Misiones*, should take an active part in seeing that the criminals who may appear in those *Pueblos* shall not go unpunished, and that Chief having left to my disposition those that he has taken for the dangerous rebellion that they incited; will your Honor take charge of those sent to you by the Commander General thereof, and forward them to the Town of Paraná, assured that this small sacrifice will bind me to a like service which you may ask on account of your Province.[3]

The Governor of *Misiones*, who had had differences with the Governor of Entre Rios, made an agreement with him on the 12th of May, 1823, in which both States recognized their dependency upon the State of Buenos Ayres. Article IV said:

Convention of 1823.

[1] See this document in "Argentine Evidence," Vol. I, page 458, and in the "*Coleccion de Datos y Documentos*," pages 325 and 326.
[2] The Spanish text is in the "*Coleccion de Datos y Documentos*," pages 188 and 189.
[3] The Spanish version is in the "*Coleccion de Datos y Documentos*," etc., page 241, document 102.

The Government of Entre Rios offers to the Government of *Misiones:* First, to request from the Government of Buenos Ayres all possible protection to the agriculture, industry and commerce of *Misiones;* Second, to request the proper authorities to recognize the boundaries of said province; Third, to protect its freedom and general prosperity.[1]

<small>War with Brazil, 1825.</small>

The Portuguese continued to occupy the Province of Montevideo. They had in 1818 attempted to annex it to Portugal but the effort was resisted by the people. Meanwhile the Argentine government concentrated all its forces to put an end to the war with Spain and to consolidate the nationality proclaimed in 1816; only awaiting the fortunate issue of these vital purposes in order to turn its arms against the Portuguese and liberate the Province of Montevideo which they had usurped. This opportunity came in 1825, and the Argentine congress passed a law, dated on the 25th of October of that year, declaring war against Brazil in defence of the Province of Uruguay.[2]

<small>The disputed Territory and this war, 1825.</small>

The Argentine government had previously taken action during that same year in view of the Brazilian advance upon the Territory of *Misiones* now in controversy.[3]

In May, 1825, the National Congress ordered the defence of the strategetical line of the river Uruguay, as follows:

ART. 1. The Government of the Province of Buenos Ayres is authorized, as for the time being in charge of the National Executive Power, to provide for the defence and safety of the State, and it is especially recommended *to reinforce at once the line of the Uruguay* as a precaution against the events that the war may produce which has been started in the *Banda Oriental* of the Rio de la Plata.

ART. 2. For this purpose and in consideration of the urgency and national interest of this matter, while in the meantime the National Army will be organized as soon as possible, the Executive Power in the name of the Congress will stimulate the zeal and patriotism of the Governments of the Provinces, so that with the least delay they may place at its disposition all the troops of the line not absolutely required for the interior security of these Provinces.

<small>[1] There are other Articles of political and ecclesiastical jurisdiction. See the "Argentine Evidence," Vol. 1, page 159, and Official Register, Argentine, Anno 1823. Also Group C of Manuscripts, document No. 6.
[2] Argentine Official Register, in the Legation at Washington, Anno 1825, page 89.
[3] See "*Coleccion de Datos y Documentos,*" etc., page 462, and following documents: 222, 223, 229, 230, 233 and 234 (very interesting).</small>

September, 1825. The head of the Nation and General-in-Chief of the Argentine army explained to the Governor of the Province of Corrientes the plan of defence of the Territory situated on the West of the Uruguay, saying:

> The National Executive Power, inviting the Provinces of the Union to contribute to the formation of the Army of Observation against Uruguay, has nevertheless deemed it proper, in the wisdom of its counsels, that the organization of this Army shall be made by the Nation, which worthily and ably presides over the duty of its own preservation and over the defence of the country and the honor of its obligations.

November 7, 1825. The Territory now in dispute was invaded by a Brazilian force of 600 men, and the Governor of Corrientes marched against them. The troops of Brazil retreated, passing to the East of the Uruguay, without an encounter. The Argentine General issued a proclamation to his troops announcing that the Territory was free of enemies. The following are some of his words:

> The eternal enemy of our independence has just given a new proof of his hatred. A division of Brazilian troops, numbering 600 men, under the command of Ventos Manuel, crossing the Uruguay advanced into our Territory on the morning of the 5th instant. But having received news on the same day of this hostile invasion, we set forth on the march with the forces gathered in Curuzú-Cuatiá against the enemy, who as soon as they learned of our movement retreated with the utmost precipitation.

December, 1825. Circular of the Minister of War of the Argentine Republic to the Governors of the Provinces, notifying them that the Brazilian army had been defeated at the battle of *Sarandí*, and ordering the mobilization of the National Guard of Corrientes.

Finally, I will record the series of acts connected with the defence of *Misiones*, which testimony can be found, as well as that already referred to, in the official work entitled, "*Colección de Datos y Documentos*," etc., page 529, section 44, grouped under the following title:

Defence of *Misiones*.

> Documents referring to the Campaigns against Brazil, in which under the orders of Generals Rodriguez, Balcarce and Alvear the Corrientes contingent in the National land and sea forces assisted in the defence of the Territories of the Provinces *Oriental* and *Misiones Oriental* [Eastern *Misiones*], and in aid of the forces which Corrientes especially put in the field as a military observa-

tion corps for the protection of its territory and frontiers and those of the *Misiones Occidentales* [Western *Misiones*], which Territory Ventos Manuel was obliged to evacuate after he had beaten the forces of the *Guaranies* with Aguirre at their head.

War of 1826. During the year 1826 the war continued to be confined to the *Estado Oriental* (Uruguay), and the now disputed Territory of *Misiones* was not even threatened by Brazil. The war for independence was ended, and the Argentine Republic, whose troops were scattered from the Rio de la Plata to Colombia, began concentrating them in Buenos Ayres, and could devote more attention to the internal organization of the country and the war against Brazil. The General Constituent Congress passed the National Constitution on the 24th of December, 1826. This Constitution bears at its foot the signatures of the Deputies of each of the Provinces, and among them these:

Argentine Constitution, 1826.

For the *Province of Misiones*: Manuel Pinto, Vicente Ignacio Martinez.

For the *Province of Montevideo*: Manuel Moreno, Mateo Vidal, Silvestre Blanco, Cayetano Campana.[1]

Brazil and the rivers Uruguay and Paraná, 1827. Brazil dispatched a powerful squadron with the purpose of controlling the rivers Uruguay and Paraná, but it was entirely defeated by the Argentine squadron in February, 1827, and in the decree of March 2d the Argentine Government proclaimed that the dominion over these rivers should remain assured to the Argentines forever.[2] As above stated, the invading army of Brazil was at last attacked by the Argentine troops and obliged to evacuate the city of Montevideo, so much coveted by the Portuguese. The Brazilian army retreated toward the imperial territories, but was overtaken by the Argentines at the stream called the *Ituzaingo*, and entirely destroyed in the bloody battle of February 20, 1827.[3] The Rio de la Plata thus became once more free from the Portuguese, and the complete and positive sovereignty of the Argentine Government was confirmed over the course of the rivers Paraná and Uruguay and the territories adjacent to them, which belonged to it according to the titles and possession held by Spain. The result of this victory was the long negotiation for the Treaty of Peace, signed on the 27th of August, 1828, in which the following was stipulated:[4]

Final defeat of Brazil.
Evacuation of the invaded territories, February 20, 1827.
Treaty of peace, 1828.

[1] Official Argentine Register, Anno 1826, page 162, in the Argentine Legation at Washington.
[2] *Idem.*, 1827, page 178.
[3] *Idem.*, 1827, pages 180, 181.
[4] *Idem.*, 1828, pages 227, 228.

The troops of his Majesty the Emperor of Brazil shall evacuate the Province of Montevideo, including "*La Colonia del Sacramento*" [Sacramento Colony], within the precise and positive period of two months, to be counted from the day on which the exchange of ratifications of this Convention is made, retiring towards the frontiers of the Empire or embarking by sea, except a force of 1,500 men which the Government of the said Sovereign shall be allowed to keep in Montevideo until the Provisional Government of the said Province is established, under the express obligation of withdrawing this force within the fixed term of four months after the establishment of such provisional government at the latest, such evacuation to leave the city of Montevideo *in statu quo ante bellum* under competent Commissioners authorized *ad hoc* by the legitimate government of that Province.

The Argentine Republic, mistress of an immense territory, was in duty bound to dedicate its scanty population and resources to its own organization under the new régime of free institutions. It was considered, therefore, more advantageous to the maintenance of peace that every pretext of conflict with the recently founded Empire of Brazil should be taken away; and this generous and wise purpose was attained by interposing a third sovereignty between the frontiers of these two growing nationalities. Such was the origin of the condition in the Treaty of Peace of 1828, imposed by the Argentine Republic, providing that the Province of Montevideo should be declared independent. The Argentine Republic thus made a spontaneous sacrifice of its lawful title and of its possession over that ancient Territory of the Spanish Viceroyalty of Buenos Ayres, in behalf of its own national consolidation, as well as of the civilization of South America, to the progress and honor of which she has dedicated herself.

<small>Independence of the Estado Oriental. (Uruguay.)</small>

This peace, the document of which can be examined in the official collection of treaties of the Argentine Republic, effectively ended the pretensions of Brazil over the territories of the Rio de la Plata and to the control of the course of the rivers Uruguay and Paraná. During the war between 1816 and 1828, the Argentine Republic did not neglect to exercise its sovereignty over *Misiones*, and the proof of this is seen in the following duly authenticated documents, accompanying this Argument in Volume I of the "Argentine Evidence."

<small>The *Misiones* and the Peace of 1828.</small>

I. Conventions made between the Governments of the

---

¹ 7 September, 1822.

Provinces of Entre Rios and Corrientes and Santa Fé, to assist with all their resources to expel the armies of Brazil from the basin of the Rio de la Plata.

II. Message of the Governor of Corrientes to the Legislature of the Province concerning the adoption of means for the reestablishment of order among the Indians of *Misiones*.

III. A very comprehensive document giving the Manifesto of the Government of Corrientes to all the Argentine *Pueblos* in regard to the war they carried on in defence of their rights against the so-called government of *Misiones*, formed by Aguirre, Aulestia and their successors. (This is an episode of the civil war, for Corrientes maintained its colonial titles to govern *Misiones*, although the Constituent Congress of 1826 had considered it as an autonomous Province, and admitted its deputies.)

IV. Compact between the Provinces of Buenos Aires and Corrientes to defend the national territory and reciprocally sustain each other.

V. Documents relating to the political representation of the Territory of *Misiones* in the Constituent Convention, denied by the Province of Corrientes, which refused to acknowledge the Deputies who, in representation of the Province called *Misiones*, had introduced themselves into that National Assembly.

VI. Laws commanding the re-establishment of the order disturbed by the civil war in the Territory of *Misiones*.[1]

Argentine Dictatorship, 1830 to 1852. After the conclusion of the war with Brazil, it is a matter of historical notoriety that the Argentine Republic entered upon a period of frightful anarchy, which only ended by the downfall of the Dictator in 1852. During more than twenty years of bloodshed and ruin, spread in all directions, the Territory of *Misiones* continued in a condition of misery, often also stained with blood, and under the direct government of the Province of Corrientes, which was constantly the field of this implacable civil war. During this time Brazil committed no act of hostility against the Argentine Republic, but on the contrary contributed as an ally of the Revolution of Freedom to the overthrow of the dictatorship at the battle of Caseros, on the 3d of February, 1852.

Acts of jurisdiction during the anarchical period 1828-1852. The truth of the preceding statements is proved by the following acts of jurisdiction over the Territory of *Misiones*:[2]

1828. The Governor of Corrientes declares that the *Oriental Misiones* of Uruguay (now the State of Rio Grande of Brazil) remains reincorporated in the Provinces of Corrientes. He says:

[1] "Argentine Evidence," Vol. I, pages 461 to 468.
[2] See "Argentine Evidence," Vol. I, page 468. Also "*Coleccion de Datos y Documentos*," page 326 *et seq.*

DEPARTMENT OF GOVERNMENT, *August* 18*th*, 1828.
The re-establishment of the *Oriental Pueblos* of *Misiones by the power of the Argentine Republic* on its incorporation being so laudable and conducive to the general welfare, and the Government being desirous of strengthening immediately the relations of fraternal friendship and reciprocal understanding with the people of that province, in all that may tend to the promotion of the happiness of the inhabitants of both territories, now decrees, etc.

1830. Agreements made by the Commissioners of the Government of the Province of Corrientes and the Representatives of a part of the *inhabitants of the ancient Misiones Occidentales*.

1832. Law concerning the preparation of "*yerba-mate*" (a kind of native tea) in the Territory of *Misiones*, dated October, 1832, of which Art. 1 says:

"The H. R. of the Province considering that the time had arrived to permit the preparation of the '*yerba mate*' in the Territory of this Province, including the ancient *Misiones*, at the session of this date has made a decree having the force of law, as follows:

"Art 1. Farms of '*yerba-mate*' are permitted in the Territory above indicated, but on account of the present state of war the producers will pay to the State ten per cent of that article."

1832. Decree proclaiming the preceding law. Its first article reproduces the text of the first part of that above quoted.[1]

In 1841 the Dictator of Buenos Aires closed the free navigation of the rivers Uruguay and Paraná to all vessels which did not carry an Argentine register.[2] On the 9th of February, 1843, the adjoining Confederated Provinces of Corrientes and Entre Rios made a treaty by which they provided for the conservation and government of the Territory of *Misiones* while the condition of anarchy which desolated the Republic continued. This treaty said:[3]

<small>Rivers closed to navigation, 1841.</small>

<small>Treaty between Corrientes and Entre Rios.</small>

ARTICLE VII.—*In the Territory of Misiones will be stationed a military force from the Province of Entre Rios* under the command of an officer appointed by said Government, until the National Congress shall convene and decide as to the rights of the people of *Misiones to be considered as constituting a Province*.

[1] "Argentine Evidence," "*Coleccion de Datos y Documentos,*" etc., page 351.
[2] Argentine Official Register, Anno 1841, page 418.
[3] "Argentine Evidence," Vol. I, pages 172 and 473. Official Argentine Register, Anno 1843, page 426.

ARTICLE VIII.—Until that time, the *Territory of Misiones* will be represented by two Deputies in the Congress of Corrientes.

ARTICLE IX.—The administration of the *Territory of Misiones* shall continue to be exercised, as up to this time, by the Government of Corrientes, until the time specified in the Seventh Article or until it shall contain a sufficient population to become a Province. The military force of Entre Rios which shall occupy it until then shall be paid by the Government of Corrientes.

<small>Triple Alliance of 1851.</small> In 1851 the Argentine revolutionary party, united against Rozas, negotiated the Treaty of Triple Alliance between the Argentines, Brazilians and Uruguayans, in order to combat the Dictatorship in the territories of the Republics of Argentine and Uruguay, which were under its domination. Brazil, the Province of Entre Rios, which was the headquarters of the Argentine revolution, and the city of Montevideo, supported by Argentine, signed that treaty, which was the precursor of the memorable victory of Caseros. It was said in Article XVII:[1]

> As a natural result of this agreement, and desirous of leaving no pretext for the least doubt in regard to the spirit of cordiality, good faith and disinterestedness upon which it is based, the allied States mutually guarantee their respective independence, and the integrity of their territories, without prejudice to acquired rights.

Brazil asked for nothing after this victory in the matter of boundaries and recognized the *acquired rights of Argentine*. The rules of international law settled the fact that these rights are such as descended from the respective European sovereignties from which came each colony that has become independent. Brazil thus acknowledged that the *Misiones* belonged to the Argentine Republic in virtue of the rights it inherited from Spain.

<small>Colonization of Misiones, 1854.</small> The Argentine National Government approved, on the 12th of December, 1854, a colonization contract with a French subject, Dr. Don Augusto Brougnes, Article VI of which said:

> The locality granted by the government of Corrientes for the establishment of the colonies is situated on the banks of the Paraná and Uruguay *in that part called "Misiones,"* where in the places indicated Mr. Brougnes shall make his choice among the lands that are public property.[2]

---

[1] Official Argentine Register, 1851, page 472, and "*Coleccion de Tratados de la Republica Argentina,*" presented to the Arbitrator.

[2] Official Argentine Register, 1854, page 183.

After the downfall of Rozas the Argentine Government made treaties of friendship, commerce and navigation with foreign nations. In the treaty with the United States of America, in 1853, it guaranteed the free navigation of the rivers Paraná and Uruguay, the natural route for *Misiones* to communicate with the rest of the world. By the treaty made on the 25th of June, 1856, with the Empire of Brazil, both countries were bound to respect the integrity of their respective territories, in the following terms: Treaty with Brazil, 1856.

ARTICLE II. Each of the high contracting parties promises not to support, directly or indirectly, any attempt at the annexation of any portion of the territories of the other, nor to allow the establishment therein of any independent government in disregard of their legitimate sovereignty and authority, respectively.

The Argentine Republic was again divided into two parties and given up to the horrors of civil war. The wealthy and powerful State of Buenos Ayres had separated itself from the National Government, reassuming its authority over its foreign affairs, while the thirteen other states of the Confederation remained faithful to the National Government, of which the capital was the city of Paraná. Under these unfavorable circumstances the Empire of Brazil took part in the Argentine civil war, offering its assistance to the National Government in subduing the State of Buenos Aires, as well as a loan of three hundred thousand dollars in gold.[1] On its part the National Government was to sign a boundary treaty with Brazil, recognizing as belonging to the Empire what Spain had refused to Portugal in 1759 and 1791, that is to say, part of the *Misiones*, between the Paraná and the Uruguay rivers, now submitted to the Arbitrator. The project failed because the Argentine National Congress, as will be shown later, refused, by a unanimous vote of both the Senate and House of Deputies, to sanction such a policy. Proposed Boundary treaty. 1857.

After its unsuccessful military campaign from 1816 to 1828, the Empire took no further steps to usurp the coveted territories in the basin of the Rio de la Plata. It, however, so arranged its boundaries with the new and small Republics of Uruguay and Paraguay as to deprive it of large areas of country, without any title, or historical, legal or political justification for so doing. Regarding the Argentine Republic its conduct was more prudent. The treaties of alliance and friendship of 1851 and 1856, above quoted, contained explicit declarations recognizing First attempt by Brazil at territorial extension after 1828.

---

[1] Official Argentine Register, 1857, page 79.

the integrity of the Argentine territory, and nothing ever indicated the slightest intention of incorporating under the Empire the *Misiones* of the *Yguazú* and the *Pipiry Guazú*. The first act in this direction was the diplomatic question of 1856, in which Brazil attempted to take advantage of and increase the misfortunes of Argentine at the price of a zone of her territory. I shall give elsewhere the details of this episode, which warned the Argentine Republic that its questions with the Brazilian Empire were not settled, notwithstanding the frank and conclusive declarations of the treaties of 1826, 1851 and 1856.

San Xavier and Corpus.
It has been already stated[1] that the *Pueblos* of *Corpus* on the Paraná and of *San Xavier* on the Uruguay were both founded by the Jesuits in the time of their Republic, and that they exercised full jurisdiction over the Territory submitted to the Arbitrator. It may now be added that they were, except San Pedro and Paggi, the only towns in existence down to 1870 anywhere near the Territory in controversy, and that Brazil declares that it never had down to that time any city, settlement, or fort near that Territory. The books cited by the Visconde de Porto Seguro and by Southey recognize this fact, and the "*Historia de las Misiones*" (History of *Misiones*), by Gay, which was officially published by Brazil, states it with equal frankness. On page 203, Volume XXVI, of the "*Revista do Instituto Historico do Brazil*," presented to the Arbitrator,[2] Father Gay narrates the foundation of San Xavier, and in the note (22) to this chapter says (page 253):

> As the city of San Francisco Xavier was the first one founded among the Indians in the Paraná and Uruguay country, of which this history treats, it is proper to preface the matter with the following statement.

This is followed by a narration of the sufferings endured by the founders of this Pueblo. At page 445 Gay publishes the official census of 1767, giving to *Corpus* 4,587 inhabitants and to *San Xavier* 1,527. He confirms the preceding data in the geographical description of *Misiones* on page 736, the language of which is decidedly favorable to the Argentine Republic, and adds at page 824 the following information:

> In the village of *San Xavier* the Jesuits had a printing office. I personally possess a work entitled, "*Sermones e exemplos em la lingua Guarani, por Nicolas Yapuguai*" (Sermons and specimen

[1] See page 55 of this Argument. [2] See this Argument, page 43.

articles in the Guarani language), printed in the *Pueblo* of San Xavier in the year 1727.

At page 661 Father Gay says:

The churches of *Corpus* and of *Santa Rosa* were the most splendid in the Jesuit settlements.

On page 792 he adds:

The Jesuits embarked the products (*Yerba*) they exported at *San Xavier*, and some of them at *Santo Tomé*. The manuscript referred to says that a Spaniard, who lived in *Misiones* ever since the last years of the past century, stated that the inhabitants of Entre Rios (that is to say, the Entrerrianos and the Correntinos) and particularly the inhabitants of the Pueblo of *Martyres*, used to ascend the Uruguay from *San Xavier*, for eight days, in boats, carrying dried meat and corn and other provisions, shortly afterwards coming back with from two to four thousand arrobas[1] of *Yerba Maté*, which they carried on rafts, only taking two days on their way home.[2]

The jurisdiction exercised by San Xavier over the Territory submitted to the Arbitrator is proven for all international purposes by Spain and Portugal in the documents relating to the demarcation of the boundaries according to the treaties of 1750 and 1777. Those documents make the general headquarters for the operations the *Pueblo* of San Xavier, close by the land in controversy. See in corroboration this Argument.

The Argentine Republic has always held and still holds this port in the service of the commerce growing out of the "*Yerba*" produced by the Territory submitted to the Arbitrator, thus completing three centuries and a half of uninterrupted possession and jurisdiction, which was not even questioned down to 1857. And to that jurisdiction the acts and documents which are cited below refer, for the better understanding of which this digression was necessary.

The Government of Corrientes issued a decree on the 8th of May, 1856, creating a Special Police service in order to watch over and protect the "*Yerba*" trade in the Territory now in dispute. This decree said:

Police of Misiones, 1856.

The Government, desiring to establish in the "*Yerbales*" of

---

[1] A weight of 25 pounds. [2] See map of "*Descubrimientos*," etc.

Misiones a police force to protect the workingmen and public interests, has appointed von Military Chief of *Misiones*, and in charge of the police inspection of that Territory.[1]

<small>Official reports on *Misiones*, 1863.</small> The Argentine government, having been warned of the new Brazilian pretensions by the negotiations that have been narrated, which occurred in 1857, asked the Federal Government of Corrientes for all the necessary data concerning *Misiones*. The Governor of Corrientes answered in the following terms:[2]

> I have the honor to acknowledge the receipt of your esteemed favor of the 13th of June, in which information is asked for concerning that region in the territories of this Province which is known as "*Misiones*," for the purposes stated.
> In my note of April 14th, in reply to the Circular of that Department regarding the boundaries of the Province, your Excellency will find all the data needed to make that subject clear, so as to settle the matter with the prompt attention which the National Government seems disposed to give to the question relating thereto, with the Governments of Paraguay and Brazil, thus avoiding gradual usurpations to which its neglect might give rise.[3]

In a subsequent note of the same origin, dated April 14, 1863, presented to the Arbitrator in the same works, we read:

> The boundaries of the Province have been fixed upon the South by the bar which the rivers " Mocoretá " and " Guaiquiraró " form at their junction with the river Uruguay, and the fall of the Guaiquiraró into the river Paraná, and the Sierra (mountain range) of the Cuchilla Larga or Cañada (ravine) of "Basualdo," in the intermediate country between said rivers. On the West and North it has for a boundary the river Paraná, from the bar of the Guaiquiraró to the junction of the "*Yguazú*," or river *Curitiba*, and the rivers *San Antonio-Guazú* and *Yguazú*, and the *Pepiry Guazú*, down to its mouth in the river Uruguay. On the East it has for a boundary the river Uruguay, from the junction of the "*Pepiry Guazú*" to the bar of the Mocoretá where it joins the Uruguay.
> This Province has always been and is now in actual possession

<small>[1] "Argentine Evidence," Vol. I, page 474; and "*Colección de Datos y Documentos*," etc., page 316, document 145.
[2] See this Argument, page 85.
[3] "Argentine Evidence," Vol. I, pages 475 and 476; "*Colección de Datos y Documentos*," page 501, document 241.</small>

of the Territory included within the boundaries above designated.

Another note from the Government of Corrientes on April 6, 1863, referring to public roads over the entire territory, says: <small>Roads and possessions in Misiones. 1863.</small>

> We refer to the means of communication between this Capital and the Territory of the *Upper Misiones*, that valuable portion of the Argentine territory which on account of the immense riches it contains in its bosom demands the special attention of the Government of the Nation.

It describes the existing roads, and adds:

> Of these roads, without any doubt, the first is of much more importance and interest for Corrientes and for the whole of the Republic; since on the one hand it affords greater facilities and more advantages as an outlet for the products which are gathered in *Misiones*, and on the other hand this road is a strategic route which it is very important should be preserved with all its advantageous conditions, in order to protect this valuable portion of our territory from the coveted absorption with which it is threatened by Brazil. . . .
> *From San Xavier to our disputed frontiers with Brazil, where upon the right bank of the Pepiry-Guazú exists the " Yerba-Mate" farm of Don Carlos Kasten, there is no overland road of any kind, but only a very difficult means of communication by way of the River Uruguay.*[1]

This document conclusively proves that the industrial Argentine establishments extended, in 1863, as far as the boundary with Brazil along the river which is contended for in this Argument.[2]

The Legislature of Corrientes passed another law on July 13, 1863, ordering roads to be constructed in the "*Antiguas Misiones*" (*ancient Misiones*).[3]

In 1864 the State of Corrientes adopted its political Constitution, the second article of which said: <small>Declaration of Boundaries.</small>

---

[1] "Argentine Evidence," Vol. I, page 477; " Colecciòn de Datos y Documentos," page 357, document 179.
[2] See map of "Discoveries," etc.
[3] "Argentine Evidence," " Collection of Data and Documents," page 358, Doc. No. 180.

The limits of its territory are the following : . . . On the East, the Uruguay river; on the North, the Paraná river as far as the Pepiri-Guazú and San Antonio Guazú.¹ . . .

Lands reserved in Misiones, 1864. The document that follows the preceding one in the first volume of the "Argentine Evidence," and in the corresponding "Group of Manuscripts," reserves from this conveyance some portion of the lands to the *Regulation of the Yerbales, 1865.* north of San Xavier. This is followed by another very important document regulating the farming of the "*Yerbales*" (Yerba Mate fields) North of *San Xavier* and *Corpus;* that is to say, on the Territory submitted to Arbitration.

Political Chief of Misiones, 1865. The *Misiones* formed a Department of Corrientes, according to the previous Constitution, but its police jurisdiction was divided amongst the different *Pueblos*. In 1866 the Government of Corrientes decided to concentrate the police power, and by the decree of February 20, 1865, appointed Don Manuel B. Rocha, *Jefe Politico* (Political Chief or Marshal) of *Misiones*. This Police force extended its supervision over the Territory as far as Brazil, according to the Argentine claim of the location of the boundary, and was never opposed by the Empire.²

New districts, 1869. The Legislature of Corrientes created a new district, called "*Candelaria,*" on the 7th of November, 1869, in giving the boundaries of which it was said :

. . . and from there until reaching at the source of the river *Yguazú* the boundary with the Empire of Brazil.

Another law of Corrientes, passed in the same year, divided the District of *Santo Tomé* into sections. Section 8 was bounded on the North by the "*Pepiry-Guazú,*" and on the West by the River Uruguay.³

Decree as to Boundaries, 1871. In May, 1871, the Government of Corrientes, in accordance with the preceding laws, decreed that a survey of the legally established boundaries should be made.⁴

¹ "Argentine Evidence," Vol. I, page 480 ; Group G of Manuscripts, document No. 14.
² "Argentine Evidence," Vol. I, page 482 ; Group A of Manuscripts, document No. 17.
³ "Argentine Evidence," Vol. I, page 482; "*Coleccion de Datos y Documentos,*" page 314 ; documents 143 and 151 (bis).
⁴ "Argentine Evidence," Vol. I, page 482; "*Coleccion de Datos y Documentos,*" page 320, Doc. 152 ; Manuscripts, Group C, No. 21.

In 1871 the Argentine Congress passed a law that had been pro- *Argentine Congress and the Boundaries*
posed by a Commission directed to examine questions of the boundaries
of the States, of which Article IV reads as follows:

> IV.—On the East the Territory bounded by the 58° Meridian West of Paris, which territory must be previously ceded by the province of Corrientes, bounded also by the Paraná River on the North-west; by the Yguazú River on the North; by the Brazilian frontier on the East, and by the Uruguay River on the South and South-east; said territory to be named *Territory of Misiones.*¹

The increase in the demand for "*Yerba Mate*" required new admin- *Commissioners and regulations of the Yerbales of Misiones,*
istrative measures, and the Government of Corrientes divided the Terri- *1876*
tory submitted to the Arbitrator into two administrative sections,²
bounded by the rivers Yguazú, Uruguay, San Antonio-Guazú and
Pepiry or Pequiry-Guazú. Two Commissioners were appointed with
the duty of preparing regulations concerning the exploitation of the
"Yerba Mate."²

On the 9th of June, 1877, the Government of Corrientes decreed the *Geographical map, 1877*
preparation of the official map of *Misiones,*³ which map, signed by the
Engineer, Don Valentin Virasoro, accompanies the geographical maps
of the "Argentine Evidence."⁴

The Judge of *Santo Tomé* in the district of San Xavier made a re- *Judicial action, 1877.*
port to the Government of Corrientes on the 24th of July, 1877, in
which he said:

> In regard to the action of the civil and police authorities of this Department, I can answer the Commission that it makes itself felt as far as the natural boundaries of the province, that is to say, as far as the Pepiry-Guazú on the Eastern side of the Sierra of the *Yerbales,* denominated Cordillera Central. Into those dense forests police patrols sometimes enter, for the purpose of capturing robbers. These are land police, however, as the fluvial police are in the hands of the National Inspection, in whose jurisdiction my authority can only be felt by consent of the National Revenue Collector of this place.

---

¹ "Argentine Evidence," Vol. I, page 483; "*Colección de Datos y Documentos,*" page 282; Doc. 122.
² "Argentine Evidence," Vol. I, page 483; and Group G of MSS.; Doc. No. 18.
³ "Argentine Evidence," Vol. I, page 486; and Group A of MSS.; Doc. No. 21.
⁴ "Argentine Evidence;" Portfolio of Maps, official map of Corrientes, XIX Century.

Desiring to contribute to the defence of our territorial rights, I have appointed an experienced person to collect all documents relating to that subject, which documents will be remitted to that Commission at the earliest opportunity. May God bless you, etc.—Cipriano Romero, Acting Justice of the Peace.[1]

Concession for Colonization 1877.

The following document in the "Argentine Evidence" is a legal contract granting lands for colonization in the Territory now submitted to the Arbitrator. Some of the pertinent articles are as follows:

1. The following concessions of lands are granted to Messrs. Firmat, Napp and Wilcken, for the exclusive purpose of colonizing them: One and one quarter parts of a concession (each section being of 20 kilometers on the side), at the confluence of the Yguazú river, bounded on the West by the Paraná river, on the South by the Uruguay stream and on the East by whatever the surveyor may determine in order to complete the area petitioned for.

2. One quarter of a section (that is to say, ten kilometers in front and ten deep) at the confluence of the Pepiry-Guazú with the Alto Uruguay.

3. One quarter of a section of equal dimensions at the confluence of the Paraná and Yguazú with the Alto Paraná.[2]

The location of this concession of lands, as well as reports of the acts referred to in this Argument, were officially published, without opposition, claim or protest on the part of Brazil.

Political, ecclesiastical, administrative, and judicial jurisdiction, 1881.

The following documents, issued by the authorities of Corrientes, prove the peaceful exercise of ecclesiastical, political, administrative, military and judicial jurisdiction over *Misiones*, and are presented to the Arbitraitor in Volume I, page 490, of the "Argentine Evidence," and the corresponding Group of Manuscript Documents.

YEAR 1881. (*a*) Decree appointing a collector of revenue at San Xavier.

(*b*) Decree appointing an Accountant-Appraiser at the Receiver's Office at San Xavier.

(*c*) Resolution approving the contract for post mail service between San Xavier and Santo Tomé.

(*d*) Law fixing the boundaries of the Province of Corrientes.

Misiones are proclaimed National Territory, 1881.

An act of the utmost importance occurred during the same year 1881; this was the declaration by the Argentine government that

---

[1] "Argentine Evidence," Vol. I, pages 486 and 487; and "Collection," etc., official, pages 402, 192; MSS. Group G, No. 22.

[2] "Argentine Evidence," Vol. I, page 187; "Coleccion de Datos y Documentos," etc., page 375, Doc. 188.

the *Misiones* were to be thenceforth separated from the Province of Corrientes, thus forming a National Territory or inchoate *State*. This law is published in the National Register of the Argentine Republic, for the year 1881, page 682, on file in the Argentine Legation in Washington, and also in the Library of the Department of State. It reads as follows:

DEPARTMENT OF THE INTERIOR,
BUENOS AIRES, *December* 22, 1881.

The Senate and House of Deputies of the Argentine Nation, in Congress assembled, have passed the following

LAW:

ART. 1. The boundaries of the Province of Corrientes shall be, and remain, as follows: On the North the Upper Paraná; on the East the small streams (arroyos) Pindapá and Chimiray on the two sides and the line most directly uniting them, and the river Uruguay; on the South the river Mocoretá to the small stream (arroyo) "Las Tunas," by this to its sources and a line cutting the Cuchilla of Basnaldo to the sources of the small stream (arroyo) of the same name; by this stream to its junction with the river Guayquiraró, and by the Guayquiraró to the place where it empties into the Paraná.

ART. 2. The Executive Power will submit to the Congress the organization, administration, and government which is proper for the part of the Territory of Misiones which remains outside of the boundaries of the Province of Corrientes.

ART. 3. Until the Congress shall provide properly for that Government the Executive Power will organize a General Government and will regulate its functions, being authorized to expend for this purpose the sum of seven hundred dollars monthly, which will be appropriated by the present law.

ART. 4. The general and district taxes due in said Territory will be paid to the new authorities till Congress provides otherwise.

ART. 5. Let this be communicated to the Executive Power.

Given in the Session Hall of the Argentine Congress, in Buenos Aires, on the 20th of December, 1881.

FRANCISCO B. MADERO,   MIGUEL GOYENA,
CARLOS M. SARAVIA,   MIGUEL SORRONDO,
Secretaries of the Senate.   *Secretaries of the House of Deputies.*

The object of this decided attitude of the Argentine Congress was to consolidate its civil authority over the *Misiones*, for since 1879 Brazil had been putting forth its pretensions, scarcely outlined until 1881.

It must be remembered that in 1879 a bloody civil war was started in Argentina, which only ended in 1880, and that, as had happened in times past, the Empire took advantage of these profound disturbances experienced by the Argentine nation, on its way to a definitive organization, to attempt to make aggressions upon its territory. Fortunately this military episode put an end to the Argentine civil war that had begun in 1810, for the Congress and the whole country gave the political organization the needed temporary equilibrium, establishing the Capital of the Republic in the city of Buenos Aires. The country and the people being pacified, the action of the government was directed towards the maintenance of its sovereignty in *Misiones*. Brazil neither discussed nor protested against, nor contested by its arms, these new acts of Argentine sovereignty over Misiones. It respected them as it had always done in former years, and as Portugal had done during the three centuries that Spain had maintained its jurisdiction there.

Consent of Brazil

On the first of January, 1882, in the execution of this law of the Congress, the Province of Corrientes withdrew its officials from the Territory in controversy and adjacent districts, and the Argentine National Government appointed as governor of the same Col. Don Rudecindo Roca, who immediately assumed the national possession of *Misiones* at the head of the third battalion of infantry of the line. The Empire of Brazil neither protested against this act nor discussed it.[1]

Governor of Misiones, 1882.

The boundaries given to the National Territory of Misiones by the law, and its regular decree in accordance with the Spanish precedents and with the jurisdictional acts of the Province of Corrientes, were as follows:

Legal Boundaries, 1882.

DEPARTMENT OF THE INTERIOR,
BUENOS AIRES, *March* 16, 1882.

It being necessary to determine the point where the authority of the central Government of the *Territory of Misiones* should be located therein, and the different administrative sections into which it should be divided,

The President of the Republic

Decrees:

ART. 1. There is designated for the Capital of the Federal Territory of *Misiones* the pueblo of Corpus, which will be officially called the "City of San Martin."

[1] Official Argentine Register of 1882.

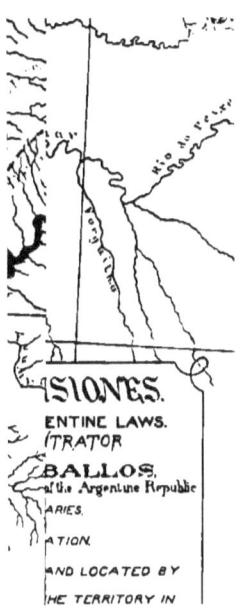

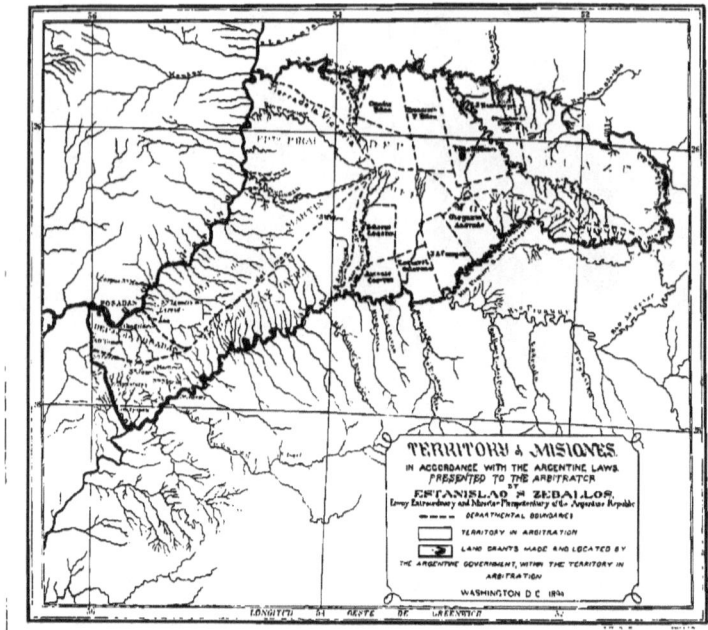

ART. 2. The *Territory of Misiones* will be divided administratively into five Departments, under the following names:

Department of San Martin (Corpus), bounded on the South by the neighborhood and fields of San Juan, on the North by the rivers Paraná and Piray, on the West by the *arroyo* (small stream) Pindapoy, and on the East by the continuation of the southern Sierras.

Department of Piray, bounded on the South by the river Piray, on the North by the Sierras of Victoria in their prolongation towards the Yguazú river, on the West by the river Paraná, and on the East by the Sierras included in the prolongation of the river Yguazú and the Sierras of Victoria.

Department of San Xavier, bounded on the North by the Sierras and the fields of San Juan, on the East by the rivers Uruguay and Acaraguay, and on the West by the *arroyo* (small stream) of Chimiray.

Department of Monteagudo (Paggi), bounded on the North by the Sierras, on the South by the river Uruguay, on the West by the river Acaraguay in its prolongation to the Sierras of Victoria, and on the East by the river Pepiry-Guazú.

Department of the Yguazú, bounded on the North by the river Yguazú, on the West by the Sierras of Victoria, on the East by the river San Antonio-Guazú, and on the South by the Sierras.

ART. 3. The Governor of *Misiones* will determine the points where the local authorities of each Department shall reside.

ART. 4. Let this be communicated, published, and inserted in the National Register.[1]

[Signed]   ROCA.
     BERNARDO DE IRIGOYEN.

The ancient Jesuit city of *Corpus*, which has been referred to, was made the Capital of the National Territory, as we have seen. Shortly afterwards this Capital was located at the place called "*Posadas*," in honor of the representative of the first Argentine Executive Power, who in 1814 put this same Territory under national jurisdiction.   *The Capital of Misiones 1882.*

The reports of the Minister of the Interior of the Argentine Republic for the years 1881, 1882, and 1883 contain various chapters explaining the measures adopted to improve the police, schools, and the general public administration of this Territory. These reports are at the disposal of the Arbitrator, in the Archives of the Argentine Legation   *Administrative organization. 1881 to 1883.*

---

[1] This document is translated from the "*Registro Nacional*" of the Argentine Republic, for the year 1882, which is on file in the Argentine Legation in Washington, p. 156.

in Washington, and are also to be found in the Library of the Department of State of the United States. To the preceding proofs there is added in the "Argentine Evidence," Vol. I, page 490 et seq., the following official documents, the Spanish text of which can be consulted in Group C of Manuscripts.

a. Decree ordering the registration of the concession of lands made by the Province of Corrientes to Don José Maria Frias, before the passage of the law placing *Misiones* under Federal authority.
b. Decree recognizing the rights of Don Daniel Molina to the concession of two sections of land in *Misiones*, made by the Government of Corrientes, before the Territory came under Federal authority.
c. Decree of the National Government in regard to land in *Misiones*.
d. Decree recognizing the rights of Don S. G. Fontenelle to the concession of two sections of land in *Misiones*, made by the Government of Corrientes.
e. Decree recognizing the rights of Don Nicasio Pujol to the concession of two sections of land in *Misiones*, made by the Government of Corrientes.

<small>Acts of jurisdiction from 1883 to 1891.</small> During the year 1883, among numerous measures referring to the progress of *Misiones*, the following were adopted :[1]

1. Decree approving the contract for transportation of the mails from San Xavier to Santo Tomé.
2. Decree appointing a Lieutenant, parish priests and sacristans in the National Territory of *Misiones*.
3. Decree ordering the contract for the surveying of two colonies of one hundred square kilometres each, situated in *Misiones*.
4. Decree directing the post service to be performed by certain telegraph offices.
5. Decree ordering the registration of the concession of grant of lands in *Misiones* made in favor of Don Clemente Ferreyra by the Government of Corrientes.
6. Decree authorizing an expenditure of three thousand pesos for the construction of a branch telegraph line, to connect Pueblo Rosa with the *Misiones* telegraph line.
7. Decree declaring expired the concession made in favor of Don P. Bravo of a quantity of land in *Misiones* that he was to colonize.

---

[1] See "Argentine Evidence," Vol. I, page 490 et seq; and Group G of MSS.

8. Decree increasing the salary granted to the Surveyor, Hernandez, by the amount of his fees for the measurement of two colonies in *Misiones*.

9. Decree appointing a Secretary for the Receiver and Justice of the Peace of San Xavier and Rural Commissioner of the district of Concepcion (*Misiones*.)

10. Decree approving the contract made with Don Pedro M. Cernadas to colonize three sections of land in *Misiones*.

11. Decree appointing an Inspector of Forests in the Territories of El Chaco and *Misiones*.

12. Decree ordering the registration of a title to lands in *Misiones* issued by the Government of Corrientes in favor of Donna Rosa Caceres de Chaim.

13. Law accepting the cession made by the Province of Corrientes of the Pueblo of Posadas, with the quantity of land ceded by that Province.

14. Decree appointing a Post Office Administrator for San Xavier.

15. Decree appointing the First Assistant to the Commission to examine into the proposed railroad to *Misiones*.

16. Decree allowing the sale to E. Puck of the lands held by him in *Misiones*.

17. Decree appointing the Assistant Rector of the Government of *Misiones*.

18. Decree ordering the necessary surveys to be made with a view to an extension of the railroad to Posadas.

19. Decree appointing the Receiver of Rents of San Xavier.

20. Decree appointing the Governor of the National Territories.

21. Decree appointing the Inspector of "*Yerbales*" in the *Territory of Misiones*.

22. Decree authorizing Messrs. Clark & Co. to begin the construction of the Posadas Railroad.

23. Decree ordering the execution of the contract made by the Province of Corrientes in favor of Don Ricardo F. Hardoy, granting to him ten leagues of land in *Misiones*.

24. Law declaring that the settlers of *Misiones* shall receive the benefit of the law of October 27, 1884, and authorizing Don José Silveira Marquez to acquire 7,500 hectares of land in that locality.

25. Decree authorizing Don Serafin J. de Paula to acquire 3,500 hectares of land in *Misiones*.

26. Decree ratifying the proprietary deed of 25 square leagues in *Misiones* in behalf of Don Francisco Comas.

27. Decree appointing a Commissioner for the Department of Yerbales (*Misiones*).

28. Decree appointing the Rent Receiver of San Xavier.

29. Law authorizing the Executive Power to make deeds for several lots of land in *Misiones*.
30. Decree approving the contract made with Don Nicolas Picardo, selling to him a tract of land in *Misiones*.

Census of 1888. Finally, about the same time, the Argentine Government ordered an official census to be made in the *Territory of Misiones* as far as the boundaries with Brazil as claimed in this Argument. I present to the Arbitrator the following official Argentine books, which contain the results of the explorations:

"*El Territorio de las Misiones, por Ramon Lista,*" Buenos Ayres 1883. (The Territory of *Misiones*, by Ramon Lista, etc.)
"*Mis Exploraciones en el Territorio de Misiones. Resultados Estadisticos y Economicos, segun el Censo levantado en 1888, con ayuda del Sr. Gobernador General D. Rudecindo Roca,*" etc. (My Explorations in the Territory of Misiones, Statistical and Economic Results, according to the Census taken in 1888, with the assistance of the Governor General, D. Rudecindo Roca; by Gustavo Niederlein, Inspector of the National Department of Agriculture.

In the second book by Professor Niederlein, who is now engaged at the Scientific and Industrial Museum of the city of Philadelphia, may be found the census and a complete statistical description of the Territory of *Misiones*.

Brazil recognizes and approves the acts of Argentine jurisdiction. In the Memoir of the Department of Foreign Affairs of the Argentine Republic for the year 1891-1892, presented to the Arbitrator, translated into English, in the "Argentine Evidence," Vol. I, page 676 and following, we find these observations:

The decree of March 16, 1882, organized the new Government, fixing our rights at the boundaries claimed. The capital remained where it had been in Corpus, the old Mission which was called San Martin.

This decided attitude of the Argentine Government occasioned a very urgent agitation of the matter in Rio de Janeiro, and the Baron de Cotegipe,[1] the head of the parliamentary opposition at that juncture, wrote to the "*Globo*"[2] a letter in which he asserted that the Imperial Government had been guilty of neglect in this grave international question. The Government was obliged to defend itself, and there appeared in the "*Diario Oficial*" (the Official Journal) of May 13, 1882, a declaration that far from

---
[1] Several times President of the Council of Ministers, and the Brazilian statesman most hostile to the Argentine Republic.
[2] Official organ of the Conservative Party in Rio de Janeiro.

neglecting the question of its boundaries with the Argentine Republic it had been followed with the same lively interest with which the Baron de Cotegipe had treated it. It added that the action of the Argentine Congress was awaited and its results.

The Baron de Cotegipe replied energetically, in a letter in the "*tiloho*," of May 13, 1882. The Government had also declared that the Minister of Brazil in Buenos Aires had been ordered to protest against the law confirming our possession and occupation of *Misiones*, but that he had not done so on account of considerations which appeared weighty. The Baron de Cotegipe commented upon this official language and very properly understood that the action of Brazil meant the tacit acceptance of the possession of *Misiones* by the Argentine Republic. The "*tiloho*" prefaced the letter of that eminent public man with the following:

"To console us for this humiliating attitude which our Government assumed, unwillingly and only in deference to its diplomatic agent, who nevertheless was not right, it assures the country that 'no Argentine law can extinguish the existing controversy between the two states, nor establish any jurisdiction which the Imperial Government will recognize.' We are not treating of such a trifle. What we censure in the Government, and what it also censures in its Envoy, *is to have allowed important acts of sovereignty to be consummated on the part of the neighboring Republic without any objection on our part*."

The same letter of the Baron de Cotegipe concludes in this wise:

"It also remains in evidence that at the present time there exists no act on our part which shows that we have asked for explanations or have done anything to save our rights or to protest."

Shortly afterwards, in July, the discussion of the estimates for the Department of War and Navy offered a pretext to examine the attitude of the Imperial Government, which had consented to the strengthening of the occupation of *Misiones* by the Argentine Government. The two celebrated statesmen from the North took part in the debate, Baron de Cotegipe and Councillor Saraiva, and also a notable orator from the South, Silveira Martins. All were agreed as to the necessity of preparing the Empire for war, and for this purpose the estimates were voted. The newspaper inspired by the Baron de Cotegipe, the "*tiloho*," said, on July, 13th:

"The three notable orators and eminent politicians who were heard, the Baron de Cotegipe, Saraiva and Silveira Martins, agreed in all vital matters, merely differing as to the manner of utilizing, rapidly and effectively, our means of defence and of aggression in case of necessity."

<small>The Parliament of Brazil recognizes and respects the Argentine possession of Misiones.</small> These facts, showing how the governing class of Brazil acknowledged the actual possession by the Argentine Republic of the Territory now in question, can be confirmed by the course of the Brazilian Parliament on different occasions. I shall confine myself to a citation from a note from the Argentine Minister in Brazil, in which he refers to one of the numerous interpellations which were caused in that body by the peaceful exercise of the Argentine jurisdiction. The following document, the original of which remains in the Archives of the Argentine Legation at the disposal of the Arbitrator, proves these facts: 1. That the Brazilian Parliament had knowledge of the Argentine possession of *Misiones*. 2. That although urged by some of its members to take action in the matter, it did not do so.

ARGENTINE LEGATION IN BRAZIL.
(Confidential.) No. 222.
Rio de Janeiro, March 15, 1879.

To His Excellency, Dr. D. Victorino de la Plaza,
Secretary of State, Department of Foreign Affairs.

SIR: There is now pending in the Brazilian Parliament the initiative of a matter which is intimately connected with Argentine interests. Señor A. E. Camargo, Deputy from Rio Grande do Sul, on the 13th inst. presented the following question to the Minister of Foreign Affairs, which appeared in the "Diario Oficial" on the 14th:

"There was read and supported the following question:

"I request that the Minister of State for Foreign Affairs will respond, on the day and hour designated, to the following points:

"1. What is the condition of our international relations with the adjacent countries in regard to boundary questions?

"2. What proceedings or adjustments have been undertaken by the Government for the definitive demarcation of the boundaries between the Empire and the Argentine Confederation?

"3. In case of a negative reply, what are the difficulties in the way of a settlement of the pending questions?"

This movement is not new, nor is it an isolated one. The inhabitants of the Province of Paraná have been for two years agitating the matter of boundaries with the Republic for the Province of Corrientes, as stated in my confidential letter to you of February 19, 1877, and in the official communications No. 86 in May of the same year, and No. 150 on March 12, 1878. What was then said in the Press of that province and in correspondence sent to it from this Court was exactly the same as the statements which have been made in the Parliament at the present time, in a session some days previous to the question offered by Señor Camargo.

A Deputy from Paraná, Alves de Araujo, speaking on the 5th instant in the discussion concerning the forces in the field, indicated the necessity for founding military colonies upon that frontier; "at the point," he said, "where the river Ygnazú joins the one which gives its name to the Province (the Paraná) and in its northern part. Here is the key that should close the door against any hostile attempt and bounds us with Paraguay and Corrientes. And its strategic, administrative and commercial advantages are easily understood, since we make use of the road that leaves the coast and from the gate of Palmeira to reach the free navigation of the Ygnazú, or seeking this river by navigating the river Negro, thus greatly facilitating the commerce of Palmas Guarapnava. *Along that frontier the people of Corrientes*[1] *make incursions upon the Province of Paraná*, and the question of boundaries with Buenos Aires is one that requires some care and some forethought on the part of the Brazilian Government. We take the Treaty of San Ildefonso of 1777, but I call your attention to it and to the movements that are taking place on the frontier."

In the Senate, Señor Correa, ex-Minister of Foreign Affairs and a Senator from the same Province, called the attention of the President of the Council to the immediate necessity of definitely fixing the boundaries of the Empire with the Argentine Republic.

"The difficulties," he said, "that arise in the demarcation of boundaries with the Argentine Republic can, I think, under the present favorable circumstances, be removed by the noble President of the Council invoking the patriotism of the Government of that Republic, which surely will not fail to recognize how important to it also is the solution of that which we are considering, being mindful of that which has happened in relation to its boundaries with Chile and with Paraguay!"

I recollect that afterwards the President of that Province, Oliveira, indicated the advantage of establishing a Military Colony in Santa Maria, on the lower Ygnazú, in the Report which he made to his successor Marcondes at the beginning of 1878, and that the latter sent an official communication to the Cabinet of the Empire in September of the same year, repeating the same. The Report of Oliveira refers to the same fact of which I gave an account at the proper time, and says:

"With regard to the question of boundaries, more serious care should be aroused by the proceedings of our neighbors in Corrientes, who under innocent pretexts are crossing surreptitiously our frontiers.

"Already at the beginning of the past year the Municipal Council of Guarapnava took official action, giving notice of an exploring party, composed of nine persons, who were present in

---

[1] Federal State of the Argentine Republic.

Campo-Eré, having set out from the bar of the Pirahy on the bank of the Paraná, and which, being increased by 16 more men, turned and opened a way for communicating with the fields of Palmas from the frontier of Corrientes.

"It is a fact that this path or way is to-day a regular road for freighters, and that the Argentines make use of it to transport wood and yerba-mate, gathered in the province.

"It is also a fact that different emissaries have come to those parts on commercial pretexts, engaging the business of the place for the Republic, and suggesting to the populace of Guarapuava the idea of gaining a port of embarcation on the Paraná, with the small distance of 50 leagues."

"All these facts are very significant, and ought to call the attention of the government to those regions, which cannot remain abandoned without grave prejudice and danger to the country."

"As a temporary means it would be of great advantage to have a Military Colony established in Santa Maria, on the lower Yguazú, which would communicate with Guarapuava by the road opened by the Engineer Beaurepaire. That Colony would be, on account of its position, the guard of our frontiers with the Argentine Republic by reason of the small distance which it would be from Campo-Eré, and with the Paraguayan frontiers by the proximity of the Paraná, which to the North of the Yguazú is the boundary between this Province and the Republic."

General Osorio, the Minister of War, being present, answered in the following terms:

"His Excellency spoke of the circumstances which might be called political in which the frontier of the Paraná is found. These circumstances are of ancient date. *The Governments in past times, or some of them, took measures which were never carried out because it was possible that they would involve acts which might lead to great disagreements with our neighbors and which would be smoothed away in better times.* The present Government has not overlooked these grave circumstances, in regard to which it has sought to inform itself with great care, that means might be taken there for the defence of our territories. The Minister of War ordered the establishment of a Military Colony on the Upper Uruguay, which should be in connection with another on the frontier of the Paraná that may be located, but the Province of Paraná did not have nor has it the proper garrison."

To complete this report I beg that Your Excellency will consult my two official communications, No. 188 of Oct. 9th last past, and No. 210 of February 7th ult.

As soon as the Minister of Foreign Affairs responds to the question of Señor Carmargo, I will take care to communicate the facts.

Reiterating the assurances, etc.,

LUIS L. DOMINGUEZ.

The Argentine possession of Misiones thus continued to be recognized by the Imperial Congress. It also proves that Brazil did not occupy *Misiones* and that it did not advance into that Territory fearing international complications.

[margin note: The Government of Brazil contents itself with taking official reports of the Argentine Possession and proposing an arrangement of the boundaries.]

The Argentine possession and the knowledge and acceptance of the same by the Government of Brazil appear in the solemn document which I here present to the Arbitrator. It is the declaration made in the name of his Government by the Plenipotentiary of Brazil in Buenos Aires, stating that *in virtue of the fact that the Argentine Republic governs the Territory* now in dispute, he proposes an early arrangement of the boundary question, and invites the opening of negotiations. This decisive document in favor of Argentine right reads as follows:

> IMPERIAL LEGATION OF BRAZIL,
> BUENOS AIRES, June 2, 1882.
>
> To His Excellency Dr. D. Victorino de la Plaza, Minister of State, Department of Foreign Affairs.
>
> Sir: The Argentine Government issued a Decree, dated March 16th last, dividing into five Departments the *Territory of Misiones*, transferred a short time before from the provincial authority to that of the Nation, and a Governor has already been named for that Territory.
>
> The Imperial Government cannot agree to any act of jurisdiction whatever by the Argentine authorities in the Territory as to which there is pending the dispute between the Confederation and the Empire; and desiring to avoid complications and maintain the friendly relations that happily exist between the two countries, I charge myself with the matter of proposing to Your Excellency the opening of negotiations for a final settlement of the question of boundaries.
>
> I beg that your Excellency will give me an answer as early as the urgency of the matter requires, and take this opportunity to reiterate the assurances of my high consideration.
>
> Baron de ARAUJO GONDIM.

If the Government of Brazil had ever possessed the Territory in dispute, as pretended, if it had ever had any clear or substantial right over it, then it would have rejected, by its arms or in some other way, the possession of Argentine, instead of contenting itself with merely giving an invitation to negotiate, which amounted to acquiescence by inaction; but the actual conduct of Brazil proves very clearly that its Government recognized that the Argentine Republic had an immemorial possession and a perfect right of sovereignty over the Territory in controversy. The highest authorities of the Empire knew of, discussed and accepted the Argentine possession without protest, nor did they oppose it, but confined themselves to extending an invitation to the Argentine Government to discuss the law of the matter and decide the difference by means of diplomatic negotiations.

<small>Principal Argument of Brazil overthrown.</small> The principal argument of Brazil opposed to the claims of the Argentine Republic asserts that Spain never had possession of the Territory situated between the two rivers, Uruguay and Paraná. The international document which I present to the Arbitrator in the Second Volume of the "Argentine Evidence," marked "No. 6," and entitled "Counter-Memorandum," is a statement of the pretensions of Brazil in this matter, presented to the Argentine Government in the year 1884. It comes properly authenticated. On page 116 of this pamphlet Brazil formulates its vital argument in these terms:

"*A Hespanha nunca possuiu um palmo de terra entre os rios do litijio.*" (Spain never possessed a hand's breadth of land between the rivers of the dispute.)

The preceding exposition overthrows in the most conclusive manner the effect of this assertion, and demonstrates the meagre examination given to this subject and the trivial character of the arguments with which Brazil has defended its claims in this international question.

PART THIRD.

AGGRESSIONS OF THE PORTUGUESE ON THE TERRITORY OF
SPAIN.
1596—1810.

PART THIRD.

AGGRESSIONS OF THE PORTUGUESE ON THE TERRITORY OF SPAIN.

1596–1810.

After the foundation by the King of Portugal of the "*Capitania*," or jurisdiction of the Captaincy-General of San Vicente, on the East of the Line of Demarcation of the Bull of Alexander VI and of the Treaty of Tordesillas, the Portuguese and the Mestizos settled the surrounding country, soon forming a characteristic race, a sort of nomadic tribe of adventurers and criminals. Properly speaking, they were subject to no authority, for the Portuguese authorities were incapable of controlling them, and they only obeyed the laws of the primitive instincts of man. The means of action upon which they depended were their arms and their horses, the latter being the great and decisive element which controlled in the heroic period of South America. *[The Paulistas or Mamelukes.]*

The territory under the Captaincy of San Vicente[1] was too narrow for their development, so the *Paulistas* crossed over to the West of the territorial boundary, thus invading the lands of the King of Spain, which had belonged to that Crown ever since the beginning of the Sixteenth century. These hordes of South American arabs at first limited their efforts to attacking the Indians, with or without any just cause, and plundering their villages. Later on their depredations covered a vast field of action, extending as far as the sources of the Paraná, upon the banks of the *Tieté* and along the *Paraná-Panema*, finally going even West of the Paraná and threatening Asuncion, the capital of the Government of the Rio de la Plata. *[Their criminal action.]*

As already stated in this Argument, as soon as the Adelantado Yrala was aware of the audacious excursions of these Mamelukes from San Pablo[2] into the territories of the King of Spain, he organized *[First encounters with the Spaniards]*

---

[1] See Map of Discoveries and Conquests.
[2] The city of San Pablo was on the West of the Captaincy of San Vicento, upon the frontier of the Spanish possessions and was used as a headquarters for the adventurers, who for that reason were called "*Mamelukes*" of San Pablo, or "*Paulistas*."

military expeditions, which by firmly occupying La Guayra kept them within bounds. During something less than a century the *Paulistas* respected the Spanish cities, limiting their vandalism to killing and plundering the Indians belonging to the tribes that were nearest to the city of San Pablo.

Hostilities in the 17th century. 1610-1650. When the Jesuits began in 1600, as already narrated, to organize their Republic among the Guarani Indians, the Paulistas prepared for hostilities, and from 1610 to 1650 their vandal acts assumed horrible proportions. They committed murders and plundered peaceful homes in the very heart of the colonies of the Jesuits, and these acts were followed by the capture of thousands of men, women, and children, who were sold as slaves at San Pablo and in its neighborhood.[1]

Spain takes energetic measures. 1615-1650 These acts, of course, excited the patriotic and humane sentiments of the Spaniards both of America and Europe, and the King issued his *Royal Cédula* of 1639,[2] in which he said:

> ... I have thought to advise and command you, as I do, that, should you hear that such invasions are continued and the dispositions in the said letter do not suffice, you shall, in order to remedy it, endeavor on your part, and communicating with my Viceroy of those provinces and the Governors of Tucuman, Rio de la Plata, and Paraguay, to collect the greatest force of armed people you can gather, sparing as much as possible the expenses of my royal treasury, helping one another and preventing and disposing matters so that those who thus come to make the said raids and captures, from whatever part, people or nation they may be, shall be defeated and chastised; and those of them who can be made prisoners and caught by hand, be punished judicially with all the rigor of the law, as the gravity of such enormous trespasses demands, for they who are doing this are open enemies of religion and of this Crown. For this I shall consider myself well served. ...

The attention of the Arbitrator is called to the documents following the preceding in the official work cited, which prove the horrible character of these invasions by the Paulistas and the noble abnegation with which the Bishop of Paraguay and the Jesuits defended the Indians. These documents are entitled as follows:

---

[1] See this Argument, page 49 *et seq.*
[2] Officially published by the Argentine Republic in the work entitled, "Annexes to the Memoir upon the Boundary Question between the Argentine Republic and Paraguay," by Manuel Ricardo Trelles, Buenos Ayres, August, 1867. Presented to the Arbitrator, page 47, Doc. No. 19. See Argentine Evidence, Vol. 1, page 323.

Copy of the certification of Juan Bautista de Larrazabal, Notary of the Reverend Bishop of Paraguay, Don Fray Christoval de Aresti, regarding the losses suffered in that Province by the invasions of the Portuguese, on the 11th of December, 1632.

Letter written by Father Diego de Boroa of the Order of the Jesuits to the King, Our Master, asking him to remedy the insolence of the Portuguese of San Pablo. Dated at the Sierra of Uruguay on January 28th, 1637.

Letter-Report of the Bishop of Buenos Ayres, in which he gives an account to the Pontiff of the continuous attacks of the Portuguese of San Pablo upon the converted Indians of the Reductions, and asks him to threaten them with some penalties and censure. Dated September 30, 1637.

Memorial of Father Antonio Ruiz de Montoya and following documents.

Finally the Royal *Cédula* of February 14, 1647, says:

Juan Pastor, of the Order of the Jesuits, Attorney-General of the Provinces of Paraguay, has reported to me that the Indians of Uruguay and Paraná in the Province of Paraguay, who are under the care of the Fathers of said Order in twenty-four very populous settlements, have bravely defended themselves and valiantly in these twelve years against the Portuguese of Brazil, at their expense and risk of their lives, purchasing arms and ammunition and other necessary things for their defence, in great quantity, and of value, exceeding seven hundred firearms; being compelled to thus protect themselves, owing to the invasions of the said Portuguese, who took captives to Brazil where they sold them as slaves; and that after I gave them permission to use the said weapons in their protection, they had defended their country, driving away the Portuguese and putting them twice to an ignominious flight, after which they now enjoyed peace, without the Portuguese daring again to come upon them; and that this was very greatly to my service and the defence of the Province of Paraguay, of which he feared the enemy would attempt to take possession, in view of its scant resistance, and that if any could be offered in such an event it would be by these Indians, who, when called by my Governor of the said Provinces, would come with their weapons and assistance to defend the country; he supplicated that, in view of this intelligence, I should extend some mercy to them towards lightening the taxes they pay, leaving this at your disposition or that of my President of the Audiencia of Charcas; and having been seen by my Royal Council of Indies, together with what the Licentiate Don Gerónimo de Camargo, my Attorney, said on the subject, it has been decided to charge and recommend you to use all care in procuring the alleviation of the Indians of the said Reductions, as it is just to assist them, in view of the report of their good services in the defence against the rebels of Portugal, encouraging them to continue whenever a future opportunity presents; for this is my will, and it fosters my service.

<small>Misiones in a state of war. 1640 1676.</small> The compliance with the Royal orders kept the *Misiones* in a state of war, and there were bloody engagements with the Mamelukes. The Government of the Rio de la Plata adopted energetic measures to sustain them in the war and to maintain the possession of the territories in the centre of which is found that now submitted to the Arbitrator. This is proved by the following documents which are presented to the Arbitrator:[1]

1649. Decree by the "*Cabildo*" (Council) of Asuncion, ordering that soldiers be enlisted from Villa Rica in order to send scouts and reconnoitre the points occupied by the Government of Paraguay, which according to Reports were held by the Portuguese; and directing that munitions, arms and stores should be prepared to repulse them, January 12, 1649.

1664. Royal Cédula ordering the Governor of Paraguay, Diez de Andino, to report as to the propriety of separating the Government from the Jesuit Colony of San Pedro de Terzano and San Francisco de Ybirá Pariga.

1673. Proclamation by Don Felipe de René Corvalan, Governor of Paraguay, ordering that the Royal Decree proclaimed in Villa Rica on the second of February should be obeyed.

1675. February 22. Decree of the *Cabildo* ordering troops to go out in force to restrain the Mamelukes of San Pablo and Tupis, who were capturing the Indians in order to make slaves of them. Also concerning the previous decree and measures for its execution.

1676. Letter from the licentiate Mongelo Garces to the Governor of Paraguay, giving an account of the hostile operations against the Portuguese Paulistas or Mamelukes, March 3.

1676. Edict of Governor Diez de Andino providing for the recruitment of people in order to pursue the Mamelukes, who had ruined four *pueblos* of Indians near Villa Rica.

1676. Statement made by Diez de Andino about his expedition for the purpose of expelling the Portuguese from the dominions of Spain.

1676. Decree of the *Cabildo* of Asuncion convoking a Council of War to discuss measures to be taken against the invading Mamelukes. Meeting of said Council, and measures taken to expel the Portuguese from the *pueblos* of San Pedro de Teré, Cané, La Candelaria, San Francisco, Ybua and Parijara.

[1] Argentine Evidence, Vol. I, page 335 et seq.; M88., Group B, No. 1 et seq.

1685. Edict in regard to the invasion of the Portuguese *Paulistas*.
1685. Decree and proclamation of the *Cabildo* of Asuncion upon receiving news that the Portuguese have come up the River. January 16th.

The results of this war were unfavorable to the Indians and to the Jesuits, for although they defeated the invaders and expelled the Mamelukes from their lands, yet these incessantly returned in search of plunder, so that social life and agricultural work in these Colonies became impossible beyond the intrenchments by which they were protected. The Jesuits therefore resolved, as before stated, to abandon the old and historical province of La Guayra and concentrate their *pueblos* South of the Yguazú between the rivers Paraná and Uruguay, where these great streams would oppose a natural defence against the indomitable horsemen of San Pablo. Consequences of the war in the 17th century.

The hostilities which had been carried on so long did not however cease during the Eighteenth century, although the robbers were less successful and their audacity was everywhere checked. The following documents, that I present to the Arbitrator, show that Spain resisted these attacks and protected its territories:[1] Hostilities and resistance in the 18th century.

1704 to 1734. Official papers concerning the entrance of the Portuguese upon Spanish territory.
1750. Letter from Don José de Andonaegui, Governor of Buenos Ayres, dated November 19, 1750, wherein he gives an account of the *Misiones* of Indians possessed by the Company of Jesus in the Bishopric of Paraguay and in that of Buenos Ayres.
1771. The Governor of Buenos Ayres sends copy of letters from Paraguay showing the progress of the Portuguese in the region of Gatimi; their ambitious ideas and their efforts to invade the dominions of His Majesty. Buenos Ayres, July 24.
1784 to 1795. Paragraphs taken from the Memoirs of the Viceroys of the Rio de la Plata, as to the boundary question between the Spaniards and Portuguese in America.
1790. Reflections suggested by the Report of the Intendant Governor of the fort of Coimbra and village of Albuquerque, as to the Portuguese having settled on the banks of the river Paraguay, October 13, 1790.
1791. Arredondo, the Viceroy of Buenos Ayres, informs Count Florida Blanca that he has given the necessary orders for the

---

[1] Argentine Evidence, Vol. I, page 367 *et seq.*; Group B of Manuscripts, Document No. 4 *et seq.*

expulsion of the Portuguese from the possession of Itapuca, which they had unjustly occupied, September 19, 1791.

1792. Note of the Viceroy, Arredondo, to the Conde de Aranda, complaining of the continuous advances and robberies of the Portuguese on the South of the Piratini, December 13, 1792.

The Government of Spain continued to exercise the same authority in the last years of the Nineteenth century as it had previously done in South America, as the following documents prove:[1]

1801. True statistics of the seven Eastern Pueblos of the *Misiones of Uruguay*, at the time they were invaded by Brazilians, some eighty days after the ratification of the Treaty of Peace of Badajoz. This is a translation from the original document existing in the General Archives of the Indies, a copy of which, duly certified by the Consul of the United States at Seville, forms part of Group B, No. 11, of the Manuscript Documents of the "Argentine Evidence."

1804. Communication from the Count of Campo Alange, the Spanish Ambassador at Lisbon, to the Portuguese Minister Aranjo de Azevedo, protesting against the advances of the Portuguese in the *Misiones* made after the agreements of the Peace of Badajoz, and urging upon him the making of a definitive treaty of boundaries.

1804. Note of Don Pedro Cevallos approving the conduct of the Count of Campo de Alange in the matter of the foregoing communications, inducing him to ask the Portuguese Government for the appointment of a Minister Plenipotentiary to conclude the definitive Boundary Treaty in America.

1804. Letter of the Count of Campo de Alange to Minister Pedro de Cevallos, and memorandum of reply to the same.

1804. Letter of the Count of Campo de Alange to Minister Don Pedro de Cevallos, informing the latter of an interview held with Aranjo de Azevedo, relating to the Portuguese usurpations in America.

1806. Statement about the situation of the negotiation with Portugal and the conclusion of a definitive Boundary Treaty, as shown by the preceding documents. Also a note on the same subject from the Department of State.

1804-1806. Correspondence of the Commander of the Spanish frontier, Don Jorge Pacheco, with the Viceroy of Brazil, concerning the Portuguese usurpations.

Measures taken in Europe by the Jesuits against the Paulistas, 1645-1652. The Jesuits decided to incite Europe against the Mamelukes of San Pablo, and accordingly in 1645 they sent to Spain, Portugal and Rome,

[1] "Argentine Evidence," Vol. I, pages 115 to 447. Group B of Manuscripts, No. 11 *et seq.*

Commissioners who were to present in all their nakedness the acts of vandalism committed by these nomads and ask that repressive measures be taken against them, and permanent guarantees be given for the safety of their agricultural settlements, their industries, their flocks and their herds. The documents presented to the Arbitrator in Volume I of the "Argentine Evidence," page 329 *et seq.*, refer to their action before the Court of Spain.[1] The celebrated Father Antonio Ruiz de Montoya spoke in the name of the Jesuits. He said to the King in his Memorial:—

. . . .

> which Indians have had in the last few years several well-fought encounters with the Portuguese rebels, who to this day still keep up their persistent intent to conquer those lands to gain a foothold in Peru, and over whom they have gained signal victories, killing a great number and driving them away from our borders on many occasions; several times they have gone out assisting the Spaniards in the pacification of the country against other Indian rebels, with all fidelity and success in the victories they have achieved; and all at their expense, without having any help; *nay, they have bought with their own money more than six hundred firearms and ammunition; and it is owing to their valor that the country is not in the power of the Portuguese rebels, regarding whom frequent advices are received of their designs to again subject the land; and for this reason the said Indians live in watchful practice with their arms, as is notorious*, and is confirmed by the certifications he presents.

The royal decision will be found on page 333 of the "Argentine Evidence," following the preceding document. It begins as follows:

> DECISION.—In conformity wherewith and in view of the causes and reasons set forth by the said Father Antonio Ruiz de Montoya in the Memorial herewith attached, and those present considering them true and just, wherefore, in the name of His Majesty, and by virtue of the powers and commissions that I have from his Royal person, I do receive as vassals the Indians recently converted in the Provinces of Uruguay, Tape, Rio Paraná and Itatí of the Government of Paraguay, and I declare them as such and belonging to the Royal Crown, and as men of the garrison opposite the Portuguese of Brazil, and I command that for the present they shall be relieved of "*mitas*" and personal servitude, because they assist in the said garrison, where it is considered they are quite busy in behalf of the Royal service and the public cause. . . .

---

[1] Official work of Señor Trelles already cited, page 30, Document No. 12.

International importance of these facts 1593 to 1700.

The preceding brief narration shows that during two centuries the legal possessions of Spain, lying West of the Meridian of the Treaty of Tordesillas, were plundered by the savage hordes from the Brazilian country of San Paulo, and that the Jesuits, who were the agents and representatives of the authority of the King of Spain, were obliged to retreat to the South of the Yguazú. But do these facts possess the legal character which is needed to base a claim of *possessory right* on behalf of Portugal to the territory which served as the theatre for these vandal excursions? Has Portugal ever invoked these facts, upon any occasion, as a basis on which to found an act of dominion over the territory in the border of which is located that which has been submitted to this Arbitration? Is there any treaty between Spain and Portugal that gives any legal status to these crimes?

No! The Sovereign Pontiff, the highest political authority of that epoch, and the King of Portugal himself, during these two centuries, always condemned these arab-like invasions of the Paulistas and ordered them to cease. The Paulistas disobeyed their King, as well as their Pontiff. Their acts were, therefore, merely common crimes, deserving punishment, and cannot serve as a basis for any claim or on which to found a right. The Brazilian writers, who have sustained the contrary in recent years, forget the official condemnation of these facts made by Portugal, and offend Humanity. The proof of these conclusions will be given to the Arbitrator, and taken from the most respectable Brazilian authorities.

Condemnation signed by King Don Sebastian, in 1570.

The Visconde de Porto Seguro, in his "*Historia Geral do Brazil,*" presented to the Arbitrator,[1] cites at page 322, Volume I, a law condemning these white slave hunts, signed by the King of Portugal, Don Sebastian, and adds:

> We consider this text of so much importance that we deem it our duty to transcribe it here. . . .

The substantial part of this law reads as follows:

> I prohibit and command that from this time forth there shall not be used in the said parts of Brazil the methods which until now have been pursued to make captives of the said peoples, neither shall they be taken captive by any other method or in any other manner whatsoever, *excepting only such as may be taken in a just war which the Portuguese may make against the said people,*

---

[1] See this Argument, page 20.

with my license and authority, or that of my Governor in the said regions, or those who may continue to attack the Portuguese or other people for the purpose of eating them, such as those which are called Aymorés, and the like. . . .

The celebrated official historian of the Empire comments upon this matter in worthy terms, which reveal the disobedience by the Paulistas of the commands of their King. He uses the following language:

> This law giving liberty to the Indians occasioned such noisy protests in Brazil that they were even heard in Portugal, and it was necessary to modify it by means of a Royal letter, the execution of which did not fall to Mendé Sá.

Father Gay in his official work, which I have already presented to the Arbitrator,[1] plainly confirms the statement made by Porto Seguro. He copies the Royal Cédula of Don Sebastian, dated in 1570, and adds:

> The Paulistas became mutinous on account of the order given by the Viceroy, they threatened the Judge and ill-treated Father Simas.

The Visconde de Porto Seguro also adds, at page 488 of the book cited:

<small>Condemnation by the King of Portugal. 1628.</small>

> As the Indians had taken refuge in the villages established on the left bank of the Paraná and were subject to the Jesuits of Paraguay, they were attacked there by the Paulistas and made prisoners by them. *In vain did the Court command by its decree* (on the 18th of September, 1628) *that measures should be taken against the guilty, for these paid no attention to it or to anything.* They formed themselves into bands, composed of hundreds of men, taking with them double their number of friendly Indians. *There was no authority that could restrain these tendencies of theirs,* and it was not easy to employ force, for it was more necessary to make use of all their forces in order to end once for all the hostilities of the Dutch.

These facts were energetically condemned by all the writers who treated of this subject, and were also strongly denounced by Father Gay in his official Brazilian work, cited.

<small>Condemnation by Gay and other Brazilian writers.</small>

On page 353 of that work he says:

---

[1] See this Argument, page 43.

In his "*Voyage en Amerique*," M. Alcide d'Orbigny says that it is proved by authentic documents that from 1628 to 1630 the *Paulistas* stole and sold as slaves more than *seventy thousand* inhabitants of the Jesuit settlements. Dr. Francisco Xargue relates in his book, "*Insignes Misioneros de la Compañia de Jesús en la Provincia del Paraguay*," the assault made by the *Paulistas* against the people of *Jesús Maria* in the province of Guayra. He says:—
" As the enemy could not by means of charms or sorcerers prevent the salvation of the large number of souls that were converted to God, they incited the attacks of the Mamelukes of Brazil (the name given in that country to the Paulistas), a daring and warlike people who had nothing in common with Christians except the fact of having been baptized, and who were more cruel than the very heathens. They formed themselves into companies with some of their allies and directed their steps towards the reduction (settlement) of *Jesús Maria*." [1] . . .

The enemy, composed of eight hundred *Mamelukes* and three thousand Tupis,[2] with fire-arms and other instruments of war, threw themselves like wolves upon those who received them like sheep, took them, loaded them with chains and also took away their clothes with great cruelty.

<small>Condemnation of the Paulistas by Pope Urban VIII. 1639</small> This same official Brazilian author, the Visconde de Porto Seguro, adds at page 691, Volume II, of his cited work, these very eloquent arguments in favor of the right of the Argentine Republic, which I uphold:—

The Paulistas, even before the Dutch invasion, had employed as a means of getting laborers *not only the method of subjecting the wild Indians but also that of carrying off those who lived in the villages that were under the orders of the Jesuits, on the affluents of the Paraná below the Tieté, that is to say, in the Provinces of Vera and of Guayra, and became so audacious that they went beyond the Salto Grande (great fall) of that river and invaded the Misiones of Acaray, thus threatening all the Reductions (Jesuit Settlements) of Paraguay.* In such an extremity the Jesuits decided to send agents to Rome and to Madrid begging for protection. Father Francisco Diaz went to the Pontifical court, and Father Antonio Ruiz de Montoya, Director of the Collego of Asuncion, went to Spain. For some years before he had been a Missionary in the Reduction of Loreto, near the River Paraná-Panema. . . .

Both emissaries obtained in Rome as well as in Madrid all they requested. Urban VIII ordered the publication in Brazil of

---
[1] See Map of " Discoveries and Conquests," etc.
[2] The Tupis were savage Indians from Brazil.

the Papal Bull of Paul III, in favor of the Indians of Peru, which declared that those who captured, sold, ill-treated or made use of the services of the Indians would be excommunicated. From the Catholic King was obtained the Cédula of September 16, 1639, ordering the Viceroy of Peru (the Marquis de Mancera) to see that the Indians of the Paraguayan *Misiones* were formed into regiments and armed in order to defend themselves against the Paulistas. This was the origin of an armed force in the Paraguayan *Misiones* under the orders of the Jesuits, by means of which in the middle of the following century they dared to 'oppose resistance to the accomplishment of the Royal orders. . . .

Diaz Taño presented to the ecclesiastical administrator in Rio de Janeiro, Pedro Homen Albernaz, a brief ordering to be put into practice that which was directed in the Papal Bull of Paul III.

The same scandals and crimes that were occasioned by the Royal Cédula of the King of Portugal in 1570 were reproduced in Brazil when Father Taño arrived with the Papal Bull against the Paulistas. Southey, the English Historian, cherished by the Empire of Brazil, describes with moving eloquence those shameful events. In Volume III, page 442 [Portuguese Edition] of his work, already presented to the Arbitrator, he says :

<blockquote>
Meantime Diaz Taño, having left Montoya at Madrid, proceeded to Rome and laid the state of the Missions before the General of the Order. Vitelleschi, who held that station, deeply impressed by a recital of the miseries which the Portuguese slave-hunters had caused, made him repeat the tale to Urban VIII, and that Pontiff, with a just feeling of indignation, denounced the severest censures of the church against all persons who on any pretext whatsoever should enslave the Indians, whether converted or unconverted. Having returned to Madrid, Diaz Taño found that his colleague had obtained from the Government everything which he wished, and the King promised a free passage for the missionaries whom he was about to take back with him, thirty in number. They were to embark from Lisbon. Here the slave party was more powerful than at Madrid, and the Minister, Miguel de Vasconsellos, forbade their embarcation ; but they appealed to the Duchess of Mantua, and by her interference were allowed to proceed. The ship was compelled by storms to put into Rio de Janeiro. There Diaz Taño consulted with F. Pedro Motu, the Visitor in Brazil, and with the approbation of the other clergy read the Bull of Excommunication in the Jesuits' Church. In Bahia perhaps this might have been done safely; but Rio de Janeiro was too near San Paulo, and many of its inhabitants were connected with the Paulistas, and implicated in the guilt of their
</blockquote>

abominable proceedings. These people had the rabble on their side; they attacked the College, broke open the gates, and would have murdered the Paraguay Jesuits if the Governor, Salvador Correa, had not invited the mob into the church, and persuaded them to appoint a meeting the next day for discussing the matter temperately and devising some remedy. The meeting was held in the Carmellite Church, and the Jesuits to save their lives, which were in imminent danger, suggested or consented that the enemies of the Bull should appeal to the Pope against it, which would have the effect of suspending it till his further decision should be known.[1]

<small>New condemnation by the King of Portugal, 1681.</small> As I have already said, the *Misiones* were at that time in open war against the *Mamelukes* of San Paulo, and the Government of Portugal hastened to condemn this war, so far as it concerned its subjects. Article VI of the Treaty of March 7, 1681, which is presented to the Arbitrator in another place, reads as follows :

> In order that whatever cause or motive of dissatisfaction may exist between these two crowns may be altogether extirpated, His Highness shall order an inquiry about the excesses which have been committed by the inhabitants of San Paulo *on the bordering land and dominions of His Majesty*,[2] *and punish them severely*, causing, to this effect, the Indians, cattle, mules and other things which had been seized, to be restored and set at liberty ; and *he shall forbid that henceforward such hostilities be carried on against the good peace and friendship of these Kingdoms*.

Is it possible, before the civilization of the Nineteenth century, to invoke these facts, which were condemned by Humanity, by the Pope, and by the Conquerors of the New World, the Kings of Spain and Portugal, as the foundation of pretensions which, besides violating openly the Treaty of Tordesillas, are contrary to international good faith?

<small>The question at the beginning of the 19th century.</small> The truth is, Portugal never set up any such claim in past centuries, and we come down to the Nineteenth century without this Crown, either on its own account or by an agreement with that of Spain, having produced a single judicial act referring to the disputed Territory. It has passed through the war carried on by the Jesuits against the savages of San Paulo, and through the most complicated diplomatic negotiations and the most contradictory treaties without one word reflecting upon its sovereignty, which has remained Spanish as a matter of fact, and by law and right has always been respected as such.

---

[1] English Edition in the Congressional Library, Washington, D. C., Vol. 2, page 325.

[2] *Las Misiones*, concentrated at that time precisely in the Territory now submitted to the Arbitrator, as has been shown.

It follows from this narration of facts, all of which are clearly proved, ^{Portuguese policy from 1501 to 1828} that Portugal has always pursued a policy of usurpation against the dominions of Spain in America. But at the same time we have seen that the field of these usurpations was the sea-coast, from *Yguapé* to Montevideo and *La Colonia del Sacramento*, the Portuguese being expelled from these coasts by Spanish swords at the end of the last century and by the arms of the new Argentine nation during the first quarter of the present one. Portugal and Brazil wished to rule the mouth of the immense estuary of the Plata; they therefore concentrated all their diplomatic efforts and their land and sea forces upon the coast, never penetrating or pretending to penetrate into the interior of the Territory submitted to the Arbitrator. If Portugal or Brazil had penetrated as far as that region they would not have abandoned the erroneous pretensions of their Demarcators of 1759 and 1791, but they would have occupied the disputed Territory or exercised their authority over its industries. Yet not a single document, nor solitary act of foundation of a town, nor law, nor decree, nor any act favorable to the present pretensions of Brazil, can be presented to the Arbitrator.

I shall briefly refer to the Portuguese usurpations on the littoral, simply as a new proof of the antagonism and bad faith, first of the Portuguese policy, and second of that of the Empire of Brazil as regards the Argentine pueblos.

Until 1801 Spain maintained its dominion over the left bank of the ^{Possessions of Spain in 1801.} Uruguay, that is to say over the seven *Misiones* called *orientales* (or eastern), which were founded on the territory of its old provinces, *del Tapé* and *del Campo*. It has been clearly shown that the possessions of Spain ^{European intrigues.} and Portugal in America were subject to the changes and constant intrigues of European politics in which England, France, Portugal and Spain took part. The examination of the treaties exhibited in this Arbitration immediately reveals how uncertain became the fate of the countries of South America, always exposed and liable to suffer from the consequences of European combinations. Therefore acts of sale often took place, as well as donations or exchanges of the colonies of America, Africa and Asia, in which Spain and Portugal did not always proceed spontaneously, but often under pressure or induced by the intrigues of other great powers.

The war that took place in 1801 between France and Spain against ^{European war of 1801.} Portugal, arising out of the exigencies of the Arbitrator of the World, Napoleon I, was terminated by the Treaty of Badajoz, which established the conditions of victory. Three months after this treaty, Portugal, without any previous declaration of war, invaded the Eastern *Misiones* of Uruguay, thus flagrantly violating the Boundary Treaty of 1777.

<small>Affirmation of Brazilian authors.</small> Father Gay, already cited, at page 608 of his official Brazilian work, narrates the attack upon and conquest of the seven *pueblos* of the *Misiones orientales* under the title of:

> *Conquest of the Misiones orientales* by the Portuguese. System adopted by the Conquerors in order to govern these *Misiones* until the invasion of Don Fructuoso Rivera.

Southey confirms this version at page 308, Volume VI, of his celebrated History,[1] already cited.

Finally the Visconde de Porto Seguro, in his "*Historia Geral do Brazil*," Vol. II, page 1057, says that this very important international fact was a spontaneous outburst of temper on the part of a fugitive deserter, who had not previously consulted his superiors, the Viceroy of Brazil and the King of Portugal. These are his very words:

> Stimulated by this proof of confidence, Canto sought greater honors. Considering the moment favorable and that the force of one hundred men which he had under his orders was sufficient *to subject the neighboring territory*, he undertook this enterprise, and with such success that in a few days he had reduced and subjected to his commands the *well known seven pueblos of Misiones, etc.* As a reward Canto was made a Captain, *and his record as a deserter was withdrawn*. A poor and mean reward in truth for a man who gave Brazil a territory that could by itself constitute a Province.

<small>The Viceroy of Buenos Ayres resists with an Army.</small> The Viceroy of Buenos Ayres, the Marquis de Sobremonte, immediately marched against the Portuguese at the head of an army of three thousand men, but diplomatic negotiations delayed his action for <small>Armistice 1804</small> some time, until an armistice was signed in 1804 by which Portugal recognized the violated boundaries of the Treaty of 1777. This armistice however between two subordinates of the Crowns of Spain and Portugal had no permanent effect, so that the situation continued uncertain in regard to the relations of the two Crowns and concerning their lands

---

[1] It is proper to notice here that the *Misiones* of the Jesuit Republic were divided into three groups:
1. *Misiones of Paraguay* on the right bank of the river Paraná.
2. *Misiones* between the rivers Paraná and Uruguay.
3. The *seven pueblos of Misiones orientales* (Eastern) on the left bank of the Uruguay.

in America, until the Independence of the Viceroyalty of the Rio de la Plata, which was proclaimed in 1816.

Portugal continued its usurpations against the new American government, and this diplomatic military drama only attained its denouement in 1827, when the Argentine arms finally defeated the Brazilians and the Treaty of Peace of 1828 was made. This contained the following vital condition: That the Portuguese invaders should retreat as far as the legal boundary of that nation according to the Treaty of 1777, the supreme law of South America in international boundary matters.

This historical digression is a valuable element to assist in arriving at a proper judgment, and it comes with new moral force when considered in connection with the Argentine Evidence. It is another landmark on the road that leads to a right conclusion. The matter submitted to Arbitration is one of the features of the aggressive and usurpatory policy of Brazil against the countries of the Rio de la Plata. The following documents, attached to the "Argentine Evidence," Volume 1, pages 437 to 447, and the Manuscripts presented in Group B, Document No. 18, prove this aspect of my Argument. It appears therefrom that the Spanish Commander upon the frontier with the dominions of Portugal resisted at all times the Portuguese pretensions against the territories of his Catholic Majesty.

1804-1806. Correspondence of the Commander of the Spanish frontier, Don Jorge Pacheco, with the Viceroy of Brazil, concerning the Portuguese usurpations.

PART FOURTH.

THE PUBLIC LAW OF THE CASE.

I.
TREATIES BETWEEN SPAIN AND PORTUGAL.
1493—1777.

II.
TREATIES BETWEEN THE ARGENTINE REPUBLIC AND BRAZIL.
1810—1890.

PART FOURTH.

I.

TREATIES BETWEEN SPAIN AND PORTUGAL.

1493-1777.

Having demonstrated in an indisputable manner, and confirmed by official Brazilian declarations, that Spain discovered, conquered and possessed the immense country I have described, presenting at the same time the "*Mapa de los Descubrimientos y Conquistas de España al Este del Rio Paraná*" (Map of the Discoveries and Conquests),[1] I now come to an explanation of the following historical and legal matters: Modifications of Spanish sovereignty in South America

1. Why Portugal made settlements in Spanish territory, thus violating the Meridian of Demarcation of the Treaty of Tordesillas of 1494.

2. Territorial exchanges between Spain and Portugal, and cessions from one to the other, in the part of South America we are now considering.

3. Legal status of the Territory submitted to the Arbitrator during these modifications of the respective sovereignties.

In order to examine these questions it is necessary to study the treaties that refer to them; all of which are presented to the Arbitrator.[2] Examination of the treaties

I have already demonstrated in this Argument that when the Crowns of Spain and Portugal made clear the Bull of Alexander VI, concerning boundaries, by means of the Treaty of Tordesillas,[3] the latter Kingdom gained a vast zone of land on the terrestrial Globe, for the boundary line was transferred by Spain, in favor of its rival, 370 leagues further west of the meridian of the Cape Verde Islands than had been designated by the Pope as the Line of Demarcation. The Kingdom of Portugal had been united to Spain for more than half a century, and its sub- First advance of Portugal. Treaty of Tordesillas. 1494. Portugal occupies Las Colonia 1680

---
[1] Page 27 of this Argument.
[2] "Argentine Evidence," Vol. I, page 9 and following.
[3] See this Argument, page 18, and Treaty of Tordesillas in the "Argentine Evidence," Vol. I, page 21.

jects had established commercial relations with the Rio de la Plata, prohibited to all other flags, the Spanish ensign being the only exception, and that under great restrictions. When Portugal, whose attention was attracted to the importance of the Rio de la Plata by these commercial relations, reassumed its sovereignty, it claimed to divide with Spain the dominion of this region, and ordered its officials in Brazil to locate a fort on the left bank of that great estuary. This order was a *Casus Belli*, because it was a blow at the sovereignty of Spain, violated the Treaty of Tordesillas, and evicted the Spanish possessors, who were in general *vaqueros* (cowboys).[1] The occupation took place in January, 1680, at a place called ever since "*Colonia de Sacramento* (Sacramento Colony). The Governor of the Province of the Rio de la Plata, Don José de Garro, received orders from the King of Spain to attack the Portuguese and expel them. He therefore organized an army composed of a few regular troops and 3,000 recruits from the *Misiones*, from the very *Territory a part of which is now submitted to the Arbitrator*, who after marching more than 200 leagues arrived at the Colony and heroically captured it on the 7th of August, 1681. Governor Lobo and his army were made prisoners, and the Colony continued in the power of Spain, then the sovereign of the world.

<small>Treaty of 1681.</small> This event obliged the Infante of Portugal, Dom Pedro, to initiate a negotiation, the result of which was to arrange the provisional treaty of 1681. According to Article XII of the treaty the rights of both Crowns to the legal possession of these territories were to be definitively settled, without varying the Meridian of the Treaty of Tordesillas.[2]

<small>Its significance.</small> This treaty does not imply the cession of the territory of the Colony of Sacramento to Portugal, as some inconsiderate writers have claimed. It is a noteworthy act of reciprocal good will and loyal friendship on the part of both Crowns, by which Spain gives a moral satisfaction for the violent military attack against the Portuguese army, and Portugal

---

[1] See the work of the Publicist Don Carlos Calvo, entitled "*Coleccion Completa de los Tratados, Convenciones, Capitulaciones, Armisticios y otros actos diplomaticos de todos los Estados de la America Latina, comprendidos entre el Golfo de México y el Cabo de Hornos, desde el año 1493, hasta nuestros dias, precedidos de una Memoria sobre el estado actual del America, de cuadros estadisticos, de un diccionario diplomatico y de una noticia historica sobre cada uno de los tratados mas importantes.*" Paris, 1862. (Complete collection of the treaties, conventions, etc., of all the States of Latin America, between the Gulf of Mexico and Cape Horn, from the year 1493 to the present day, preceded by a Memoir in regard to the present condition of America, statistical tables, a diplomatic dictionary, and a historical notice of each of the most important treaties. Vol. I, page 176 *et seq.*)

[2] See the work of the eminent publicist Carlos Calvo, on International Law, cited,

in its turn explicitly recognizes the territorial sovereignty of Spain and the authority of the Treaty of Tordesillas for adjusting every boundary dispute. A brief analysis of the articles of the treaty will in fact show this. Its preamble declares that this treaty is provisional, until the two Crowns sign a definitive one. The second paragraph says that the object of this treaty is "*to correct the disturbance caused by this settlement* (that of the Colony of Sacramento) *to the legitimate rights of quiet and peaceful possession which His Catholic Majesty had enjoyed for nearly two centuries in that part of the Rio de la Plata, its navigation, islands, and northern and southern banks and other adjacent lands, reducing things to their primitive condition*," until an examination of the ground permitted an honest application of "*the just demarcation agreed upon in the settlement between the Catholic Sovereign and the King of Portugal which was made at Tordesillas on June 7, 1493.*"[1]

<small>Portugal recognizes the sovereignty of Spain.</small>

This is a very clear acknowledgment of the sovereignty of Spain in the entire region of the Rio de la Plata and over the Territory submitted to the Arbitrator, for that is situated several hundred leagues West of the *just demarcation* of Tordesillas.[2]

In the second paragraph of the preamble of the Treaty the King of Portugal corroborates the foregoing interpretation, declaring that it must by no means be understood that in occupying the Colony of Sacramento he had "*any purpose to disturb or to overstep the limits of the 'Demarcacion Catolica,' by occupying any port, site or place which might be understood* to belong either to his possessions (those of the King of Spain) or to his dominions," and adds—"*assuring him, in demonstration of his good faith*, of his *prompt disposition to repair whatever injury there was to the right of his Crown* which might be shown by His Catholic Majesty." He concluded by promising to arbitrate, by the agreement of both Kings, the means of securing this necessary information.[3] This, fairly interpreted, signifies that at that period the Crown of Portugal had doubts as to the true position upon the terrestrial globe of the Meridian of Demarcation of the Treaty of Tordesillas, but it was decided to submit to what a technical investigation might show in regard thereto. Very well! These investigations proved that the Colony of Sacramento was situated on Spanish territory, and the Kings of Portugal afterwards accepted the decision of science.

[1] "Argentine Evidence," Vol. 1, page 26, Paragraph 1.
[2] See " Map of Discoveries and Conquests," etc.
[3] "Argentine Evidence," Vol. 1, page 26, second paragraph.

In acknowledgment of this fundamental recognition of its sovereignty, and to facilitate the negotiation of the treaty in which this was to be stated, Spain deplored the excess of zeal on the part of the Governor of Buenos Aires in assaulting the Colony of Sacramento, the evacuation of which might have been obtained amicably (see paragraph 3, article I of the treaty).¹

Article II refers to the restitution of arms. Article III provides that the inhabitants of the Colony of Sacramento who were taken prisoners shall be returned to the Colony again. This was an act of humanity and a tribute to the civil liberties of man, although as to its international political character the same article says, at the end, that they shall remain there simply as *guests*, having neither public nor private effect upon the lands; and "*they shall not raise any other kind of new fortification, neither build new houses of stone or with mudwalls, nor any other sort of durable or permanent buildings.*"²

Article IV limits in the same way the public action of the Portuguese inhabitants returned to the Colony of Sacramento, for it forbids them to accumulate materials of war, to increase their numbers or to do any commercial business.³ Article X, already quoted,⁴ categorically recognizes the rights of Spain to the Territory now submitted to the Arbitrator. Article VII guarantees to the inhabitants of Buenos Aires, that is to say to the Spaniards, the enjoyment in the Colony of Sacramento of civil rights, particularly those of a commercial character, of which they had been deprived by the Portuguese.⁵

Article VIII is still more explicit, for it provides that the maritime commerce of Spain should have control, full and free, under the sovereign authority of that Crown, over the Colony of Sacramento, its port, coasts, and surrounding country, without consultation or previous permission from the Portuguese.⁶

Articles IX and X are of no interest, merely referring to previous laws. Article XI establishes the military authority of the Governor of Buenos Aires in the Colony of Sacramento.

Article XII declares and repeats that all this is without prejudice to the ultimate rights of either Crown, whose precise rights were to be decided from the results of the examination of the Demarcation Com-

---
¹ Argentine Evidence, Vol. I, page 26, third paragraph, Article I of the Treaty.
² Argentine Evidence, Vol. I, page 27, Art. III.
³ Ibid., Art. IV.
⁴ See this Argument, page 118.
⁵ Argentine Evidence, Vol. I, page 27, Art. VII.
⁶ Ibid., Art. VIII.

missioners whom it was agreed in Article XII to appoint to delineate upon the Globe the line of the Treaty of Tordesillas.[1] It installs as Arbitrator the Sovereign Pontiff, who was to decide any difference between the Commissioners.

This treaty is, therefore, essentially favorable to Spain and to its heir, the Argentine Republic, for the following reasons:— *The treaty of 1681 favorable to Spain and the Argentine Republic.*

1. Because the King of Portugal recognized the Spanish possession, during two centuries, of the lands which were the subject of the treaty.

2. Because the King of Portugal declared that his only doubts were as to the boundaries fixed by the Treaty of Tordesillas; but that he would accept the result of its location upon the ground, adding that when he occupied the Colony he had no intention of remaining there if the rights or possessions of Spain were to be affected thereby.

3. Because the King of Portugal recognized as existing in all its vigor the Treaty of Tordesillas, the unchangeable foundation of the rights of Spain.

4. And because, finally, the King of Portugal acknowledged that the *Territory of Misiones*, now submitted to the Arbitrator, was situated within the sovereignty of Spain.

The course of political intrigue in Europe was preparing a coalition of England, Austria and Holland against France and Spain. Portugal hesitated, but was inclined to take part in the coalition as a means of weakening Spain and obtaining advantages in the demarcation of its dominions in America. Spain, seeing the danger, attracted Portugal to her own cause by the promise of ceding to her the Colony of Sacramento, with the lands that its inhabitants could cultivate around it. Europe thus remained divided into two camps: France, Spain and Portugal on one side; and England, Holland and Austria on the other. This was the origin of the Treaty of 1701, the Fourteenth Article of which contains the said territorial cession.[2] Having secured the Colony of Sacramento, that is to say having at last lawfully put its foot upon the mouth of the Rio de la Plata, which it had coveted for two centuries, Portugal only two years later acted in bad faith toward Spain by going over to the ranks of the hostile European coalition. The Visconde de Porto Seguro states this without any ambiguity in his "General History," etc., already quoted, Volume II, page 774: *European intrigues and the Colony of Sacramento. 1701.*

---
[1] *Ibid.*, page 28, Art. XI. The demarcation was attempted, without any positive result, but the Geographers of the Academy of Sciences of Paris, directed by the celebrated La Condamine, traced the line of the Treaty of Tordesillas, and this neutral authority shows that Spain was entirely in the right.

[2] "Argentine Evidence," Vol. I, page 35, Article XIV.

In this way came about the alliance of England, Austria and Holland against France and the Duke d'Anjou (Philip V of Spain), and those nations offered Portugal great advantages to induce her to join them, among which was that of agreeing to guarantee the frontiers of its colonies in both extremities of America. Taking advantage of the fact that France could not afford the naval protection to its dominions which it had promised, Portugal joined the said three Powers, and entered their great alliance by a triple treaty, signed in Lisbon by the celebrated Mathuen on the 16th of May, 1703.

<small>Sacramento Colony attacked and taken. 1705.</small> War having been kindled anew by this action, the Governor of Buenos Ayres attacked the Colony of Sacramento, which surrendered unconditionally in October, 1705, thus re-establishing anew the sovereignty of <small>Negotiation of the Peace of Utrecht.</small> Spain upon both banks of the Rio de la Plata.[1] This state of war lasted until 1713, when Queen Anne of England intervened to obtain a truce. This was agreed upon, under the guarantee of that sovereign, in the compact of 1713. One of its most important clauses provided that the Queen of England should employ her influence to have the Colony of Sacramento restored to Portugal.[2]

<small>Peace of Utrecht.</small> The Peace of Utrecht was at last arrived at, being signed on the 6th of February, 1715.[3] The right of the King of Spain to preserve his sovereignty upon both banks of the Rio de la Plata was recognized in this solemn document, while at the same time it was declared that the King of Portugal should be indemnified for the material sacrifices made in the settlement of the Colony of Sacramento. For this purpose Article VI of that treaty provided as a starting point that the seat of government of that Colony and its territory should be restored to the King of Portugal,[4] but Article VII authorized the King of Spain to keep these possessions provided he gave the King of Portugal an equivalent indemnification in some other region.[5] The pretensions of the King of Portugal to dominate the mouth of the Rio de la Plata were thus once more substantially rejected.

<small>The treaty of Utrecht in the Rio de la Plata.</small> The conditions of the preceding treaties served the necessities of European politics and the American territories were used as makeweights in the balance in arranging changes on the map of Europe. American interests were not regarded, and the cession of the Colony

---

[1] The Visconde de Porto Seguro—"*Historia Geral do Brazil*," Vol. II, page 801.
[2] "Argentine Evidence," Vol. I, pages 37 and 38.
[3] *Ibid.*, page 39.
[4] "Argentine Evidence," Vol. I, page 41, Art. VI.
[5] Idem, Art., VII.

of Sacramento was an act of force against Spain, committed by the Great Alliance, which thereby violated the solemn Treaty of Tordesillas, depressing the Spanish power in the best regions of South America, in the Rio de la Plata and in Peru.

The treaty of Utrecht, considered in this point of view, was in fact simply the triumph of the interests and suggestions of England, which obtained thereby great advantages amid the irreconcilable discords of Spain and Portugal. The Visconde de Porto Seguro, the official historian of Brazil, already quoted, says [Vol. II, page 883]: *Suggestions of England to favor its commercial interests in South America.*

> It is known that it was at Utrecht that England secured the privilege of furnishing African slaves to Spanish America, to which countries, down to 1740, she sent as many as 140,000, the product of which gave her the capital she afterwards invested in India. One must believe that the interest she afterward took in the general extinction of this inhuman traffic was caused on her part by her keen remorse of conscience.

Portugal and England were thus being united in Europe against Spain. They remained associated in order to mortally wound Spanish commerce in the Rio de la Plata, absolutely forbidden to foreigners. With the Colony of Sacramento as a port, and the English ships masters of the seas, smuggling was openly carried on in South America.

A new European war, occasioned by the Polish question, in which Spain and France took an active part, induced Portugal to send a military expedition to the Rio de la Plata. It did not attempt to reinforce the Colony of Sacramento, but established itself at the place now called Montevideo. The Governor of Buenos Ayres, General Don Bruno de Zavala, attacked the Portuguese, who for the third time departed from the Rio de la Plata, defeated and expelled by the arms of Spain. In order to finally guarantee the possession of Spain on the Eastern shore of the great estuary, Zavala founded the city of Montevideo, now the Capital of the Republic of Uruguay. *Portuguese expedition to the Rio de la Plata, 1723. Foundation of Montevideo, 1723.*

Spain also attacked the Colony of Sacramento in 1734, supporting her forces in Montevideo, but the first secret steps taken by the Kings of Spain and Portugal towards the negotiation of a definitive treaty put an end to these hostilities. Portugal had won a very important position at the Court of Spain. The Infanta Doña Barbara, the sister of the King of Portugal, had married the King of Spain. While she weakened the acts of the latter and opened ways for conciliation, Portugal committed new usurpations in South America and advanced *Attack on the Colony of Sacramento, 1734. New intrigues and aggressions of Portugal, 1737.*

its troops into the old Spanish Colonies of Yguapé, San Francisco and Santa Catalina. The above-quoted Visconde de Porto Seguro, the official Historian of Brazil, says:

> On this occasion the military occupation of the Island of Santa Catalina was decided upon, a subaltern Captaincy being thus established.[1]

England fo-ments discord

This movement was encouraged by England, because its commerce needed a base of operations on the South American coast and the Rio de la Plata, and this had disappeared with the foundation of Montevideo, which closed the mouth of that river to her ships. On occupying the ports of the Rio Grande, England had opened to her clandestine trade the route of Alvar Nuñez, which penetrated the interior from Santa Catalina, going towards *Misiones*, Paraguay and Peru, passing through great populations of consumers of European manufactured goods.[2]

Preliminaries of Peace, 1750

Nevertheless Queen Doña Barbara gained ground in her plans to soften the heart of the Spanish monarch in favor of Portugal, and to gently bring him to make peace and a treaty.

Boundary Treaty, 1750

Such was the origin of the most important boundary treaty made up to that time between the two rival Crowns. The boundaries between the two nations were subject, until 1750, to the rules laid down in the Bull of Alexander VI, and in the Treaty of Tordesillas. The Line of Demarcation had only been modified by the conventions held between Spain and Portugal as to their northern possessions in the region of the Amazon, and in the Rio de la Plata only in the case of the Colony of Sacramento. The sovereignty of Spain over the Territory now submitted to the Arbitrator was recognized and ratified in all the treaties signed by the two Crowns. The Boundary Treaty of 1750 made a regular exchange of territories, and fixed new rules for the location of boundaries, declaring null all those which had preceded it.

Its preamble

The preamble of the treaty sets forth the claims of each Crown and both declare they have resolved—

> ... to forget and not to use all titles or rights which might belong to them by virtue of the said treaties of Tordesillas, Lisbon and Utrecht, as well as of the deed of Zaragoza or any other fact or argument adapted to bear upon the division of their dominions

[1] "*Historia Geral do Brazil,*" etc., Vol. II, page 880.
[2] Map of *Discoveries and Conquests.*

by a meridian line; and it is their wish that this subject shall not be further argued upon, the boundaries of both monarchies to be fixed by the present treaty, etc.[1]

The "*ánimo*" or *purpose* of the Monarchs (to employ the very words of the preamble quoted) in making this treaty was declared to be—

... that this treaty shall carefully contrive two ends; the first, and the chief one, being to fix the boundaries of both dominions, using for boundaries, to avoid all confusion and dispute, the best known places, such as the sources of rivers and their course, and the most notable mountains; the second end being that *each party is to keep what it actually possesses, excepting the mutual cessions to be stated at the proper place, which shall be executed by mutual agreement.*

This clause controls the treaty; it is of vital importance and conclusive as a guide to its understanding and application. The first Article defines the legal situation of the boundaries, acknowledging and annulling the preceding Papal Bull and treaties. The new agreement was to be the supreme law of both Kingdoms. It runs as follows:

<small>Prior treaties annulled</small>

ART. I. The present treaty shall be the only basis and rule to be henceforth followed for the division and boundary of the dominions in all America and Asia, and in virtue thereof any right and title which might be adduced by the two Crowns on account of the Bull of Pope Alexander VI, of happy memory, shall remain void, as well as the treaties of Tordesillas, Lisbon and Utrecht, the deed of sale drawn at Zaragoza, and all other treaties, agreements and promises, which, in so far as they concern the Line of Demarcation, shall be of no value and effect, as if they had not been agreed upon, the rest of the treaties remaining in full force and vigor; the question as to the above-mentioned line to be dismissed for the future, and all argument based on it to be discountenanced in any decision upon the boundaries that may occur, the frontiers prescribed in the present articles being the only and invariable rule, and much less subject to controversies.[2]

Article II granted to Spain the Philippine Islands and their surroundings, the King of Portugal renouncing forever all pretensions or <small>Exchanges in Asia and America.</small>

---

[1] "Argentine Evidence," Vol. 1, page 52, paragraph II, lines 23 and following.
[2] " Argentine Evidence," Vol. 1, page 53, article I.

right to them, or to the money paid for them in accordance with the contract referred to made at Zaragoza on April 22, 1529. By Article XIII Portugal retired forever from the Rio de la Plata, and gave up any future claim to it, consequently ceding to Spain the Colony of Sacramento, with all its territories. Finally Portugal ceded to Spain all the land that extends from the western mouth of the river Yapurá and is located midway between this river and the Marañon or Amazon river, and also the navigation of the river Yza and all that the grantor possessed to the westward thereof.[1] As a matter of fact the King of Portugal had paid to Spain 360,000 "*cruzados*"[2] for the Moluccas and the possession and dominion of the Philippine Islands.

As a compensation for the preceding cessions, the King of Portugal was to receive:

1. The territories that he occupied in the northern portion of South America, on the river Marañon or Upper Amazon, to the West of the Bull of Alexander VI and the Treaty of Tordesillas.[3]

2. The Portuguese usurpations made on the North of the Paraguay, in the dominions of this Spanish province, were to be known thereafter by the name of "*Matto Grosso*."[3]

3. The territories possessed by Spain during two centuries, from 1516 to 1715, on the coast of Brazil and known by the names of the Provinces of "*Campo*" and "*De los Tapes*," afterwards called "*Las Siete Misiones Orientales*" (the Seven Eastern Missions), and the Island of Santa Catalina.

4. The territories of the primitive Jesuit Republic situated North of the river Ygnazú, and between it and the river *Tieté*, adjoining on the East with San Paulo and with the ancient Spanish Province of Campo.[4]

Enormity of the cession made by Spain.

Whether from ignorance as to the territories in America, or weakness amidst the European complications that were driving Spain rapidly down the declivity of its decadence, the fact is that Portugal gained under this treaty enormous advantages, entirely disproportionate, and in truth incomprehensible. In the accompanying "Map of the Discoveries and Conquests of the Spaniards," the dividing line of 1750 has been traced in conformity with the official map that served to

---

[1] Argentine Evidence, Vol. I, page 53 and following, Arts. II, XIV, XV.
[2] A "cruzado" was worth ten reales of Vellon de Castilla, or about fifty cents, more or less.
[3] Argentine Evidence, Vol. I, page 53, Art. III.
[4] *Idem*, pages 53 and 54, Arts. IV, V, VI, and VII of the Treaty of 1750.

prepare that document. The vast extent of country given up by this line included probably one-fourth of the South American continent, and lands of the best quality on account of the mildness of their climate, the fertility of their soil, the inexhaustible resources and variety of their productions suited to the use and progress of man, and with the most charming landscapes. The Philippines cannot even be taken into consideration when compared with what Spain gave up for them. As to the Colony of San Francisco, it was a Spanish place, and Portugal did not give up anything in acknowledging the unquestionable sovereignty of Spain in the basin of the Rio de la Plata.

Article XIV of the treaty shows clearly that Spain did not give up any territories that were disputed or over which her dominion was doubtful, but only what was hers in fact, by possession and legal right, according to the declarations, made before the occupation of these territories, by the Bull of Alexander VI and the Treaty of Tordesillas. *Acknowledgment of the rights and possessions of Spain.*

Its text is as follows:

XIV.—His Catholic Majesty in his name and that of his heirs and successors gives up forever to the Crown of Portugal all that which is occupied on the part of Spain, or which by any title or right may belong to him, in any part of the lands that by the present articles are declared as appertaining to Portugal, from the Castillos Grandes mountains and their southern slope and sea shore up to the head spring and main source of the river Ybicui, and also cedes all the towns and settlements that may have been made on the part of Spain on the corner of land comprised between the northern bank of the river Ybicui and the eastern one of the Uruguay, and those which may have been founded on the eastern bank of the river Pepiry, and the town of Santa Rosa, or any other town whatever that may have been founded on the part of Spain on the eastern bank of the river Guapore.[1]

The clearness and exactness with which, in this historical and important document, the territories and settlements reciprocally given up are designated, attracts attention. In none of the Articles of cession is there any doubt left as to the boundaries or situation of what is exchanged, in the Philippine Islands, the basin of the Amazon, or the valley of the Rio de la Plata. Nothing is said as to the territories of *Misiones*, possessed by Spain, neither are they mentioned in the preamble of the Treaty, in which both Crowns set up their claims, their injuries and their wars. They could not have been omitted *Misiones and the Treaty of 1750*

---

[1] Argentine Evidence, Vol. I, page 56, Art. XIV.

through ignorance, for the name of the "*Republica de los Jesuitas del Paraguay*" (Jesuit Republic of Paraguay) or *Misiones*, filled the world with its fame, occasioning envies and political jealousies at the Court of Spain and in the Cabinets of the great powers of the two camps into which Europe was divided. Nor could they have been omitted as insignificant, for they formed the wealthiest, most powerful, most intelligent and most populous colonial group of the two monarchies in Asia and America. But the treaty did mention a part of the *Misiones* of the Jesuit Republic in restrictive terms, so as to segregate this portion from the remainder of them. I refer to the cession of seven of the Spanish settlements, known in the diplomatic history of South America under the name of "*Los siete pueblos de las Misiones Orientales del Uruguay*," (The Seven Villages of the Eastern Missions of the Uruguay) which were situated on the eastern bank of the river Uruguay and separated by it from the Territory submitted to the Arbitrator. The Fourteenth Article (above copied)[1] mentions these facts in very clear terms when referring to the acquisitions of Portugal at this point, and the Sixteenth Article adds:

> The "*missioners*" shall leave the towns or villages which His Catholic Majesty cedes on the eastern bank of the river Uruguay, carrying with them their movable property and effects, and taking with them the Indians, to settle on other lands of Spain.[2]

The Eighteenth Article reinforces still more energetically the interpretation which I place upon the matter, as follows:

> The day in which the mutual delivery of the Colony of Sacramento and adjacent territory and of the lands and towns comprised in the cession that His Catholic Majesty makes on the eastern bank of the river Uruguay, will be agreed upon between their Majesties.[3]

The Royal *Cédula*, published by the Spanish Monarch on December 28, 1743, seven years before the Boundary Treaty (presented to the Arbitrator at page 51 of this Argument)[4], enumerates the thirty Pueblos of *Misiones*, directed by the Jesuits in the name of their sovereign at Madrid, and gives a sort of political constitution for their municipal government. The seven pueblos, the dominion over which the King

---
[1] See this Argument, page 135.
[2] "Argentine Evidence," Vol. I, p. 56.
[3] *Idem*, page 59.
[4] "Argentine Evidence," Vol. I, page 263.

of Spain resigned in favor of that of Portugal, in the Articles already commented upon, formed part of these thirty pueblos, the lawful possession of which by Spain no nation had ever questioned. Consequently the treaty of 1750 recognizes and confirms the sovereignty of Spain over the thirty pueblos, setting apart seven of them, those located in the ancient province *del Tape on the East of the River Uruguay*, and leaving the twenty-three remaining *Pueblos* under the sovereignty of Spain. The Territory which is now submitted to the Arbitrator included within it a part of these twenty-three *Pueblos* or villages. And not only was the sovereignty of Spain over this Territory definitively established, but the Government of Portugal guaranteed the quiet and perpetual enjoyment of this sovereignty, obligating itself to employ its arms, if that should become necessary, together with those of Spain, in order to make this arrangement effective "*which will last indefinitely as far as it concerns the interior of America;*" that is to say, the region where the Territory is located which is the subject of the present dispute.[1]

The care with which each Article of the treaty of 1750 was written reveals not only previous study of the local geography of these regions by the plenipotentiaries, but also a generally exact knowledge of the places, woods and rivers selected to serve as boundaries. In that part of the introduction to this document, above transcribed and commented upon, it is declared that the boundary shall follow the best known places.[2] All this had in fact been maturely prepared by Portugal herself and reduced to the graphic form of a map, constructed in 1749, during the tedious period of the secret negotiations between the two Sovereigns.[3]

The "*Mapa de las Cortes.*" 1741-1751.

There is, indeed, a document, or complementary treaty, which is explanatory of, and proves the origin and existence of, the map referred to, which map is known in the History of Diplomacy as the "*Mapa de las Cortes*" (Map of the Courts). I present this document to the Arbitrator, at page 76 of Volume 1 of the "Argentine Evidence," under the title of --

International proof of this fact.

Declaration signed at Madrid, dated the 12th of July, 1751, by the Plenipotentiaries of Their Most Faithful and Catholic Majesties, *on the margins of the geographical map which served*

---

[1] Argentine Evidence, Vol. 1, pages 59 and 60, Art. XXV.
[2] "Argentine Evidence," Vol. 1, page 52.
[3] See this Argument, page 148.

for the adjustment of the Treaty of Boundaries of the conquests of 13th of January, 1750.[1]

The second paragraph[2] declares that this map was prepared *at the beginning of the conferences that preceded the adjustment and conclusion of the boundary treaty of the conquests.* The importance of this map results from the following declarations that were made in the complementary treaty itself by the Ministers of Spain and of Portugal—

<blockquote>... that it would be impracticable to proceed in the serious affair of their commission, before they should examine and reduce to a demonstrative map what countries were until then occupied by the subjects of each of the two Crowns, so that according to the demonstrations of the same map they should negotiate and conclude that which each of these should deliver and receive.[3]</blockquote>

So as to leave no doubt whatever as to this the complementary treaty adds:

<blockquote>That with it before them, the said Plenipotentiaries had continued their conferences.[4]</blockquote>

This map is, consequently, an integral part, the *alma mater* so to speak, of the Treaty. The Treaty cannot be discussed nor interpreted, nor even clearly understood, if each one of its Articles is not read with the map in view. And it was not an arbitrary map, nor one taken up by chance; it had been prepared by scientific authorities, as is affirmed by the complementary treaty itself in this formal clause:

<blockquote>That in fact the said map was drawn by engineers, geographers, and skillful and well-informed persons of both nations.[5]</blockquote>

The plenipotentiaries submitted it to their careful examination, the result of which is attested by the document in the following terms:

<blockquote>... that having been by both well examined and compared, it was by common agreement approved and agreed to by the same respective Plenipotentiaries, *to serve as* GUIDE AND BASIS *to*</blockquote>

[1] "Argentine Evidence," Vol. I, page 76, bottom of the page.
[2] Idem, Vol. I, page 77, 2d paragraph.
[3] Same paragraph.
[4] "Argentine Evidence," Vol. I, page 77, 1st paragraph.
[5] Idem, Vol. I, page 77, 1st paragraph.

No. 1.
The True "*Mapa de las Cortes.*"

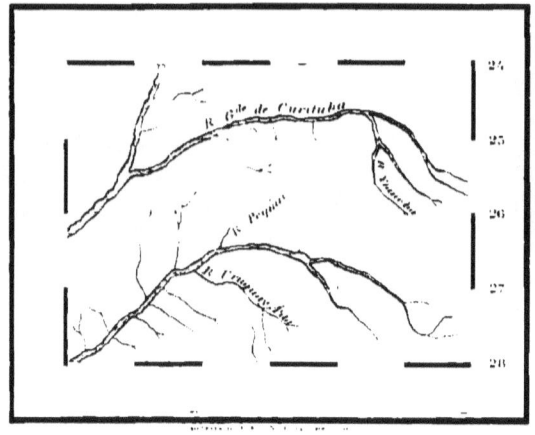

No. 2.
The False "*Mapa de las Cortes.*"

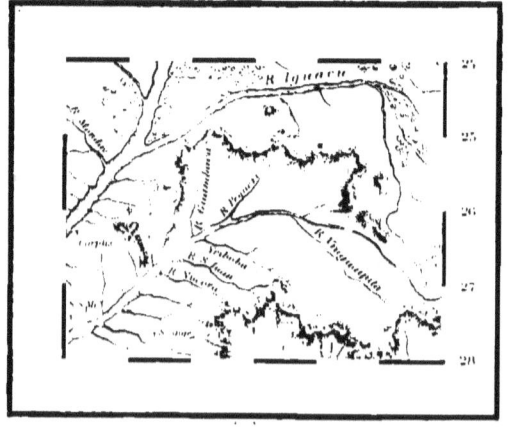

the said Treaty of Boundaries, the conclusion of which was its object.[1]

Finally, this map cannot be confounded with any other map, because the Plenipotentiaries took careful measures to guarantee its authenticity for all time. Concerning this the complementary treaty of 1751 says:

> ... that the said map was legalized and perpetuated by the said two Plenipotentiaries with the declarations on its margin written in Portuguese and Spanish by the two respective Secretaries: That the said declarations were signed by the said Plenipotentiaries and provided with the seals of their arms, for perpetual memory of the authenticity of the said map, and to be kept in the archives of the two contracting Monarchs.[2]

The preceding treaty was confirmed by another additional treaty, dated January 17, 1751, which I will discuss further on, and which is conceived in such terms as to give to the "*Mapa de las Cortes*" a vital importance in this Arbitration, for it is conclusive proof in favor of the Argentine Republic. *Probative Force of this Map.*

The Brazilians have not denied the existence of the "*Mapa de las Cortes*," but they have recently expressed doubts as to its authenticity. In the "*Collecção de Tratados*" (Collection of Treaties), published by Borges de Castro, presented to the Arbitrator, a pretended copy of this map was published at the end of Volume III. It is evidently altered in favor of Portugal. The accompanying engraving represents the true "*Mapa de las Cortes*" (No. 1), and the *supposed* "*Mapa de las Cortes*" which was published in the said "*Collecção*, etc.," is represented by No. 2. *Does the "Mapa de las Cortes" exist?*

The difference between these maps is evident even to those who are unprepared for geographical difficulties. The "*Mapa de las Cortes*" gives little data on the "*campo limpio*" or open field, because it only delineates the particulars then known, while the apocryphal one abounds in sketches of those regions which no one had ever formally explored up to that time, so that these details are imaginary. It gives besides erroneous locations to well-known points, such as *Santo Angel*, which the true map represents with exactness. Still grosser and more important, politically speaking, is the alteration traced in the apocry- *Altered Publication of the Map in 1856. Comparison with the True Map.*

---
[1] "Argentine Evidence," Vol. I, page 77, 1st paragraph.
[2] Idem, 2d paragraph.

phal map as to the tributaries of the river Uruguay. For example, it changes the name of the *Uruguay-Pitá*, which is one of the guides of the Line of Demarcation, and calls it *Yribohuí*, while it gives the name of the former to a river that flows into the Uruguay above its junction with the *Pepiry*. The true map, however, situates the *Uruguay-Pitá* in its exact position, as revealed by the international explorations of 1783–1791 and of 1885–1891, both agreeing upon this point. Nevertheless the modification of the true "*Mapa de las Cortes*" was made with such want of care that the river Pepiry keeps its true general course of North-east to South-west in the false map instead of running from North to South, as the river Guarumbaca runs, situated below the Uruguay-Pitá, claimed by Brazil. Finally, the apocryphal map bears on its back a declaration of the Plenipotentiaries different from that which they in fact signed, and which can be read on the original.[1] It appears that a stupid omission has been made, thus depriving the "*Mapa de las Cortes*" of its value and its adaptability to the ground. Here are both texts compared:

True Protocol.	False Protocol.
This geographical map which is to be kept in the Royal Archives of Portugal, as well as another original which is to be kept in the Royal Archives of Spain, is the one which the Minister Plenipotentiary of His Faithful Majesty used to adjust the treaty of division of the boundaries in South America, signed on the 13th of January, 1750. And because in said map there is found a red line which indicates and passes by the places where the demarcation had to be made, *that being anterior to the Boundary Treaty which was made afterwards, the line does not conform with the treaty in passing by the foot of the Monte Castillos Grandes in search of the sources of the Rio Negro, and following it until it enters the river Uruguay, trying to find the principal source of the river Ybicuy in conformity with said treaty;* It is declared that the said line only serves so far as it is in conformity with the treaty referred to; to remain for a testimony forever.	This geographical map is a faithful and exact copy of the first upon which was made and adjusted the Boundary Treaty signed on the 13th of January, 1750. And because in that map is found a red line, which indicates and passes by the places where the demarcation had to be made, it is declared that the said line only serves in so far as it conforms with the treaty referred to; and so that it shall remain a testimony forever, we the Ministers Plenipotentiary of His Catholic and Faithful Majesty sign and seal it with our Arms. In Madrid, the 12th of July, 1751. *Viscount Thomás da Silva Tellez. Joseph de Carvajal y Lancaster.*

[1] See apocryphal map in the Collection of Borges de Castro, at the end of Vol. III, and the authentic and true map presented in the "Argentine Evidence," portfolio of maps XVIII Century, document Nos. 12, 13, 14 and 15.

We the undersigned Ministers Plenipotentiary of His Faithful Majesty[1] and Catholic Majesty have affixed our hands and seals. Madrid the 12th of July, 1751.
Viscount Thomaz da Silva Telles.
Joseph de Carvajal y Lancaster.

The true text declares that the red line is valid over the entire frontier on which it is traced, except in the space included between the sea and the river Uruguay, where it was modified after the map was made, by agreement of both Ministers, while the apocryphal map suppresses this exception, which is italicized in the true text, and its statement is to the effect that the demarcators shall apply the line or not, according as to whether or not in their opinion it conforms with the treaty. The legal text does away with every pretext for discussion; while the false text on the contrary furnishes a reason and leaves room for contention. The first declares that the Demarcators must follow the line traced on the map. The second leaves this optional, according to their judgment. The first contains a local exception as to the dividing line; but the second applies this local exception to the entire frontier from the Rio de la Plata to the Orinoco, thus converting it into a general rule.

The general opinion in the Argentine Republic was that the true map had disappeared from the Archives at Madrid at the beginning of this century, during the occupation by Napoleon. It was in fact searched for by Argentine agents in the Archives of Madrid and Lisbon, but the answer to inquiries always was that this document did not exist. Nor had the Brazilians any better knowledge of the original map. Some of their statesmen cited it in favorable terms, led into error by the falsified copy in the Collection of Borges de Castro.

Some others, and certainly of great authority, such as the Baron de Capanema, the head of the Demarcation Commissioners from Brazil, who in company with those from the Argentine Republic explored the Territory (1885–1891), have made official publications. I present to the Arbitrator one which appeared in 1893 under the title of "*Questao de Missões* (Question of Misiones).[2]

In this work he puts in doubt the existence of the "*Mapa de las Cortes*" in the following terms: *The Brazilians doubt the existence of the "Mapa de las Cortes."*

[1] The King of Portugal.
[2] This argument was published in the "*Jornal do Commercio*," an important newspaper of Rio de Janeiro, in 1892. The file of said paper remains in the Argentine Legation at Washington, at the disposition of the Arbitrator.

Even if the "*Mapa de las Cortes*" did exist as is said (but which I doubt, for having asked my very distinguished and always careful colleague, Colonel Garmendia, for a copy, he answered that he only had the map of Olmedilla, nor did I ask him to give me a copy of this, because it was an Argentine argument and support), this map also loses its value on account of the Treaty of January the 17th, 1751, etc.

<small>Presentation of the Map under the authority of France, Spain, and Portugal.</small> This doubt from the highest and best authorized of the Brazilian officials who has intervened in this question in regard to boundaries which has been submitted to the Arbitrator still prevails in 1893, but is entirely dissipated by the copies of the original maps taken from the Archives of France, Spain, and Portugal, which I now present to the Arbitrator.

The Chief of the International Boundary Commission on the part of Brazil adds:

> These quarrellers (the Spaniards) say that the Pepiry is situated above the Uruguay-Pitá, and that this is proved on their manuscript "*Mapa de las Cortes*," which, as we have already seen, by the Treaty of January 17, 1751, is unworthy of any confidence.

It seems to me quite natural that this map should have lost the "*confidence*" of the Brazilian Statesman. But it was relied upon by the King of Portugal and the King of Spain, whose treaties are now binding upon their heirs. The French government also had confidence in it when they opposed this map to Brazil in 1845 in the Guayana <small>Brazil suspects the "*Mapa de las Cortes*" of being a falsification.</small> question.[1] Finally, this same Demarcation Commissioner says:

> The map of Olmedilla is the "*Mapa de las Cortes*," of which many copies exist *urbi et orbi*, and is not a manuscript that anyone may bring forward, that may have been substituted in some archive or other or even falsified ("*desfigurado*").

This is an argument unworthy of a loyal and serious Statesman. Neither Spain nor the Argentine Republic merits such a degrading suspicion. Civilized nations have always conducted themselves with the dignity and good faith which are required by the fundamental laws which secure moral order in the world. It may be that their statesmen might be mistaken in their interpretation of a document, but they never would be guilty of the abominable crime insinuated in this

---

[1] See the Relatorio de Negocios Extrangeiros do Brazil, 1857. . . .

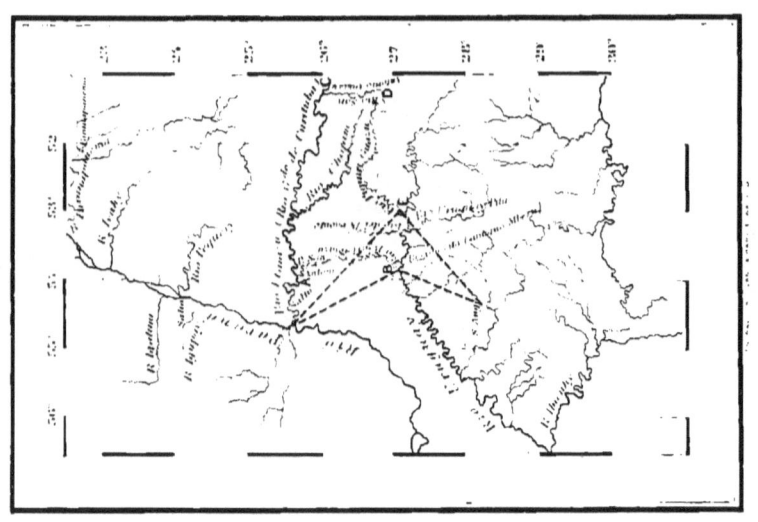

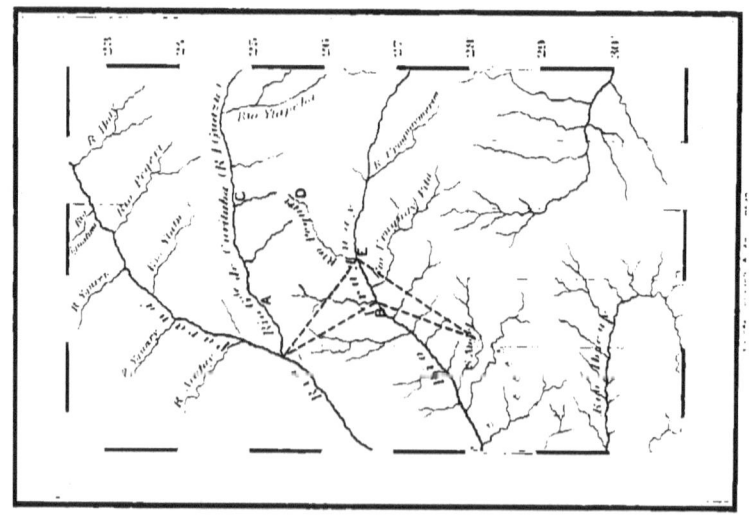

careless phrase. But these arguments, signed by one of the highest _{Brazil pleads ignorance.} functionaries of the Empire, who has managed this international controversy, show that Brazil too late perceives that it has disputed without reason, that it was ignorant of the true sources of right applicable to the case, and that its Statesmen have lost their self-control in the midst of the struggle.

The author of this Argument was Minister of Foreign Affairs of the Argentine Republic in 1892, and being convinced of the value of the "*Mapa de las Cortes*," determined to find it in Europe, for it was not credible that the numerous authentic copies of this document should all have been simultaneously destroyed or rendered useless in the Archives of Spain and Portugal, as well as in the private archives of the Boundary Commissioners who received them. Therefore Dr. Tomas Lebreton was commissioned to search for this map in the National Library at Paris, under the supposition that the French carried it away from Spain in 1802. There it was, in fact, found! And after this fortunate issue the map was also found in Lisbon and in Madrid. I have presented it to the Arbitrator in the Portfolio of Maps of the "Argentine Evidence," under the triple authority of the governments of France, Spain, and even Portugal itself. _{How the "Mapa de las Cortes" was found.}

The "*Mapa de las Cortes*" coincides in an extraordinary way with the map of the *Territory of Misiones* prepared in 1885-1891 by the official commissions of Argentines and Brazilians, appointed in virtue of the Treaty of 1885, to which I shall refer later on.[1] This coincidence, after so much time and notwithstanding the progress of geographical methods, conclusively proves that Brazil is wrong in sustaining as the boundary a small stream situated much further West. _{Commentary on the "Mapa de las Co tes."}

The two accompanying engravings each contain an extract from one of these maps, so that they can be compared.

The "*Mapa de las Cortes*" of 1749 contains a red line that follows along the river *Pequiry* upward, to the East of the Uruguay-Pitá, that is to say, following the direction C. D. E. The boundary which the Brazilians claim follows along the small streams A. B. Their mistake is palpably demonstrated by the simple examination of the two documents. The differences in the details between the locations of the places and rivers on the two maps are small and entirely accounted for by the progress which has been made in geographical methods and instruments, and also because the explorations that were made in the preparation of this map in 1749 were very _{The boundary according to this Map, the base and guide of treaties.}

---

[1] See this Argument; chapter on *Demarcations*, etc.

hasty. The Jesuits, military men, and travellers who journeyed along the rivers Paraná, Uruguay, Yguazú, and Pequiry, made observations at their junctions and at certain points in their courses, and upon these general data the map of the Territory was prepared, the interior of which was occupied by Indians and Spaniards who were incompetent to make scientific observations. The Map of 1891, on the contrary, is the fruit of very careful work, made in the field and in the office during six years of labor (1885–1891) by numerous commissioners, engineers and boundary demarcators, selected among the best qualified men of both countries.

Confirmation of the "Mapa de las Cortes" by the international exploration of 1883–1891.
But, notwithstanding this circumstance, the differences are insignificant in a legal and technical point of view. Examining the "*Mapa de las Cortes*," it is found that the Pueblo of Santo Angel, on the left bank of the Uruguay river, as a point scientifically observed, differs very little in its latitude from the true location of that Pueblo as found by the official exploration of 1891. The Upper Paraná was quite well known in 1749, and this accounts for the fact that the latitude of its junction with the river Yguazú being also very exact.

The river Uruguay-Pitá, which had been well explored about its sources, was officially described in the instructions given by Vertiz, the Viceroy of Buenos Ayres, to the Demarcators.[1] It was therein stated that the frequented road from *Santo Angel* to *Vaquería* passed by the sources of the said Uruguay-Pitá. Other old maps corroborate these data, and clear away all doubts as to the possibility of confounding the river mentioned with any other.[2]

That portion of the river Uruguay which bounds the Territory in controversy was not described otherwise than by the references of travellers and of the Jesuits; and those who prepared the "*Mapa de las Cortes*" accepted these data, which have been shown in general to be accurate by recent explorations, so far as they came in conjunction. Various Jesuits and Spanish "*Yerba*" merchants used to travel frequently along the river Pequiry, that of the boundary agreed upon in 1750. Rui Diaz de Guzman had, on the other hand, drawn it upon the map of 1612, and a Spanish Indian colony had its capital, *Pueblo*, at a short distance from its right bank.[3] In 1612 Rui Diaz de Guzman had also described it in his historical work as the "*Mas caudaloso*" (the largest, or carrying the greatest volume of water) of the western

---
[1] See this Argument; chapter on *Demarcations*.
[2] See road of "*las Vaquerías*" on the map of *Discoveries, etc.*
[3] See this Argument, page 40.

tributaries of the Uruguay. It was therefore impossible to confuse it with the small stream of the line " A. B." claimed by the Brazilians. According to these facts the course of the Pequiry was traced on the "*Mapa de las Cortes.*" The international explorations of 1885-1891 show that the position of that river is in general exact. This is proved by its general direction on both maps, northeast to southwest, and its situation above the Uruguay-Pitá given in the two charts. Rui Diaz says:

> In this region empties the large river of the Uruguay, which I have mentioned, and which has there a mouth of about three leagues, and within it a small river called the San Juan, connected with another San Salvador, a very good port; and ten leagues farther on one that is called the Rio Negro, above which on either side a great many come in, and especially one "*caudaloso*" (of great volume), which has the name of Pepiry, of which the fame is very wide-spread, there being a great many people on it that have gold in quantity, which this river carries in its sands.[1]

Finally, I present to the Arbitrator an official document of the Brazilian Empire which is a still further proof of its contradictory and irregular method of argument in regard to the question of its boundaries as opposed to the Argentine Republic. In fact, I have proved already that down to 1892 prominent statesmen of Brazil asserted that the "*Mapa de las Cortes*" was an imaginary or a false document. Did they sincerely believe that statement? Nevertheless this same map was considered by the statesmen of Brazil as authentic and the only rule for the demarcation of the boundaries between the Empire and the Republic of New Granada, simply because there it was favorable to their claims. I present to the Arbitrator the work, entitled:

<small>Brazil invokes the Map of 1749 in the Boundary Question with New Granada, 1870.</small>

Memoir upon the Boundary Question between the Empire of Brazil and the Republic of New Granada, by Councillor Duarte da Ponte Ribeiro. Rio de Janeiro. 1870.

The text of this work is preceded by the following statement:

Explanatory statement of the Maps annexed to the report made to the General Assembly upon the Boundary Question pending between the Empire of Brazil and the Republic of New Granada, by His Excellency the Minister and Secretary of State for Foreign Relations, in office on the 27th of August, 1870.

---
[1] Rui Diaz de Guzman. Argentine History, etc. Presented in this Argument, page 31. See Book 1, Chap. III, page 7. Books of "Argentine Evidence."

In this work Brazil sustains the line of the Treaty of 1750, reproduced in that of 1777, and to apply it to the ground exhibits the "*Mapa de las Cortes*," although taking it from the apocryphal copy published in the "Collection of the Treaties of Portugal," cited. Page 7 of this large quarto is devoted to the eulogy of that map opposed to New Granada as a supreme argument. The perusal of this page is recommended to the Arbitrator as it clearly shows why the Argentine Republic should succeed in this Arbitration.

The river Pequiry or Iguiry in the "*Mapa de las Cortes.*"
Besides in 1749, before signing the treaty, and in 1751 after it was signed, the Geographers and Plenipotentiaries of Spain and Portugal desired the boundary line to run in that place along a river that was to have these characteristics; 1st. It must empty into the Uruguay above, that is to say to the East of; the river Uruguay-Pitá. 2d. It must have a course SW. and NE. 3d. It must be a river "*caudaloso*" (of large volume) and not a small stream. 4th. It must have a wooded island in front of its mouth. 5th. It must have a reef inside of its bar.

The International Hispano-Portuguese explorers of 1791, and the Argentine-Brazilian Demarcators of 1885-1891, when surveying the ground in accordance with the treaties of 1777 and 1885, found such a river, that is to say the river "D E" (see preceding engraving), agreed upon, traced and pointed out by the Kings to the Commissioners and Boundary Demarcators in the Map of 1749, which was the *basis* and the *guide* of the treaties of 1750 and 1777. The question is thus solved. In

Clear solution of the Dispute by the "*Mapa de las Cortes.*"
order to complete the boundary it is sufficient to follow up the course of this river in search of "*las vertientes mas cercanas*" (the springs or sources in closest proximity) of a river that runs to the Yguazú, the boundary then following this river.

General Agreement of the "Mapa de las Cortes" and the Map of 1891.
Besides this there is also another important circumstance, namely, that the river the Brazilians claim to be the boundary from the point "B" towards the North does not have its sources or springs near or close to the river that empties at "A" into the Yguazú, but nearer another river called the "*Urugua—y*," a tributary of the Paraná.[1] This fact will be also proved later on by international documents and by an official Brazilian declaration made by General Cerqueira, Minister Plenipotentiary of Brazil in the present Arbitration, who was one of the explorers of the Territory as a member of the International Argentine-Brazilian Commission. It therefore seems to be demonstrated by two explorations, made with an interval of one century between them:—

[1] See the international map of *Misiones*, page 5 of this Argument.

1. That there exists on the ground the river adopted as an international boundary by the treaty of 1750. 2. That said river was mapped in 1891 by an international commission, with the result that its position and general direction on this map is the same that it had on the "*Mapa de las Cortes*" of 1749, which served as the *basis* and the *guide* of the treaties, these being also the same as those found by the Demarcators of 1791.[1] 3. That it has close by the counter-sources of a river that empties into the Yguazú. 4. That the boundary line supported by the Argentines in the direction "C D E" is the same one agreed upon by the sovereigns in 1750 and drawn from "E" to "D" on the Portuguese map of 1749 to which the Protocol was added in 1751 by both Crowns. 5. That the line "A B" claimed by Brazil has no legal antecedent, either on the map of 1749 or in the treaties of 1750 and 1777.

The small difference as to shape that appears in the two maps in the area submitted to Arbitration is accounted for by scientific reasons and the lack of detailed explorations. I have in fact stated that both maps coincide as to the situation of the following principal references: 1. Settlement of the Spanish Pueblo of Santo Angel. 2. Junction of the rivers Paraná and Yguazú. 3. Situation of the river Uruguay-Pitá, to the south or down stream from the boundaries agreed upon in 1750. 4. Situation and shape of the Territory submitted to the Arbitrator.

Besides, if we examine carefully the course of the rivers Ybicuy, Uruguay-Pitá, part of the Uruguay and others, we will see that all of them have been delineated with an error of 22° 30' when compared with the true magnetic direction given by the exploration of 1891. This constant variation on the Map of 1749 reveals a constant error, either due to the observers or to their instruments, or it may be to the methods employed. If this error is corrected, or if in imagination we move the map of 1749, so as to make the drawing run 22° 30' from South to North, we find that the rivers Ybicuy, Uruguay-Pitá, Uruguay and others will take the inclinations that belong to their true courses, according to the Map of 1891, and that the mouths of the rivers Uruguay-Pitá and Pepiry will remain in a situation that is almost identical with that which they occupy upon the ground.

Finally, there is a geodesical proof of the fundamental agreement between the two maps, which is furnished by the magnetic courses

---

[1] See the "*Mapa de las Cortes*," and of the Exploration of 1885 1891, in this Argument, page 5; and the "Argentine Evidence," Maps, XIX Century, No. 55.

which are traced in dotted lines on both maps. And, indeed, if we trace the magnetic courses from the Spanish Pueblo of Santo Angel to points "B" and "E" of the Map of 1749, and from "B" and "E" to the junction of the Yguazú with the Paraná, the result will be two triangles united by their base "B E," analogous to those obtained by making the same tracing from Santo Angel to the same points "B" and "E" and the mouth of the Yguazú upon the map of 1891.

<small>The "Mapa de las Cortes" was made in Portugal and accepted by Spain.</small> We must also bear in mind that the "*Mapa de las Cortes*" was prepared by the Portuguese and accepted *bona fide* by the Spaniards.[1] The Portuguese received gratuitously by the Treaty of 1750 a quarter part of South America. There was no object for them to raise a question for twelve hundred square leagues more, which is the area included between the four rivers of this dispute. It was the Portuguese who selected as the boundary the Pequiry or Pepiry of the East, the *large one*, and they drew it on the "*Mapa de las Cortes*," where it is favorable to the Argentine Republic, while its political heirs now deny it, discussing the matter and surrounding it with confusion and doubts.

In the public archives of Spain there is preserved a precious document that I present to the Arbitrator.[2] It is the report of the Regent of the Jesuits of the Rio de la Plata concerning the boundaries of the <small>Portugal explores in detail the Territory in controversy.</small> treaty of 1750. This narration is well worth reading. It expresses with prolixity the laborious plan developed by the Portuguese to explore the dominions of the King of Spain, and it proves that they knew perfectly well the principal points and rivers of the boundary. It adds at pages 10 and 11 of the manuscript and at page 503 of the book cited :

> . . . who, notwithstanding all this, ceased not to explore by means of this and other stratagems, from the year 40 up to the year 50, at which time they had received such complete information of all the territory of the future survey, that they made the full map which was afterwards signed by the Kings in the adjustment; after the map was made, it was observed that all incursions of idle Portuguese ceased for good, and almost at the same time, negotiations with great earnestness were begun at our Court for adjusting the Treaty ; in this they finally succeeded about the beginning of 1750.

Therefore the "*Mapa de las Cortes*" is, judicially and scientifically considered, a decisive document if right and good faith are to govern the solution of this question.

<small>Groundless observations against the "Mapa de las Cortes."</small> Some Brazilian statesmen have impugned the value of the "*Mapa de*

[1] See this Argument ; chapter on *Demarcations*, etc.
[2] "Argentine Evidence," Vol. 1, page 495 ; Group D of Manuscripts, No. 1.

las Cortes," fearing it might exist and be some day presented in an arbitration case. They remember the agreement additional to the Treaty of 1750, signed on the 17th of January, 1751, the text of which is as follows:

> We, the undersigned, Ministers Plenipotentiary of their Most Faithful and Catholic Majesties, in virtue of the full powers which we have communicated and acknowledged reciprocally to our satisfaction, declare that, whereas we have been governed by a manuscript geographical map to formulate this treaty and the instructions for its execution, for that reason there is to be furnished a copy of this map to every party of Commissioners of each Sovereign for their government, all of them signed by us, since by it and conformably to it are explained all the expressions. We also declare that although from the information received from both of the Courts we consider very probable all the things which are noted in said map, also agreeing that some of the territories marked out, even though no persons living have gone over them, and others were drawn from the maps of trustworthy persons who have frequented them, but at the same time with little skill to make the demonstration in the sketch, for which reason there is likely to be some evident variations upon the ground, in the situation of the mountains as well as in the origin and course of the rivers, and even in the names of some of them, because each nation of America used to give them different ones, or on some other account, yet the contracting Sovereigns desire and agree that whatever variation there may be shall not prevent the course of its execution, but it shall proceed in everything conformably to the Treaty which shows the purpose and intention of their Majesties, and particularly according to the Articles 7, 9, 11 and 22, following it all precisely. And we, the said Ministers Plenipotentiary, thus declare it in the name of our Sovereigns and in virtue of their orders and full powers we sign it. This declaration will be ratified at the same time and place as that of the extension of the term and the instructions, and a copy of it will be given to the Commissioners of both Sovereigns. In Madrid the 17th of January, 1751.
>
> VISCONDE THOMAS DA SILVA TELLEZ.
> JOSEPH DE CARVAJAL Y LANCASTER.

The last part of this protocol has been misunderstood by Baron de Capanema, the head of the Brazilian demarcators, and also by other Brazilian statesmen. Knowing that the situation of the rivers on the "*Mapa de las Cortes*" was unfavorable to them, they therefore declared that this map was erroneous. Such a declaration was arbitrary, and its value is entirely destroyed by the preceding scientific proofs.

Interpretation which would annul the treaties. They also add a forced interpretation of the text copied in 1751, saying that the Demarcation Commissioners of the boundaries could change their situation if they found when on the ground names of places or rivers in a situation different to that indicated by the *red mark* on the official map. Such an interpretation leads to the annulment of the treaty, for it would have authorized subordinate Demarcators to modify the *purpose and intention* of their Majesties (the exact expressions used in the additional treaty of 1751), by enlarging or diminishing the "*actual possessions they were to preserve*" (the expression used in the Treaty of 1750).[1] In fact the *red mark* on the map marked the boundary of that which each Crown desired to maintain within its dominion. Moving this line towards the West, as the Brazilians claimed should be done, in order to find the river they supported, would result in a violation of the predominating idea of the Treaty; that is to say, it would enlarge the dominions of one Monarch by diminishing those of the other. It would have been, furthermore, the only instance in Political History when mere subordinates, on their own volition, proceeded to decide questions involving the enlargement and cession of territories, which are matters of sovereignty and prerogatives of the Crown in an Absolute Monarchy, or belong to the Congress in a Parliamentary Monarchy and a Republic.

Interpretations which entirely destroy the act under examination are unprecedented. It seems to me that a fair application of the additional treaty of 1751 is favorable to the Argentine claim and that it should be construed as follows: The Demarcators shall go to the ground, and where it is possible that the places named on the map that serves them as a guide may be called by other names by the inhabitants or the Indians, in such case they shall not hesitate, but continue their work, and shall carry the line by the mountains, fields and rivers their Majesties have indicated with the *red mark*, in conformity with the *spirit and intention* manifested by them. We have seen at page 133 of this Argument that the *spirit and intention* of the high contracting parties was thus manifested in the preamble of the Treaty of 1750:

> It being their purpose (*animo*) that they shall attend with care to two results:
>
> . . . .
>
> Second, that each party shall keep that which he actually possesses. . . .

[1] See this Argument, page 133.

The only document signed by both Crowns up to that time which indicated primarily the boundaries of what each possessed, was the "*Mapa de las Cortes*," for the additional treaty of July 12, 1751, already cited, says:[1]   *The intention and purpose of the Sovereigns.*

> . . . that it would be impracticable to proceed with the important affair before the Commission (to make the Treaty of 1750), until they should have examined and should have *reduced to a demonstrative map, which were the countries that had been occupied until then by the vassals of each one of the two Crowns*, so that conformably to the showing of each map they could negotiate and conclude. . . .

Therefore the best way of respecting the purpose and intention of their Majesties, according to the additional treaty under discussion, was simply to trace the boundary line where it was already drawn, even if the places happened to have other names, and the authority of the Demarcators was limited to changing these names if there should be a place for them, which is a very different matter from changing the location of the boundary, thus altering the possessions reciprocally acknowledged and protocoled by both Crowns.   *How the Demarcators should proceed in accordance with the Royal purpose and intent.*

Another objection has been made by Brazil to the "*Mapa de las Cortes*," founded on the declaration written on its back and subscribed by the Plenipotentiaries of Spain and Portugal, which is copied at page 140 of this Argument. The Brazilians assert that the "*Mapa de las Cortes*" was only to be followed upon the ground when the names found there corresponded with those in the sketch, and that whenever a case to the contrary was found it was to be abandoned. This is a new and absurd interpretation, and the same observations above made would be applicable if we were considering a general declaration. But such is not the case, for it is only a partial one. In fact, when the Plenipotentiaries ordered this map to be prepared they had agreed that the boundary should start from the Rio de la Plata, on the heights called "*Castillos Grandes*," which would remain the property of Spain, but when the treaty was signed, a year after the map was made and protocoled, they agreed to alter the first boundary that had been arranged in the part *between* "*Castillos Grandes and the river Uruguay*. The meaning of the protocol written upon the margin of the map, is this: *en este parte el Mapa no vale, valga el tratado*,"—(in this part the map is void, but the treaty is valid); or, in other words,   *Another unfounded objection to the official Map.*

[1] See page 138 of this Argument.

making this exception the line ought to be applied to the whole frontier; and this was to be done from the Uruguay to the North, because the Protocol of the alterations locates the modification in what is now the Republic of Uruguay.

Imperative character of the "Mapa de las Cortes."
On the other hand, there could be no disagreement between the Map and the Treaty, for the latter declared it had been prepared in conformity with the former document, except in the part referring to "*Castillos Grandes*," and the same Protocol in the margin, so arbitrarily interpreted by Brazil, declares once more, as if to exclude any such unfounded deductions, that—

> ... in said map there is found a red line, which indicates and passes by the places *where the demarcation had to be made*,[1] ...

"*Por onde se ha de fazer a demarçao*,"—or where the demarcation had to be made, is imperative and admits of no discussion. But this point was also studied by the negotiators of the Treaty of 1750, and it was settled in the Additional Treaty of January 17, 1751, made—

> ... between their Catholic and Most Faithful Majesties, which determines the instructions for the Commissioners of the two Crowns in the Demarcation of the respective boundaries in South America in execution of the Boundary Treaty.[2]

The instructions for the Demarcators.
If we attentively read Article X it will convince us that both Crowns had but one doubt as to the rivers selected to direct the location of the boundary, and that was in the case of the river *Ygurey* to the northeast of the Paraguay. It is, therefore, only reasonable to say that their confidence in regard to the situation and general course of the Pequiry was complete, for otherwise they would have dedicated a special article to this doubt, as they did in the case of Article X.

Case analogous to that of the River Pequiry decided by the Courts favorably to Argentine interpretation.
But the most important part of this Article is the solution it gives, in the event that the river followed in that region by the *red mark* of the "*Mapa de las Cortes*," under the name of *Ygurey* might not prove to have that name given it, but another, given by the Indians and neighboring people. This is exactly the case of the stream said by the Indian Guide of 1759 to be the Pequiry or Pepiry river of *Misiones*. The Brazilians claim that the river along which runs the *red mark* has been erroneously called "Pequiry" by the "*Mapa de las Cortes*." How shall a difficulty of this kind, foreseen in the Additional Treaty of

---
[1] See page 140 of this Argument.
[2] Argentine Evidence, Vol. I, page 61.

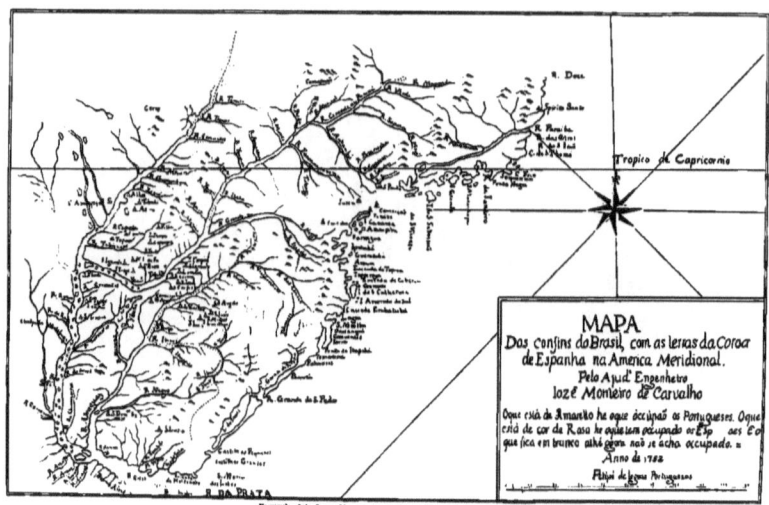

Instructions under discussion, be solved upon the ground? Ought the Demarcators to abandon the course followed by the *red mark* and carry it to the rivers that in a different and more or less distant position should have upon the ground the common name (under the supposition that there was an error) registered on the map that was the *basis* and *guide* of their operations? No! That would be to alter the substance of the treaty, injuring one dominion in favor of the other. For that reason the treaty provided in the second paragraph of Article X, as follows:

> And although this river is not called *Ygurey*, it shall be noted as the boundary, with whatever name it may have upon the ground, or it shall be given a name by common consent.[1]

The letter and spirit of this solution were obligatory upon the Demarcators in the case of the Pequiry, and it could be said:

> And although this river is not called *Pequiry*, it shall be noted as the boundary, with whatever name it may have upon the ground, or it shall be given a name by common consent, . . .

for this was the only way to carry out the *purpose* and *intention* of their Majesties.

Article XXVIII provides that preference must be given to the rivers "*Mas Caudalosos*," or of largest volume,[2] notwithstanding which the Brazilians undertake to substitute for the river of the "*Mapa de las Cortes*," which is located on the ground, one that hardly carries one-fifth of its volume of water.

Some very curious documents may be added, taken from the Archives of Portugal, which reveal what the purpose and intention of the King of Portugal was in regard to the position of this boundary. These documents are three letters, exchanged between the Marquis de Pombal, Minister of Foreign Affairs of Portugal, and the Portuguese Embassador in Madrid, Senhor Silva Tellez, who negotiated the treaty of 1750. To this correspondence was added *a map, on which the King of Portugal traced in a line of red dots the boundary he wished to maintain*. These materials for a decision were to be communicated in the greatest secrecy to the sister of the King of Portugal, Doña Barbara, who was the Queen of Spain, so that she might influence her husband

<small>New Documents.

Revelation of a State Secret, wherein the King of Portugal decided the question in favor of the Argentine claim.</small>

---

[1] "Argentine Evidence," Vol. I, page 64, bottom of the page.
[2] "Argentine Evidence," Vol. I, page 68, Art. XXVIII.

in favor of the claims set up by Portugal.¹ The Secret Map of the King of Portugal of 1752, referred to in these documents and presented to the Arbitrator, is exactly the same as the "*Mapa de las Cortes*" of 1749, protocoled in 1751, which remains intact, as the solemn and authentic expression of the intention of the Monarchy at Lisbon to solve the boundary problem which is now submitted to the President of the United States. And that intention was favorable to the claim of the Argentine Republic.

Attempt to mark the boundary. 1750-1759. Both Crowns having appointed the Commissioners who were to trace the boundaries agreed upon in Article XXII ² of the Treaty, they went to the field and began their labors. In 1757 this expedition of Demarcators was broken up. It had committed several fundamental errors, which were sufficient to render its acts of no effect.

In a special chapter I will give the Arbitrator a brief and clear scientific analysis of the operations of the International Demarcation Commissioners of 1759, of 1791 and of 1885 to 1891. Meanwhile, as a synthetical conclusion to this chapter, I will enumerate here the substantial errors that were committed by the Demarcators of 1751 and 1759:

Reasons for the failure.

1. Instead of following the demarcation up to the river *Uruguay-Pitá*, on the East of the Uruguay, so as to clearly establish the situation given by the "*Mapa de las Cortes*," they made a mistake and confounded this river with another one situated much further to the South, called at that time "*Mberay*" and now known as "*Guarita*."

2. Having thus made a mistake as to the first point which was to serve as a reference and guide, the mouth of the river *Uruguay-Pitá*, up stream from which was to be found the *Pepiry* or *Pequiry* of the boundary, they also made a mistake when looking for this river, and going up the Uruguay from the *Mberay* they called *Pequiry* the river *Guarambaca* of the old maps. The engraving at page 143 clearly explains the error made by the Demarcators of 1759. The rivers "A. B." are those put forward by them and "C. D. E." are the rivers of the Treaty of 1750, which they ought to have followed.

¹ I present these documents, copied from the original, to the Arbitrator under the authority of the Consul-General of the Argentine Republic in Lisbon.—"Argentine Evidence," Vol. I, page 516. The map reproduced in this chapter is to be found in the Portfolio of Maps, No. 16. The originals are in the private archives of the Count da Videgueira, and the Argentine Government has considered the amount of £15,000 which he asks for them as excessive. Group D of Manuscripts, No. 23.

² Argentine Evidence, Vol. I, pages 158 and 159.

3. The Demarcators themselves acknowledged their mistake, for in the paper they drew up concerning the river falsely called *Pequiry*, they said:

> We declare we recognize this as the river Pepiry designated in Article V of the Boundary Treaty as the frontier of the dominions of their most faithful and Catholic Majesties, and consequently that *the demarcation commenced in the city of San Xavier* and followed up the Uruguay until the month of the aforesaid river must continue following its course as far as its sources, *although it is not found that its position* in fact conforms to that given by the Map of Demarcation furnished by the Courts.[1]

4. Notwithstanding this they insisted upon altering the possessions declared by both Crowns on the "*Mapa de las Cortes*," thus enlarging the dominions of Portugal and diminishing those of Spain.

5. They thus violated the express and clear text of the Treaty of 1750 and of the additional Treaty of January 17, 1751, which required them to carry into the field the "*Mapa de las Cortes*," and to keep it there and respect it as the guide of their operations.[2]

6. They also violated the additional treaty of July 12, 1751, explanatory of the preceding map, which establishes—

> That after the same had been well examined and compared by both (Plenipotentiaries) it was by a common accord approved and agreed upon between the same Plenipotentiaries respectively in order to serve as the *guide and basis for the said boundary treaty*.

And the Demarcators destroyed this basis, declaring at the same time that they did so knowingly.

7. They failed in geographical veracity when they affirmed that above the true Uruguay-Pitá, and East of the river erroneously accepted by them as the boundary, there did not exist another river that might be the one mentioned by the treaty of 1750, because the international Hispano-Portuguese Commission (1783-1791) and the international Argentine-Brazilian Commission (1885-1891) confirmed the existence of the large river a few leagues above the place where the Demarcators of 1759 had stopped.

---

[1] This Article is confirmed by what is said at page 86 of this Argument as to the jurisdiction San Xavier exercised over the disputed Territory.

[2] See this Argument; chapter on *Demarcations, etc.*

8. They thus clearly showed that they lacked the necessary courage to bear the fatigues of the journey,[1] and that they were especially negligent in the fulfilment of such solemn duties.

9. They violated the spirit of the additional treaty of instructions of January 17, 1751, which settled the matter in Article X.

10. They thus originated the boundary question that has continued to disturb the greater part of South America during a hundred and fifty years.

Nullification of the Treaty of 1750, and of the Demarcation of 1750.

The demarcation thus attempted had therefore an irremediable organic vice; it was void. The Courts of Portugal and of Spain, for this and analogous reasons referring to South America, agreed to nullify the treaty of 1750 and its results. The causes of this nullification were discussed for a long time, and both Brazilians and Spaniards

Palace Intrigues about these boundaries.

have arrived at these historical conclusions: 1. Spain desired the annulment. 2. Portugal was opposed to it. The King of Spain influenced by his wife, the Portuguese Infanta Doña Barbara, had, as I have said, negotiated with great secrecy the Treaty of 1750. His Ministers and Councilors were ignorant of this fact. The domestic influence of the sister of the King of Portugal on the one hand and the personal ignorance of the King of Spain as to his immense dominions in America and Asia on the other, explains the disadvantageous exchange of a third part of South America for the Philippine

Errors of the King of Spain made evident.

Islands. But this mistake was soon made evident, for the Jesuits brought the matter up and prominent men of the Court at Madrid endeavored to effect the nullification of this exchange. The Jesuits have been accused of engaging in intrigues. The Portuguese unjustly accuse them, for they were right and were doing an exceedingly important service to the King, their Master, by employing their knowledge of South America in order to maintain in his power the immense territories that belonged to the Crown of Spain. They rightly and justly agitated Europe and America by preaching armed resistance among the inhabitants of the *Misiones* that had been given up to Portugal by this change of sovereignty agreed upon in 1750. The influence of the Jesuits triumphed at last and they obtained the nullification of this treaty.

The Jesuits of Spain and Portugal and the boundaries.

The official historian of Brazil, the Visconde de Porto Seguro, already cited, acknowledges that even the Jesuits of Portugal admitted those of Spain to be in the right. This he expresses in the following terms:

---

[1] In their Journal, as we shall see further on, they excuse themselves, saying that the navigation of the Uruguay was very trying on account of the frequent falls and reefs.

Matters having arrived at this point it was not difficult to know how the King of Portugal would solve the dilemma, which solution had depended for many years on his deciding either in favor of the Company of Jesus or in favor of his Prime Minister, who had hitherto brought so much glory to his reign. The complete triumph of Pombal was manifested by the royal sanction given to the law of September 3, 1759, that abolished in the kingdom of Portugal the order of the Jesuits.[1]

This was in revenge for the opposition made by the Jesuits of Spain and Portugal to the cession of the South American territories by the Treaty of 1750, made by the former Crown for the benefit of the latter. A sterile vengeance! The same official historian of Brazil, at page 927 of the volume cited, adds:

> Indeed, so many were the difficulties and intrigues, that the two Cabinets, disgusted, tired and exhausted by so many expenses, at last resolved by common accord to cancel, break and annul the treaty of 1750 by a new adjustment, signed at Pardo on the 12th of February, 1761.

The King of Portugal did, in fact, yield at last, but did all that he could to maintain the disproportionate advantages that were given to him by the treaty of 1750. This is proved by the secret documents I present to the Arbitrator in this Argument. *Impartial Brazilian testimony to my statements.*

Southey, in his "History of Brazil," cited, says:

> The Queen was believed by the Spaniards to favor her native country more than was consistent with the interest of Spain; and to her influence they attributed a treaty which was now made for adjusting the long disputed boundaries in America. No such treaty would have been concluded if an amicable disposition had not existed on both sides; and that disposition had certainly been produced by this happy marriage.[2] . . .
>
> But there was a fatal fault committed in the treaty, and Spain and Spanish America and Brazil feel at this day its baneful consequences.
>
> The portion of Territory eastward of the Uruguay, which was ceded to the Portuguese, contained seven flourishing Reductions, inhabited by about thirty thousand Guaranies, not fresh from the woods or half reclaimed, and therefore willing to revert to a savage state, and capable of enduring its exposure, hardships, and privations; but born as their fathers and grandfathers had been,

---

[1] "*Historia Geral do Brazil*," etc., presented to the Arbitrator. Vol. II, page 926.
[2] See Southey's "History of Brazil," Vol. III, Chap. 39, page 443.

in an easy servitude, and bred up in the comforts of regular domestic life. These persons, with their wives and their children, their sick and their aged, their horses and their sheep and their oxen, were to turn out, like the children of Israel from Egypt into the wilderness, not to escape from bondage, but in obedience to one of the most tyrannical commands that ever were issued in the recklessness of unfeeling power (page 449).

In the complete collection of treaties concluded between Brazil and foreign nations and officially published in 1864 by the Superintendent of the Public Archives of the Empire, Don Antonio Pereyra Pinto, which I present to the Arbitrator among the books of the "Argentine Evidence," may be read the following commentary concerning the causes of its invalidity which the Treaty of 1750 contained within itself:

In spite of these tendencies the Treaty of 1750 encountered opposition among the Portuguese and also among the Spaniards. The former made a point of honor of keeping the Colony of Sacramento as an ancient claim to the possession of the northern bank of the Rio de la Plata, and they did not therefore accept it with pleasure. The latter, seeing themselves despoiled of a great extent of territory that they actually occupied, such as the *Oriental Misiones*, of Uruguay, and others to which they considered they had legitimate rights, regarded it with covetous eyes, attributing the actual situation to the instigation and national predilections of the Catholic Queen. . . .

But in reality of what value was the maintenance of the Colony of Sacramento, situated on the confines of Brazil and *enclosed in the centre of the Spanish dominions*, exposed to continuous irruptions from that people, and a constant apple of discord between both nations, *when compared with the acquisition of the Misiones of Uruguay, of the Eastern bank of the Uruguay, of the vast territory between the river Paraná and Paraguay and all Portuguese* "UTI POSSIDETIS" *in the province of Matto-Grosso and in the basin of the Amazon?*

To pretend that besides these advantages the possession of the Colony of Sacramento should also be granted to Portugal, was to demand a "*contrato leonino*," or "lion-like" contract, in which all the advantages should be exclusively for one of the parties only; and for this very reason the contract would contain within itself the reasons for its own dissolution. And the fact is these very reasons were used by Spain to attack the treaty, notwithstanding the cession of the Colony of Sacramento.[1]

---

[1] *Data for International Law, or Complete Collection of Treaties made by Brazil with different foreign nations*, accompanied by an *historical and documentary* notice of

The armed opposition made by the South American *pueblos* thus violently transplanted was not long delayed, and the war called "*Guaranitica*" which broke out in the Government of the Rio de la Plata lasted, properly speaking, from 1752 to 1761. Southey says the Spanish colonists issued a manifesto in these terms:

> By the Royal letters of Philip V, which, according to his own injunctions, were read to us from the pulpits, we were exhorted never to suffer the Portuguese to approach our borders, because they were his enemies and ours. Now, we are told that the King will have us yield up to these very Portuguese this wide and fertile Territory, which the Kings of Spain, and God and Nature have given us, and which for a whole century we have tilled with the sweat of our brows.[1]

Such were the causes for the cancellation of the Treaty of 1750, signed at Pardo on the 12th of February, 1761. This new document[2] begins by confirming the reasons for the invalidity which I have just stated, and takes away the authority of the Brazilian statesmen who attribute this nullification to the results of European politics, which in this case had nothing to do with what was done. It acknowledges, therefore, that upon applying the Treaty of 1750 to the ground there were found so many and such great difficulties that it was not possible to get over them, for the action of the Sovereigns depended on the reports of many persons employed at different parts for this purpose, the disagreement between which no one had been able to reduce to any concordance, but they let it be known that the boundary treaty referred to clearly and positively stipulated for the establishment of a perfect harmony between the two Crowns, and an unalterable union between their subjects, although since the year 1752 they had given and would give in the future many and frequent reasons for controversies and retorts opposed to such a desirable end.[3]

The Sovereigns alluded to the claims set up by the Portuguese Boundary Commissioners and to their usurpations of territories in *Misiones*, on the Ygurey and in the basin of the Amazon, thus altering the possessions of each Crown by moving the red mark of the "*Mapa*

---

the most important Conventions. By Antonio Pereyra Pinto, Director of the Public Archives of the Empire and former member of the Historical and Geographical Institute of Brazil. Rio de Janeiro. E. S. Pinto & Co., 1864. Vol. III, pages 280 and 281 (*Official Work*).

[1] Southey, History of Brazil, Vol. III, page 159.
[2] "Argentine Evidence," Vol. I, page 79.
[3] *Idem*, pp. 79 and 80.

de las Cortes" to different locations. These tendencies were resisted by the Spanish Demarcators, as has been demonstrated, and by the *Pueblos* whose inhabitants were threatened by this change of home, property and sovereignty.

Treaty of 1761. Article 1 of the treaty of nullification says:

> The aforesaid Treaty of Boundaries in Asia and America between the two Crowns, signed at Madrid the thirteenth of January, one thousand seven hundred and fifty, with all the other treaties or conventions which as a consequence of it were eventually adjusted to settle the instructions of the respective Commissioners hitherto employed in the demarcations of the above-mentioned boundaries, and all that in virtue of them may have been performed, are given and remain in consequence of the present one, annulled, abrogated and cancelled, as if they had never existed or been executed; and everything concerning the boundaries of America and Asia is restored to the terms of the treaties, pacts and conventions which had been made between the two contracting Crowns before the said year of 1750; so that only the treaties, pacts and conventions made before the year 1750 stand henceforward in their force and vigor.[1]

Article II provides for the execution of the Royal will so that there shall not be left upon the ground even the vestiges of the condemned and cancelled work of the Boundary Demarcators of 1759, for which purpose the Governors and Commissioners in South America were ordered to—

> ... cease the operations and acts respecting its execution, destroying the monuments erected in pursuance of it, and evacuating immediately the lands occupied under the shelter or by reason of the treaty referred to, demolishing the habitations, houses or forts, which in consideration of it may have been erected by one party or the other.[2]

This Article closes by recommending to the respective Governors the faithful observance of the preceding treaties, that is to say the Line of Demarcation of the Treaty of Tordesillas, founded on the Papal Bull of Alexander VI, and the partial agreements concerning the small area of the Colony of Sacramento on the Rio de la Plata.

Article III declares, and this is of vital interest, that—

---

[1] "Argentine Evidence," Vol. I, page 80.
[2] Idem, page 80.

... the present treaty, and what by it is agreed and contracted, shall have perpetual force and vigor between both aforesaid Most Serene Kings, all their successors, and between both Crowns. ...

It is evident that the rights of Spain, based on the Meridian of Demarcation of 1493, and the possessory rights maintained by its soldiers and its colonists ever since 1516, were thus re-established in full force and effect, so that in consequence thereof its dominions in the region of this controversy extended towards the North as far as the Tieté and towards the East as far as the coast of the Atlantic Ocean. The Territory now submitted to Arbitration was therefore located anew in the very heart of the dominions of Spain, and the Argentine Republic, its heir, far from admitting any abridgment of this Territory, as is claimed by Brazil, ought rather on the contrary to plead for its enlargement as far as the neighborhood of San Paulo and Curitiba, where the boundaries of Portugal were at that period located, according to the declarations made by its King on the "*Mapa de las Cortes.*" Legal consequences.

The "*Pacto de Familia*" (Family Compact), signed in 1761 by Spain, Naples and France against England, led to a new war between Portugal (allied to the latter power) and the first of these. Thereupon General Don Pedro de Ceballos sailed from Spain in 1762 in command of a squadron and six thousand soldiers. As previously stated,[1] this campaign was rapid and successful, for in a few days he vanquished and defeated the Portuguese forces, expelling them from the territories they had occupied on the frontier, in the interior and along the coast of the ocean at Yguapé, San Francisco and Santa Catalina.[2] European war of 1761.

England, the ally of Portugal, fomented this strife in order to extend its commerce in South America by the influence of the latter, as well as to secure a foothold in Rio de la Plata at the first opportune moment, as she in fact attempted to do in Buenos Ayres in 1805 and 1807, when she was heroically defeated by the inhabitants and her generals and soldiers compelled to surrender. But when Portugal claimed the effective assistance of England, in order to defend its South American encroachments, that ally refused to compromise herself. The official historian of Brazil, the Viscondo de Porto Seguro, says that when Spain was operating against the Island of Santa Catalina, the head of the Portuguese Cabinet wrote a remarkable official paper— English intervention in the Rio de la Plata

---

[1] See this Argument, pages 56 and 57.
[2] See this Argument, page 57; and Collection of Treaties of Brazil, cited, Vol. III, page 287.

... complaining of the cold attitude and inaction of England, always a tardy ally.[1]

<small>Armistice in Rio Grande, 1763.</small> Meanwhile the Spanish General, being victorious in Rio Grande, the ancient Spanish Province del Tape, signed on the 6th of August, 1763, an armistice with the Portuguese, which document affirmed the power of Spain over the territories occupied by Portugal.[2]

<small>New treaty, 1777.</small> The Crown of Portugal, scarcely aided at all by its allies, and defeated in all its attempts to enlarge its South American territories, determined to treat anew upon bases less onerous for Spain, and which should respect some of the legitimate rights and the notorious facts founded upon the Bull of Alexander VI and the Treaty of Tordesillas. The acquisitions Portugal obtained through Doña Barbara, and which Brazil has officially designated as "*leonine*," or all on one side, were omitted in the new agreement signed at San Ildefonso on the 1st of October, 1777.

<small>Examination of the treaty.</small> The preamble and the first Article proclaim perpetual friendship between the two Crowns, and their desire to fix their boundaries in a <small>Causes of discord eliminated.</small> clear and unequivocal manner.[3] The second Article provides the restitution—

... likewise, as well the goods and effects seized, together with the prisoners, and the territories whose dominion happened to lie according to the present treaty within the demarcation of the Sovereign to whom they are to be restored.[4]

<small>Controlling Clause favorable to Spain.</small> The third Article contains the controlling clause of this treaty. By it Portugal recognized that it had no right to claim jurisdiction over the Rio de la Plata or over the river Uruguay. It consequently abandoned its claims to the Colony of Sacramento and to the seven eastern *pueblos* on the latter river. It uses this language:

As one of the chief causes of the differences between both Crowns *has been the Portuguese settlement of the Colony of Sacramento, San Gabriel's Island and other ports and territories pretended to by that Nation on the Northern bank of the Rio de la Plata, navigating this river in common with the Spaniards, and even that of the Uruguay*, both high contracting parties, for the mutual benefit of both nations, and in order to assure a perpetual peace

---
[1] *Historia Geral do Brazil*, presented to the Arbitrator, Vol. II, page 955.
[2] Argentine Evidence, Vol. I, page 83.
[3] Argentine Evidence, Vol. I, pages 85 and 86.
[4] *Idem*, 86 and 87.

between both, have agreed that the said navigation of the Rio de la Plata and the river Uruguay, and the lands of their two banks, Northern and Southern, may solely belong to the Crown of Spain and to its subjects, up to the place where the river Pequiry or Pepiry-Guazú flows into the aforesaid Uruguay by its Western bank. . . .[1]

It is unnecessary to study the new boundary agreed upon between the Uruguay and the Rio de la Plata, for this matter belongs to the boundary question between Brazil and the Republic of Uruguay. Calling the attention of the Arbitrator to the facts connected with the question submitted to his decision, he will examine the close of the above quotation from Article III. In it both Crowns allude to their boundary on the west of the Uruguay, and state that it begins on the river *Pequiry* or *Pepiry-Guazú*. But in the treaty of 1750 and in its supplement of 1751, already examined, this river is simply called the "*Pepiry*" or "*Pequiry*." The treaty of 1777 adds the qualificative "*Guazú*" (large). This circumstance is of vital importance. It tends to confirm and reinforce the selection of the river of the "*Mapa de las Cortes*" and of the Treaty of 1750, which is, in fact, the largest tributary of the Uruguay, excluding the small stream *Guarumbaca*,[2] which, by a proved mistake and against the evidence, the Demarcators of 1759 took for the Pepiry or Pequiry. It agrees, besides, with the first map of these territories, that of Governor Rui Dias de Guzman, of 1612, which delineates the river Pequiry or Pepiry as the largest affluent of the Uruguay. It finally settles that it is to be adjusted in conformity with the criterion of the twenty-eighth Article of the treaty of instructions given to the Commissioners in 1751[3], which orders that preference be given in making the demarcation to the rivers "*mas caudalosos*," or that have the greatest volume of water. In the same Article and in the following ones, each time that the treaty alludes to the river Pepiry or Pequiry it calls it "*Guazú*." It ends by declaring that Portugal renounces all its pretensions to the Spanish possessions and even to the cessions made to it by the King of Spain in the Treaty of Utrecht.[4]

The fourth Article provides that the boundary from the Rio de la Plata up to the Uruguay shall be "*a line drawn so that it shall cover the Portuguese settlements up to the emptying of the river Pepiry-Guazú into*

---

[1] "Argentine Evidence," Vol. I, page 87. [2] See this Argument, page 151.
[3] See this Argument, page 68. [4] Idem, page 130.

<small>The possessions that should save the boundary.</small> *the Uruguay, and shall likewise save and cover the Spanish Misiones and settlements of said Uruguay,* which are to remain in the present state in which they belong, to the Crown of Spain."[1]

The Spanish settlements extended as far as the river *Uruguay-Mini* on the Northwest, and to the *Matto Castelhano* on the Southeast. The latter is a large forest situated upon the sources of the Uruguay-Pitá. On the North and West of the Uruguay the Spanish settlements extended to the Territory submitted to the Arbitrator, which, as has been shown, had *pueblos* of Spaniards and Indians very near the red mark of the "*Mapa de las Cortes.*"[2] Therefore, in order to fulfil the requirements of the Treaty of 1777, *to cover the said possessions of Spain*, following the rivers "*mas caudalosos,*" that is, of greatest volume, it was logical and necessary to follow the banks of the River Uruguay-Pitá in its sources, then separating from them and going towards the North to the Uruguay-Mini, and then towards the Pepiry or Pequiry of the "*Mapa de las Cortes,*" or the great river *Pepiry* or *Pequiry-Guazú* of the Treaty of 1777, as is shown in the dotted line on the accompanying engraving, over its entire course.

The eighth Article confirms the preceding interpretation in the following terms:

> The possessions of both Crowns, up to the entrance of the river Pequiry or Pepiry-Guazú into the Uruguay, having been already pointed out, the High Contracting Parties have agreed that the boundary line shall follow up the stream of the aforesaid Pepiry to its main source and thence by the highest ground, according to the rules stated in the sixth Article,[3] shall continue to find the waters of the river San Antonio which drains into the Grande of Curitiba, otherwise called Yguazú.[4] . . .

<small>Erroneous interpretation of this Article by Brazil.</small> The Brazilians have pretended to find in this Article some puerile foundation for their pretensions, because it gives the name of "San Antonio" to the river the watersheds of which correspond to those of the Pequiry or Pepiry-Guazú, forming the boundary. This argument is simply ingenious. I have already stated, and it will be proved at the proper time, that the rivers claimed by the Brazilians, the "Guarumbaca" and the "San Antonio" of the Demarcators of 1759, do not have their origin near nor corresponding among themselves.

---

[1] "Argentine Evidence," Vol. I, pages 87 and 88.
[2] Page 40.
[3] Rules purely topographical.
[4] Argentine Evidence, Vol. I, page 89.

MAP SHOWING THE ERROR OF 1759.
The rivers in black are drawn according to the "*Mapa de las Cortes.*"

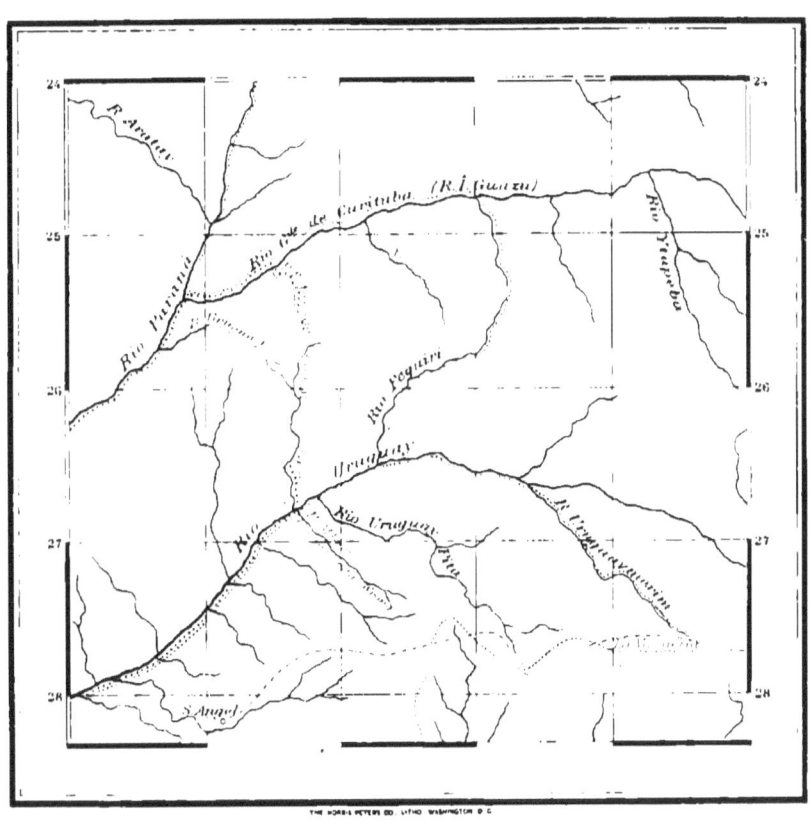

Note
1 .... Error of 1759
2   Real boundary of 1759
3   Ancient road to "La Vaqueria"

The springs of the "San Antonio" of the mistake of 1759 correspond to those of the river Urugua-y, which empties like the former into the Paraná, that is to say, it has the same sources; and it is required that its sources should be the nearest and correspond to those of a river which was a tributary of the Uruguay, to be admitted into the fluvial system of the boundary.[1]

On the other hand, since 1759 the river on the North that should correspond to the Pepiry or Pequiry-Guazú has been called theoretically "San Antonio," without this however solving the question of its geographical position, which is not given by the "*Mapa de las Cortes*" like that of the latter, and without any intention of subordinating the boundary to the names. On the contrary I have demonstrated that in 1759 the Sovereigns agreed that in these cases the names should follow the boundaries; so that the river having its sources opposite the sources of the Pepiry or Pequiry-Guazú being theoretically called the "San Antonio," it is only needful to find its location on the ground in accordance with the antecedent facts and the "*Mapa de las Cortes*," which is the text and the spirit of the treaties. The "*Mapa de las Cortes*," never nullified, gave clearly and irrevocably two rivers as the basis by which to trace the boundaries; the Uruguay-Pitá and above this the Pepiry or Pequiry-Guazú. It gave no name to the other river, nor did it give it any importance, leaving it subordinate to the Pequiry or Pepiry. It limits itself to directing, in effect, that when the vital river *Pequiry* or Pepiry is found, the Demarcators shall follow its course to its principal spring, and then find the nearest neighboring spring of another river, whatever may be its name,[2] which empties into the Yguazú.

Consequently the boundary river in these parts, before unknown and in 1759 called the "San Antonio," scarcely even known and explored in 1885-1891 by the Commissioners of the Governments in this controversy, ought to be found in the necessary proximity and correlation of sources with the river which serves as the basis of the drawing, the Pequiry or Pepiry-Guazú. Another interpretation, subordinating the officially selected river, known and proved by two international explorations, to the problematic river still to be found, leads to an absurdity, because it tends to alter the areas respectively possessed by the two Crowns, and

Interpretation that does not destroy but given vitality to the Treaty of 1777.

---

[1] See this Argument, page 146.
[2] Article V of Treaty of 1750 expressly re-enacted by that of 1777. Argentine Evidence, Vol. I, page 54.

expressly guaranteed by the treaties of 1750, 1777 and 1778, which are perfectly in harmony upon this point.

Guaranty of both dominions. The provision of the sixteenth Article confirms, if there were any need for it, the preceding observations. It says (and this is very significant):

> The Commissioners or persons appointed under the terms expressed in the preceding article, besides the rules established in this treaty, shall bear in mind in regard to what may not be specified in it that their objects in the demarcation of the boundary line must be the reciprocal security and perpetual peace and tranquillity of both Nations, and the total extirpation of the contraband trade that the subjects of either of them carry on in the dominions or with the subjects of the other, so that attending to these two purposes, the necessary order shall be given to them in order to prevent disputes which may injure *the actual possessions of both Sovereigns.*

Further on it adds, accentuating the purpose and intention of their Majesties, then the same as in 1750—[1]

> . . . The purpose of both august Sovereigns being that, in order to obtain a true peace and friendship, to the perpetuity and intimacy of which they aspire for the reciprocal tranquillity and welfare of their subjects, ATTENTION BE ONLY PAID, *in those vast regions through which the boundary line is to be described, to the maintenance of what each one may remain in possession of by virtue of this treaty.*[2]

Respective possessions at the Period of the Treaty. What were the respective possessions of the two countries at the moment when the Treaty of 1777 was signed ? Spain could rely *stricto jure* on the treaty of nullification of 1761, which declared in full vigor the Pontifical and Tordesillas demarcations. Its possessions occupied in fact the vast country it had discovered and settled during the preceding centuries.[3] General Ceballos maintained the maritime littoral in Santa Catalina at one extreme, and also the interior regions ; the Jesuits were civilizing the tribes around the sources of the Paraná and Amazon, up to the line drawn in the Treaty of Tordesillas.[4]

The Treaty of 1750 had limited these possessions, but this compact being annulled, Spain was recognized as the legal as well as actual

---

[1] See this Argument, pages 150 and 151.
[2] Argentine Evidence, Vol. I, Art. XVI, page 92.
[3] See Map of Discoveries and Conquests.
[4] See this Argument, page 44.

sovereign of these almost measureless dominions. The Treaty of 1777 must therefore have followed some criterion, in order to limit in its turn the possessions of both Crowns. That criterion was, as to the Territory submitted to Arbitration, the Treaty of 1750; that is to say, the *red mark* of the "*Mapa de las Cortes*."

It is a legal principle, accepted by Brazil, that the interpretation of facts should always be favorable to, not restrictive of, the right of one who has already ceded a part of his lands. Spain had, in fact, ceded a large extent of territory in accepting the line of 1750, for by so doing it renounced its undisputed sovereignty, not even doubted by Portugal or by Brazil, over the extensive regions situated between the Yguazú on the South, the Tieté on the North, and the Paraná on the East. In regard to the doubt raised by the Portuguese about the River Pequiry or Pepiry, so clearly dissipated by the "*Mapa de las Cortes*," if this solution had not existed the interpretation would nevertheless have been favorable to Spain by excluding the tendency to take more territory. The Rio San Antonio, so called theoretically, as the complement of the boundary, to facilitate the preparation of the treaties and the necessary discussions, cannot therefore be located to the West of the Pequiry or Pepiry-Guazú, which was the sign or line declared by both Crowns as the boundary of what they possessed and wished to keep. Nor can it be the river so called by the erroneous demarcation of 1759, for this survey was disapproved of, as it was not rightly done, other rivers than those of the treaty having been selected, as is explicitly stated in the preamble of the treaty of nullification, already quoted.¹ The contrary would change the Royal wills, which had been maintained without any discrepancy, as to those possessions, in the agreements of 1750 and 1777.

The boundary between the two Crowns on the margin of this Territory was, therefore, that fixed by the Treaty of 1750, confirmed by the one of 1777, and delineated officially and with royal authority upon the "*Mapa de las Cortes*" in 1749. The Spaniards had reasons for being opposed to the Treaty of 1777, for if it did grant less South American territory to Portugal than the Treaty of 1750, yet it nevertheless abandoned to that nation immense rich and hospitable regions. The Argentine Republic cannot, however, sustain any claim beyond the line traced by Spain and Portugal in their treaties, for it recognizes these agreements as incorporating the "*Derecho de Gentes*," law of

---
¹ See this Argument, page 159.

nations, which must be respected, for it is the basis of the sovereignty of new nations. It, therefore, places itself on the safest ground in defending the faithful application of the *red mark* of the "*Mapa de las Cortes*" of 1749, sanctioned by the treaties of 1750 and 1777.

<small>Object of the Treaty of 1777, according to its Negotiators.</small> On the other hand, the true spirit of the Treaty of 1777, its fundamental purpose, was made known by the official reports of the same Plenipotentiaries who negotiated and signed it, which are presented to the Arbitrator in the " Argentine Evidence," Vol. I, page 536 and following. The examination of these documents clearly authorizes us to affirm—

1. That the King of Spain corrected with his own hand the project of the Treaty of 1777 in the part submitted to the Arbitrator and in the Rio Grande, and that these corrections were admitted by Portugal because the Spanish Monarch declared that he would not sign it unless they were accepted. Such was the origin, then, of the addition of the adjective "*Guazú*" (large) to the name of the Pepiry or Pequiry of the Treaty of 1750. (*See the " Evidence" cited, page 537 ; Letter of Souza Coutinho, Portuguese negotiator of the Treaty of 1777, MSS, Group D, No. 4.*)

2. That the Treaty of 1777 is the same as that of 1750, and it was so stated in a secret Article proposed by the King of Portugal. (*Same document and book, end of page 536 and beginning of page 537.*)

3. That the Treaty of 1777 was very convenient for Portugal, for the Portuguese negotiator Souza says :

> . . . we shall regulate our America, *and profit by the fruitful lands of Rio Grande,* which being well handled will be more convenient than the principal ports of Brazil, *and finally we shall suppress forever the epithet of usurpation* which was connected with the establishments made in the dark times of the past, *the memory of which would always be disagreeable.*

The negotiator of Portugal, therefore, recognized that the Portuguese possessions on the *sea-coast,* to the West of the Meridian of Tordesillas, were usurpations, which it was desirable should be legalized once for all, by the signature of the Treaty of 1777. (*Same document and book, page 537.*)

4. That a secret Article was prepared by the King of Portugal relative to these treaties, which is referred to in paragraph 2 above and may be read at length by the Arbitrator at page 539 of the same document and book.

5. That the Minister of Foreign Affairs of Spain sent to the Spanish Minister at Paris reports concerning the new treaty, in which he said:

> We could not have reached this arrangement if we had not given up the rights which this Crown founded on the Treaty of Tordesillas. For this reason the King resolved that we should try to make up for it in the region of La Plata and the Uruguay rivers, *reserving to ourselves their exclusive navigation, embracing within the boundaries of Castile all the rivers that empty into the one or the other*, and those having their sources within these districts up to the end of their course, as well as the lands that they include, retaining the seven villages ceded by the Boundary Treaty of 1750, and in fact fixing the boundaries so as to avoid in the future any new matters of discord between the two countries and all pretexts for usurpations by one or the other.

It was not possible to assure the results of the royal purpose, leaving in the jurisdiction of Portugal the largest tributaries of the Uruguay, the Pepiry or Pequiry-Guazú and the lands cultivated by Spanish subjects to the East of that river. (*See "Argentine Evidence," Vol. 1, pages 543 and 544.*)

6. That the terms of the Treaty of 1750 were explained so that all doubt should be avoided. It was stated:

> Otherwise the same general direction is observed along the boundary fixed by the cancelled Treaty of 1750, only differing in that it has been specified in clearer and more positive terms than before (as in the case of the Pepiry or Pequiry-Guazú). (*Idem*, 544.)

7. That Spain did not gratuitously give up the Island of Santa Catalina on the coast of Brazil, which was in the possession of Portugal at the time the treaty was prepared, without other right than that of simple usurpation. Portugal, on the contrary, recognized these rights of Spain in the Treaty of 1777 and exchanged the Island of Santa Catalina and the Brazilian coast for the Islands of Annobon and Fernando Po. This is the language:

> In consideration of the relinquishment of the Island of Santa Catalina, and of the magnanimity of the acts of the King with regard to all the points of this friendly agreement, Portugal cedes in favor of Spain two islands, the Island of Annobon on the coast of Africa and the Island of Fernando Po in the Gulf of Guinea. (*Idem, page 545.*)

Official declarations of Brazil upon the Treaty of 1750

This same interpretation has been maintained in official publications made by Brazil. In fact, in the work cited at page 158 of this Argument, containing the "Collection of Treaties of Brazil," etc., (Vol. III, pages 280 and 281,) will be found eloquent and conclusive statements, which are quoted in this Argument.

It should also be remarked that among the advantages obtained by Brazil in this Treaty, which are enumerated in the official Brazilian work in the clearest manner, nothing whatever is said as to the Territory situated between the rivers Uruguay and Paraná, now submitted to the Arbitrator.

Confirmation of these ideas by Brazilian statesmen. They admit the boundary of 1777 is the same as that of 1750, and therefore the one in the "Mapa de las Cortes."

The Statesmen of Brazil confirm this Argentine criterion, which is based not only on what has been said above, but upon the clear and explicit text of the third Article of the guaranty Treaty of 1778, presented to the Arbitrator in the "Argentine Evidence," Volume 1, page 97. Brazil acknowledges, in fact, that the Treaty of 1777 confirmed that of 1750, so far as it referred to the boundary now submitted to Arbitration. The Visconde de Porto Seguro says, in his "Official History of Brazil," cited, that—

> ... from the Pepiry onward the demarcation was approximately the old one of 1750, and it is useless to take the trouble to occupy ourselves with its small differences.[1]

These in fact only amounted to rejecting the errors of the Demarcators of 1750, saying that the boundary river of the Territory in dispute was not an "*arroyo*," or small stream, nor a *small river*, but the *great river Pequiry* or *Pepiry*. It was natural that the Brazilian Historian should not care to notice the circumstance unfavorable to his cause. He adds:

> And the new treaty was drawn up twenty-seven years after the first one, and when the territory was much better known.[2]

And this new information proves that the Pequiry or Pepiry and the Uruguay-Pitá of the "*Mapa de las Cortes*" were in general perfectly well delineated. In the "Collection of Treaties of Brazil," a publication presented to the Arbitrator,[3] Volume III, page 295, may be read the following commentary upon the Treaty of 1777, after an analysis of the boundary agreed upon from the sea to the mouth of the Pequiry or Pepiry-Guazú, where it empties into the Uruguay:

---
[1] "Historia Geral do Brazil," Vol. II, page 991.
[2] *Idem*, page 992.
[3] See page 158 of this Argument.

In the interior, from the Pequiry to the Jauru, the line follows the same course (as in the treaty of 1750); from this river onward, the point where the middle distance has to be counted from was not the same as that of the treaty of 1750, from the junction of the Pararé and Guaporé, but from the junction of the Guaporé and Mamoré, etc.

And in a note (page 303) this official work ratifies these statements, saying:

As to the tracing (referring to the treaty of 1750) in the part relating to the Pepiry onward, the frontier is the same as that of the Treaty of 1777, etc. . . . .

The illustrious diplomat Paranhos, Minister Plenipotentiary of the Empire of Brazil, in order to negotiate a boundary treaty with the Argentine Republic in 1857 presented a Memoir in which he said, discussing the Treaty of 1777: [Diplomatic declarations accepting the boundary of the "Mapa de las cortes."]

Wherefore it is evident that the purpose of the two Courts was to adopt in that region the same division stipulated in the unsuccessful Treaty of 1750.[1]

The Plenipotentiary of the Brazilian Empire, the Baron de Araujo Gondim, in the *Memorandum* presented to the Argentine Government on the 29th of July, 1882, suggesting an arrangement of the boundaries between the two countries, took the position that Article VIII of the Treaty of 1777 *re-established in the Territory of Misiones the dividing line indicated by that of* 1750.[2]

Finally, the Brazilian Government confirmed the preceding interpretations in the report presented to Congress by the Minister of Foreign Affairs of the Empire, in which he said, after copying the eighth Article of the Treaty of 1777:

In this article the frontier maintained the direction given to it by the Treaty of 1750.[3]

---
[1] Report presented to the General Legislative Assembly of Brazil, at the First Session of the Twentieth Congress, by the Secretary of Foreign Affairs, Rio de Janeiro, 1886, page 8, Books of the "Argentine Evidence."

[2] See Volume II of the "Argentine Evidence," pamphlet Contra-Memorandum, entitled "Document on the *Misiones* question," page 13.

[3] Report presented to the General Legislative Assembly at the First Session of the Twentieth Congress, by the Minister of Foreign Affairs, the Baron de Cotegipe, Rio de Janeiro, 1886, page 8, "Argentine Evidence" books.

Declaration of the Republican Government of Brazil on the rehabilitation of the Treaty of 1750 by that of 1777.

There may be added to the facts already stated a document presented by the Minister of Foreign Affairs of Brazil to the Congress of that country at the session of 1891. It reads as follows:

DEPARTMENT OF FOREIGN AFFAIRS.
1ST SESSION, No. 3.
RIO DE JANEIRO, *April* 24, 1890.

I acknowledge the receipt of your official communication of March 24th last, and in reply confirm the dispatches of the 2d and 5th inst. It does not appear necessary at present to make copies of the correspondence. The purpose manifested by the Plenipotentiaries to renew the Treaty of 1750 is proved by the Treaty of 1777 when it reproduces the frontier described in the other.

Health and fraternity.

S. BOCAYUVA.

To Señor José Antonio de Freitas.

This conclusive note upon this point was directed to the Commissioner of Brazil charged with the search for documents in the Archives of Portugal.

Favorable results to the Argentine Republic. Therefore Brazil officially admits the "*Mapa de las Cortes*," and tracing the boundary according to it, the river San Antonio should be sought in the counter-sources, on the opposite watershed, in the "*San Antonio-Guazú*," as it was called by Oyarvide, supported by the Argentines. If the boundary is traced along the San Antonio of the mistake of 1759, as maintained by the Brazilians, the result would be an absurd boundary, as indicated by the adjoining engraving, which shows this in a line of crosses.

Permanent character of the Treaty of 1777. It is worth while to notice in the Treaty of 1777 the attribute of perpetuity which both Crowns attached to its clauses, not only as the basis of a new and definitive treaty, but also as a rule to control the future relations between the two powers in South America.

The preamble seeks to establish, in fact, perpetual harmony between their respective possessions;[1] and the twentieth Article endeavors to secure the unchanging authority of the treaty.[2]

The Treaty of March 11, 1778, "*de garantia*" (of Guaranty), confirms and protects the perpetuity of the rules laid down by both Crowns in the document of 1777 for their boundaries in America.[3] Their

---
[1] Argentine Evidence, Vol. I, page 85.
[2] Idem, 93.
[3] Idem, 97; Treaty of El Pardo, March 11, 1778.

Majesties wished to prevent, by this new agreement, all misunderstandings, distrusts and struggles between their vassals in America, as well as dangers that had been occasioned by certain ambiguities or doubts in the preceding treaties, by saying:

> ... we have resolved to establish the most intimate and indissoluble union between both Crowns, to which they are naturally inclined by their situation and vicinity, the ancient marriages and relationships of their respective Sovereigns, the identity of origin and the reciprocal interests of both nations. . . .[1]

They consequently agreed for themselves and their heirs, in accordance with the object expressed in the preamble and in Article I,—

> ... not to contemplate the one against the other, nor against their states in any part of the world, any kind of war, alliance, treaty, or council, nor to allow entrance to their ports or lands, nor the direct nor indirect help or subsidies for it, of any sort whatsoever, nor to permit their respective vassals to do so. . . .[2]

Article III of the Treaty of 1778 is of vital importance. It says that both Monarchs agreed together to reciprocally guarantee their dominions in Europe,— *The treaties of 1750 and 1777 and their perpetuity guaranteed by the Treaty of 1778.*

> ... as also to renew and revalidate the guaranty and other points established in the twenty-fifth Article of the Treaty of Boundaries of the 13th of January, 1750, which will be copied at the end of this. . . .[3]

Article XXV, already quoted, says:

> For the further security of this Treaty both high contracting parties agree to give to each other guaranty for all the frontier and adjacencies of their dominions in South America, as it has already been expressed.

That which had "already been expressed," was the boundary line, the *red mark* of the "*Mapa de las Cortes*," which in the zone of the present dispute follows the course of the River Pequiry or Pepiry in search of a river "*contravertiente*" (i. e. one having its

---

[1] Argentine Evidence, Vol. I, page 98.
[2] Idem, 98, and Article I of the Treaty.
[3] Idem, Vol. I, page 99.

sources opposite to the former, and adjacent thereto), which empties into the Yguazú on the counter watershed (Article XXV of the Treaty of 1750). This article ends thus:

> ... But with regard to the interior of South America, this obligation shall be *indefinite*, and in any case of invasion or insurrection both Crowns shall help and succor each other until affairs may reach a peaceful settlement.

The Sovereigns of Spain and Portugal confirm the boundary of 1750 and of the "Mapa de las Cortes."

I have left without commentary the language of the third Article, which precedes the foregoing and in which both sovereigns declare, in order to exclude all doubt, that the boundary of the Treaty of 1777 is the same as that of the Treaty of 1750. This declaration was necessary to begin Article XXV of the treaty last mentioned, because the reciprocal guaranty of their dominions being stated therein, it was necessary to fix boundaries for them. Therefore it said:

> For a further security of this Treaty both high contracting parties agree to give to each other guaranty for all the frontier and adjacencies of their dominions in South America, *as it has already been expressed*, obliging themselves to help and succor each other against whatever attack or invasion, until each may effectively rest in the peaceful possession and free and full use of that which was intended to be usurped; and this obligation, with regard to the sea-coasts and neighboring countries, on the part of His Most Faithful Majesty, shall extend up to the banks of the Orinoco on both sides and from Castillos to Magellan's Strait, and on that of His Catholic Majesty it shall extend to the borders of both banks of the river Amazon or Marañon, and from the above mentioned Castillos to the port of Santos. But with regard to the interior of South America this obligation shall be indefinite, and in any case of invasion or insurrection both Crowns shall help and succor each other until affairs may reach a peaceful settlement. [Art. 25 of the Treaty of 1750, quoted in Art. 3 of the Treaty of 1778.]

I have already shown that both Argentines and Brazilians agreed that the boundary line was the same between the Rivers Paraná and Uruguay, and that the only terms of the compact of 1759 explained by that of 1777 were those of "Pequiry or Pepiry." The explanation consisted in the addition of the qualificative "*Guazú*" (large), in order to exclude the small stream selected by the Demarcators of 1759. At the same time the third Article of the Treaty "*de Garantía*" of 1778, imports the ratification of the boundaries of the "*Mapa de las*

Cortes" of 1749. It was called "*Preliminar*" (preliminary) in its preamble, and therefore some Brazilian statesmen argue that it has no permanent character and that no definitive agreement having been made this one is void. But "*Preliminar*" does not mean temporary. The preamble explains the reason why this word was employed, and this explanation gives to this treaty the character of firmness and perpetuity which I have already shown. It is in fact a bringing together of fundamental and permanent rules for the tracing of boundaries. After these rules had been applied to the ground and the character, names, and other special facts concerning the boundaries had become known, the final treaty was to be drawn up, individualizing by their names, character, or nature the features of the soil which the Treaty of 1777 could not designate excepting in some regions. It therefore said:

<blockquote>
... they have resolved, agreed, and adjusted the present Preliminary Treaty, *which shall serve as basis and foundation to the definitive one of boundaries*, which is to be committed to writing in due time with the details, exactness and necessary information. . . .[1]
</blockquote>

The Treaty of 1777 is therefore substantially conclusive as a rule of Public Law for both Nations and only *preliminary* as to its topographical details. When a litigant resists without reason various lawsuits against the same property he often sets up matters which may favor him in one case but prejudice him in another. Contradiction and confusion are inevitable. And this is what has happened to the Empire of Brazil in its anxiety to extend its territory without right, from the Rio de la Plata to the Orinoco, all over South America. The Republics of Venezuela, Colombia, Ecuador, Peru, Bolivia, Paraguay, and Uruguay have struggled against the Empire for sixty years in defence of their territories. The Republic of Peru, supporting the validity of the Treaties of 1750 and 1777, after its independence, said:

<blockquote>
The consequence of not having taken into account these stipulations, and of having substituted for them the second Article of the Treaty in question, is clearly to be perceived by any one who casually examines the map of the localities. *Far from being a light matter for Peru and for Bolivia, it means the absorption by Brazil of nearly ten thousand square leagues, where some very im-*
</blockquote>

---

[1] "Argentine Evidence," Vol. I, page 86.

portant rivers are to be found, such as the Purus, the Yuma, the Yutay, the commercial future of which will no doubt be immense.[1]

The map that accompanies this page eloquently demonstrates to every right-minded person the enormity of this and other imperial usurpations against the Republics of South America. This map shows the boundaries of Brazil according to the Treaties of 1750 and 1777 and its present boundaries. It still remains for Brazil to settle its boundary questions with France in Guayana, with Venezuela, Colombia and Ecuador, and with the Argentine Republic in *Misiones*.

---

[1] Protest of Peru against the treaty made between Bolivia and Brazil, on the 27th of March, 1867, dated in Lima Dec. 20, 1867, "*Coleccion de los tratados, &c., del Peru;*" officially published by the Department of Foreign Affairs, Lima, 1890; Vol. I, page 387. State Department Library.

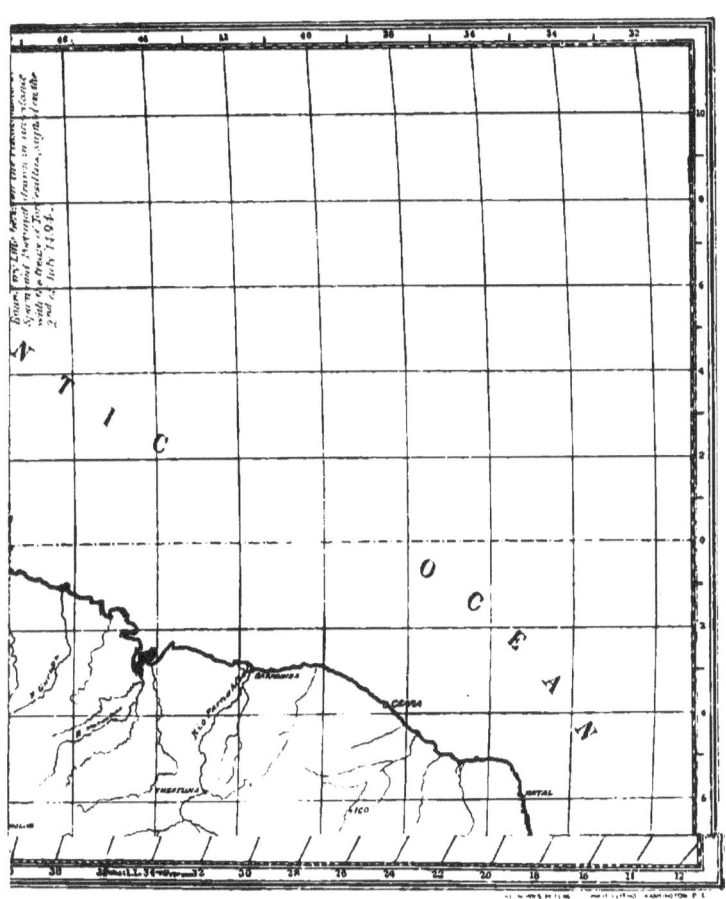

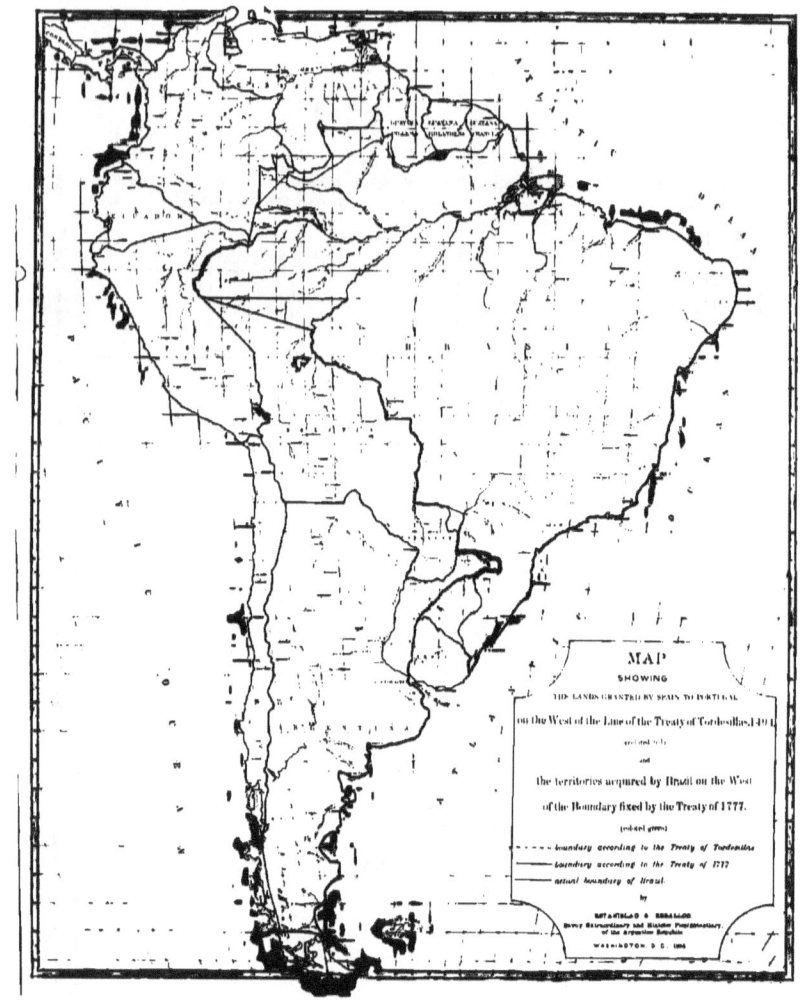

II.

TREATIES BETWEEN THE ARGENTINE REPUBLIC AND BRAZIL.

1810-1890.

The Argentine Republic has always taken the position that the question to be determined was one of law; and Brazil has agreed to that position in various documents and among others in the very treaty submitting the subject to arbitration. The question at issue one of law.

Having demonstrated that the matter submitted to the Arbitrator is one of *Law*, he will without doubt ask this question: *What is the legal criterion applicable to the demarcation of the boundaries between the South American Republics and Brazil after their independence?* Spanish America has solved this question. All the Republics, from Venezuela to the Rio de la Plata, have maintained the boundaries that corresponded to the Spanish possessions at the time of their emancipation. They have legally inherited from Spain their territorial patrimony, and have taken their possessions under the boundaries agreed upon by Spain and Portugal in the treaties of 1750 and 1777. Law applicable to South American boundary lines after the Independence.

The Republics of Venezuela, Colombia, Ecuador, Peru, Bolivia, Paraguay, Uruguay and Argentine have set up these treaties against Brazil as a basis for ascertaining their respective boundaries. The Arbitrator may corroborate this fact in the official work issued by the Republic of Colombia, which contains a complete and learned study of these questions, published by the Government of that country under the title of:

> *Boundaries of the Republic of the States of Colombia; by J. M. Quijano Otero, etc., Vol. I, Sevilla, 1881. General basis; the Hispano-Luisitanian Treaties, etc.*[1]

The doctrine of all the Spanish American Republics, officially stated by the government of Colombia, is in perfect harmony with that which the Argentine Republic has hitherto asserted, as follows:

---
[1] Page 360, and following. In the Argentine Legation at the disposal of the Arbitrator.

From all which it results that the line described in these treaties (of 1750 and 1777) including in favor of Colombia the part that is held to have been usurped by Brazil, must have been the "*uti possidetis*," the adoption of which is heralded by the second article. Because one of two things must be true :—either the "*uti possidetis*" is the basis or it is not. If it is the basis the Colombian rights descend according to the line in Articles X, XI and XII of the Treaty of 1777, and this is the legal *line to-day, not only for Venezuela, but also for all the Spanish Colombian states*, Brazil being obliged to make all the restitution necessary in order that it may be effective. . . . And this line of the Treaty of 1777 is the one the Commission find Venezuela ought to sustain. Ever since the states that formed Colombia were emancipated from Spain, they have in their fundamental laws fixed for their territories the boundaries that had been marked out by the Metropoli, *and this right can only be derived from the existing treaties, and these treaties give the delineation of the "uti possidetis" that all these states have invoked.*

This was also the judicial rule implicitly adopted in 1888 by the President of the United States, Grover Cleveland, as Arbitrator in the questions submitted to him by the Republics of Costa Rica and Nicaragua.

<small>Frequent contradictions of Brazil on this point.</small> While all the rest of South America has constantly maintained a profound conviction and a uniform criterion in this long struggle inherited from the mother country, the Empire has neither held convictions nor observed a straight line of conduct, but has sustained both the *pro* and the *con* of the same question of law and right in its disputes with the different countries with which it contested for territory. In fact, in the Report of the Minister of Foreign Affairs of the Argentine Republic published in 1892 [1] may be read the following concerning the boundaries of Bolivia and Brazil :

In 1834, General Armaza, in behalf of Bolivia, opened negotiations, proposing to the Emperor as a primary basis of the boundary treaty, that of San Ildefonso of October 1, 1777. . . .

In 1837, Brazil was in accord with such attitude, for the diplomatic representative of the Empire in Peru and Bolivia, Señor Duarte da Ponte Ribeiro, demanded, in October of the same year, the extradition of several criminals sheltered upon Bolivian territory, on the strength of the Treaty of 1777, just as Councillor Paranhos did, later on, from 1856 to 1859, on the Rio de la Plata. . . .

[1] Argentine Evidence, Vol. I, page 692.

During the negotiations between Brazil and Paraguay, from 1855 to 1856, the validity of the treaties between Spain and Portugal was contested by the Brazilian Cabinet. . . .

Brazil, the heir to Portuguese usurpations of different territories in South America, had invoked in solemn boundary debates with Venezuela, Peru and Bolivia, the principle of *uti possidetis*. Paraguay, favored by such principle, invoked it in its turn, and Brazilian diplomacy was momentarily surprised and entangled in its own nets.

Councillor Paranhos, who had not yet touched the territorial knot with the Argentine Republic, changed his tactics upon the field, and remembering the treaties of 1750 and 1777, which Brazil rejected when discussing with New Granada, said:

"How then recognize upon the ground the dominion of one country or the other, on the territory extending beyond their towns and settlements, in the extreme points where substantial proofs of their possession are not found? *The old treaties would afford a plain and evident proof;* and in order to get at this knowledge, the Imperial government understands that it is necessary to resort to that which was acknowledged and signed by the Courts of Spain and Portugal.

. . . .

"Let us see what was the right of Portugal, and what that of Spain to the Territory now disputed between the Empire and the Republic. This examination clears up the question, and decides the same with the best evidence.

"The Boundary Treaty of October 1, 1777, marked out the region beyond the frontier in Articles VIII and IX, which are transcripts of Articles V and VI of the treaty of June 13, 1750, with some explanations indicated by the surveys made by the Demarcators of this last treaty."

"Finally, I will state that in the Treaty of October 4, 1844, concluded between the Governments of Brazil and Paraguay, which was not ratified for other reasons, the Imperial diplomacy accepted Article XXXV, reading:

"The high contracting parties bind themselves to appoint Commissioners to examine and survey the bounds pointed out by the Treaty of San Ildefonso of 1777, so that the definite boundaries between both States shall be established accordingly."

The boundaries marked after the fall of Rozas between the Empire and the Republic of Uruguay, did not follow the lines as given by the Treaty of 1777, because that demarcation, made under abnormal circumstances, was rather a consequence of the war than a regular free convention on the part of the country, weak and exhausted, which accepted its neighbor's claims; . . .

<small>Other contradictions of the Brazilian Empire.</small> In its debates with Venezuela, Ecuador, Peru and Uruguay, the Empire of Brazil rejected the treaties which it accepted as the only rule in the case of the dispute with Paraguay, and which it accepted in its quarrel with New Granada. In the question now submitted to the Arbitrator the inconsistencies of the Empire have been still more striking. In 1857 Brazil accredited to the Argentine Republic the illustrious Minister Paranhos, for the purpose of negotiating a boundary treaty. That diplomat opened the discussion with the Memoir already quoted, in which he said:[1]

> The last stipulations adjusted and concluded between the two Crowns for the demarcation of their dominions in the New World were those of the Preliminary Treaty of October 1, 1777, the greater part of which provisions were copied from the Treaty of January 13, 1750, which was modified and made clear by the former. The Treaty of 1777 was destroyed and nullified by the war that intervened in 1801 between Portugal and Spain, and so remained forever. . . .

<small>Conflict with France.</small> But there came up about the same time the boundary question between French Guiana and the Empire of Brazil. France invoked the *secular possession* of the territory. The Empire then forgot that when settling its boundaries with all the Republics of South America it had founded its arguments upon the deeds of its soldiers, and frankly condemned all its diplomatic past and its recent territorial acquisitions. It condemned the acts of France, resting its claims upon legal right, invoking the treaties previous to the emancipation of South America, and the discussion between the two nations was reduced to an interpretation of the Treaty of Utrecht, which had alluded to this question of boundaries. I present to the Arbitrator a copy of the Protocol, signed in 1855, by the Ministers of Brazil and France who discussed this matter. The copy of this protocol has been officially certified by the French Government.[2] It set forth in substance—

1. That Brazil opposed to France the treaties prior to its Independence, the Treaty of Utrecht of 1715 and that of 1795.

---

[1] "Argentine Evidence." Vol. II, pamphlet No. 6.
[2] "Argentine Evidence." Group D of Manuscripts, No. 24, in French. *Relatorio da Repartição dos Negocios Estrangeiros*, of Brazil, etc., 1857, page 58. (Books of the "Argentine Evidence.")

2. That by accepting in 1855 the validity of these treaties, Brazil condemned its own doctrine that the prior wars between Spain and Portugal had nullified the agreements between these two nations, for in those same wars Portugal and France took part, the former as the ally of England, and the latter as that of Spain.

3. That the Empire acknowledged that there ought to be general rules or principles of law to regulate the boundaries of South American sovereignties, other than the edge of the sword and the thunder of cannon.

4. That these rules were the treaties signed by the Sovereigns, and obligatory upon their colonies now independent, for when the territories changed their masters they still carried with them all the antecedents of their dominion, their Royal Law and their Public Law. Here we have the Empire defending itself by means of these treaties in the Amazon Valley against France, as well as in the Matto Grosso country against Paraguay, and then condemning these very treaties in the South in its dispute with the Argentine Republic.

It had no possession of the ground, nor consummated acts of violence, to invoke against the Argentine Republic, and yet there, on the banks of the same river Paraguay, it once more changed its tactics and accepted anew the treaties that the Argentine statesmen upheld as the only basis of discussion. The Empire yielded, and its Minister of Foreign Affairs, the great politician of his time, who was most familiar with the boundary controversy submitted to the Arbitrator, presented to the Imperial Congress in 1882 a Memorandum in which he recognized the validity of the Treaty of 1777 in the case of *Misiones*, and copied it at the end as an illustrative annex.[1]

New contradictions of Brazil.

The same Minister abandoned this declaration four years later, in 1886, fearful of its consequences, for the treaty of 1777 is clear and favorable to the Argentine cause. He, indeed, says in his conclusions upon the imperial arguments:

<blockquote>12. Thus is proved the nullification of the Treaty of 1777, on which the Argentine Government bases its right, and which is au-</blockquote>

---

[1] The Baron de Cotegipe, in his official work entitled "Points in regard to the Boundaries between Brazil and the Argentine Republic." Rio de Janeiro, 1882. Presented to the Arbitrator, with a copy, in the same cover with the note of the Argentine Minister in Brazil, authenticating the book, which may be read in the "Argentine Evidence," Vol. II, pamphlet No. 6. See "Argentine Evidence," Vol. I, page 640.

nulled by the *uti possidetis*, as a fact anterior to the treaty of 1750, recognized and respected in it.[1]

What a series of contradictions! If the Treaty of 1777 is in conformity with that of 1750, and if the latter is to rule the case, why reject its concordant, that is to say, the Treaty of 1777?

But these contradictions lead the Empire of Brazil into an abyss. Indeed, studying the possessory acts which are acknowledged, prior to the Treaty of 1750, we ought to apply the "*Mapa de las Cortes*" of 1749 as the only document in which, since the Treaty of Tordesillas, both Crowns fixed a royal boundary to the dominions they possessed and held by each of them. The "*Mapa de las Cortes*" is therefore the monument over the grave of the Brazilian cause, voluntarily accepted.

<small>Positive attitude of Brazil accepting the legal Argentine doctrine.</small> At last the Brazilian Congress rejected the entanglements of the Imperial diplomacy and accepted frankly and definitively the validity of the treaties, in the session of the House of Representatives of August 8, 1891,[2] in the following terms:

5. *For it is Article VIII of the treaty of October, 1777, that regulates the boundaries of Brazil with the Argentine Republic in this region*, notwithstanding its being a preliminary treaty, and notwithstanding it was not renewed by the treaty of Badajoz in 1801; notwithstanding the fact that the Brazilian Government affirmed its nullity, and notwithstanding these treaties were obligatory only upon the contracting parties, and were made between Portugal and Spain.

Article VIII of the Treaty of 1777 is in full force, because the Argentine Republic accepted it; because the Brazilian Government although denying its *absolute validity accepted it in this particular*; finally, because invalid treaties can be renewed and re-established by the mutual consent, either expressed or tacit, of the contracting parties; *and Brazil and the Argentine Republic* have declared more than once in public documents, which must be given faith, the latter that the treaty of October 1, 1777, known as the Treaty of San Ildefonso *has always been valid, and has always been sustained as such*, and the former although considering it void admits Article VIII in order to settle the question of boundary.

<small>Causes of the pretended nullity.</small> It is scarcely necessary to add any other observations as to the

---

[1] Report of the Minister of Foreign Affairs of Brazil, 1886, page 11. See books of the Argentine Evidence.

[2] "Journal of the National Congress," etc., 1891, No. 52, page 627; presented to the Arbitrator among the documents of the "Argentine Evidence." Group D of MSS., No. 25.

validity of the Treaty of 1777 as a matter of International Law, in anticipation of the possibility that the defender of the Brazilian cause may assert its nullity. Its validity has been upheld, as I have demonstrated, by all the nations of South America; and the same imperial diplomats have, in the question with Argentine, vacillated between the validity and the nullity of this agreement, finally concluding to accept it, although with bad grace. And in fact the alleged cause of its nullity, the war of 1801 between Spain and Portugal, is not well founded. The great American authorities upon treaties maintain that a war either leaves territorial interests as they were before or expressly modifies them. In the first case it is useless to allude to these interests in the Treaty of Peace. Silence signifies clearly that the matter was settled *ante bellum* and that it is not altered. In the second case the modifications import simply a *conquest*, an exchange or a sale, and they must be clearly expressed in the Treaty of Peace, of exchange or of sale, otherwise there would be no conquest, nor peace, but usurpation and a latent state of war, which is contrary to the fundamental principles upon which rest the welfare of peoples and of men. [Opinion of American authorities upon treaties. Wars and boundary treaties.]

According to John Quincy Adams war dissolves such obligations of treaties as are transient (II Wharton, Int. Law, Sec. 135[1]), but does not abrogate treaties which contain permanent declarations of right, such as those relating to boundaries and fisheries. This doctrine was energetically sustained by Gallatin, Rush, Buchanan and other eminent statesmen of the United States of America. England has upheld the same doctrine.[1]

The peace that put an end to the war of 1801 was settled by the Treaty of Badajoz, which confirmed in its third Article the pre-existing boundaries between the two Crowns in Europe and in America, with the exception of the town of Olivenza, of which single and only alteration of the Treaty of San Ildefonso of 1777 there is made express mention. The treaty of 1777 is the supreme law in this dispute, according to the unanimous decision of South America and the authoritative writers on the Law of Nations, and even by the acknowledgment of both Imperial and Republican Brazil, the latter more frank than the former. [The War of 1801, and the Treaties.]

[1] A Digest of International Law of the United States, taken from Documents issued by Presidents and Secretaries of State, and from Decisions of the Federal Courts and Opinions of Attorneys-General; edited by Francis Wharton, in three volumes. Washington (Government Printing Office), 1886.

184

The treaty of 1777.

The treaty of 1777 governed the question up to 1857, when Brazil opened negotiations with the Argentine Republic to decide the inherited dispute. The Argentine Republic was at the time divided into two camps, owing to the separation of the State of Buenos Ayres, which has been referred to. The National government, at the head of the Provinces of the Confederation, had its seat in the city of Paraná, and the foreign nations had accredited their representatives to it.

The Councillor José Maria Silva Paranhos, Envoy Extraordinary and Minister Plenipotentiary of Brazil near the government of Paraná, presented the *Memoir* dated on the thirtieth day of November, 1857, promoting the settlement of the question of *Misiones*. This Memoir contains a superficial exposition of the antecedents of the long diplomatic debate held between the sovereigns, presenting them in a manner favorable to Brazil. Señor Paranhos said to the Government of the Confederation that His Majesty the Emperor lacked a written right to sustain his territorial claims on the neighboring States, and was opposed to the precedents set forth in the treaties and instructions of the Courts, because the statement that the Pepiry or Pequiry-Guazú had its mouth above the Uruguay-Pitá was contrary to his claims. Señor Paranhos went on in his unfounded argument so far as to deny the authority of the "*Mapa de las Cortes*," adopted by expressed declaration and authenticated by a protocol written upon it; but this feature of the Memoir serves only to demonstrate the injustice arising from the lack of a written right on which to base the system of territorial enlargement it supported. It says, in fact:

> If the map of the courts showed the Pepiri as *up stream from the Uruguay-Pitá, other printed maps, and some manuscripts of the Indians* in the times when they navigated those places, placed the same river otherwise.

But when independent governments solemnly determine to adopt international rules in such important matters as the division of territories, it is not possible to destroy these royal agreements by vague references to private maps or Indian manuscripts.

Señor Paranhos initiated the settlement in an untimely moment. The Republic being divided by an unfortunate civil war, public

---

[1] I refer in this connection to the Memoir of the Department of Foreign Affairs of the Argentine Republic, presented to the Arbitrator in the Argentine Evidence, Vol. I, page 619.

sentiment lacked the necessary repose and homogeneity to pass upon grave matters of sovereignty. The Government of the Confederation had, however, committed the error of supposing that this was a favorable opportunity to insist upon its imprudent desire to mix up Brazil in the internal contentions of the Rio de la Plata and of Paraguay, and it appointed its ministers of Foreign Affairs and of the Interior to negotiate with the shrewd diplomatist of the empire. The Memoir of Señor Paranhos was not answered, and fourteen days later, that is, on the fourteenth day of December, 1857, the boundary treaty was formulated with these provisions:

ART. I.—Both high contracting parties, being in accord as to fixing their respective boundaries, agree to declare and recognize as the frontier of the Argentine Confederation and of Brazil, between the rivers Uruguay and Paraná, that which is hereinafter designated.

The territory of the Argentine Confederation is divided from the Empire of Brazil by the river Uruguay, all the right or western border to belong to the Confederation, and the left or eastern border to Brazil, from the mouth of the affluent Cuarahim to the mouth of the Pepiry-Guazú, where the Brazilian possessions occupy both sides of the Uruguay.

The boundary line follows by the waters of the Pepiry-Guazú to its principal source; from whence it continues through the highest ground, to find the principal head of the San Antonio, as far as its entrance into the Yguazú or Rio Grande de Curitiba, and by the latter as far as its confluence with the Paraná.

The lands which the rivers Pepiry-Guazú, San Antonio and Yguazú separate, toward the eastern side belong to Brazil, and toward the western side to the Argentine Confederation; the waters of the two former rivers above mentioned throughout their course being common property of both nations, and the waters of the Yguazú only from the junction of the San Antonio as far as the Paraná.

ART. II.—Both high contracting parties declare, to avoid any doubt, notwithstanding the designations of the first Article are well known, *that the rivers Pepiry-Guazú and San Antonio spoken of in the said Article are those which were recognized* (in 1759) *by the Demarcators of the treaty of January* 13, 1750, *made between Portugal and Spain.*

This treaty made a deep and unfavorable impression on the Paraná. Influential members of Congress pronounced against it, and the resistance went so far as to promote parliamentary opposition, as well as in the press. The debate began in June, 1858. The Committee on

National Argentine opposition to the Treaty.

Legislation and Constitutional Affairs of the Senate reported on the 8th, in favor of ratification. On the 28th the matter was brought up for discussion, and Doctor Don Vicente Saravia, Senator from Salta, objected to the general declaration of the river Uruguay as the division of the two sovereignties. Señor Saravia stated that the Crown of Portugal had never possessed either all or any part of the Territory of Misiones, since all of these settlements belonged to Spain, by which they were organized into Provinces, uniting them to the political jurisdiction of Buenos Ayres.

Dr. Don Martin Zapata, Senator from the province of Mendoza, said that—

> ... he was not acquainted with the explanations made by the Minister of Foreign Affairs within the bosom of the committee, to which the said committee made reference in its report, and consequently he did not know upon what data, upon what practical knowledge, and upon what preliminary studies the making of this treaty had been proceeded with. That if such data did not exist, and if, as he believed, those studies had not been made; and if it was established by the protocol of the conferences that the former treaties between Spain and Portugal (*which were the only documents to serve as a starting point*) were worthless; it was necessary to make other studies and practical surveys, in order to avoid being obliged, for want of them, to give up a large portion of the Argentine territory, as was yielded, according to his judgment, by virtue of this treaty; ... that he saw that the Argentine plenipotentiaries, with good judgment, had saved that principle which the Brazilian plenipotentiary wished to establish with regard to the islands of the Uruguay; but at the same time he was sorry to see that while that right had been saved in reference to the uninhabited islands, the same principle had not been recognized with regard to the valuable Territory of *Misiones* which, for thousands of reasons, ought to belong to the Confederation.
>
> . . . . .

<small>Substantial modification of the Treaty.</small> The opinion of the Senate caused a deep reaction, to the extent of demoralizing the Committee which upheld the treaty; and one of its members, Senator Bustamante, from Jujuy, moved to substitute for the second Article of the Committee the following one, which frustrated the easy victory of the Brazilian negotiator:

ART. II.—It is understood that the rivers Pepiry-Guazú and San Antonio, which are designated as boundaries in the first Article of the Treaty, *are those which are found further East* with these names, according to the operation referred to in the second Article of the same.

The Senate approved, by thirteen votes against two, this fundamental amendment; and its action brought about the disapproval of the treaty by the Executive Power. The two dissenting votes were radical; they rejected any treaty in regard to a thing of which the Nation was already in possession. Though the debate took place in secret sessions, it leaked out rapidly. The opposition members had consulted together and were conducted skilfully. The orators designated to lead them represented the groups of Senators from the different frontiers of the Republic. In all the provinces the press pronounced itself in the same sense. In September the House of Representatives deliberately endorsed the corrective action of the Senate and sanctioned the modification of the second Article.[1]

The antecedents of the Treaty of 1857, brought to light for the first time in the Memoir of the Minister of Foreign Affairs of the Argentine Republic in 1892, unjustified reservations having caused publications to be made in Brazil which were incomplete and void of historical truth, show *that the said compact*, far from receiving the open approbation of the Congress of the Paraná, as Brazilian writers have repeatedly asserted during thirty-four years, *suffered a substantial modification.*

An illustrious Brazilian diplomatist, Enrique C. R. Lisboa, has lately published a study on the *"Question of Misiones before the Court of Arbitration,"* and treating in a masterly manner the point relative to the Treaty of 1857, says:[2]

Opinions of Brazilian diplomatists upon this precedent.

> Some defenders of Brazil in that question pretend to strengthen our right, attributing to the treaty of the fourteenth day of December, 1857, and to the *memoranda and protocols* accompanying it, moral value,—to demonstrate the acknowledgment by the Argentine Republic of our occupation and possession of the territory in dispute, and of the solemn acceptance by that republic of the just application of the *uti possidetis* in our favor. No matter how advantageous that interpretation may be to us, a sense of justice and impartiality, which must preside over our discussions, does not admit of its acceptance. It is at this very moment a risky recourse. The ratifications of the treaty of 1857 were, as a matter

---
[1] The original papers of these parliamentary proceedings are in the Argentine Legation in Washington at the disposition of the Arbitrator. This part of the matter has also been discussed at length in the Memoir of the Argentine Minister of Foreign Affairs, cited, "Argentine Evidence," Vol. I, page 649 and following.

[2] "Argentine Evidence," Vol II.

of fact, never interchanged, and, therefore, such treaty never existed as an international contract. The most that can be made out of its negotiation, and of those memorable protocols, is that the Argentine negotiators admitted our *claim*.

That personal opinion, however, does not bind the Argentine nation in any way, because it did not accept it officially, neither can a single presumption constitute a right, much less a solemn acknowledgment of our dominion by the republic.

<small>Interpretation of the modifications of the Treaty of 1857</small> The Article added through the initiation of the Senate has, in fact, two well-defined parts, the first essential, the second a matter of form. The first one says:

> ART. II.—It is understood that the rivers Pepiry-Guazú and San Antonio designated as boundaries in the first Article of the treaty, *are those which are found further East, with these names.*

The question of *Misiones* arises out of the claim by Brazil that the boundary is the river that enters into the Uruguay *below* the Uruguay-Pitá, and a line seeking the nearest sources of the opposite river flowing into the Yguazú; while the Argentine Republic, a lawful heir of the Crown of Spain, holds that which was given to the latter by the treaties made between it and Portugal, and by the "*Mapa de las Cortes,*" which served as the basis in drawing up those documents; and the said treaties provide that the boundary shall run by the system of rivers situated *above* the Uruguay-Pitá. The former are the *western rivers*, and the latter the *eastern rivers*. The Paranhos-Lopez and Derqui treaty pointed out plainly the *western rivers*. The Congress of the Confederation substituted the Article adopting the *eastern rivers*. Can it be affirmed that this acknowledged the claims of Brazil?

<small>The Minister of Brazil accepts the modification favorable to the Argentine Republic.</small> The Argentine Republic, on the contrary, will always invoke with success the note of the illustrious negotiator, Paranhos, demanding the ratification of the compact *thus modified* as a frank admission of the amendment, and consequently of the system of *eastern rivers*, or Pequiry-Guazú and San Antonio Guazú, of Oyarvide, named arbitrarily *Chapecó* and *Yangada* by the modern Brazilian writers.

The second and last part of the second Article could not be invoked in an unauthorized sense. It reads:

> According to the operation referred to in the second Article of the same.

The operation alluded to is the Demarcation of 1759, which clearly raised the presumption of the existence of a second system of rivers, that of the east, which was not the one delineated in the "*Mapa de las Cortes*," and accepted in the compacts of 1750 and 1777.

On the 14th day of June, 1859, the amendment of the compact having already been agreed to by both houses of Congress, and the Minister of Foreign Relations being called upon by Señor Paranhos to make the interchange of the ratifications, the Government showed opposition to the original negotiation, thus disclosing the nature of the internal policy that had guided it. The communication said:

> Your Excellency, knowing the good faith of my Government and its friendly feelings towards the Government of His Majesty the Emperor of Brazil, and knowing furthermore *the excitement produced in the whole country by the sanction of those treaties*, will do it justice in the appreciation of the noble spirit which this resolution implies, and the reasons of prudence which counsel the same.
>
> Your Excellency will not fail to notice that in the present excitement of the personnel of the House, and public opinion being stirred by the comments of the Press against those treaties, their immediate ratification would be very inconvenient. This unfavorable result, which the Government desires to prevent, will appear to your Excellency all the more probable, *if he remembers the serious opposition which the Government met in the Houses, although the discussion was held under the impression that the adoption of those treaties carried the implicit condition that the Government of His Imperial Majesty would lend to the Government of the Confederation its moral and material co-operation to obtain the reincorporation of Buenos Ayres into the bosom of the Nation*.[1]

Councillor Paranhos replied on August 1st, deploring, in the name of the Imperial Government, the idea of the extension of time, and demanded in unequivocal terms the interchange of the ratifications of the treaty, *as sanctioned by Congress*. He said: [Imperial Diplomatic reasons for acceding in this case.]

> *Approved as those agreements are by the Government and by the Congress of the Confederation*, what else do they need to have full effect? Only the exchange of the respective ratifications. . . .
>
> The undersigned, in the name of his Government, requests the Government of the Confederation that it will deign to *reconsider* the said determination.

Councillor Paranhos and the Imperial Government explicitly accepted the treaty *sanctioned by Congress*, which adopted as the inter-

---
[1] Argentine Evidence, Vol. I, page 657. The original Manuscript is in the Argentine Legation in Washington, at the disposal of the Arbitrator.

national boundary the system of *eastern rivers* of Oyarvide; and if the Government of the Confederation committed an error, it was in not exchanging the ratifications, hesitating to drag the Empire into a military revolt against Buenos Ayres.

Señor Paranhos, with high and far-sighted political views, wished by all means to put an end to this question just when Brazil was engaged in conflicts with Paraguay, and in the demarcation of its boundaries with the Eastern State of Uruguay. That eminent statesman asked, and took advantage of, the effectual aid of the Government of Paraná, especially in the Paraguayan question; and in his notable speech upon the subject, delivered in the Brazilian Parliament on the fourth day of August, 1858, he said:

> Sir, I cannot take my seat without giving from this place an expression of recognition, in the name of my country, for the frank and friendly co-operation which the government of the Argentine Confederation lent to us for the friendly and honorable solution of our differences with the Republic of Paraguay (*Seconded, very well*). That aid was offered us with the best intentions, and it was very effective, so that our just claims should be heard by the Government of Paraguay without distrust or prejudice.
>
> The Government of the Confederation, besides the said assistance lent to us, negotiated two important treaties with the Empire. The treaty on boundaries which recognizes and indicates the frontier of the Province of Paraná with the Province of Corrientes, and the treaty of extradition of criminals and for the surrender of runaway slaves, a need urgently demanded by the Province of San Pedro de Rio Grande do Sul. . . .
>
> Señor Bello: *Seconded.*
>
> Señor Paranhos: . . . treaties without which the friendly relations between the two countries could not be considered as solidly established (*very good*). I, therefore, feel obliged in the name of my country, for the help received and the friendly disposition which I met in the Government of the Argentine Confederation (*very good*).

These words explain Brazil's interest in settling the difficulties with the Argentine Republic, and this fact, together with the lack of value of the territory comprised between the two systems of rivers, perhaps influenced the mind of Señor Paranhos and his government *to accept the ratification of the treaty as modified by Congress*, which cleared up the political horizon and spared Brazil the dangers of an Argentino-Uruguayan-Paraguayan coalition.

Señor Paranhos had a capital interest in compelling the Argentine Republic to surrender the runaway slaves. The Southern provinces of Brazil demanded this measure as a vital and urgent one. The treaty of extradition was made along with the one on boundaries. But if the latter had caused strong resistance the former was also opposed for being in contradiction with the constitutional principles and text of our political system, and Señor Paranhos, who saw danger threatening the two results obtained by him, and Brazil, being isolated in its questions regarding Paraguay and the Eastern State of Uruguay, had to make skilful concessions to save these results.

<small>The Surrender of slaves preferred by Brazil.</small>

This attitude, not yet well known by Brazilian diplomacy in 1858 and 1859, has been accepted by another of the most notable diplomatists of the Empire, who treated the question at Buenos Ayres in 1876: Señor Baron Aguiar d'Andrada, who died in the United States, where he represented Brazil in this dispute, published a letter in Lisbon on the 19th of September, 1882, in refutation of an article by the Argentine Minister to Italy, Dr. del Viso, concerning the question of *Misiones*, which appeared in the "*Revista Sud-Americana*" (South American Review) of Paris. Baron Andrada uses the following language:

> Later on, in the year 1876, I had the honor to be charged with the negotiations to settle said questions. I proposed in the first place, as a basis of the demarcation of the respective frontiers, the provisions of the treaty of Paraná of 1857, not pretending, as Señor del Viso avers, *but asserting as a fact, evidenced in the official documents of both countries, that this treaty was signed by the Argentine plenipotentiary* AND APPROVED BY CONGRESS, and that the lack of ratification, for the reason already explained, did not alter the existence of this compact.

Some Brazilian statesmen having become alarmed, owing to the decisive importance of these antecedents against their pretensions, expressed doubts as to the existence of the text of the treaty sanctioned by the Congress of the Confederation.

Councillor J. M. N. Azambuja, in a book published by him in 1891 at Rio de Janeiro, under the title "*Questão Territorial com a Republica Argentina*," says on page 50:

<small>Authenticity of the Treaty of 1857. Doubts of Brazil.</small>

> It is fair to doubt the authenticity of such a document, which, on the other hand, is contradictory, because, if the designated rivers are those situated *further East* with the names of Pequiry-Guazú and San Antonio Guazú, according to the operations referred to in the second Article of the treaty, and if this Article

refers to the operations made by virtue of the treaty of the thirteenth day of January, 1750, in which operations no other Eastern rivers were demarcated or surveyed, the sense of the proposed amendment is not comprehended. For twenty-four years nobody knew of such documents.

I must suggest a suspicion with regard to the document that the Brazilian Cabinet has well guarded the State secret of its attitude in 1858 and 1859, which was not favorable to it. In the Argentine Republic the following document was published in 1858 in the shape of approbative law, in accordance with the Constitution.

The Senate and House of Representatives, etc.

Art. 1.—The stipulations contained in the five articles of the treaty of boundaries between the National Executive Power and His Majesty the Emperor of Brazil, through their respective plenipotentiaries, in the Capital, on the fourteenth day of December, 1857, are hereby approved.

Art. II.—It is understood that the rivers Pepiry-Guazú and San Antonio, which are designated as boundaries in Article I of the treaty, *are those situated further east with these names*, according to the operation referred to in Article II of the same.

Art. III.—Inform the Executive Power.

Hall of the Congress of Paraná, provisional capital of the Argentine Nation, the twenty-fourth day of September, 1858.

Pascual Eschagüe, Mateo Luque,
Carlos M. Saravia, Benjamin de Igarzabal,
Secretary. *Secretary.*

Department of Foreign Relations.

PARANÁ, September 26, 1858.

Let it be taken for law, and have it published.

URQUIZA.
BERNABÉ LOPEZ.[1]

The Treaty of 1857, in its primitive form, invoked by Brazil. The last argument of certain statesmen in reference to this treaty has already been refuted by a Brazilian diplomat, Señor Lisboa. They have, in effect, asserted that the Treaty of 1857, in its primitive form sanctioned by the Executive Power, with the rivers which the Empire claimed as boundaries, was a moral precedent contrary to Argentine right. That is, however, a mistake. This act was not a spontaneous

[1] Memoir of Department of Foreign Affairs, of the Argentine Republic, cited in the "Argentine Evidence," Vol. I, page 660. Manuscript in the Argentine Legation, at the disposal of the Arbitrator.

legal declaration by the Argentine President that Brazil was right in the boundary debate. There was no discussion as to that. It was a negotiation—a bilateral contract. The Argentine President ceded the Territory in dispute to Brazil, *on condition* that Brazil would put its armies, squadrons, and treasures under his orders, as they were placed at the orders of the same Argentine General for the overthrow of Rozas in 1852, so that he might attack and defeat the powerful State of Buenos Ayres, then separated from the Nation, and which had resumed independent control of its foreign relations.[1]

Brazil did not carry out its promise of furnishing military assistance, and General Urquiza, condemned by Congress and by the Country, yielded. This precedent is favorable to the people of Argentine, whose Congress saved its territorial integrity, and whose President, blinded for a moment by political passion, nevertheless signed the reform of his own work which had been passed by the Congress.[2]

This negotiation was an extraordinary one. It began by the cession of the Territory in favor of the Empire by the Argentine Government, *on condition* of a military alliance and of a loan, and it ended in an absolutely contrary and unexpected way, for the Empire *recognized the Argentine right as far as the eastern rivers* (C. D. E. of map on page 143 of this Argument) are concerned, on condition that the Argentine Republic, disregarding its Constitution, should pursue and return the fugitive slaves of Brazil, a matter which was, in fact, of greater material, political and moral importance to the wealthy and industrious Brazilian States than the Territory of *Misiones*.

From 1857 to 1865 Brazil did not bring up the question of the *Misiones*, which the Argentine Republic possessed, as I have shown. In 1865 Paraguay and Brazil became engaged in a formidable war. Paraguay, which had, ever since 1856,[3] recognized Argentine sovereignty over *Misiones*, asked permission of the Argentine Government to cross this Territory with an army of fifty thousand men, in order to attack Brazil from the rear. If this plan had been carried out Brazil would have been defeated and perhaps divided by Paraguay, whose dictator Lopez, at the head of eighty thousand heroic soldiers, revealed the

The integrity of Brazil saved by the Argentine Republic 1865 1870.

War with Paraguay.

---
[1] Brazil began by loaning $300,000 to the Argentine Government, as stated at page 85 of this Argument, and as set forth in the Memoir of the Minister of Foreign Affairs of Brazil for the year 1858, page 23, Annex II, presented to the Arbitrator.
[2] All the documents quoted in this chapter are presented to the Arbitrator in Vol I, page 649 *et seq.* of the "Argentine Evidence."
[3] Arbitration on the Chaco, already quoted.

tendencies of a Conqueror and was in search of sea-coasts for his country, shut up in the centre of South America. The military debility of Brazil was such that ten thousand Paraguayans invaded and rapidly dominated part of the most warlike state of the Empire, Rio Grande do Sul. The Argentine Government undoubtedly considered that Brazil had been the ally of Argentine in 1852 for the overthrow of the Dictator, and that there was a community of civilized interests between Argentines and Brazilians, while the Dictator of Paraguay was a menace to both, and so it denied to the latter the permission which had been requested. The Argentine Republic thus saved the Empire; but it paid dearly for its action, for the infuriated Paraguayan Dictator immediately declared war against it. This lasted for four years, cost the Argentine Republic thirty-five millions of dollars in gold, left twenty-five thousand dead in its campaigns, and set back its incipient progress for ten years; nor did it furnish any moral or material compensation for all this, either in the extension of its territories, or by any pecuniary indemnification from exhausted and agonized Paraguay; nor did it even obtain from Brazil the abandonment of its unjust quarrel about *Misiones*. On the contrary, as soon as the war was over, the astute diplomats of the Empire exerted their skill in intrigue against their disinterested ally, so candidly governed, seeking to annex Paraguay, and more than once the peace existing between the Argentine Republic and her Imperial ally was seriously threatened.

Brazil reopens the debate 1876.

From 1870 to 1875 the legal aspect of the question continued the same. The Argentine Republic was demoralized by a recent civil war. The moment seemed propitious to the Empire, and the distinguished diplomat, Baron Aguiar d'Andrada, accredited near the Government of the Republic of Uruguay in 1876, was charged with the special mission of going to Buenos Aires to open the discussion of the question of *Misiones*.[1]

The proposition submitted by the Argentine Government to the Brazilian Plenipotentiary on the 28th of March, 1876, was as follows:

> To name the Commissioners who shall trace the frontier, bearing in mind that the demarcation of the dividing line should regard, as stipulated by the governments of Spain and Portugal on the 10th of October, 1777, the preservation of that which each one possessed in virtue of the treaty cited.

[1] The account of these negotiations has been published by the Argentine Government in the "Report of the Foreign Department," 1892. See **Argentine Evidence, Vol. I, page 661.**

That was the application of the "*Mapa de las Cortes*" of 1749. Brazil did not accept this, but during this negotiation it was established:
1. That the Empire of Brazil feared the inherited treaties as a royal law applicable to the territories that had become independent from Spain and Portugal. 2. That the Empire sustained the doctrine of *uti possidetis*. Both points of view are favorable to the Argentine Republic.

After the emancipation of the Spanish colonies, as they had to divide between themselves the territories of North and South America which Spain had conquered, it became necessary to adopt a judicial criterion, and that was the *uti possidetis* of 1810. Each one of the new republics was to continue in possession, according to this rule, of the territories that corresponded to its internal jurisdiction under the government of Spain at the moment of its independence.

But it is proved that Brazil never possessed the Territory in dispute. From 1516 to 1810 it was held by Spain, and this fact and the rights derived therefrom passed with the Territory to the Argentine Republic, when it became independent. Brazil had no settlements whatever in the past centuries anywhere near the Territory. The official maps already presented and the Histories by Gay and the Visconde de Porto Seguro,[1] clearly show that the Portuguese possessions scarcely began to extend beyond the sea-coast at the end of the eighteenth century, and during the first quarter of the present one. All the Brazilian settlements near the *Misiones* now in question were made after 1840, as is proved by the official table of foundations given in the work by Gay, which is presented to the Arbitrator. What *uti possidetis*, therefore, can Brazil invoke?

Between independent Nations the *uti possidetis* signifies the possession of territories by one with the *tacit* or *express* consent of the other. It is *tacit* when a country knows that its territory is usurped and does not defend it, nor protest against such aggression, either through weakness or for any other reason. It is *express*, when it is authorized either by documents or international treaties, until a final solution is arrived at.

In the Argentine-Brazilian question the possessions of the two Crowns were established by the red mark upon the "*Mapa de las Cortes*," which was incorporated into the treaties of 1750 and 1777.[2] At the same time its possession is unquestionably favorable to

[1] See this Argument, page 62.
[2] See this Argument, page 140.

the Argentine Republic, because it actually possessed in fact, through Spain, territories which were situated much further East of the red mark of the "*Mapa de las Cortes*," and in fact and with legal right the entire zone situated to the West of that mark thus delineated. Since 1810 Brazil has not possessed, nor pretended to possess until within the last few years, the Territory in question.

Unfriendly and astute attitude of the Empire, 1876. Two countries bound by such solemn ties as the alliances of 1852 and 1865, by the first of which Brazil contributed to assure the liberty and national organization of the Argentine Nation, and by the second of which the Empire was saved from defeat and territorial dismemberment by Argentine, could have found easy ways open for the settlement of this question. And it was urgent that it should be settled. The consequent intranquillity and reciprocal distrust occasioned an armed peace and enormous financial sacrifices for these two new countries, whose progress is founded upon labor and the use of credit for their development. The alarm extended beyond the frontiers of the two countries. Paraguay, Uruguay, and Bolivia would be involved in the conflict between the two disputing nations, for territorial and political reasons. Chile itself was not exempt from this general distrust. It was said that there was a secret understanding between Brazil and Chile as against the Argentine Republic, and the Empire did not lose any opportunity of making a display of its weakness, flattering Chile with acts calculated to indirectly authorize these prejudices. Chile, a wise and considerate country, was a friend to the Argentine Republic, if not by the sympathy of its masses, at least through the influence of the peaceful disposition of its statesmen.

The moral considerations affecting alike the Argentine Republic and the Empire, their finances, their progress and their endeavors to attract European immigration to populate their wild lands, the welfare of South America and the small importance of the question at issue when compared with these vital interests, all demanded a settlement of the matter, if not by an absolute treaty, at least by a friendly arrangement or by Arbitration. The head and for many years the director of the Imperial diplomacy was the Baron de Cotegipe, who always managed the dangerous probability of a war with the Argentine Republic as a resource in the necessities of the internal politics of that country, and who had the design of keeping on hand, like a firebrand near fuel, the question of boundaries. He had himself sent a Minister to Buenos Aires with the object of obtaining advantages from the Argentine political crisis of 1876. On seeing that his plan was of no avail, he retreated from this position, abruptly recalling the negotiator. The uncertainty continued and the large armaments were still kept up and increased. The Minister of Foreign Affairs of the Empire advised his agent in Buenos Aires in the following terms:

The armaments are continued.

> Therefore, I recommend you to state to Dr. Irigoyen that the Imperial Government cannot accept his last proposal, and considers the negotiation with which you have been charged as closed. It is convenient that Your Excellency should hasten your departure, etc. . . .[1]

The Argentine Government determined to insist, and the Minister of Foreign Relations gave instructions on January 30, 1877, to Señor Luis L. Dominguez, Envoy Extraordinary and Minister Plenipotentiary of the Republic in Rio de Janeiro, to propose an Arbitration. He was not able, however, to make any headway against the deliberate policy of unreasonable delay in international matters, and in February, 1880, he wrote a despatch to the Minister of Foreign Affairs explaining the failure of his action, in which he said:

The Argentine Republic hurries the settlement and proposes Arbitration 1877.

> I held a conference with the Baron de Cotegipe, in which he told me that it was best to wait for more favorable circumstances to obtain, purely and simply, the ratification of that treaty (of 1857). . . .[2]

This was simply a pretext. The treaty was unfavorable to Brazil. The Imperial Government was aware of this, but made a show of being ignorant of it. If the Argentine Government had proposed a ratification, as I think it ought to have done, the Empire would have rejected it, basing its refusal upon the fact that the modification introduced by the Congress destroyed its claims, and it would have thus had an open road to pursue its object, that of postponing matters, hoping that the frequent Argentine discords would at some future day allow the coveted Territory to fall into its hands, as it had already secured tens of thousands of square leagues of territory from the other adjoining republics when they were torn by civil wars.

Brazil decides for uncertainty and an armed peace in South America.

The Minister of Foreign Affairs of the Argentine Republic, in his report upon the progress and state of this question which was presented to Congress in 1892, comments upon the attitude of the Empire in 1876 and 1877 in the following terms:

---

[1] Argentine Evidence, Vol. I, page 666. Señor Irigoyen was the Minister of Foreign Affairs of the Argentine Republic.
[2] Argentine Evidence, Vol. I, page 192.

The Baron de Cotegipe foresaw that Argentine politics would continue in a state of agitation and that civil war would present itself as the only settlement upon the horizon of the historical Presidency of Dr. Avellaneda. His anxiety was, therefore, to gain time. . . .

Brazil attempts to occupy the Territory in question.
About that time Brazil began, in fact, the foundation of military colonies upon the Territory in question. These acts endangered peace, and the Argentine government protested against them and affirmed the possession of the Territory, enacting laws to that effect, completing investigations which confirmed its rights.

I have said that peace was threatened, and this prudent minister [Mr. Dominguez, the Argentine Minister in Rio de Janeiro] thought that it was his duty to intimate it to the government in a private note of December, 1879, counseling a firm and sensible policy.

"At this present moment," he said, " I do not see any imminent danger; but presuming to know the policy and the means the statesmen of this country control and have always availed themselves of, I would always adjust the conduct of my country to the principle just mentioned. I would try to avoid giving them such pretext. I would spare no exhibition of friendship and justice towards them, but would maintain our forces on sea and land under a perfect organization and ready for defence, just as they hold theirs in readiness for aggression." . . .

The Argentine Civil War and the Empire, 1879.
A new, bloody and formidable civil war commenced in the Argentine Republic in 1879, and the Empire endeavored to occupy the disputed Territory, as stated in the "Memoir of the Minister of Foreign Affairs" of that country. It will be considered in a separate chapter in order to show how the Empire retreated from the position it had taken and disavowed its own acts, after giving entire satisfaction to the Argentine Nation. The civil war ended sooner than had been expected and its influence disappeared from the minds of the people with

Situation of both Nations.
the same rapidity. The Argentine Republic then began to devote itself to labor and to the perfecting of its institutions, as if it had not been agitated by such important events, and after the Federalization of Buenos Aires[1] the wealth and power of the country attained a most surprising development.

Meanwhile Brazil was following an opposite road. The monarchy was beginning to decline. The gradual emancipation of the slaves, which with all honor to his name was made by the Em-

[1] See this Argument, page 94.

peror, alienated from him the enthusiastic support of the wealthy and laborious classes, as well as of the planters and those engaged in industrial enterprises, who controlled the economic life of Brazil. The infirmities of the Emperor obliged him to make frequent journeys, and regencies did not make matters better, so that, favored by this bad state of affairs, the republican party increased. The germs of the downfall of the Empire were already incubating.

Under these circumstances it was imprudent to think of international adventures, so the Emperor put aside his old and notable political leader, the Baron de Cotegipe, who was always inclined to play with gunpowder.

The Memoir of the Minister of Foreign Affairs of the Argentine Republic, already quoted, speaking of this matter,[1] says that the interviews of Señor Dominguez with the Emperor and with the Minister of Foreign Relations, to which reference is made in the note cited of March 11, 1880, revealed a reaction in the Imperial policy against the plans of Baron de Cotegipe, and the Argentine minister advised that advantage be taken of it. The impossibility of agreeing upon the basis of the Treaty of 1857 was a serious obstacle in the way; but Señor Dominguez found it cleared up by the Imperial Minister, in the conferences of the third and seventh of March with the Emperor and with the Minister of Foreign Relations, in which they offered him a frank and clear opening for a *direct settlement* or *compromise*.

The Empire initiates a boundary arrangement.

Señor Dominguez addressed the Minister of Foreign Affairs of the Empire in April asking that he would determine the matter which had been discussed in the conference of March 7th. The Imperial Government, doubtless with the intent of paralyzing any action by the Argentine Government in respect to the military colonies, hastened to give instructions to the Baron Aranjo Gondim, its Minister to Buenos Aires, to treat for the arrangement of the question.[2]

A publication made by the Imperial Government in the "Diario Oficial" (Official Journal) on May 13, 1882, closed with a vital and very important declaration for the Argentine Republic. From reports asked for by the Cabinet about the true situation of the military colonies, it appeared that they were *outside of the disputed Territory.* The publication stated:

Brazil declares the Colonies outside the Territory in question.

---
[1] Argentine Evidence, Vol. I, page 674.
[2] Memoir of the Department of Foreign Affairs, Argentine Republic, 1892. Argentine Evidence, Vol. I, page 675.

The foundation of our military colonies cannot be a cause for protest, *because those colonies are situated outside of that Territory*, according to the memorandum presented by Councillor Doria to the General Assembly.

The uniform earnestness with which the Imperial Cabinets disapproved of the foundation of these colonies *upon the disputed Territory*, gives to the fact actually found to exist by the international survey and exploration ended in 1891 a clandestine character, opposed to the ostensible policy of the Government of Brazil, which grave circumstance must be considered in connection with the matters already stated, and clearly takes away all substance or effect from such foundations or alleged colonies.

Baron Cotegipe energetically replied to the publication in the *Official Journal* in a letter published in the "Globe"[1] of May 13, 1882. The Government also declared that the Minister of Brazil in Buenos Aires had been ordered to protest against the law confirming our possession and occupation of *Misiones*, but that he had not done so for reasons which seemed weighty. The letter of Baron Cotegipe, referred to, closed in the following manner:

Argentine action consummated.

> *The claim of the Argentines, meanwhile, subsists in all its vigor. It is true that one law, or one decree, does not give them any right; but it is a symptom, if not a proof, of a lack of consideration towards us that they pretend to cut the knot with the sword. It remains also in evidence that for the present there does not exist any act on our part demanding explanations, or taking any exception or making any protest whatever.*

The possession of the *Misiones*, which the Argentine Republic held uninterruptedly since the national organization was consummated, came from its Spanish inheritance. The Argentine law of 1881 was the exercise of a conclusive right of sovereignty, sanctioned historically and legally, and the Empire did not protest against nor object to the occupation which invalidated the clandestine acts of its employees.

Brazil instigates new negotiations, 1882.

The Brazilian Plenipotentiary in Buenos Aires, the Baron Araujo Gondim, received the instructions offered by Señor Dominguez in regard to the arrangement of the question.[2] On June 2, 1882, he notified the Argentine Government that—

[1] A daily Journal of Rio de Janeiro, and the organ of the Conservative Party.
[2] Memoir of Foreign Affairs, 1892, cited.

... wishing to avoid complications, and in order to maintain the friendly relations which happily exist between the two countries, he was charged with proposing to the Argentine Government the opening of negotiations for a definite adjustment of the question.¹

The negotiation was prolonged until 1884 without any result. Brazil was gaining time. Its political debility on the one hand, and the ardor of Argentine partisanship during the presidential campaign of 1885 on the other, led it to adopt this waiting policy. After the former failure Brazil adopted a new means to prolong these uncertainties. It in fact followed a double-faced policy. Its Minister in Buenos Aires suggested the postponement of the settlement of the matter, and that a third exploration be made of the Territory in dispute, by commissions composed of Engineers from both countries. Meanwhile in Rio de Janeiro the Emperor and his Minister of Foreign Affairs proposed to the Argentine Government a direct and immediate compromise. This double diplomatic action should be briefly examined, as a moral element affording a means of judging the policy of the Empire. The Minister from Brazil to the Argentine Republic made, in 1885, the following proposition: *Double-faced Policy of the Empire, 1885.*

> And wishing, on his part, to give a further token of his feelings, and conscious of his right, he has resolved to propose to the Argentine Government, as he does hereby propose, that both governments shall appoint a joint commission, composed of competent persons, in like number, to survey the four rivers Pepiry-Guazú, San Antonio, Chapecó and *Chopin*, which the Argentine Government calls Pequiry-Guazú, and San Antonio-Guazú, and the zone comprised between the same, preparing an accurate map of the rivers and all the disputed zone.²

When it is remembered that the map had been made in 1749, in 1759 and in 1791 by Geographers of the Crowns of Portugal and Spain, it will be easily understood that this proposition was simply a means of gaining time. The Arbitration frankly proposed by the Argentine Government in 1877 was preferable. *Basis for an arrangement.*

Meanwhile the Argentine Plenipotentiary in Rio de Janeiro wrote about the same time to his government that at the end of 1884 the Minister of Foreign Affairs of the Empire had presented to him a basis

---
¹ See this Argument, page 103.
² The facts here related in my Argument are documented in the Memoir of Foreign Affairs, cited, Vol. I, page 675 *et seq.*

for a direct arrangement or compromise. The Argentine Minister secured the paper, forwarded it to Buenos Aires, and in a confidential letter asked instructions after it had been examined, and that any modifications of form or counter proposals which seemed proper should be indicated.

The Empire proposes to divide the Territory equitably. The Argentine Government signed and issued on January 5, 1885, full powers, so that its Minister in Rio de Janeiro might start in earnest the conciliatory negotiation proposed by the Imperial Council for the division of the Territory of Misiones in an equitable manner, upon the basis of submitting to arbitration the doubtful questions of law and according a pecuniary indemnity to the losing party in that suit.[1]

The conferences continued. The Argentine Minister noted meanwhile that the Imperial Council was playing a double game, which has been intimated before in this Argument. In Rio de Janeiro it presented the draft of an immediate compromise, in Buenos Aires, the postponement of the negotiation, suggesting the method of a treaty for the prior exploration of the Territory.

The President of the Council of Ministers, Councillor Dantas, the Baron de Cabo Frio, *a traditional authority upon the matter, and a part of the Ministry were in accord with the Argentine Minister in regard to the compromise, and so pledged themselves, officially and privately, by acts and words.*

The Council of State having been convened, the arrangement was approved by the majority, but the minority was in favor of a previous survey. The Imperial government, however, did not reply to the counter proposal or modifications suggested by the Argentine Minister in the plan of the Ministry of Foreign Relations, and keeping him in ignorance of the favorable report of the Council of State, he was told that the Government deemed it necessary to reply to an Argentine *Counter Memorandum* before deciding upon the arrangement.

The Emperor personally manages the affair. When this reply was in the hands of the Argentine Government, and the invitation given by the Imperial Minister in Buenos Ayres to stipulate for the previous survey was favorably accepted in that city, the government of Rio stopped its progress towards the arrangement; and the Emperor, having deviated for a moment from the diplomatic and constitutional practice of his Court, took advantage of a visit of social courtesy of the Argentine Minister to give the latter, quite suddenly, the reply that he should have received through the Minister of

[1] Argentine Evidence, Vol. 1, Memoir of the Department of Foreign Affairs, cited, page 698 *et seq.*

Foreign Relations of the Empire, and which he had been long looking for, about the direct settlement. The Emperor was in favor of the previous survey, and left the other negotiation in abeyance.

The Argentine diplomats were candid, and showed their good faith. The negotiation of a direct arrangement was put in protocols. I present to the Arbitrator in the "Argentine Evidence," Group D, No. 26, these protocols, in virtue of which I have made the preceding narration, corroborated furthermore by the Argentine Memoir of 1892.

The treaty providing for the third or fourth official exploration of the Territory was signed in 1885, and when referring to the demarcation I shall examine it. Substantially it said: *Treaty for International Exploration of the Territory, 1885*

> The Joint Commission appointed by the two Commissions referred to shall, in accordance with the instructions annexed to this treaty, survey the rivers Pepiry-Guazú and San Antonio and the two lying East of the same, known in Brazil by the names of Chapecó and *Chopin*, and which are called by the Argentines Pequiry-Guazú and San Antonio-Guazú, as well as the territory contained between the four.[1]

Meanwhile, I will state that the Commissions of Brazil and the Argentine Republic, presided over by Baron de Capanema and by Col. José Ignacio de Garmendia, respectively, began their operations on the 28th day of September, 1885, and finished the same on the 24th day of September, 1891, without a single break in their harmony.

The previous treaty of exploration indicated clearly the ignorance of the geographers, the people, and both governments as to the natural characteristics of part of the Territory in controversy. And, in fact, the treaty was confused to such an extent that instead of indicating the San Antonio-Guazú, or river "C. D.," as the eastern boundary of the Territory above the Pepiry-Guazú of the Spaniards, that is the river "D. E.",[2] it gave as the boundary (A) a *fifth river called Chopin*, which had never before appeared in this international controversy. It was of course a new element of disturbance, for it diminished the area of the disputed Territory in prejudice of the claim of the Argentine Republic and in favor of Brazil. *Errors of both governments in the Treaty of 1885.*

In the plan referred to in the preceding paragraph the diminished Territory is delineated in lighter black lines and is enclosed between the rivers "C D E" and *Chopin*. In the engraving it bears the letter "A."

[1] "Argentine Evidence," Vol. 1, page 113 and following.
[2] See engraving in this Argument at page 143.

Brazil recognizes its error   On arriving on the ground the Argentine Commissioners claimed the rectification of the treaty as to the mistake committed. The Brazilian commissioners recognized the mistake but refused to rectify it without a previous order from their Government, confining themselves to simply respecting the express text of the Treaty of 1885. And in fact there was reason in their position. It was a matter requiring to be settled by both governments, as it was, and this settlement declared that the Argentine Commissioners were right. The Treaty of 1885, so carelessly drawn up by both Cabinets, was corrected, and it was declared that the disputed Territory extended West as far as the "*San Antonio-Guazú*" of Oyarvide (rivers "C D" of the plan, page 143 of this Argument) lately called "Yangada" by the Brazilians. The fact is stated in the Memoir of the Minister of Foreign Relations of Brazil for the year 1888, pages 11 and 13, which is presented to the Arbitrator, and in the Arbitration Treaty, Article I.

Near the settlement, Decline of the Empire.   In 1888 matters became worse in Brazil. The Emperor, an upright man, beloved and prudent,—the only basis of the Empire,—was rapidly losing his physical strength and moral force. The end was approaching for him and for his work of fifty years, as reactionary agitations began to move the social currents. The Argentine Republic, on the contrary, was wealthy and strong, proud of having passed ten consecutive years in peace and of the extraordinary progress made in its internal affairs. The *Misiones* question then entered a new period; it was nearing its final settlement.

The Empire initiates a compromise.   The Argentine Government, perceiving at last the double game which had preceded the negotiation of the treaty of postponement of 1885, had assumed a severe and dignified attitude towards the Empire, and on its part closed all negotiation. The new Argentine Minister in Rio de Janeiro carried, in fact, the following instructions:

> The discussion between the Republic and the Empire in regard to the boundary line of the Territory of *Misiones* being located in this capital, it is proper that Minister Moreno take no notice of it, and in case he should be invited to confer upon the same, decline all intervention, confining himself to stating that, pending the discussion at Buenos Aires, his Government has not given him any instructions upon the subject, and that any proposal that the Imperial government may be pleased to make, it can do so, as heretofore, through its plenipotentiary.[1]

[1] "Argentine Evidence," page 143.

On April 25, 1889, the Argentine Minister in Brazil communicated to his Government the fact that the Empire was inclined to arrange the matter, and the Minister of Foreign Affairs made the following propositions:

 Let us sign a compromise that shall contain the following propositions: Proposition for friendly arrangement.

 FIRST. The negotiations between the Argentine Plenipotentiary and the Brazilian Plenipotentiary shall be closed within thirty days.

 SECOND. Should there be no direct and definite solution found during the said lapse of time, a convention shall be signed on the last day of the stipulated term, and the matter shall be submitted to arbitration.[1] . . .

This direct proposition was followed by the promise of the Minister of Foreign Affairs of the Empire to go to the Rio de la Plata and to there join his Argentine colleague in Montevideo, the Capital of the Republic of Uruguay, for the purpose of discussing the compromise, for which reason the latter answered in a confidential note, which stated: The Imperial Minister of Foreign Affairs promises to go to the Rio de la Plata to make the arrangement.

 I consider of great importance what Your Excellency communicates to me in regard to Señor Rodrigo da Silva's attitude in the question of *Misiones*. . . .

. . . .

 An equitable settlement would meet with no opposition by public opinion in this country; far from it, it would be applauded by everybody, regardless of political colors. I understand that such would be the case with you. Can it be obtained without resorting to third parties? I think so, and the Government prefers this method, which shows that both Argentines and Brazilians have sufficient prudence to settle their differences themselves, avoiding unpleasant discussions.

 I am happy to learn that Señor Rodrigo da Silva has no objection to going to Montevideo, and that we shall meet there to settle the old dispute; but I think we ought not to take that step without a previous agreement; that is to say, we should not meet without some assurance of an understanding.[2]

The Memoir of the Argentine Department of Foreign Affairs, cited, narrates the facts in detail, which are only briefly referred to here, and

---

[1] "Argentine Evidence," Vol. I, page 708 and following.
[2] "Argentine Evidence," Vol. I, page 709.

that document will be found in the latter part of Volume 1 of the "Argentine Evidence."

Reserved attitude of the Argentine Government towards the new projections.

Consequently, the Argentine Government replied under reservations, accepting the negotiation, but insisting upon its withdrawal from Rio de Janeiro.

Treaty of 1889.

Both Governments having agreed to compromise their differences, they sought to fix upon the bases of the treaty. The meeting of the Ministers of Foreign Affairs of both countries, which had been arranged for in Montevideo, did not take place on account of the political tempest which had arisen in Brazil. The Minister of the Empire frankly informed the Argentine Government of this by a telegram which was presented by the Brazilian Minister in Buenos Aires, and read as follows:

> Telegram to the Brazilian Minister in Buenos Aires. May 7. 1889. Inform Dr. Quirno Costa[1] that I cannot leave the Empire on account of political labors.
>
> RODRIGO DA SILVA.

The Cabinet was dissolved. The new Ministry accepted, nevertheless, the pending negotiation, and on the 7th of September, 1889, the Preliminary Treaty was signed. It is included in the "Argentine Evidence" and the substance of it may be stated as follows:[2]

> The discussion of the legal right which each of the high contracting parties claims to have to the Territory disputed between them, shall be closed within the term of ninety days from the conclusion of the survey of the ground where the headwaters of the rivers Chapecó or Pequiry-Guazú, and *Jangada* or San Antonio-Guazú, are situated. . . .
>
> *If the term of the preceding article should expire without a friendly solution*, the question shall be submitted to the arbitration of the President of the United States of America, to whom the high contracting parties shall apply within the next following sixty days, requesting him to accept the charge.

Brazilian suggestion for a friendly solution.

A few days later the Argentine Minister informed the Government

---

[1] Foreign Affairs Minister of the Argentine Republic.
[2] The document referring to the matter discussed here has been published officially by the Argentine government. See Memoir of the Foreign Office for 1892, already quoted. Argentine Evidence, Vol. 1, page 717.

that the Minister of Foreign Affairs of the Empire had suggested a friendly arrangement or division of the Territory. His note said:

In the course of a conversation I had yesterday with Minister Diana I understood that they would accept a direct settlement which would fix the natural boundaries, and establish the obligation to pecuniarily indemnify the contracting party who, by the decision of the Arbitrator, should have lost some territory in marking out the dividing line.
A price shall be set per square kilometer of the Territory in dispute.
The legal question once determined by the President of the United States, and the kilometric extent of the whole disputed ground and of the zone which shall be agreed upon beforehand for each one of the contracting parties having been accurately ascertained, the country most favored in territorial extent shall pay to the other for the excess of land received.

The letter reached Buenos Aires just at the time when the Portfolio of Foreign Relations had been intrusted to me by the President of the Republic. The Argentine Government was animated with the generous impulses that tended to a compromise, honorable for both countries; but it could not forget the teachings of experience. Therefore I summoned the Argentine Minister at Rio de Janeiro to come down to Buenos Aires, and in a general meeting of the Cabinet on the 28th day of October, 1889, after a rigid examination of the situation, the Government approved the plan which I had the honor to submit, and the essential points of the question.

Instructions given to the Argentine Minister.

Accordingly, the following official instructions were prepared, which the Argentine Minister at Rio de Janeiro received and was required to comply with:

BUENOS AIRES, *October* 28, 1889.
To the Argentine Minister in Brazil, Don Enrique B. Moreno.

The treaty of arbitration between the Republic and the Empire of Brazil having been approved and exchanged, this government remembers with pleasure that you sent in your confidential note of the ninth day of September last a general form of settlement, which was presented to you by His Excellency Councillor Diana, Minister of Foreign Relations of Brazil.
Though said form, based upon a pecuniary indemnification of the party losing by the arbitration, which it leaves in force, is not admissible, this Government thinks that His Majesty's Government will not on that account modify its noble purpose of hasten-

ing the definite conclusion of the question, discussing other combinations.

Therefore you will signify to Councillor Diana, referring to the form of his confidential note of September 9th, that this Government does not deem it proper to make a question of which the legal right has always been upon the side of the Republic, the subject of pecuniary indemnification; but that it would be pleased to reciprocate the noble purpose of His Majesty's Government by discussing a direct settlement upon the general basis, plainly and distinctly understood, that a frontier shall be fixed which will put an amicable end to the dispute. This frontier would pass by the prominent and known features of the Territory in dispute, being established in a manner agreeable for both countries.

In view of the good will and harmony of the diplomatic relations of both nations, this government believes that the solution indicated will be easily attained; and if His Majesty's Government should accept the negotiation in that form, you will propose to Councillor Diana the holding of a telegraphic conference with the undersigned to fix the said frontier.

Your Excellency may hint in such a case, that this Government is moved by the desire of facilitating with generous views a fair settlement, for this treaty will permanently consolidate the union of two brotherly peoples, who are united by sacrifices of blood and by the highest ideals of civilization. You may add that with such feelings we would accept a frontier which could be marked out between . . . in the conference before indicated, and its survey upon the ground would be entrusted to a joint commission. To illustrate this part of the instructions a plan is enclosed, sealed by the Sub-Secretary of this Department, which will serve as a basis for the interchange of ideas which you are authorized to make. You may state, if necessary, that this government does not deem it indispensable, in order to treat on the direct settlement, that the surveys now being made at the *Misiones* should be terminated.

Should the Government of His Majesty entertain different views, Your Excellency must be reserved, without advancing any declaration in the name of this Government, and communicate the facts for proper action.

ESTANISLAO S. ZEBALLOS.

At the same time the Emperor had in mind projects for the division of the Territory. An authorized publication made by the "*Jornal do Commercio*" of Rio de Janeiro, on July 24th, 1891, said:

<small>Proposition made in Brazil and accepted by the Emperor.</small>

It has been alleged that the Emperor had entertained a project devised by Señor Andrés Rebouças. This project substantially provided:

" The parallels shall be taken between the four rivers Pepiry,

San Antonio, Chapecó, and Yangada, and the geometrical meridian shall be marked by a line of points.

b To transfer it to the ground and build up a railroad on it, which will be done by a committee of five members, two Argentines, two Brazilians, and one drawn by lot between the two countries.

c The expenses to be equally divided by the two nations, as well as those of the survey; the profits also being divided.

d The marginal zones to be neutralized and distributed in lots of twenty and thirty *hectares* for settlement by European immigrants, who would be installed therein.

e Both countries to be forbidden forever to build permanent or temporary fortifications between the rivers Paraná, Uruguay or Yguazú.

f Both countries to be bound to adopt as a guide this procedure of technical arbitration for all other boundary questions.

There is no doubt that such a project was sent to the Secretary of Foreign Relations.

Dr. Nilo Peçanha, a National Deputy, wrote to the "*Gazeta de Noticias*," of Rio de Janeiro, in connection with the discussion about the existence of this project, a letter, in which he said:

I append below the project of technical arbitration of Doctor Andrés Rebouças, endorsed by the Emperor a few months before the revolution of the fifteenth of November. Had the Republic not been proclaimed on that day the project would have been converted into a treaty. Dom Pedro thought it excellent, and referred it to the Minister of Foreign Relations through Baron de Loreto, Minister of the Empire at the time, and the Viscount de Cabo Frio passed judgment upon it. It is, therefore, an official document.

The Council of State took up this matter in 1889. The idea of omitting the Arbitrator and settling the question directly by a spontaneous international act was submitted to the Cabinet and to the Council of State, according to official data authorized by the ex-ministers of the Empire and published by the Press of Rio de Janeiro. The opinions of the Ministers and members of the Council were printed in the "*Jornal do Commercio*" of July 10, 1891.[1]

The Viscount of Ouro Preto, President of the last Imperial Cabinet, gave the following opinion: <small>Opinion of the Council of State in favor of a compromise.</small>

To the first Article I reply: *A compromise, having as a basis the division of the Territory in dispute, is acceptable; however, not*

[1] In the Argentine Legation, at the disposal of the Arbitrator.

as proposed by the Argentine Government, but as counselled by the learned Baron de Cabo Frio. . . .

The Visconde de San Luis of Maranhao, in reply to these questions, prepared, as indicated, by the Chief of the Imperial Cabinet in order to consult the judgment of the Council of State, agreed with the opinion of the Viscount of Cabo Frio, and thought that "Brazil ought not to oppose any reasonable proposal of compromise, tending to the division of the Territory." He added:

> Notwithstanding the full conviction we have of our rights, and even if we lose a part of the Territory which legitimately belongs to us and which we have always claimed, yet we cannot advocate any other policy; but it is necessary that the agreement to be entered into shall be governed by the principles of equality, imposing sacrifices on both parties, so that one shall not be benefited at the expense of the other, thus offending the dignity of the nation.

Councillor Manuel Francisco Correia expressed his opinion in this manner:

> Any proposal having as a basis the division of the contested Territory is not a matter that can be rejected *in limine* in the settlement of the boundary question. The question is as to the fixing of the extreme points, in view of which the dividing line is to be traced, or, in other words, in the just division of the Territory in dispute.

The Viscount of Cabo Frio, Sub-secretary of the Department of Foreign Relations, who has preserved in that capacity the traditions of the *Misiones* dispute, and whose authority is respected by Brazilians of the Empire and of the Republic, was also an advocate of a direct settlement, dividing the contested Territory by a natural line, excluding the fraction of territory comprised between the Yangada and the Chopin.

Finally the National Deputy, Brigadier-General Dionisio de Castro Cerqueira, a Boundary Commissioner,[1] solemnly affirms in a letter published by the "*Jornal do Commercio*" of July 21, 1891, that in starting for the exploration of the Yangada, or San Antonio-Guazú of Oyarvide,

---

[1] Now Brazilian Minister in Washington and one of the Ministers accredited to defend the Republic of Brazil before the Arbitrator in this case.

in 1889, he went to the Emperor, to receive his orders, and the latter told him in the presence of several personages:

> Go and finish that matter as soon as possible, for we can determine the question ourselves without having recourse to a third party. We do not need any Arbitrator.

The Ministers and Councillors of the Empire disclosed in the meeting their fundamental purpose to exclude war from the possible solutions, preferring a direct settlement with the Argentine Republic, which had demanded it as a condition of peace. This political plan is explicity stated in the words of the President of the Cabinet, the Visconde de Ouro Preto.

This was the state of the negotiation for a compromise, or equitable division of the disputed Territory, when suddenly came the downfall of the Empire which had promoted and discussed it. On the 15th of November of the same year, 1889, there was proclaimed the establishment of the Republic of the United States of Brazil. *Downfall of the Empire.*

During the first days of uncertainty and uneasiness of the new Republic, her elder sister in South America gave her encouragement and helped her on her way. The Argentine Republic was, in fact, the first conutry which recognized the advent of the new Republic, and entered into diplomatic intercourse with it. This was done by virtue of the decree of December 3, 1889, which the Brazilian people hailed with joy, as a firm support in those initial and solemn moments. The Republican Government of Brazil hastened to give testimony to this patriotic feeling, ordering the Argentine colors to be hoisted at the mainmast head of its men-of-war, while its fortresses saluted them with the royal homage of their guns. The Argentine decree can be read at page 730 of the first Volume of the Argentine Evidence. *Argentine-Brazilian confraternity.*

This action, which was taken spontaneously, produced a deep political impression in Rio de Janeiro. Señor Bocayuva, the mouthpiece of the Brazilian Republic and its first Minister of Foreign Affairs, acknowledged it in the last publications which he made, and the minds of Brazilian statesmen of the Revolution were inclined to carry out acts evincing a spontaneous and sincere feeling of confraternity with the Argentine Republic.

The Argentine government on its part affirmed the instructions given to its Minister on the twenty-eighth day of October,[1] and when *Diplomatic attitude of the Argentine Government.*

---
[1] See page 207 of this Argument.

it considered that the new Republic had been definitely established and in regular relations with other countries, the Cabinet at Buenos Ayres sent to the Argentine Minister in Rio de Janeiro the following despatch :

BUENOS AIRES, *December* 2, 1889.

Continue diplomatic service, as per instructions received by you in this city.

Advise me of any news regarding authority I give you in this telegram.

E. S. ZEBALLOS.

The Republican policy repudiates the errors of the Monarchy.
The high officials who had founded the Brazilian Republic were remarkable men from all points of view, soldiers, journalists, professors, jurists. Their names and occupations in the new government were as follows :

The Marshal Deodoro de Fonseca, head of the Provisional Government ; Aristides Lobo, Minister of the Interior ; Benjamin Constant, Minister of War ; Dr. Rui Barboza, Minister of Hacienda ; Quintino Bocayuva, Minister of Foreign Affairs ; Dr. Campo Salles, Minister of Justice ; Eduardo Wandelkolk, Minister of Marine ; and Demetrio Ribeiro, Minister of Agriculture.

They condemned by sincere and eloquent acts the policy of postponement, alarms, and an armed peace, which had been always astutely sustained by the Empire, and disclosed a new horizon for American international relations, proclaiming equity, good faith and friendly sentiments as the diplomatic resources which should assure the future and glory of free institutions in that region of the world.

Brazil proposes a division of the Territory.
When the Republican government took up the consideration of ordinary business relating to its foreign relations, the Argentine Minister presented to it a private memorandum, of which the Argentine Government had not nor has it now any official record, recalling the condition in which the *Misiones* dispute had been left at the time of the downfall of the Empire, and the negotiations for direct arrangement or compromise. The Argentine Government officially published a statement of the facts concerning the matter in the Memoir of the Foreign Office for 1892, already quoted.[1]

At the session of the Chamber of Deputies of Brazil which was held on August 6, 1891, to discuss the Bocayuva-Zeballos Treaty,[2] that

[1] Argentine Evidence, Vol. I, page 735.
[2] Señor Bocayuva, negotiator of the treaty, referred to below as Minister of Foreign Affairs.

eminent Brazilian republican confirmed the statements which have been made.

The published extracts read as follows :

His Excellency postponed the question, thinking that it was premature at the moment of a struggle against serious internal difficulties.

Upon a subsequent examination of the advantages that would result for American politics, and especially for the international policy which Brazil ought to uphold in this part of America, Your Excellency judged that it was really of national convenience to determine this question, so that the relations between both peoples should be thoroughly cemented.

The Government communicated this officially to the Nation, advising it of the making of the treaty in an article published under the head of "*A questão de Misiones*" (The question of Misiones) in the "*Diario oficial*" (Official Journal) of February 18, 1890, which said :¹

The Provisional Government having found, among the *spoils* of the Monarchy, and therefore pending, the settlement relative to the *Territory of Misiones*, deemed it convenient to examine it at once, in order to decide it in accordance with the dictates of patriotism, which amounts to saying in harmony with the great interests of the Nation.

Placed thus in the presence of a diplomatic quarrel of unquestionable importance, and which presented itself with a certain urgency for a speedy decision, as it had been the subject which had engaged the attention of the old régime in the last days of its existence, *the present government resolved, at the initiative and suggestion of the proper Minister*, to examine it thoroughly, submitting it to discussion in successive conferences, in which the members would have an opportunity to study its different features and give their opinion as to how it should best be decided. It was thus by this full and complete understanding and collective Government action, sealed with the stamp of its entire approval, that the resolution was prepared by virtue of which the Minister of Foreign Relations was to proceed to Montevideo, the place selected for the meeting of the representatives of the Brazilian and Argentine governments.

The Argentine Government recognizing this attitude of the Republic of Brazil, the Minister of Foreign Affairs addressed to his agent in Rio de Janeiro the following telegram :

Treaty of Division of the territory. 1890.

---

¹ Books of the "Argentine Evidence."

BUENOS AYRES, *January* 3, 1890.

Significance of news transmitted pleases greatly. Complying with instructions, arrange day and hour for telegraphic conference with Minister of that government, you bringing plan signed by this Department.[1]

ESTANISLAO S. ZEBALLOS.

The Argentine Government refers to the facts stated in the Memoir cited and to the negotiation through its Plenipotentiary *ad hoc* the Minister of Foreign Affairs, for the full details of this matter.[2]

After the telegraphic conference of January 7, 1890, in which we agreed upon the basis of the treaty, I sent to Señor Bocayuva a despatch inviting him to a meeting in an intermediate place, at Montevideo for instance, in order to give it a definitive form. He replied:

> Thanks for your Excellency's kind words. I shall soon proceed to Montevideo; will advise date of departure. I reiterate my high appreciation.
> BOCAYUVA.

Treaty of Montevideo.

Upon Señor Bocayuva's arrival at Montevideo, in company with the Argentine Minister to Rio de Janeiro, at the first meeting the former handed me a project of a treaty, the original of which I kept and which is on file in the archives of the Department of Foreign Relations. It contained in the text of the first Article, and in the guise of accidental phrases, solemn and important clauses, which had not been mentioned by Señor Bocayuva during the interrupted conference, nor by the Argentine Minister in his communications.

The clause to which my attention was particularly called in the first Article was the one reading as follows:

> The frontier line shall be drawn between each of the extreme points and the central point, in such a manner that, SPARING THE BRAZILIAN SETTLEMENTS, the best natural boundaries shall be made use of, *the same to be constituted* by straight lines only where they may be inevitable. . . .

At the telegraphic conference Señor Bocayuva proposed quite the contrary to me, that is to say, to draw the straight line in preference. If such wording had been proposed to me by telegraph in its entirety, it would not have been accepted, on account of the vagueness of the criterion given to the future Demarcators to make use of natural

---
[1] Of October, 1889. See page 207 of this Argument.
[2] See Argentine Evidence, Vol. I, page 736 *et seq.*

boundaries which were not designated, describing curves in preference, to save the *Brazilian settlements*.

My proposition of the central point had a plain and clear object: that the boundary line should leave in our jurisdiction the Colony of *Campo Eré*, founded in 1880 by the Brazilians in the contested Territory. By the wording of the treaty prepared at Rio de Janeiro this result could not be attained, because the clause about drawing curves to save the Brazilian towns would have created, among the Demarcators at least, a fundamental misunderstanding.

I therefore proposed to Señor Bocayuva to make clear the phrase setting forth that the boundary should spare the *Argentine or Brazilian settlements* which it found *in its path*, from the mouth of each river to the central point. My colleague accepted this amendment, and the Argentine sovereignty over the Colony of *Campo Eré* was thus recognized.

I added other minor modifications of detail which were accepted, and which are indicated by italics in the comparative texts following:

SEÑOR BOCAYUVA'S PROJECT PRESENTED IN MONTEVIDEO.	DEFINITE TEXT AGREED UPON AND SIGNED IN MONTEVIDEO.
ARTICLE 1.	ARTICLE 1.
The frontier of the Republics of the United States of Brazil and Argentine in the contested Territory of *Misiones* begins at the mouth and right bank of the Chapecó on the Uruguay, crosses the watershed of the waters of the Yguazú and of the Uruguay, between Campo Eré and Campo Santa Ana at the nearest point to the one situated at 26° 20′ latitude South, and 53° of longitude, according to the map of the Joint Exploring Commission of the said Territory, and ending at the mouth and left bank of the Chopin on the Yguazú.	The frontier of the Republic of the United States of Brazil and of the Argentine Republic in the contested Territory of *Misiones* begins at the mouth and right bank of the Chapecó or *Pequiry-Guazú* on the Uruguay, crosses the *divortia acquarum* of the Yguazú and of the Uruguay, between Campo Eré and Campo Santa Ana, *at the middle point of the distance between the settlement of Coelho in the former Campo, and the bridge over the river Santa Ana upon the road to the Sierra de la Factura*, according to the map of the Joint Exploring Commission of the said Territory, and ending at the mouth and left bank of the Chopin, on the Yguazú.
Between each one of the extreme points and the central point, the frontier line shall be drawn in such a manner that, sparing the Brazilian settlements, the best natural boundaries shall be made use of, it being constituted by straight lines only where it is inevitable, and leaving in the exclusive possession of Brazil, in all their course, the said rivers Chapecó and Chopin.	Between each one of the extreme points and the central point the frontier line shall be drawn, *making use of the best natural boundaries, and sparing the settlements of both nations that it may find in its path*, it being constituted by straight lines only where it is inevitable. The said rivers Chopin and Chapecó shall remain, in all their course, in the exclusive possession of Brazil.

Article II.

The high contracting parties bind themselves to respect the possession of the settlers who, after the dividing line shall have been traced, may remain on one side or the other, and to grant to them property deeds, provided they prove that they were settlers one year prior to this date.

Article II.

The high contracting parties bind themselves to respect the possession of the settlers who, after the *frontier line* shall have been drawn, *remain* on one side or the other, and to grant to them property deeds, provided they prove that they were settlers since one year prior to this date, *with settlements of a permanent character.*

Article III.

The two high contracting parties shall, in due time, agree upon organizing a Joint Commission which shall trace the dividing line, and shall furnish it, by common accord, with the necessary instructions.

Article III.

The two high contracting parties shall in due time agree upon organizing a Joint Commission which shall trace the dividing line, and shall furnish it, by common accord, with the necessary instructions.

Article IV.

The Joint Commission shall submit what direction is proper to be given to the dividing line, in conformity with Article I of the treaty, and with the instructions referred to in Article III, and the proposition being approved by both Governments, if they judge the demarcation to be necessary, it shall be proceeded with, subject to the instructions which shall be given them.

Article IV.

The Joint Commission *shall project the tracing that corresponds to the dividing line, in conformity with Article I of this treaty,* and with the instructions referred to in Article III, and *the said project being approved by both Governments, the demarcation upon the ground shall be proceeded with, if the high contracting parties deem it necessary.*

Article V.

This treaty shall be ratified and the ratifications exchanged at Rio de Janeiro with the shortest possible delay, after it shall have been approved by the Argentine Congress and the Constituent Assembly of the United States of Brazil.

Article V.

This treaty shall be ratified and the ratifications exchanged in the city of Rio de Janeiro *immediately after its approbation* by the Argentine Congress and by the Constitutent Assembly of the United States of Brazil.[1]

The Government of Uruguay and the Treaty.

When ready to sign the Treaty at the House of the Argentine Legation, we agreed to do it in the halls of the Uruguayan Government, whose distinguished hospitality had been tendered to both missions. We, therefore, sent the following communication:

Montevideo, *January* 24, 1890.

Sir: The undersigned, Ministers of Foreign Relations of the Argentine Republic and of the United States of Brazil, have received with the highest consideration the offer of the halls of the Palace of the Government to perform the international act for which they have met in Montevideo, and although they had agreed

---

[1] The text of the treaty appears in the "Argentine Evidence," Vol. 1, page 125.

to do this in the House of the Argentine Legation, they take pleasure in informing Your Excellency that, as a token of respect and cordiality towards the Eastern Republic of Uruguay, they will meet for the purpose stated at the Palace of the Government.

In communicating this we beg that you will present to His Excellency, the President of the Republic, our feelings of gratitude, and our best wishes for the welfare of the nation and of his person.

With the assurances of our distinguished consideration, we greet Your Excellency.

ESTANISLAO S. ZEBALLOS.
QUINTINO BOCAYUVA.

To His Excellency, the Minister of Foreign Relations of the *Republica Oriental del Uruguay*, Don Oscar Hordeñana.

Signing of the Treaty.

The Chiefs and adjutants of the respective Boundary Commissions were present, and therefore I proposed to my colleague that Colonels Garmendia and Cerqueira should exchange the maps of the *Misiones*, drawn by their respective parties, and mark out on the copies the stipulated boundary, signing the maps, and making a record thereof.

Señor Bocayuva accepted this suggestion, as tending to prevent any doubt in the future. Colonel Garmendia produced the general plan of *Misiones*, according to the labors of the Commission under his orders, and Colonel Cerqueira exhibited the corresponding Brazilian map. The work of both having been compared, they were found to be remarkably accordant. Colonel Cerqueira proceeded to draw on both the central point, sketching the boundary with his own hand; and this done, both Boundary Commissions signed the maps and exchanged the same. The Brazilian Minister received that of Argentine, and I kept the Brazilian one. This is the document which was drawn up:[1]

On January 25, 1890, at the Government Palace of the Eastern Republic of Uruguay, in Montevideo, the President of the Argentine Republic being at the time Señor Doctor Don Miguel Juarez Celman, and the Chief of the Provisional Government of the Republic of the States of Brazil being Marshal-General Don Deodoro da Fonseca; there met together Colonels Don José Ignacio Garmendia, First Commissioner and head of the Argentine Boundary Commission, and Don Dionisio Evangelista de Castro Cerqueira, Third Commissioner of the Brazilian Commission, and chief *pro tempore* of the same:

And they declared authentic the plans of the Territory in dispute between the two countries, drawn by the Joint Commission, signed by them and presented to the Ministers of Foreign Rela-

---

[1] See the Map, page 5.

tions of the two Republics, Doctor Don Estanislao S. Zeballos and Don Quintino Bocayuva.

By these plans the agreement of the months of the rivers Pepiry-Guazú, or Chapecó, and Chopin, and of the intermediate point, situated half way between the bridge over the river Santa Ana and Coelho's farm on the road leading from Sierra de la Factura to Campo Eré, is verified.

José Ignacio Garmendia.   *Dionisio E. de Castro Cerqueira.*[1]

This document and the practical work upon the plans rendered unnecessary for many years the setting of landmarks upon the intermediate lines between the centre and the extremes. It was for that reason that the Article of the project providing for the demarcation was modified.

The officials of the Government of Uruguay assembled in the hall of the President of that Republic and awaited the termination of the act. We went in to greet them, exchanging reciprocal and cordial congratulations. The President said that the Republic of Uruguay considered this matter one of great importance, and that he desired to celebrate it with an official banquet. This took place at the Government Palace, the Argentine Republic occupying a place on the right.

The Minister of Brazil in the Argentine Republic.

We then proceeded to Buenos Aires, where Señor Bocayuva and his suite were warmly received. The illustrious guest signified his desire to go to Córdoba and salute the President of the Republic, who was there during his vacation, and the excursion was extended over the neighboring provinces amid flattering demonstrations for the Brazilian republican.

The general political views of both Cabinets being perfectly harmonized, new and extensive prospects were opened for the advancement of South America when Señor Bocayuva returned to his country to report the result of his mission. The monarchical party declared, through Baron de Ladario, that this treaty "is one of the greatest crimes of the Revolutionary *Junta*, which History will record with amazement."[2]

Rejection of the Treaty in Brazil.

The President of the Argentine Republic stated in his message in May, 1891:

> There is no record in the history of questions concerning the Rio de la Plata of a more full or solemn debate. All the Brazilian

---

[1] "Argentine Evidence," Vol. I, page 125.
[2] This Argument, page 12.

Press took part in it, *the dethroned Emperor and the old chiefs of the Cabinet, State Ministers, Plenipotentiaries, geographers, publicists and boundary demarcators, who during the last ten years have been concerned in the politics of Brazil.*

The compact was brought before the Congress under such auspices and was rejected, in spite of the spirited and glittering arguments of the negotiator, Señor Bocayuva. The confidence in the strength of the Argentine title explains why that long campaign and great diplomatic agitation did not produce in the Argentine Republic any unpleasant impressions.

The rejection of the treaty, which Marshal Deodoro and his Cabinet had initiated and unanimously approved after its conclusion, was the first symptom of the loss of prestige and the approaching downfall of that Government. Monarchical passions found an outlet in the negotiation, and with less concern for future events than for the interest of the moment, the feelings of the negotiator, Señor Bocayuva, were wounded in a merciless manner, and the negotiation was condemned.[1]

The judgment of the Special Committee of the Chamber of Deputies could not, however, avoid certain declarations which affirmed the Argentine titles, inasmuch as they recognize the validity of the documentary right between Spain and Portugal.[2] Parliamentary Declarations favorable to the Argentine Republic.

I have already explained in the first pages of this Argument the causes which were so foreign to the first candid action of the new and yet unsteady republican government and which finally resulted in the rejection of this noble work. But it nevertheless remains as a moral element of conviction and as a high example of the noble sacrifice which the Argentine Republic was resolved to make in deference to Humanity and the citizenship of South America. Causes of rejection.

Shortly after the rejection of the treaty of Montevideo had been obtained, the situation of Brazil grew worse. Marshal Peixoto, the Vice-President of the first republican government, preserved due respect for the work of the Republic which had been annulled by the monarchical majority, thought he could bring about a final settlement of the *Misiones* dispute, and renewed the rejected compromise through his Minister in Buenos Aires, who opened confidential and verbal negotiations to this effect. The President of the Argentine Republic, Dr. Don Carlos Pellegrini, with whom the Brazilian Minister spoke personally, in the presence of the Minister of Foreign Affairs, New attempt made by Brazil to arrange the matter, 1891.

---

[1] "Argentine Evidence," Vol. I, page 749.
[2] See the documents in the "Argentine Evidence," Vol. I, page 749.

stated the facts in the terms of the testimony that I present to the Arbitrator in Vol. I of Argentine Evidence, page 637 et seq.[1]

Second attempt, 1891

In 1891 the author of this Argument, being for the second time Minister of Foreign Affairs of the Argentine Republic, the Brazilian Minister suggested in a private and confidential manner a new arrangement. It is set forth in the quoted Memoir of the Foreign Office.

The Government of Marshal Deodoro having been overthrown and replaced by that of the Vice-President, General Floriano Peixoto, at the opening of the National Congress it announced that the Boundary Commissions had finished their labors, *and, if necessary, the question would be submitted to arbitration.*

At the same time a Brazilian diplomat sought the opinion of the President of the Republic and mine, in a personal way, concerning a new direct settlement. I had the honor to state then that this form of settlement was not desired by us, and that we relied on the Arbitration; but if Brazil had any new proposal to offer, it must be subject to the previous acceptance of these three conditions:

1st. The proposal to be officially initiated by the Brazilian Government.

2d. The proposal must carry with it the declaration that the treaty would be approved by the Congress at Rio de Janiero before being submitted to the Argentine Congress.

3d. The areas that each country would obtain by the new transaction to be similar to those of the Zeballos-Bocayuva treaty, though the position of the boundary line might vary.

This same fact was communicated to the Argentine Minister in Rio de Janeiro in the following terms:[2]

DEPARTMENT OF FOREIGN RELATIONS,
(Private) BUENOS AIRES, *December* 29, 1891.

SIR: I send herewith a note wherein I advise Your Excellency of the initiative of Señor Cyro de Azevedo, Envoy Extraordinary and Minister Plenipotentiary of the United States of Brazil, in the direction of reaching a compromise in the matter of *Misiones.*

I place such antecedents within the knowledge of Your Excellency in order that you may know accurately what has occurred, availing yourself of the first opportunity to acquaint the Minister

---

[1] The original document authenticated by the American Consul is to be found in the "Argentine Evidence," MSS. Group D, No. 22.

[2] Argentine Evidence, Vol. I, page 754; and Group D of Manuscripts, document No. 22.

of Foreign Relations of that country with the conversations that have taken place here. Your Excellency may add that the Argentine Government has no interest whatever in delaying the arbitration, and that it anxiously wishes, as is expressed in the said note, to bring about a solution of the controversy, recurring to the said resource as soon as possible.

At the conference which you may have regarding the matter with the Minister of Foreign Relations, you may read the said note if you should consider it advisable, but without leaving him a copy.

I repeat the assurances of my distinguished esteem.

(Signed)   ESTANISLAO S. ZEBALLOS.

To His Excellency, Don AGUSTIN ARROYO,
*Envoy Plenipotentiary of the Argentine Republic
in the United States of Brazil.*

There is quoted at the same place a document, following the foregoing, which gives the explanation of the matter.

In the Brazilian Congress there had been manifested, among the members of the Monarchical party, certain hostile tendencies towards the Argentine Republic, possibly in order to create foreign difficulties for the Government of Marshal Peixoto, which would aggravate its situation in the midst of the civil war already begun and alienate the monarchical opinion in some of the larger States. The Argentine Government decided to put an end, once for all, to the old system of permitting the politicians of Brazil to make use of international peace and of the *Misiones* case in particular as a means of breeding domestic rancor, and resolved to insist that the matter should be immediately submitted to the President of the United States of America.[1]

The Argentine Republic decides to hasten Arbitration. 1892.

Such are the legal antecedents of the question submitted to the Arbitrator, briefly expressed, suppressing numerous details and proofs, which may be read in the Documents and papers accompanying this Argument. But as an incident of the legal question it still remains to analyze the declarations made by the Brazilian Government in the discussion of the Treaty of Montevideo.

I present to the Arbitrator the "*Diario Official*" (Official Journal) of Brazil, which shows:

Official Brazilian proofs of the Policy of its Republican Government

1. The reception of the Brazilian Minister of Foreign Affairs in Montevideo, and speeches of the Minister of Foreign Affairs of the Republic of Uruguay, in which the latter stated that the Republican

---
[1] Argentine Evidence, Vol. I, page 756.

Government initiated a policy of international cordiality (Vol. for January, 1890, pages 42 [and 141).

2. Declaration of the Republican Government that it initiated the treaty for the division of the Territory, and that it was unanimously approved (Vol. for February, 1890, page 737).

3. Declaration of the Government of Brazil affirming that the Treaty of Montevideo, dividing the *Misiones*, was negotiated with a perfect agreement upon the bases unanimously approved by that Government (Vol. for March, 1890, page 1137).

4. Declaration signed by all the members of the Republican Government contradicting alarming reports circulated by the Monarchists, and declaring that the Cabinet accepted with unanimity the responsibility for all the acts of Marshal Fonseca, the first President, and considered them valid and subsisting (Vol. for September, 1890, page 4033).

5. Declaration of the Republican Government, informing the country that the Treaty of *Misiones* would be submitted to the Congress (Vol. for November, 1890, page 9).

6. Speech of the Minister of Foreign Affairs of Brazil, the negotiator of the Treaty of 1890, in the Senate of the Brazilian Republic, declaring that the treaty was only antagonized "in a violent and perfidious manner by the enemies of the Government of the Republic" (Vol. for February, 1891, page 475).

7. Proclamation by the President of the Republic of Brazil, declaring that the majority of the Congress were "*facciosa*" (factious or rebellious), composed of the elemental debris of the overthrown monarchy; that this majority sought to break the ties of international unity, and finally that the idea of a restoration of the monarchy was gaining ground on account of the lamentable conduct of the Congress, for which reason he dissolved it (Vol. for November, 1891, page 4564 et seq.)

<small>Discussion of the Treaty of Montevideo. Declarations favorable to Argentine right.</small> Among the most important declarations was the speech of the Brazilian Minister who negotiated the treaty. The newspaper of the most authority in Rio de Janeiro, the "*Jornal do Commercio*," published, on August 7, 1891, an official extract from the Secret Session in which the Treaty of *Misiones* was discussed. It is presented to the Arbitrator in the "Argentine Evidence," Vol. III, under the title: "Discussion of the Treaty of Montevideo." The negotiator of the treaty, the Minister of Foreign Affairs of Brazil, said:

I regret to say that I do not feel the same confidence in our rights that others feel, and do not know how they can affirm that they are clear and positive. For my part I must declare that I have very profound doubts. If I had confidence in the right of our claims to the point of not fearing the result of their arbitration, I would be the first to ask the rejection of the treaty with the consideration of which we are now preoccupied. I will say further that the Monarchists, who are now fighting the Republic upon this ground, have twice been at the point of making a compromise.

He then proceeded to analyze the value of the "*uti possidetis*" in the Territory, and declared that they did not have it or at the least it was very doubtful. He also quoted from Pasquale Fiori various passages to explain what ought to be understood by the true doctrine of the *uti possidetis*, and from Bluntchli and other authors which he had before him, who maintained the same opinions. He therefore affirmed in view of these facts that he did not understand whence arose the blind confidence expressed in the Brazilian right over *Misiones*, and analyzing the history of the question asserted that it was very much confused, obscure and intricate, reading from other documents, showing that there were arguments for their side as well as for the Argentine claims.

The same Journal, on the following day, August 8, gave out an official extract of the second Session, which is presented to the Arbitrator in the same volume. At this Session the negotiator of the Treaty read extracts from the Memoir of Oyarvide, of the Second Party of Demarcators, which he considered excellent, thus answering several of the matters referred to. He showed the confusion in which the whole subject was entangled and stated that he read from the documents to indicate the doubts and uncertainties which arose in his mind, and that any Arbitrator who should undertake to judge the question must read all the documents, and from the contradictions with which the history of it is surrounded he would find it very difficult to sign a decisive opinion in favor of Brazil. He proceeded to say:

> From the long statement I have made of the manner in which the Monarchy in recent times managed the question, it will be seen that a settlement of it was imminent which would have divided our territory. In the meantime there arose a great outcry against the Treaty of Montevideo, a most unfriendly campaign on the part of some who were on the point of doing worse. It is clear that the fight is now being made against the Republic, and that

this treaty is only used as a pretext by those who are combating it.

In his peroration the orator called the attention of the House to the serious and grave character of the internal political situation, showing that the monarchical reaction was every day increasing and that the people should build a wall against it.

These solemn declarations by the illustrious propagandist of the Brazilian Republic, whom the Republicans call "Our Master and Chief," reveal:

1. That Brazil has not had the possession claimed of the Territory.
2. That its arguments have always been confused and unfavorable.
3. That if the Minister of Foreign Relations of Brazil, Señor Bocayuva, had given judgment as an Arbitrator, the result would have shown that the Argentine Republic was right.

<small>The Republicans retire from the Brazilian Congress on seeing the Majority against the Treaty of Montevideo.</small> The day for the vote finally arrived. The monarchists were compactly united against the treaty and the republicans, who were in the minority, preferred to retire and not vote. The "*Jornal do Commercio*" of August 11, 1891, presented in the same volume as the preceding citations, gave an official account of the Session and closed by giving the names of forty-three republican deputies who refused to support with their votes the old imperialistic political tendencies, which the Republic nobly repudiated.

<small>Chiefs of the Monarchist Cabinet who also repudiated the old policy.</small> But justice compels the statement that the noble frankness with which the Brazilian Republic recognized, to say the least, the want of clearness in the reasons adduced by the Empire against the Argentine Republic, was before that emulated by one of the most illustrious chiefs of the Cabinet under the Imperial rule. Councillor Octaviano, President of the Council of Ministers of Brazil, delivered a speech at the Session of the Imperial Parliament of May 1, 1865, in which, referring to the boundary questions of the Rio de la Plata, he said: (See Journal of the Brazilian Congress for 1865.)

> Gentlemen: Let us put aside once for all this antagonistic attitude of our country, this superstition of what is called our traditional policy, which has only led us into struggles and produced frightful divisions in the body politic, putting us finally in a position of isolation by reason of lack of confidence. This isolation is the result of that policy which would sacrifice all the present for an uncertain future. (Applause.)
> Prudent England abandoned its traditions, its errors, and the preconceived ideas of its statesmen in respect to the Jews and

Catholics, in respect to the direction of educational matters, its navigation laws and system of imposts, and even to the giving up of its colonial policy, its methods of competing with France and its interference in the affairs of other states. France, Austria, all the great nations, relinquished their traditional policies, and the only instance in Europe in which it has been adhered to is in the case of Russia in its relations with Poland. Let us not pursue the phantom of an ambition that we have not, and with which our sincere and generous character has never been profaned. Let us concentrate our efforts in promoting our domestic welfare, beginning by a practical development of the liberties which the institutions of our country promise to us. *Let us lead away the spirit of our people from ideas of influence over the territory and the government of other nations,* excepting only that which flows naturally from good examples of honest industry and from disinterested service.

Instead of having the notoriety of being ambitious and sharp, let us rather seek the reputation of being honest and just. Such are the sentiments that I see already dominating the minds of the greater part of our public men and which must prevail in Brazilian politics. . . . *Therefore if it were necessary to cede a small portion of land, the sacrifice would amount to nothing, for it would cause surprise and we would be execrated before America and the world for undertaking a war, if such an event happened, in order to contest a few leagues of land, we that as a Nation occupy more than two-thirds, or nearly 83 per cent., of all the South American Continent.*

THE DEMARCATIONS.

1753 TO 1791 1885 TO 1891.

Geographical doubts and confusion
The question submitted to the Arbitrator has been complicated by Portugal and by Brazil, in order to surround with doubt and confusion its legal basis, otherwise so clear and precise, as we have seen. It is necessary therefore, to simplify it. In fact this lively and protracted debate has two cardinal aspects, one *legal* and the other *geographical*. *Legally* speaking, the terms are precise and definite. There was a perfect agreement between the Courts of Spain and Portugal and a uniformity of purpose in their international contracts. *Geographically*, however, Argentines and Brazilians had so entangled the question, one pulling to the East and the other to the West, that instead of loosening the knot it became with all this controversy yet tighter. It is unwise and useless to dispute about geographical points in regard to which the two high contracting parties never agreed. It is proper, however, to bring these contradictory facts to judgment, or confront them with the international acts which are internationally established by the sovereignty and joint will of the Sovereigns, that is to say, with the *legal* question, maintaining those which harmonize with it, and declaring null and void and eliminating those which are not found to do this, because they are the true elements of confusion and useless for any good purpose in this controversy.

Basis and Guide of the Demarcation of 1759.
In 1759 the Demarcators appointed in conformity with the Treaty of 1750 went to work upon the ground. Their proceedings were regulated by additional treaties. That of January 13, 1751, declared that the fundamental treaty had for its basis an official geographical map.

> . . . That in fact the said map had been drawn by *engineers, geographers, and skilful and well-informed persons of both nations;* that with it before them the said Plenipotentiaries had continued their conferences; that the same map having been by both *well examined and compared*, it was by *common agreement approved and agreed to* by the same respective Plenipotentiaries, to serve as *guide and basis* to the said Treaty of Boundaries, the conclusion of which was its object; that the said map was legalized and perpetuated by the said two Plenipotentiaries with the declara-

tions on its margin written in Portuguese and Spanish by the two respective Secretaries. . . .[1]

The additional treaty of January 17, 1751, provided that the said *basis and guide* of the Demarcation should be carried with them by the Commissioners for their respective governments.

It said:

> We . . . declare that, whereas *we have been guided* by a manuscript geographical map to *formulate this treaty and the instructions for its execution*, a copy of this map is therefore to be furnished to every party of Commissioners of each Sovereign for their guidance, all of them signed by us, as the boundaries are explained by it and according to it. . . .[2]

The "*Mapa de las Cortes*" was, as already shown, the exclusive work of the Portuguese, who had studied the region we are now considering during the ten years that preceded the treaty of 1750, and who knew the country with certainty. The official explorations of 1789–1791 and those of 1885–1891, on the other hand, show that the "*Mapa de las Cortes*" actually conforms to the peculiarities of the ground, that is to say, it is exact, and the Demarcators should have applied it, simply and scrupulously.

On applying the "*Mapa de las Cortes*" in the field the rules provided by the ninth Article of the additional treaty of instructions of January 17, 1751, should have been observed, that is— _{Itinerary traced for the explorers. 1751.}

> The first party shall survey from Castillos Grandes to the emptying of the river Ybicuy into the Uruguay, as it is prescribed in the fourth Article of the treaty. The second shall survey the boundary running from the mouth of the Ybicuy to the place which on the eastern side of the Paraná lies oppposite to the mouth of the River Ygurey, according to the fifth Article. . . .

The *second* detachment was commissioned, therefore, to examine the boundary in the region now submitted to the Arbitrator. Its itinerary traced by the international compacts was evidently as follows:[3] Having met at the mouth of the Ybicuy, and having opened the "*Mapa de las Cortes*" in order to apply it to the ground, the detachment was

---
[1] Argentine Evidence, Vol. I, page 77. See this Argument, page 138.
[2] Argentine Evidence, Vol. I, page 74.
[3] By looking at the "*Mapa de las Cortes*" and following the red mark the locations will be clearly comprehended.

to *follow the red mark up the river Uruguay* until it reached the most important of its eastern tributaries delineated upon that Map, the *Uruguay-Pitá*. Verifying the geographical situation of the junction of the two streams, and finding that it conformed with the "*Mapa de las Cortes*," (as it did exactly, as we know,) the problem was solved, according to the Boundary Treaty. Article V of that document says:

> It shall ascend from the mouth of the Ybicuy following the waters of the Uruguay until it finds the mouth of the river Pepiry or Pequiry, which flows into the Uruguay on its western bank. . . .[1]

And still following up the Uruguay from the mouth of the Uruguay-Pitá they were to find coming in upon the eastern bank of the former a river "*Caudaloso*," or carrying much water, called the Pequiry or Pepiry. There it is, in fact, according to the official explorations of the eighteenth and nineteenth centuries. Having proved its geographical situation to be in conformity with what was drawn on the "*Mapa de las Cortes*," (as it is), the Demarcators ought to have read Article V of the Treaty of 1750, which they were then tracing upon the ground. It says:

> . . . and they shall continue up the stream of the Pepiry to its principal source, from which it shall continue through the highest ground to *the main head spring of the nearest river* which flows into the Grande of Curitiba, otherwise called the Ygunzú, through the waters of the said river nearest to the source of the Pepiry.[2]
> . . .

The Demarcators neglect the "Mapa de las Cortes." Their errors.

The Demarcators charged with such a clear and indisputable mission showed that they were cowardly and weak in the presence of the dangers and fatigues of the enterprise, and that they were hasty, negligent and without perspicuity in the accomplishment of their technical task. In fact, they closed the "*Mapa de las Cortes*," and in doing so disobeyed the express text not only of the fundamental Boundary Treaty, but of the additional treaties directing their proceedings, which have been quoted. They substituted for the purpose of the Sovereigns expressed therein the confusion of their own ignorance, and for the *basis and scientific guide* of the demarcation, the "*Mapa de las Cortes*," they accepted the childish remembrances of an Indian.

[1] Argentine Evidence, Vol. 1, page 54
[2] *Idem*, page 54.

Such were the causes of the errors committed by these Boundary Commissioners, whose acts have produced a long and unjustified international quarrel, which has threatened the peace of two nations. Their proceedings were expressly annulled by the Treaty of 1761,[1] and did not result in any prejudice to the Argentine Republic, because that treaty considered them null *and as if they had never existed.* Organic and legal nullity of their acts.

That country desires, however, to have a still stronger protection than even the legal declaration of their invalidity. An act which has been annulled may have been just and reasonable in its origin, and under such a view of the matter Portugal would have been in the right as against Spain in the boundary incident prior to 1759.

I shall demonstrate that such was not the case, but that the proceedings of the Demarcators in that year are void not only because both Crowns declared them so in 1761, but also because they were absolutely invalid *before* this manifestation of the Royal wills, on account of an incurable organic vice in the acts themselves. The Sovereigns did not create the causes of the invalidity of the proceedings, but they recognized their pre-existence and so declared in a solemn treaty.

As a matter of fact the Demarcators in tracing the line followed an "*arroyo*," or small stream, situated down stream from the *Uruguay-Pitá*, and which they called "Pepiry." This was not the river of the treaty, described and exactly delineated in the "*Mapa de las Cortes*," which empties into the Uruguay above the Uruguay-Pitá. The careful studies which we possess to-day of this region prove that this "*arroyo*" was the *Guarumbaca*, known since 1650, as will be seen in the geographical maps presented, and in the engraving at this page. The river accepted as boundary, the Guarumbaca.

The Spanish Commissioner concurred in this mistake in a hesitating and undecided way, signing the paper in which it was declared that the "arroyo" *Guarumbaca* was the *Pipiry* or *Pequiry* of the Treaty of 1750.

Upon this gross error the Portuguese and Brazilians have founded their claims to other lands of Spain and the Argentine Republic, besides the thousands of square leagues which they unjustly and gratuitously received by the Treaties of 1750 and 1777. The Brazilian arguments, deduced from these void and mistaken facts, were solemnly presented to the Congress of Brazil, in 1886, by the Minister of Foreign Affairs, the Baron of Cotegipe.[2] They are substantially as follows: Brazilian arguments.

---

[1] Argentine Evidence, Vol. I, page 79.
[2] Report presented to the General Legislative Assembly, at the First Session of the 20th Legislature, by the Minister of State for Foreign Affairs, Baron de Cotegipe, Rio de Janeiro, National Print, 1886.

1. The Demarcation of 1759 and 1760 was made very regularly and in entire conformity with the Treaty of 1750, with the instructions sent for its execution, with the local traditions and with the map prepared and published by the Jesuits in 1722 and 1726.

2. It fixed by these and recognized as belonging to Portugal all the territory situated on the East of the rivers Pepiry-Guazú and San Antonio.

3. The fact of possession prior to 1750 existing, and the Demarcation not having been set aside, this, as a practical expression of the right of Portugal, ought naturally to govern whatever new adjustment may be made.

Refutation.

The vital argument made is that—

... the "demarcation" of 1759 and 1760 was made very regularly and in entire conformity with the Treaty of 1750, and with the instructions sent for its execution, *with the local traditions and with the map prepared and published by the Jesuits in* 1722 *and* 1726.

Brazil is here condemned by the voice of the most high-minded of its diplomats of later years, and the one who has most studied and agitated the *Misiones* question. I will analyze this first argument, and take each part separately.

The foregoing pages demonstrate that the demarcation was not made with entire conformity, nor even with partial conformity, to the Boundary Treaty of 1750 and its additional treaties of instructions of 1751. Arguedas, the Spanish Commissioner, who with so little success and capacity had fulfilled the arduous mission which had been confided to him, wrote to the Minister of Foreign Affairs of Spain, the Marquis de Valdelirios, an account of what occurred at the "*arroyo*" or small stream of *Guarombucu* (falsely called Pequiry or Pepiry). I present this narrative to the Arbitrator, copied from the official archives of Spain. If its text and its spirit are studied scrupulously, it gives the impression of a private confession by one who, having perceived his errors, sought to exculpate himself and explain them. This document also reveals all the vices and the invalidity inherent in the demarcation of the Treaty of 1759. It is as follows:

Letter of Don Francisco de Arguedas, addressed to the Marquis de Valdelirios, dated at the mouth of the Pepiry, March 27, 1759, wherein are told all the incidents relating to the survey of said river.[1]

MON TRÈS CHER AMI: With double pleasure would I write you if

[1] This is a translation from the original document existing in the Central Archives of Alcala de Henares. A copy duly certified by the United States Consul at Madrid, forms part of Group D, No. 3, of Manuscript Documents of the "Argentine Evidence."

instead of the difficulties which oblige me to stop the demarcation here and return to *Misiones*, in order to ascend the Paraná to battle again with reefs and currents, it could be in my power to avoid this trouble and delay; but it being necessary to do this, it only remains for me to become reconciled with adverse fate, which your good example has taught me to endure.

The fifteenth of last month I sent you a short letter from the Fall of the Guaraí, by means of a raft from the pueblo de Santa Maria, which was returning from the Itacaraí. Afterwards we pursued our journey with success, but encountered continual reefs and currents, which were the more troublesome on account of the scarcity of water in the Uruguay; this continued until the twenty-fourth, when we arrived at a distance of a league and a half from the great Fall, where the whirlpools and strong currents begin, and with great difficulty we proceeded a little further, but seeing it would be impossible for the rafts to proceed, we determined to leave them there with the men who could be spared, and with the Commanders of the troops. Some of the rafts were unloaded, and with ten different canoes for the officers of each party, we proceeded on our journey. Accompanying us, at the request of Alpoym, came Friar Francisco and Dubois, the Chaplain and Surgeon remaining to take care of the men who were left. While the canoes were being prepared Captain Vega went by land and returned with the information that the Fall could not be passed even with canoes, nor could it be passed by land, following the Eastern bank of the river, where we then were. For this reason we resolved to send the geographers by the said bank, to draw a plan of the river, and ordered Captain Antonio Rodriguez to go with Marron to the opposite bank and find out if the Fall could be passed by the Western bank or by land. They brought the news that with difficulty the canoes could be dragged to a place where they would not be injured by the Fall; so, with great trouble, clearing rocks and cutting down trees to force a passage, we managed to carry the canoes with the help of thirty men who pulled them with a rope, while others pushed them from behind, until we reached a height of thirty fathoms and a distance of twenty-four fathoms. At this point the canoes were thrown into a small lake formed by the rise of the waters of the river, and repeating the above operation three times more, we reached a place where the waters are quiet, and where the water flows in cataract form to the principal channel of the river, at which point the latter becomes so narrow that it cannot be more than twenty yards in width. Looking at the fall of the water I was reminded of the "Peines" of Lima, although the latter are more beautiful, having a greater volume of water and the height from which it descends being also greater. We finally managed to overcome the difficulty and continued our march.

Upon our arrival at the Fall we were told by *the Guide of San Xavier, the only Indian of Misiones who had ever been beyond the Fall*, that the very day we should leave the Fall we would reach the Pepiry. In fact, the next day we found a river *which the Guide said was the Pepiry*. The news soon spread among the Portuguese soldiers, and their Commissioners topped at the river, awaiting the arrival of my canoe which had remained behind. As soon as I came Alpoym told me the news. *Observing the small volume of water of the river*, though its mouth was wide, *I said I doubted that the river in question was the Pepiry*. I landed, and calling again the Guide who was coming in Milhaú's canoe, I asked him in the presence of the officers of the two Nations the name of the river at which we had arrived, and he said it was the Pepiry, under which name he had known it years before when he had been to Espia, and that it was so called by the Indian guides who at that time were of the party.

Although I found the river to be in conformity with the position given it in two maps of San Xavier, which I had, one of which I had found to be, as to the rest of the river, more exact and truthful, *yet seeing it was a small river which could not be navigated, I said it did not correspond with the river represented in the "Mapa de las Cortes," because we had not seen anywhere along the Western bank the river Uruguay-Pitá which said map places before the Pepiry, nor was the latitude where we were, 27° 9', the same as that given by the map in question, which represents the Pepiry as being at 26° 40' latitude, and finally, that it was difficult to believe the Sovereigns could have taken as the boundary such a small river as that one appeared to be, although its mouth was thirty-nine fathoms wide, when I knew the Pepiry was navigable and had been navigated by Father Delgado in search of Indians, as proven by his map, which I produced, as well as the "Mapa de las Cortes."*

Alpoym and his officers stood by the testimony of the Guide, *the only one there who could determine the name of the river*, and upon the declaration of the Plenipotentiaries to the effect that more faith should be placed in the Treaty and instructions than in the *"Mapa de las Cortes,"* when the latter should not conform with the ground, as in the present case, when we found the Pepiry before the Uruguay-Pitá.

While my canoe was on the way, Alpoym had explored the river for some distance, and he told me it was a large river which further on had the same width as at its mouth. I asked him if it had *a fall near its mouth* (because I knew it should have one through information given me by Father Candiel); he said he did not know, but that his Geographer had proceeded further and he would be able to tell upon his return. In fact, the Geographer brought word that at a distance of half a league from the mouth of the river *there was a large reef which prevented* the canoes from proceeding any further. This information justified me in believing it was the Pepiry, in the face of the previous information I had of Father Candiel, *but from the existence of the reef I gathered the river could not be navigated*, and I insisted that we should go that afternoon *to personally survey the reef. We did so and found the reef*, and the river had so little water at that point that it was difficult to believe its source could be far distant. *I then spoke to Alpoym, assuring him the exigencies of our honor demanded that we leave there the boats*, and that the officers should proceed in the canoes and survey the Uruguay further on. He assented to it, and the next day we navigated four long leagues, encountering at every moment rocks and scarcity of water until we reached a new Fall, which we could not pass without experiencing the same difficulty we had at the Fall we had passed before. At a distance of a league, and through the Western bank, flows a stream which the guide called Apiterebi, and at a distance of a league from the latter the Uruguay-Pitá flows through the Eastern bank. Upon our arrival at the foot of this second Fall Alpoym said: "It seems that we have satisfied your scruples; *this Fall does not permit us to go any further, and the river you were seeking has been found*, although a little higher up than represented in the '*Mapa de las Cortes*,' so I suppose we can now return."

The guide had told Milhau it was useless to look further for the Pepiry, as it was the river we had left behind, and upon reaching the Uruguay-Pitá *the guide told me he had never been any further and that he did not know anything more about the river;* at this I reasoned to myself as follows: "A year and a half ago the guide told me in San Xavier that he had gone beyond the Pepiry: now he assures me that he has not been beyond the Uruguay-Pitá, and has never, in fact, indicated that he had any knowledge beyond the latter river. The Pepiry, then, must be below the Uruguay-Pitá." This reasoning served to calm my fears that the contrary was the case. This reasoning, besides the difficulty of passing and going beyond the Fall, and the fact that several small streams flowed into the Uruguay river through its western bank, *which proved to me through the light of past experience that, for a long distance, further on there was no possibility of any large river flowing into the Uruguay*, decided me to assemble together the officers of the two nations and ask them if they entertained any doubts that the Pepiry was the river we had left behind, because I knew that some of our own officers attributed my actions to mere personal scruples. They all agreed there was no doubt about its being the Pepiry, and said I should not hesitate to believe the same, notwithstanding the scarcity of its waters, because the Uruguay was also dry in spite of its greater volume of water; so we decided to return to the point where we had left the other canoes.

While making some observations at that important point, I proposed to Alpoym we should send a light and small canoe to explore the Pepiry, so that we might obtain more knowledge concerning it, as we did not know anything about the interior of said river. He agreed, and the canoe was sent with the best Paulists, with provisions for four days, and with orders to explore the river as far as its source if possible, and to go on by land if it became impossible to navigate it. At the end of two days and a half they returned with the information that the river was full of rocks which began at a distance of half a league from its mouth, the first of which had been overcome with difficulty, after which the little canoe had been taken, which could be shouldered by two men and carried to a place where there was *more water*, *but they had afterwards encountered other rocks which could not be passed*. They then continued by land about two leagues further, where they saw a stream of water descending from a mountain which they could not climb, and having observed, also, fresh signs of Indians, they resolved to return.

Upon the receipt of this news I again persuaded Alpoym to send the same small canoe with good men to explore the Urugnay, and if they could not cross the Fall at which we had arrived, to go on by land, taking provisions for four days. They departed, *Corporal Reynoso going as my representative*, with orders to explore as much as they could, entering the rivers that flow through the Western bank. At the end of four days they came back with the information that they had reconnoitered the streams we had seen, and finding it impossible to cross the Fall they had left the canoes there, and that Reynoso and a Portuguese Corporal who knew how to steer, and who was provided for the occasion with a marine compass and a watch, had gone by land some distance further from the Fall, *without finding or seeing as far as their eyes could reach any river of consequence, or half as large even as the one where we were.*

In view of this new disappointment, and according to the news brought *by the Corporal who explored the Pepiry that it was impossible to navigate it beyond a distance of half a league*, which we had already explored, we decided to send an exploring party by land which should open a road as far as the source of the Pepiry, and this once found should proceed by the highest lands until it found the source of the other river which flows into the Yguazú. For the better execution of this undertaking we decided that the Geographers of the two nations should also go, with Antonio Rodriguez, Captain of Adventurers, and twenty troopers, without counting the servants and Indians who carried the provisions, as the former only would be employed in opening the road. We gave them (by common agreement) the necessary instructions, in which we included articles third and fourth of our own Instructions, charging them to proceed with great diligence and exactness, and to draw up the necessary plans.

They left on the fourteenth, and at a league from this place they abandoned the canoes and proceeded by land. On the seventeenth a heavy rain began to fall, which lasted for nearly eight days. Part of their provisions became wet, and another large portion was prematurely consumed by the Indians, so that at a distance of five leagues they wrote for more, adding that the river, although having many rocks, had nearly the same width as at its mouth, for which reason they thought its source was at a greater distance than I had imagined, and we all thought that owing to the great amount of rain which had fallen the river would become navigable. We sent them five canoes with the provisions requested and with orders to continue on with the canoes as far as they could. They left the point where they had stopped on the twenty-fifth of the month, and to this date we have heard nothing further from them. I am of the opinion that the river having risen they have been able to proceed for a long distance, and I judge the river is large, because if at a distance of five leagues it has the same width as at its mouth, which is thirty-nine fathoms wide, it cannot be very small, and only seemed so at first owing to the dryness of the weather.

This operation has shown that the Portuguese Corporal who gave the first information did not see the river, nor did he carry out his orders as he should have done, relying, perhaps, upon the supposition that the river would not be explored by us. I would have gone personally as far as possible if an indisposition of which Alpoym is suffering had not detained me. He has been for a period of eight days shedding much blood from the hemorrhoids, and is now so weak that I have not wished to trouble him, but have told him that since the river is navigable we should explore it as far as our canoes can go, and when he recovers we will do so. In the meantime observations are being made here to properly locate the mouth of the river, but the frequent mist interrupts the operations and prevents their repetition. A small island at its mouth constitutes a visible sign of identification, but when the waters rise they cover the island. On its Eastern bank, because it flows into a bend where the river runs from South to North, several trees have been cut on an elevated ground, and a cross has been placed in one which has only a large and decayed trunk, but above all the best sign is that it is the first river after passing the great Fall which flows into the Uruguay through its western bank, in which it agrees with the Gatimi, that flows into the Parana.

This is the history of my movements written in a great hurry, as I have not even the time to read it over and correct any grammatical errors which may have been made. We are all enjoying good health. The heat, which has been intense at times, is now much more bearable, and as we live under the trees the rays of the sun affect us less. Mosquitoes and other insects trouble us considerably, but not as much as I had anticipated.

I am on the best of terms with Colonel Alpoym and his officers. After we left the rafts the formality of precedence in the march was abandoned. We united our mess, and have had our meals together, I providing the provisions one day and Alpoym the next. He is open and frank and can easily be convinced with suitable arguments. Since passing the Fall I have had no reason to believe he acts in bad faith, but on the contrary believe he acts with frankness and in good faith. He thinks me somewhat overcautious, as I try not to be outdone by him, and yet he relies upon me and we are always in good humor, to which Marron contributes his share.

Owing to the dense forests which have always surrounded us from the day of *our departure from San Xavier*, since then neither we nor the Paulists, who have gone a league further, have ever seen any plains.

I am writing the Intendant to have ready the necessary provisions for one hundred *days for forty men at the pueblo of Corpus*. I do not mention jerked-beef, because I have seen how what we have has been spoilt by*the insects, and if *we find time while at Corpus* we will have fifty or one hundred "arrobas" of fresh jerked-beef prepared, and the rest of the provisions will be made up of grains, which are more useful.

Mouth of the Pepiri, March twenty-seventh, 1759. Your most faithful, "*usque ad aras.*"

ARGUEDAS.

It is unnecessary to insist further upon this point, which the sagacity of the Arbitrator will undoubtedly resolve in favor of the Argentine Republic, by a brief consideration of the documents presented.[1] The error of one man cannot be, and never could be, the cause of violation of the treaties.

On the other hand, the Government of Brazil makes in this argument a very important omission, for it does not even mention the "*Mapa de las Cortes*," declared to be the *basis and guide* of the demarcation in one of the additional treaties (that of January 13, 1751), and which the Commissioners must carry with them to the ground *for their government*, according to another of these additional treaties (that of January 17, 1751).

This silence on the part of Brazil is a proof that its position is wrong, for the "*Mapa de las Cortes*," this *official instrument*, the *basis*

[1] See this Argument, page 138.

and guide for the action of both Sovereigns, which had been compared, analyzed, approved, protocoled, and sealed by the Plenipotentiaries of the High Contracting Parties, is now for Brazil a document without any value, only fit to be thrown into the waste-paper basket, and that country now pretends that the Demarcators of 1759 could at their caprice substitute for it the childhood recollections of an Indian and the anonymous Jesuit Maps of 1722 and 1726. Such proceedings by the Demarcators cannot be sustained; no Executive of a State would ever permit its subordinate officials to substitute for protocoled maps and treaties, popular tradition and unauthorized and private maps, which were besides too old, incomplete, and badly informed to be reliable.[1]

Geographically speaking, the demarcation of 1759 was badly made. Having as a basis an official map, the logical thing to have done would have been to fully study the ground, verifying the exact position of the rivers Uruguay, Uruguay-Pitá and Pepiry or Pequiry, and stating whether they were properly delineated upon this official map, in order to proceed, if such were not the case, to the interpretation of the treaties. If the locations given to these rivers on the said map coincided with their actual locations upon the ground, there was no discussion possible, for the matter was reduced to the mere tracing of the line and marking it by monuments in the field. But instead of making this geodesic study the Demarcators called an Indian to pilot them; and what that Indian said had more influence with them and was a higher law than their duties, or the treaties, or the red mark of the official map.   Geographical errors.

The Brazilians have published the documents relating to this demarcation in an incomplete way, in paragraphs isolated from each other, and only selecting such as appeared favorable to them. The Argentine Republic, however, presents to the Arbitrator the trustworthy and vital documents of the demarcation, copied for the first time from the originals in the Archives of Spain.[2] The manner of the discovery of the river *Guarumbaca* (falsely called the *Pepiry* or *Pequiry* of the treaty) is related as follows: Documents that prove the facts.

> FIFTH DAY. The Spanish party led the way. We followed the same western bank on which we were, and turning South-Southeast as the river runs, there are in this direction two small

---

[1] This will be shown in this Argument in the Resumé of the Brazilian arguments.
[2] Argentine Evidence. Vol. I, page 522. Group D of Manuscripts. Document No. 2. 1759. Journals of the Spanish and Portuguese Demarcators.

reefs or ledges of rock close to each other. We left two streams of water that come down tumultuously over the rocks, which we judged were produced by the heavy rains of the previous night. Great labor was occasioned by the numerous rocks and shallow water of the river, which turns to the East-Southeast; and in this direction there is a ledge of rocks terminating in a small island of stones and saraudys,[1] leading to the North shore. This is covered over during the floods; and behind this, at a distance of two-thirds of a league from the Ytagoa, there is the mouth of a river that can only be seen after turning the point of the island. The Guide said that it was the Pepiry, which we were searching for.

The Commissioners had him brought before them, and bringing together all the officers of both nations, he was asked what river that one was. He again answered that it was the Pepiry, and that *by this name he had known it during the voyage that he had made a few years before* with the people of his village to the place which they called Espia. In the season there was so little water in it that it promised a very short navigation; and *as it was known from other information that the Pepiry had a reef of rocks near its mouth*, the Commissioners with the Portuguese Astronomer went to search for it, and they found it half a league from its mouth. Nevertheless, as it was seen that *we had not arrived at the latitude* in which the "*Mapa de las Cortes*" locates the Pepiry, and that the position of the river on which we were situated did not correspond with it either, as it was before the *Uruguay-pitá*, which empties on the opposite shore, whereas on the Map it appears after it, in order to rectify this map and to remove every kind of doubt that might be raised against the testimony of the guide, as being that of only one man (although he was also the only one, not only among us but among all the *Misiones* villages who could give any, as there were now no Indians remaining who had navigated above the falls), or because he might not remember well, *so many years having passed since he had gone over that ground only once*, the two Commissioners therefore agreed to go up the river the next day and to make a map of this region, in order to satisfy ourselves of his knowledge and good guidance by comparing the information that he gave us concerning the rivers Apiterebí and Uruguay-pitá, or as far as he said he had gone, with their true position.

Thermometer 29° at one o'clock, North wind, weather rainy.

Francisco Arguedas, Francisco Millan, Juan Marron, Joseph Fres. Pto. Alpoym, Antonio da Veiga da Andrada, Manoel Pacheco de Christo.

The Guide was an Indian, and was a sergeant of the Spanish police of

[1] A kind of tree growing on low ground.

San Xavier. Therefore this fact confirms the statements made in this Argument[1] as to the jurisdiction in fact and law exercised by the pueblo of San Xavier over the Territory submitted to the Arbitrator. San Xavier, according to the treaties, the instructions and the documents which have been presented, was the starting point of the Demarcation undertaken by the second party. Brazil did not have in 1759 any settlements near, nor even within a distance of a *hundred* leagues from, this Territory. This document also proves the incapacity of the Demarcators, because instead of using instruments to verify whether the latitude and longitude of the river mouth they had arrived at were those in which the "*Mapa de las Cortes*" located the mouth of the river selected by the Monarchs as the boundary, they confided the solution of the matter to the recollection of an Indian, *who when very young had only passed once by that place*. The Demarcators did not care to work and found the suggestion made by the Indian convenient, but at the same time it is evident their consciences mortified them, for their acts denote vacillations, violent interpretations of the facts, entire lack of any scientific procedure and a deplorable misunderstanding of the treaties. They did not even take the trouble to investigate as to whether or not there existed any radical difference between the *infantile remembrances of this Indian* and the "*Mapa de las Cortes*," made by engineers, geographers and well-informed people.[2] They knew (the document says) that the river of the "*Mapa de las Cortes*" had a *reef* near its mouth, and going up the *Guarumbaca*, or false boundary river, they found a *reef* at the distance of *half a castillian league* (nearly three kilometers) up stream from its mouth. Is that *near*? Near in this case should be understood as meaning *in sight*, because it refers to the characteristics of the *mouth* of a river, and a thing cannot be characterized by something which is not connected with it.

The truth was otherwise, and as a matter of fact there was no reef near the mouth of the false river, but there were a great many beginning half a league above its mouth.

But the official document exhibits its organic vice, and the incurable cause of its invalidity, in the terms in which it acknowledges that the Party had not reached the latitude of the "*Mapa de las Cortes*," nor that of the Uruguay-Pitá, nor that of the boundary river, which according to that map ought to empty into the Uruguay above the Uruguay-Pitá, and it adds that they decided to *correct the official map*.

---
[1] See this Argument, page 86.
[2] Argentine Evidence, Vol. I, page 77.

But no correction could be made in a map the exactness of which was proved in 1791 and 1891, twice in one century, by international Commissions selected by the two contracting parties. The alleged correction of the *official map* was after all simply a new statement of the Indian, which should have been sufficient in itself to have caused any circumspect person to have put him aside as a witness. He stated, in fact, that it was many years (more than thirty)[1] since he had passed through those regions, *that he had only been there once and that then he was a mere child*. Besides, the Demarcators had noticed he had been mistaken as to other rivers, as he was in the case of the most important one. The document also declares, with inconceivable candor, that he was the *only one* among 150,000 Indians of *Misiones* who could give information, against the Treaties, against the scientific instruments and against the geodetic calculations.

Doubts of the Demarcators. Explorations continued. Fortunately a wrong always carries in itself the germs of its own discredit, and the Journal of the Fifth Day is written in such a way that its text and its spirit leave intact all the arguments which advised the rejection of the opinion of the Indian and going ahead.

The Journal of the Sixth Day states that the Demarcators did in fact proceed to navigate up the Uruguay in search of the *Uruguay-Pitá* and of the true boundary river, for the Guarumbaca, in which they had stopped on the Fifth Day, was only an "*arroyo*," or small stream, carrying very little water, and the treaties required a river "*Caudaloso*," *i. e.*, of *much water*[2] or large volume. These cowardly explorers exaggerated the difficulties of the reefs and asperities of the ground, showing that they were very delicate, for before and after they were there merchants and travellers passed through the same regions, under obligations much less urgent and solemn, without complaining or retreating. Finally this day ends with the discovery of the *Uruguay-Pitá*. The Journal states it in the following terms:[3]

> SIXTH DAY.—The Commissioners, Astronomers and Geographers of both Nations started in the unladen canoes, and at a distance of less than a quarter of a league in the northwest direction taken by the river, an unnamed "*arroyo*," or small stream, empties into it by the eastern bank, passing which there is a strong current and

---
[1] See the letter of Arguedas, page 232 of this Argument.
[2] See this Argument, page 116.
[3] Argentine Evidence, Vol. I, page 523; Group D of Manuscripts; same document as the account of the Fifth Day.

a small ledge of rocks, and a little further up, in a direction northeast one-quarter north, another one like it, also with a ledge and very little water, and in the same direction on the western bank a glen comes in. The river then turns east-northeast and then inclines southeast one-quarter east, and in this direction it has another ledge one-quarter of a league in length, with very little water. This was passed in the usual manner, with the people in the water, where besides the sharp points of rocks that hurt the men's feet, various kinds of mosquitoes troubled them greatly by attacking their naked bodies in swarms. A small island of rocks and sarandys may be seen in the middle of this ledge, and after passing it there empties on the western bank, at a distance of a league and a quarter from the Pepiry, a not very large river, which the guide called the *Apiterebi*.

After passing the ledge the river turns again with a slight current to the south-southeast, where a ravine comes in on the same bank, and inclining again to the southeast it has a slight current, in the middle of which there are large rocks, some rising out of the water; others are very superficial, slightly covered by the water; on their sides the water in some places was very deep and in others very shallow. Between them a passage was sought for, to avoid the powerful current of the channel, which runs very rapidly under the south shore. The river follows its turn toward the northeast and northeast one-quarter north, and at the beginning of this course, at a distance of nearly two and one-third leagues from the Pepiry, a large river empties on the eastern shore, which the guide said was the *Uruguay-pitá*. This was the extent of his knowledge. We followed it up a little distance to see if the color of its waters corresponded with its name, meaning *Uruguay-red*, and it was found that the color was somewhat like this.[1] Its width, measured a short distance above its mouth, is forty-nine fathoms, four feet, and its depth six, eleven, fourteen, sixteen feet (del Rey), and navigated up a distance of half a league it preserves the depth of twelve feet; the waters of the large Uruguay, being so much further down, have nothing to do with it and could not control those of the Pitá, *which is the largest river we have met since leaving San Xavier.*

We continued the navigation of our river up stream, and in the same direction it has another reef which occupies its full width; and after passing it a small stream empties on its opposite shore, and a little further on in a direction East-northeast another, which is followed by another rapid current with a rocky reef. After passing this we halted for the night on the Eastern shore, having travelled a distance of three leagues. . . .

---

[1] All the rivers of this region have the same color, on account of the soil, which is a reddish sand, similar to that along some portions of the Potomac.

Rivers erroneously explored.

The demarcations of 1791 and of 1891, made by mixed Commissions from the two governments to this controversy, have proved that the river called in this document " Uruguay-Pitá " was the river Mberuy, situated further to the South.[1]

The Journal of the Seventh Day shows that the Commission of Demarcators was convinced that the river where they had stopped on the Fifth Day was not that of the boundary, for they sent

> ... a small canoe to examine the falls at close quarters, with orders if it was possible to get around in any way, *to continue the navigation until turning a point that could be seen in the distance*, and to notice if any river *came in on the West* along the bank *which agreed better with the "Mapa de las Cortes."* ...

Therefore, if the river had been found there the question would have been settled according to the "*Mapa de las Cortes.*" Then onward! A brief effort more! The *river of the Treaty* and of the *Map* empties into the Uruguay only eight or ten miles further on, and if they had proceeded in accordance therewith they would have found it. But they did not go farther up stream because they came to a fall or ledge of rocks which, according to their Journal, was not more than one "toesa," or four to six feet, in height, and in the presence of such an enormous (!) obstacle, which has never detained any one else since, they were terrified. Their Journal actually states this fact, which is almost incredible when it is remembered that they were tracing and fixing the boundaries of two jealous sovereignties, constantly at war.

Therefore they sought a large river, or as the treaties called it "caudaloso" (of great volume), and if they had found it they would have adopted it as the boundary. These reasons and the very substance of the matter vitiate this final act and indicate the incurably invalid character of their actions, entirely irrespective of the subsequent agreement by the Courts. Instead of continuing the comparison of the "*Mapa de las Cortes*" with the ground, they went back and adopted as the boundary the "*arroyo*" Gnarumbaca, a small and nearly dry stream, for two reasons which will certainly appear very remarkable

Unreasonable abandonment of the explorations. to the Arbitrator. The first was *because some of the officers said it would be necessary, in order to continue the navigation, to carry the canoes overland*, as they had done at the *Salto Grande* (great fall). This is the language of their Official Journal and justifies the accusation of cowardness and weakness which I have made against these

---

[1] See this Argument, demarcations of XVIII and XIX centuries.

Royal Commissioners. The second reason was *because the crew of the small canoe that had gone overland a short way had not found any river.*

The Official Journal continues, declaring that the Indian told the truth, inasmuch as he was right as to the Uruguay-Pitá. Later international explorations have proved that the Indian was wrong, and made only incorrect statements during the whole voyage, confounding all the rivers. This foundation for the important decision which they made is as wretched as the preceding ones. Deceiving even themselves, they affirmed that the river falsely taken for that of the boundary was always one of considerable size, forgetting that in the preceding and following documents they described it as an insignificant "*arroyo*," or small stream. This curious document, which contains all the causes of organic invalidity which attach to the proceeding, says, in substance, that they returned to the false Pepiry (or Guarumbaca) *because they could not find the other river of the treaty.* If it did not exist on the ground the matter might perhaps have another aspect, in equity, although it would be legally void in virtue of the Treaty of 1761. But the large or very considerable river they were looking for having been officially found, their error is evident and their proceedings invalid. This commentary will not be extended farther, but I beg the Arbitrator to carefully consider this remarkable document. The Official Journal for the next day runs as follows:

SEVENTH DAY.—We continued on our way forward on a course East Northeast, in which, at the bottom of the hill, a brook empties on the same North shore, and the river turning to the Southeast one-quarter East receives another one on the opposite side. It continues South one-quarter Southeast; and during this course, a little more than half a league further on, is found a small island, rocky and high. After passing it we saw a great fall which we judged must be one fathom high in ledges over which the water fell, violently obstructing our further passage. We stopped before the island and a small canoe was sent to examine the falls at close quarters, with orders if it was possible to get around in any way to continue the navigation until turning a point that could be seen in the distance, and to *notice if any river came in on the West that agreed better with the "Mapa de las Cortes."* Some officers accompanied it up to the foot of the falls, and they stated that in order to pass them it would be necessary to execute a manœuvre similar to the one that had been executed at the great falls, of carrying the canoes overland.

The people or crew of the canoe, who explored a little on foot, did not find any river. In view of this obstacle, and as there was no hope of a large river near by because of the many small brooks that were so frequently met with on that bank, the Commissioners called together the Astronomers and Geographers of both nations, and after they were all together, the Commissioner of His Christian Majesty *set forth the reasons that had led him to take these measures, and to doubt the statement of the guide that the said river was the Pepiry, not only because its latitude does not agree with the one given to it in the aforesaid map, but because after so many years the latter might have forgotten the ground and rivers.*

On the Eighth Day the Official Journal of the Exploration, fortunately for the Argentine Republic, was drawn up so as to set forth the legal and scientific omissions of which the Demarcators were guilty, and which I have already commented upon. The document says:

Document concerning the mistaken boundary and its errors.

EIGHTH AND FOLLOWING DAYS TO THE FOURTEENTH.—Being now convinced that we were at the mouth of the Pepiry river, the following document of acknowledgment or recognition was entered into and signed by all.

The Commissioners of the Second Party of Demarcation, Don Francisco Arguedas for his Catholic Majesty and Josef Fernandez Pinto Alpoym for His Most Faithful Majesty, after hearing the unanimous opinion of the Astronomers, Geographers and officers of both nations who (*in view of the reasons stated at the preceding meeting, and of the assurance of the Indian Guide Francisco Xavier Avirapi, sergeant of his pueblo of San Xavier*, whose acquaintance with and information regarding these rivers was proven by the agreement that was found between the information he gave regarding them and their true position)[1] stated that there was now no doubt in their minds that the Pepiry river was the one so designated by the said Guide, at whose mouth the parties were encamped, we hereby declare that we recognize this as the river Pepiry named in Article V of the Treaty of Boundaries as the boundary between the dominions of Their Catholic and Most Faithful Majesties; consequently *the demarcation begun at the pueblo of San Xavier and followed up stream along the Uruguay up to the mouth of this river.* shall follow its course towards its headwaters, *in spite of its true position not being in accordance with the one given it in the Map of the Demarcators given by the two Courts, as we ought not* to follow the declaration that appears on its reverse side, signed by their Excellencies the two Plenipotentiaries Don Josef de Carvajal y Lancaster and Viscount Don Thomas da Silva Tellez, to follow the aforesaid map only in so

[1] All the locations which he had given were false. See this Argument, Demarcations of 1789 and 1891.

far as it agrees with the Treaty.[1] And in order that this act of recognition and boundary of the division of limits may be known for all time we made this present declaration, signed by all of the undersigned. Mouth of the Pepirí river, March 8, 1759.—*Francisco Arguedas.—Francisco Milhau.—Juan Marron.—Josef Fernandez Pinto Alpoym.—Antonio da Veiga da Andrada. Manuel Pacheco de Christo.*

If, as is just, there is applied to the preceding facts the criterion which is derived from the literal and philosophical examination of the treaties, as has been done in this Argument, it produces absolute conviction that the text and spirit of those documents were violated by the Demarcators, for which they should have been severely punished. The legal consequences of their acts were:

<small>Violation of the text and spirit of the treaties.</small>

1. They altered the areas which each Crown desired to keep (Preamble of the Treaty of 1750).
2. They disobeyed the Treaty of January 13, 1751, which gave to the "*Mapa de las Cortes*" the character of a *basis and guide* for the demarcation.
3. They forgot the treaty of January 17, 1751, which ordered them to govern their march according to this same map.
4. They disobeyed Article V of the Treaty of 1750, which traced the itinerary of their operations.
5. They forgot Article XXVIII of the Treaty of Instructions of January 17, 1751, which stipulated that the boundary should follow the river "*mas caudaloso,*" *i. e.,* of greatest volume.
6. They did not recognize the true locations given by the "*Mapa de las Cortes*" to the rivers *Uruguay-Pitá* and *Pepiry* or *Pequiry,* but they substituted for them incorrect locations, founded upon the childish recollections of an Indian, whose grave error was proved without any discussion by the High Parties to this controversy both in 1791 and in 1891.
7. They violently interpreted the text of the protocol signed upon the very "*Mapa de las Cortes*" itself by the negotiators of the Boundary Treaty, in which it was stated that the *red line* traced on that document was valid *from the Ocean* (*Castillos Grandes*) *to the junction of the rivers Ybicuy and Uruguay only so far as it conformed with the text of the treaty,* leaving it *absolutely* valid from the Ybicuy toward the North. This exception was made necessary by modifications made in the agree-

---

[1] Only in the part between the Sea and the Uruguay.

ment after the Map was made, and it did not effect nor attach to the part now submitted to the Arbitrator. I have explained this incident at pages 141 and 150 of this Argument.

8. And lastly, they paid no attention to the identical case of the Ygurey, in Article X of the Treaty of Instructions of January 17, 1751, upon which I have also commented at page 153 of this Argument.

Conclusions. Having demonstrated the nullity of the basis of their proceedings, it is unnecessary to occupy ourselves with their consequences. If the small stream called the Guarumbaca is not the river of the boundary, then neither is its correlative, its counter source upon the opposite watershed, which empties into the Yguazú, a boundary. Whether the latter was well or carelessly explored by the Demarcators of 1759 (the "*arroyo*" or small stream they called the "*San Antonio*") I shall not discuss. I simply say that it was a useless exploration.

Brazil sets up, then, as the basis of its pretensions and arguments the gross errors of two subordinate employees of Spain and Portugal. This basis lacks any probative force as against the Argentine Republic, because it was expressly annulled by the Treaty of 1761, and also because that of 1777 only ratified that part of the Treaty of 1750 which refers to the boundary line, and so expressly declares. But if the facts of 1759 cannot be adduced as legal arguments against the Argentines, they can be presented as moral elements in equity, which should appeal to the fair judgment of the Arbitrator. In this point of view they are also favorable to the Argentine Republic, for the mistaken Demarcators, condemning themselves, left proofs of their incapacity, weakness and lack of reason in the very documents upon which Brazil relies.

Second Brazilian argument. The second deduction drawn by the Empire from the error of the Demarcators, according to which "they recognized as belonging to Portugal all the territory situated to the East" of the "arroyo" or small stream mistakenly explored, is also without foundation. Far from declaring anything of the kind the two Crowns annulled the proceedings by the Treaty of 1761, presented to the Arbitrator.[1]

Third Argument. The third argument of Brazil, which follows the preceding on page 230 of this Argument, is simply a deduction from the first two. The worthless character of these being shown, the third conclusion also remains entirely refuted.

Demarcation of 1789-1791. The Treaty of 1777 put in the field new parties of Demarcators.

---

[1] "Argentine Evidence," Vol. I, page 79.

Their instructions obliged them to respect the *red line* of the Map of 1749 as a boundary of the dominions which the two monarchs not only reserved to themselves but which they guaranteed to one another in Article III of the Treaty of March 11, 1778. They were to proceed so that the navigation of the Rio de la Plata and the Uruguay should remain exclusively reserved to the Crown of Spain (Article III of the Treaty of October 1, 1777). In case of any doubts arising while they were on the ground, they were to be submitted to the decision of the two Courts (Article XV of the Treaty of 1777). If in consequence of such doubts any subject belonging to either of the Powers interested were to occupy any land belonging to the other, the act would be considered void, and the author punished at the pleasure of the offended Power (Article XIV of the Treaty of 1777). This provision accords with Article II of the Treaty of March 11, 1778.

<small>Instructions of the Demarcators.</small>

I have demonstrated that in the disputed region the boundary of the Treaty of 1777 was the same as that of the Treaty of 1750, ratified by the compact of 1778. Brazil has admitted these facts,[1] consequently the Demarcators of the Treaty of 1777 had a very clear mission—that of rectifying the errors of the Commissioners of 1759 by scrupulously exploring the ground in order to declare officially and definitively whether the rivers Uruguay-Pitá and Pepiry or Pequiry did exist or not in the locations where they were supposed to be, and where they were delineated by the two Courts upon the map of 1749 and Treaty of 1750.

If the Treaty of 1777 is attentively examined, comparing it with that of 1750, it will be discovered that the former is much clearer and more prolix in the description of the boundary than the latter. This prolixity, according to Article IV of the Treaty of 1777, was for the purpose of avoiding the confusions and disagreements of the prior Demarcators, and it recommends that the boundary be traced by *the most important peculiarities or features of the ground*, such as the mountains and *large rivers*.

<small>Clearness and fullness of the Treaty of 1777.</small>

The first dispute occurred in 1759 regarding the sources of the rivers that originate in the Estado Oriental (Uruguay) and flow into the Uruguay, or in that part of the boundary that lies between the Ocean and this river. The matter was minutely analyzed and resolved in Articles III, IV, and V of the new treaty, in such a manner that the operations in the field were reduced practically to the mere mechanical acts of a land surveyor.

[1] See this Argument, pages 172 and 173.

The new Treaty and the error of 1759.

The first doubts which arose in 1759, up to the Uruguay, thus being settled, the treaty considered the second dispute of the Commissioners, concerning the Territory situated between the Uruguay and the Paraná, and resolved it categorically, rejecting the "*arroyo*" or small stream of the Guarumbaca, or false Pequiry, as the Treaty of 1761 had already done, and insisting that they seek the Pequiry or Pepiry-Guazú, that is to say, the "Grande" or large one, which is the river of the "*Mapa de las Cortes.*"[1] It directs, in continuation, that there must be sought the principal source of the nearest river of the opposite watershed which empties into the Yguazú, to which it gives the name of "San Antonio."

Forced interpretations by Brazil.

The Brazilians wish to infer from this name the approval of the errors of the Demarcation of 1759, and they assert that this is the boundary river the source of which should correspond to the "*arroyo*" *Guarumbaca*, or the false Pepiry, on the opposite watershed. This interpretation is a violent one. The Treaty of 1750 has been expressly incorporated into the Treaty of 1777 in the particular of the boundary now submitted to the Arbitrator, and so also has the "*Mapa de las Cortes,*" which both Crowns declared to be an *integral part* of the former treaty in a protocol signed upon the very map itself. The situation of the boundary river Pepiry or Pequiry, which should be a large river (*Río Grande*), being given on that map, and it being demonstrated in 1791 and in 1891 that this river actually exists in the field in the same position in which it is delineated upon the map, it is clear that the boundary must continue by the principal headwaters of the nearest river upon the opposite watershed which empties into the Yguazú.

The false Pepiry of 1759 is therefore expressly rejected by this treaty and its antecedents, and, of course, the opposite "*arroyo,*" which was termed the "San Antonio," also stands rejected. Farther on it will be proved that the Brazilian and Argentine Demarcators of 1891 found that the watershed of the false Pepiry or "*arroyo*" of Guarumbaca and the counter or opposite watershed of the San Antonio were not *near one another* and did not correspond, as was strictly required by the treaties of 1750 and 1777.

The "arroyo" and the river San Antonio.

The demarcation, therefore, is guided by the rivers *Uruguay-Pitá* and *Pepiry* or *Pequiry-Guazú*; and the river *San Antonio*, which must be the river corresponding thereto upon the opposite watershed, flowing

[1] See this Argument, p. 163.

into the Yguazú, is entirely dependent as regards its location upon the situation of the first rivers, the *basis and guide* for the operations of the Demarcators. The name of "San Antonio" given by the Treaty of 1777 to the river that might be found in this position was, therefore, a name without any previous geographical determination, only being adopted to facilitate the discussion and the drawing up of the documents, it being understood that it would be applied on the ground to the *unnamed river* which they were looking for. It has been clearly shown that the two international explorations of 1791 and 1891, without any discrepancy, demonstrated that the "*arroyo*" Guarumbaca (false Pepiry) and the "*arroyo*" San Antonio of 1759, claimed by Brazil as the boundary, did not fulfil the conditions required by the treaties as to the correlation and close proximity of their respective watersheds; while these requirements are fully met, as has been proved by observations, by the relations found to exist between the *Pepiry or Pequiry-Guazú* and the *San Antonio-Guazú* of Oyarvide, which are maintained by the Argentines.[1]

On the other hand the original documents of the annulled Demarcation of 1759, which I have presented, always speak of the Pepiry. If the Treaty of 1777 had wished to consider the operation well done and to adopt the boundary arrived at therein, it would have preserved the same names and said so in express terms, in order to leave without effect the annullment made by the Treaty of 1761. But from the third Article of the former treaty, before mentioning the boundary in question, each time it had to refer to the river Pepiry or Pequiry it abandoned entirely the name given to it in the Treaty of 1750 and the documents of the erroneous Demarcation of 1759, and employed another and a new and descriptive name. Articles III and IV call it several times the Pepiry or Pequiry-Guazú, as well as in Article VIII which refers to the question. This precaution of never repeating in any case, not even incidentally, the name of the river wrongly adopted in 1759, throws light upon the Treaty of 1750. On applying it to the ground the Demarcators of 1759 called an "*arroyo*" or small stream the Pepiry. The treaty of 1777 declared substantially that the river Pepiry of the "*Mapa de las Cortes*" and of the boundary was a *large river*, and in order to avoid doubts on the part of the new Demarcators it added this descriptive term, which excluded the "*arroyo*" of

---

[1] See this Argument, page 255.

1759 and required the "*Rio Grande*" or large river officially drawn on the Map—the Pepiry or Pequiry-Guazú.

Application of the Treaty, 1759-1791.
The Demarcators went upon the ground and after three years of fruitless discussion they suspended their operations because they could not come to an agreement, and submitted the case to the deliberation of the two Courts, in virtue of Article XV of the Treaty of 1777. The Portuguese Commissioners insisted on carrying the boundary along the "*arroyos*" or small streams mistakenly explored in 1759. The Spanish Demarcators maintained the rivers of the "*Mapa de las Cortes*" and of the treaties, which they had just explored with their Portuguese colleagues. The Royal Courts did not settle the case, for Spain and Portugal were involved in the military crisis produced in Europe by Bonaparte, and soon after this came the political emancipation of South America. The nations that inherited these regions from Spain and Portugal, have, as I have shown, been on the point of settling this conflict between the Demarcators by a division of the disputed territory.

Results of the demarcation of 1789-1791.
But if this demarcation did not give a definitive result, it nevertheless advanced the general knowledge concerning the geographical facts, and in a very important manner, because it cleared up doubts and reinforced the solutions of the "*Mapa de las Cortes*" and of the Treaty of 1750. As a matter of fact, the Demarcators of 1759 retreated to the "*arroyos*," or small streams, wrongly selected, convinced that the *large river* called the "Pequiry" on the "*Mapa de las Cortes*" did not exist. But the Demarcators of 1789 scrupulously explored the ground and they found the rivers *Uruguay-Pitá* and *Pepiry* in the very places and positions indicated by the official Map. Therefore the vital consequences resulting from the exploration of 1789[1] were two, that is to say—

1. To correct the errors of the Demarcators of 1759, who confounded the river Mberny with the Uruguay-Pitá, situated further up.

2. To rectify the mistake of these same Commissioners, in declaring that they did not believe in the existence of the large river, "*Rio Grande*," of the official map.

These corrections were made by common explorations on the part of the Spaniards and Portuguese, as may be seen by examining the maps of 1789 and of 1891, which were signed by the agents of both governments. I present the Arbitrator with an unauthenticated

[1] The exploration lasted several years, but it is named for convenience in 1789, as that was the year of the dispute. Argentine Evidence, Map No. 16.

copy of the Official Map of 1789, signed by the Commissioners of both Spain and Portugal, who were instructed to find the rivers of the Treaty of 1750 and of its *basis and guide*, the Official Map of 1749. These Commissioners were: on the part of Spain, Don José Varela y Ulloa, and on the part of Portugal, General Don Sebastian Xavier da Veyga Cabral da Camara. The copy of the original which I present to the Arbitrator, in which these boundaries are shown, bears the declaration of the Portuguese geographers recognizing that the river Pepiry or Pequiry sought existed in the location given by the "*Mapa de las Cortes*," but refused to accept that legal boundary.

This map shows the following vital features, previously questioned and in doubt:

1. The true location of the Uruguay-Pitá.
2. The river wrongly called Uruguay-pitá in 1759, with this inscription: "*Uruguay-Pitá de los Demarcadores pasados.*" (Uruguay-Pitá of the past Demarcators.)
3. The river wrongly called Pepiry in 1759, with this inscription: "*Arroyo Pepiry de los Demarcadores pasados.*" (Pepiry of the past Demarcators.)
4. The river also wrongly called Pepiry by the Portuguese Demarcator Saldanha, with this inscription: "*Rio Apetereby de los Demarcadores pasados.*" (River Apetereby of the past Demarcators.)
5. The river Pequiry or Pepiry-Guazú of the "*Mapa de las Cortes,*" and "*caudaloso*" (of large volume), with a reef inside of its mouth and an island in front of it, bearing this most important inscription: "*Rio caudaloso de 256 varas*[1] *y 2 piés de cause*, QUE TIENE APARIENCIAS DE SER EL PEPIRY VERDADERO. (A river of large volume, of 256 varas and two feet in depth, *which has the appearance of being the true Pepiry*.)
6. The Uruguay Pitá, with this inscription: "*Uruguay-Pitá verdadero*. (The true Uruguay Pita.)

Brazil has claimed that the "*Mapa de las Cortes*" was not kept in view by the negotiators of the Treaty of 1777, and further that they were guided by other maps without any official character, which will be discussed in a final chapter. The proof to the contrary exists in the Archives of Portugal and Spain. I have presented at page 153 of this Argument the facsimile of the secret map which the King of Portugal sent in 1752 to his sister, Doña Barbara, the Queen of

The "*Mapa de las Cortes,*" followed in the negotiation of the Treaty of 1777.

---

[1] A Spanish yard measure.

Spain, begging her influence with her husband that the boundaries of the Treaty of 1750 should be maintained. I also submit to the Arbitrator in the Portfolio of Maps, XVIII century, Map No. 17, copied from the official Archives of Spain and duly certified by the Consul of the United States of America, with the title of—

> The Chief of the Archives, Library, and Interpretation of Languages of the Department of State, certifies that the present photographic copy is a reproduction of the upper left-hand part of the original map signed by the Demarcators Sres. Varela y Ulloa and Veyga Cabral da Camara, and has been made by the Photographers Laurent and Co., under the inspection of the office in my charge. Witness my hand and seal in Madrid, March 8, 1893. Manuel del Palacio.

This map clearly indicates the error of the Demarcators of 1759, and the differences between the river called the Pepiry of the past Demarcators and the true rivers which are denominated Pepiry or Pequiry-Guazú and San Antonio Guazú. This map coincides with the former in putting in evidence the errors of the past Demarcators as to the rivers. It also coincides in all particulars with the "*Mapa de las Cortes*," and is signed by the Demarcators of Spain and Portugal.

Finally, I present another map, preserved in the Archives of Spain, made by agreement of the engineers of the two nations [Argentine Evidence, Map No. 15], which is entitled:

> "*Plano corográfico*," etc.—Descriptive map of the reconnoissances pertaining to the Demarcation of Article VIII of the Preliminary Boundary Treaty of October 11, 1777, made by the second Spanish and Portuguese Subdivisions in order to clear up the doubts which have arisen between the respective Commissioners.
>
> The course of the rivers that have not been reconnoitered is put in light lines and taken from the map of the past Demarcations, and the dotted lines indicate the most probable direction of the river where they appear, as in the San Antonio Guazú.

Errors of the Viceroy Vertiz inspired by Portuguese. So great was the confusion and ignorance of the two governments and their agents respecting the numerous rivers of the immense region of the boundaries, that the Viceroy, when drawing up some instructions for the Commissioners, fell into gross mistakes that increased the doubts and made more difficult the task of clearing up the entangled boundary questions. In fact, when the Commissioners appointed to locate upon the ground the Treaty of 1777 arrived at the Rio de la

Plata, the heroic Viceroy Ceballos, the conqueror of the Portuguese, had been called to Spain to take charge of the War Department and had been replaced by Lieutenant-General Don Juan José Vertiz, who had just arrived from Europe. A Portuguese officer who appeared at the same time in Buenos Aires, without any clear explanation of the reason therefor, gained the confidence of the Viceroy and came to be his most trusted counsellor in boundary matters with Portugal ! Don Custodio de Sáa y Faria was not only a Portuguese, but if the Arbitrator will open the third volume of the official Collection of the Treaties of Portugal, at page 118 he will find the following statement:

1735, May 30. Instructions that we, Gomes Freire de Andrada and the Marquis de Val de Lirios, the Principal Commissioners of their very Faithful and Catholic Majesties, have given and signed to govern the Commissioners of the Third Party of Demarcators, the Sergeant Mor Engenheiro *and José Custodio da Sáa y Faria*, and Don Manuel Antonio de Flores, Lieutenant-Colonel and Commander of the Royal Navy, so that they may be executed as is hereby prescribed.

It is thus officially proved that General Sáa y Faria was one of the Demarcators commissioned by Portugal in order to trace the boundaries of the Treaty of 1750. With a counsellor of such origin what would the Viceroy of Buenos Aires be likely to propose in favor of Spain? This Portuguese officer, his adviser and intimate, was one of the authors of the erroneous and disapproved demarcation of 1759.

Furthermore the Viceroy Vertiz had not been charged with the duty of giving instructions to the Commissioners. They brought these signed by Don José Galvez, Minister of Foreign Affairs of Spain. The Viceroy of Buenos Aires ought simply to have followed them, but notwithstanding this, under the influence of this Portuguese official, he presented a brief memoir to the King to the effect that the Treaty of 1777 was more disadvantageous for Spain than that of 1750, and proposing to correct the boundaries upon the ground. This was as a general proposition absurd, for it has been already demonstrated that by the latter treaty (1750) Spain ceded to Portugal a fourth part of South America; while it only regained a part of these territories and the Colony of Sacramento by that of 1777, with the exclusive sovereignty over the Rivers Paraná, Uruguay and de la Plata.

The suggestion of the Portuguese official is explained, therefore, by the fact that Portugal wanted to keep the cessions of 1750 which had been annulled, and all the Portuguese Demarcators of the treaty of 1777 came to the ground with the secret instruction to delay the operations and make them as difficult as possible, so as to bring about the annullment of the compact.[1] That the Viceroy was influenced by his Portuguese counsellor is shown by the following document, the original of which is in the Argentine Legation at the disposal of the Arbitrator.[2] It runs as follows :

BUENOS AIRES, *Sept.* 4, 1778.

To Exmo. Señor Joseph de Galvez:

SIR: I received the written Instructions of June 6 last directing that everything possible be done to facilitate the demarcation and settlement of the boundaries in America between our nation and the Portuguese.

This matter has received, on account of its great importance, my constant attention since my arrival in this Capital, so that I had already prepared some Instructions which may be added to the present paper, referring to the local circumstances of the countries through which the line is to be followed and other matters which have been carefully thought out. It should be stated to your Excellency that *this good result has in a large measure been brought about by the enterprise and the practical knowledge of the Portuguese Brigadier, Don Joseph Custodio Sáa y Faria.*

I include a copy of No. 1 of the additions which have already been agreed upon with the Viceroy of Rio de Janeiro, in order that in the operations in the field there should be no doubts or differences which would delay the work, and I send them at once, begging an early reply.

Wishing your Honor, etc.

JUAN JOSEPH DE VERTIZ.

The Viceroy had been in the same way induced by his Portuguese counsellor to give the Demarcators instructions that modified the boundary in accordance with the interests of Portugal in the territory submitted to this Arbitration, but in a form different from that claimed by the Demarcators of 1759 and also from that required by the treaties and the map of 1749. There was thus brought about a state of chaos which is now invoked by Brazil in support of its unfounded pretensions.

As I have said, the Viceroy was not authorized or charged to give

---

[1] See this Argument, chapter on Demarcations.
[2] See Argentine Evidence, Vol. I, page 550. [Advice given by Sáa y Faria.]

these instructions, and this act on his part was spontaneously suggested by the Portuguese official.

The instructions drawn up in these terms prove at the same time the absolute candor and ignorance of this strange Viceroy concerning the boundaries in question, the Treaty of 1750, the "*Mapa de las Cortes*" of 1749, and the substantial errors of fact and right committed by the Demarcators of 1759. Consequently the Viceroy of Buenos Aires, whom the Portuguese Brigadier led by the nose, instead of throwing light upon the treaties and the instructions drawn up by the King of Spain, of which he acknowledged the receipt, deprived them of their essential characteristics, making confused and entangled what they ordered with precision. The Viceroy in fact said, referring to the boundaries of the zone in dispute:

> In order that the Demarcators of this Party may arrive at the place indicated at the bar of the river Pepiry-Guazú, they should be guided by the course of the Uruguay-Pitá to its junction with the River Uruguay, *so that at a distance of two leagues and a third, following the bank of the river Uruguay* on the West side, will be found the opposite bank to the bar of the river Pepiry. The river Uruguay-Pitá is well known by the Indians of Misiones, especially by those of the pueblo of San Angel, who are nearest to it and pass its headwaters by the road that goes to the Vaqueria.

The confusion and error are here evident. The "*Mapa de las Cortes*" had given as a *guide* for the demarcation of the Treaty of 1750 the Uruguay-Pitá. On this point the Viceroy agreed with the map which was the *basis and guide* of the treaties of 1750 and 1777; but instead of following this guide and looking for the boundary river *above* the Uruguay-Pitá, he ordered it to be looked for *down stream*, with wrong data, giving as the distance two and one-third leagues. This was equivalent to introducing a third line of demarcation between that of 1759 and that of 1789. The Portuguese Brigadier had attained his object, for upon arriving on the ground the Commissioners of Spain wrote officially to the Viceroy of Buenos Aires informing him that his instructions were wrong, and that besides they violated the treaties. The Portuguese were well informed of all that was going on, and insisted upon adhering to the demarcation of 1759, so that the survey failed once more, as they desired it to do. Shortly afterwards the Portuguese armies invaded the dominions of Spain, as I have already stated,[1] and the intrigue against the treaty of 1777 was made evident to all fair-minded persons.

Results of the errors of the Viceroy of Buenos Aires.

Brazil deduces from these instructions the claim that the Viceroy of Buenos Aires restored and ratified the erroneous demarcation of 1759, which had been annulled, and that, consequently, the boundary fixed by it is the proper one. It is impossible, however, to reconcile justice with such facts. In public law and in civil law the nullity of official acts is not to be presumed, but it must be declared in solemn form, and this was done in the case of the demarcation of 1759 in the Treaty of 1761.[2] To restore or make valid again an act previously declared void is still more delicate, and requires the express manifestation, in a clear and solemn manner, of the intention of those who caused the invalidity. The Sovereigns did not do this in the Treaty of 1777, nor is there any additional treaty in which this has been done. On the contrary, in the third Article of the Treaty of 1778, there is a provision expressly restoring the boundary of the "*Mapa de las Cortes*," made by Portugal in 1749 and protocoled in 1751. A Viceroy, only an agent of the King, with powers limited to the administrative care of a colony and without any diplomatic character, could not make declarations that would alter existing treaties or that would affect the national sovereignty. The reports requested by the Minister of State from an employé of the Council and the opinion of the latter favorable to the instructions given by Viceroy Vertiz, the mistakes in which he could not perceive on account of his lack of geographical knowledge about this matter, are incidents of administrative procedure which cannot be permitted to modify the treaties. Besides, as a matter of fact, all this was erroneous, and the King refused to authorize it when he was informed later of such blunders.

The approval at last proposed, based upon this careless and unfounded report and the instructions given by the Viceroy of Buenos Aires, does not better the strict legal status of this document, for an international compact cannot be altered by the acts of one of the parties alone. The Boundary Treaty of 1777 was negotiated by a diplomat who was a specialist, and it related to a matter of which the King and his Minister were ignorant, for they had not like the negotiator made a special study of the subject. When the note from the Viceroy Vertiz arrived no one made a comparative examination of it, but some subordinate, thinking it was merely a matter of form, drew up

---
[1] See this Argument, page 149.
[2] Idem, page 79.

the different parts of the procedure for approval. The document remains in the Argentine Legation at the disposal of the Arbitrator. On its last page may be read the draft of a note of approval in the following terms:

> In a letter dated September 4, of the year last past, No. 28, your Excellency forwarded the Instructions dated June 5 of the same year, to which additions had been made in order to facilitate as much as possible the demarcation of the boundaries between our nation and Portugal. In these additions your Excellency gave an exact geographical and economic statement to facilitate the voyages of the surveying parties and the execution of the work incumbent upon them in regard to the direction, certainty and care of marking the boundaries according to the spirit of the Treaty; and so recognizing it, the King approves all the additions made by your Excellency to the aforesaid Instructions, and I communicate this by His Royal Order for your information and that you may provide that all those employed in the Parties that belong to your jurisdiction shall be governed thereby. May God keep you.
> El Pardo, January 12, 1779. To Don Juan José Vertiz.

As may be seen this is an ordinary paper drawn up by a clerk with the usual formalities, which was not even signed, nor is there any evidence that it was ever accepted or sent to the Viceroy of Buenos Ayres. The Royal Cédula of approval has never been presented.

Shortly after these careless administrative proceedings, the Government of Spain refused to authorize this scheme and openly opposed the errors of its subordinate, the Viceroy Vertiz. The King of Spain then decided to give the desired intervention in this case to the negotiator of the treaty, the Conde de Florida Blanca, who had prepared the Instructions which had been opposed and entangled by the Viceroy, and to declare that these Instructions were maintained as sufficient and clear. Minister Galvez did, in fact, sign in 1782 an explanation of them, which was to be sent to the Demarcators, instead of the Instructions suggested to Vertiz by the Portuguese General. *The acts of the Viceroy revoked by the Spanish government.*

The original explanations appear in the "Argentine Evidence," Group D of Manuscripts, Document No. 8. In the commentary on the fourth Article of this document the boundary line which the Portuguese official suggested to the Viceroy of Buenos Aires is expressly rejected. It says:

To the Viceroy of Buenos Ayres:

In view of the letter of your Excellency of February 5, 1779, No. 94, accompanying the opinion of *Brig. Don Custodio de Sáa y Faria*, with two plans which set forth the difficulties that would arise from establishing the boundary line through the districts designated, the Conde de Florida Blanca has sent to me, dated yesterday, the official paper which I insert here, of the contents of which you will inform our Commissioners in order that they may conform to it in all their operations.

Your Excellency:

In a note of the 13th of January of this year Your Excellency reminds me of an official note that you sent me on the 28th of May of the preceding year, sending me a letter from the Viceroy of Buenos Aires which accompanied an opinion of Brigadier Don Joseph Custodio de Sáa y Faria, respecting the difficulties which they believe would arise from tracing the line of boundaries in South America through the places prescribed in our last treaty with the Court of Portugal, and setting down, on one of the maps sent with the aforesaid opinion, the localities through which in his judgment the line should be drawn.[1]

To the end that Your Excellency *may inform the Viceroy of Buenos Aires, and he, in his turn, our Commissioners, of the true letter and spirit of the Preliminary Boundary Treaty, I will explain how it must be understood.* I think I can best do so by putting down here Articles IV, VIII and XVI, as they appeared in print, and the explanatory notes on the margin of each one.[2]

Article IV.—To avoid another source of discord between the two Monarchies, such as has been the entrance to the Lagoon de los Patos or Rio Grande de San Pedro and following it up its source as far as the River Yacui, whose two banks and navigation have been claimed by both Crowns, it has now been agreed upon, that the said entrance and navigation shall remain the exclusive property of Portugal, its domains extending along the southern bank up to the "*arroyo*" of Tahim, continuing along the banks of Lagoon de Manguera in a straight line to the sea, and on the Continent the line will go from the banks of the said Lagoon de Merin, taking a route along the first southern "*arroyo*" which enters its outlet or mouth, and which runs nearest to the Portuguese Fort of San Gonzalo, whence the Portuguese possessions will continue, without overstepping the limits of the said "*arroyo*," along the head-waters of the rivers which run towards the aforesaid Rio Grande and towards the Yacui [it does not say that the Yacuy shall altogether belong to Portugal] until passing above those of the rivers Ararica and Coyacui, which shall remain in the Portu-

---
[1] The line two and one-half leagues below the Uruguay-Pitá; this Argument, page 244.
[2] They will be placed in the text in brackets.

guese part, and those of the rivers Piratiní and Ibimini which shall remain in the Spanish part, a line [nothing is said of the line being necessarily straight] shall be traced which shall cover the Portuguese settlements as far as the outlet of the Pepiri-Guazú river into the Uruguay; and *which shall also save and cover the Spanish settlements and Misiones on the said Uruguay, which shall remain in their present condition as possessions of the Spanish Crown;* recommending to the Commissioners who are to lay out this line of demarcation to follow along its entire length the direction of the mountains along their tops or along the rivers, if there are any suitable; and to make of the headwaters and sources of these rivers the boundaries of one and the other possessions in all places *where it can be done,* so that all the rivers that rise within one possession and run towards it shall remain in favor of that Power; this can be done on the line [the expressions italicised and underlined in this Article and in the XVI prove that the line of demarcation *pointed out by Brigadier Sáa was thus imagined by him,* inasmuch as the bounds and rivers, herein indicated and in the instructions, are not prejudicial to our saving our settlements and pastures] that is to run from the lagoon Merin to the Pepirí-Guazú river, at which place there are no large rivers, crossing from one country into the other, *because wherever such occur, this method cannot be employed,* as it is evident, and such one will be followed as is specified for each respective case in other Articles of this Treaty. *For the purpose of saving the properties and principal possessions of both Crowns,* His Catholic Majesty, in his own name and on behalf of his heirs and successors, cedes in favor of His Most Faithful Majesty, his heirs and his successors, each and all rights that may pertain to him over the territories which, as is explained in this Article, shall belong to the Crown of Portugal.

Article VIII.—Whereas the possessions of both Crowns are already marked out up to the entrance of the Pepirí river or Pepirí-Guazú into the Uruguay, the high contracting parties have agreed that the line of demarcation shall continue up the said river Pepirí to its principal source, thence over the highest part of the land, according to the rules laid down by Article VI, it will continue until *it meets the waters of the river San Antonio* [nothing is said about the necessity of meeting them in a straight line, nor in front; it is sufficient for the meeting to take place in those regions in order to descend the waters of the Yguazú; but *saving the present possessions of both Sovereigns, and the plantations, mines or pastures at present in their possession that are not ceded,* as stated in Article XVI, and it is very plain that Article VIII does not cede the two pueblos of Spaniards and Indians mentioned by Brigadier Sáa] which empty into the Grande de Curitiba, otherwise called *Yguazú,* continuing along this, down the river, to its entrance into the Paraná on its eastern bank, thence to continue up stream, along the said Paraná, to its junction with the river Ygurei on the western bank.

Article XVI.—The Commissioners, or persons appointed on the terms explained by the preceding Article, besides the rules established in this Treaty, will bear in mind, in all cases not specified in it, that their object must be, in tracing out the boundary line, the reciprocal security and perpetual peace and tranquility of both nations, and the total extermination of the smuggling operations that the subjects of the one may carry on in the possessions or with the subjects of the other; therefore in view of these two objects they shall be given the corresponding orders to avoid disputes *that may not be directly prejudicial to the present possession of both Sovereigns,* or to the common or exclusive navigation of these rivers, or channels, according to the agreement in Article XIII, or *to the plantations, mines or pastures at present in their possession that are not ceded by this Treaty* [ceded specifically, stating the land, pueblo, pasture, coasts or place of cession], for the benefit of the line of boundaries, as it is the intention of both august Sovereigns, in order to attain the true peace and friendship which they hope will be perpetual and close, for their reciprocal repose and the good of their subjects, that attention shall only be given in those vast regions through which the line of demarcation shall be drawn, to the *preservation of all that which may remain in possession of each by virtue of this treaty and the final am of boundaries,* so arranging these as to avoid for all time all causes of doubt and discord.

Your Excellency will infer from the above, and will kindly so inform the Viceroy of Buenos Aires, that the line of demarcation to be traced, and the one agreed upon, is no other than that one which shall make clear the belongings and shall save the respective possessions, to which end the rivers are indicated, except in those cases where there has been a *de facto* cession of some place, pueblo or territory, as those *de jure* will not suffice, except in those cases when the party to whom the cession is made was already in possession. I have fully notified the King's Ambassador at Lisbon of all this, so that he may obtain from that Court orders in accordance with what I have stated to Your Excellency.

It is impossible to foresee all the difficulties that may occur to the Commissioners of both Crowns when they are upon the ground, but if they attend to the true spirit and meaning of the Treaty, *if they see that the subjects of their respective sovereigns shall remain in possession of those grass lands, plantations, mines and pastures, that are necessary to them,* and if they proceed in good faith in carrying out their Commission, if they come to some agreement among themselves which shall not be injurious to their august Masters, saving their present posses-

sions, they will avoid troublesome disputes, from which the least injury that could result would be the loss of time.
Dated Aranjuez, April 7, 1782.
(Signed) JOSEPH DE GALVEZ.

This document is of decisive importance, for it repudiates the errors of the Portuguese Demarcator Faria, so innocently accepted by the new Viceroy of Buenos Aires. These explanations of the meaning of the Treaty of 1777 confirm the Instructions of the author of the same, dated June 6, 1778. The commentary upon the fourth Article refers to the line drawn by the Portuguese General as the boundary. *Comments upon the new Instructions by the King.*

The maps of the reference have not been found; but it is not necessary to have them in view, since I have frankly stated that the line suggested by General Sáa y Faria was accepted by the Viceroy of Buenos Aires and that it was an intermediate line between the erroneous one designated by the Demarcators of 1759, which was annulled in 1761, and the line delineated by the "*Mapa de las Cortes.*" But the communication of the Spanish Government and the note to the fourth Article again reject and annul this line. The boundary line was therefore to be transferred from the *false Pepiry*, or the "*arroyo*" of *Guarumbaca*, to the Pequiry or Pepiry-Guazú ("*El Grande*" or large river), as the only way to save the Spanish possessions.

Article VIII is more explicit, because it speaks of the rivers of the boundary in dispute, and referring to the San Antonio does not recognize the importance given to it by the Portuguese and the Brazilians, but adds very positively that the boundary river must cover the Spanish possessions and avoid leaving the two pueblos of Spaniards and Indians existing in the Territory now in arbitration in the power of the Portuguese, since if this were to happen the treaty would be violated as to its meaning, which was that each Crown should keep the possessions agreed upon in the "*Mapa de las Cortes*" of 1759. What *pueblos* were those? If the Arbitrator will turn to page 40 of this Argument and glance at the Portfolio of Maps of the "Argentine Evidence," he will find the official map of the Government of the Rio de la Plata of 1612, and on this, in the Territory submitted to his decision, near the River Pequiry or Pepiry-Guazú of the "*Mapa de las Cortes,*" he will see a *pueblo* of Spaniards and Indians. The other *pueblo* was founded by Governor Rui Dias de Guzman in person, as stated at page 40 of this Argument, in order to exploit the gold mines which the map of 1612 indicates at the mouth of that river. Its ruins were officially recognized in 1863 by the Brazilians, as stated in this

Argument. Applying to the ground the meaning of this Article, its text and its spirit, according to the Spanish Minister Galvez, the only way of tracing the boundary was along the *red line* of the "*Mapa de las Cortes*," which saves for Spain these *pueblos*, whatever may be the situation of the river *San Antonio*.

From the new Instructions of Minister Galvez it is clear that the river Pepiry-Guazu must be taken as the *basis* and afterwards there must be connected with this a river which flows to the Yguazú, whatever it may be. Finally, the last sentences of this document reject any other boundary line which does not respect the possessions of Spain previously specified in the "*Mapa de las Cortes*" of 1749, expressly incorporated by the Treaty of 1778 in the Treaty of 1777, as it had already been by its own protocol in that of 1750.

The Viceroy Vertiz had also committed the error of trying to give an international character to the Instructions suggested by the Commissioner of Portugal, Sáa y Faria, addressing himself to the Viceroy of Rio de Janeiro, asking him to agree with them. To repudiate this act, which could not have been carried out except by virtue of authority as Plenipotentiary which he did not have, the new instructions of the King of Spain ended by stating that this Monarch had requested the King of Portugal to give instructions to his Demarcators in conformity with this interpretation of the boundary compact. Portugal did not protest against this understanding and accepted it.

Fundamental Clause. The clause at the end of the instructions directing that the "*yerbales*" and pasture fields needed for the Spanish possessions be saved is really of great importance. The documents presented, pages 40 and 87, prove that the disputed Territory contained the cultivated "*yerbales*" for the trade of San Xavier. Tracing the boundary by the Pepiry of the mistake of 1759, or by the river two and a half leagues below the Uruguay-Pitá of the Portuguese Brigadier Faria and the Viceroy of Buenos Ayres, the Treaty of 1777 was violated, for this left some of the actual possessions of Spain under Portuguese dominion.

The surveyors in the field. Their guides and instructions. I have said that shortly after arriving upon the ground where the demarcation was to be made, the Commissioners saw clearly that the Viceroy of Buenos Aires had made a mistake. The basis and guide which the Spanish Commissioners had were the Treaties of 1750 and 1777, the official map that served to draw up these treaties and the instructions already cited of the King of Spain, issued in 1778, not yet called to the attention of the Arbitrator. These instructions state in the part relating to this region that the rivers *Pepiry-Guazú and San Antonio-Guazú* are navigable. This is the language :[1]

> But considering that the work of this Division, until reaching the foot of the Grand Fall of the River Paraná, may be impracticable in the terms stated, proposed by the Court of Lisbon, by the Serranos mountains, and without any road, and rivers of very short navigation, as are the Pepiry-Guazú and San Antonio, etc.

The original documents of the demarcation of 1759 prove that the "*arroyos*" or small streams were absolutely *unnavigable*. The same Article of these instructions adds:

> And the other subdivision leaves the river Ybicuy, which has its origin in and passes by Monte Grande, and crossing by the Pueblos of *Misiones* to that of Candelaria or to that of Corpus, the last on the Eastern bank of those of Paraná, going up that in boats to the foot of the Fall of the river Yguazú or Curitiba, which is distant three leagues from its mouth in the Paraná, and stopping on the Northern bank the Canoes will be taken to the top of the Fall, navigating in them to the river San Antonio, which is the second that enters by the Southern bank.

The Portuguese and Brazilians, who always lacked any legal criterion for applying the boundary treaties to the ground, thought they had found in the last part of that phrase an argument favorable to their pretentions. And in fact, confounding the repeated declarations of the Treaties of 1750 and 1777, which ordered that the rivers of greatest volume (*mas caudalosos*) should be followed, they mistook the "*arroyos*" or small streams, lacking water and obstructed by an excess of rocks and stones, for the *navigable rivers* specified in these same instructions, and they counted the small streams that enter the river Yguazú in order to apply to their advantage the text about the *second river*. When Minister Galvez reduced the instructions to writing he must have borne in mind that according to the "*Mapa de las Cortes*" only two rivers entered the Yguazú; the two delineated upon that Map without names, and which the international explorations of 1891 have proved to be, without any question whatever, the only rivers of great volume or of importance which run through this Territory

---

[1] This document is very well known. It is published in Volume III, page 2, of the "Collection of Treaties," by Calvo, already quoted and presented to the Arbitrator.

and empty into the Yguazú. They bear the Brazilian names of *Chopin* and *Vangada*, the latter improperly, because it is the *San Antonio-Guazú* of the Demarcators of 1791.

The Demarcators of 1759 went up the Yguazú from the Paraná and arrived at the unimportant "*arroyo*," or small stream, which was called by them "San Francisco," and at the one immediately beyond this they stopped, saying it was the one of the boundary and calling it "San Antonio."

To the East of these small streams the first river of great volume (*caudaloso*) and navigable that flows into the Yguazú is that now called Chopin, delineated without name on the "*Mapa de las Cortes*," and the second one is the San Antonio-Guazú, the correlative of the Pepiry or Pequiry of the "*Mapa de las Cortes*" and of the treaties. Therefore these instructions are against the claims of Brazil which invokes them.

Geographical proofs of the preceding deductions. The comments I have made upon the documents were confirmed on the ground. The Demarcators found that the data furnished by the Portuguese official, and signed by the Viceroy of Buenos Aires, were not only contrary to the rights of Spain, but audaciously entangled. And this circumstance once more establishes, if there was any necessity therefor, that the purpose which guided the agents of Portugal in entangling the work and making it each day more confused, was to obtain the annulment of the Treaty of 1777 and return again to dominate the left bank of the Rio de la Plata, occupying the Colony of Sacramento, given back to Spain by the last compact. In fact, the Viceroy Vertiz wanted the Demarcators to find the Pepiry or Pequiry-Guazú by navigating the Uruguay-Pitá as far as the Uruguay and then descending that river a distance of two leagues and a third, where they were to find the boundary river.[1] This was a new confusion, for these indications and distances corresponded to other rivers, concerning which no question had ever been made.

There were commissioned to make this exploration the Spanish pilot Gundin and the Portuguese Geographer Dr. Saldanha. After traversing with much difficulty the great forest of the Uruguay-Pitá they arrived at the left bank of that river, in latitude 27° 17' 23" South, that is to say: near the point where it empties into the Uruguay, where they began to make ready to go on in canoes. They set out on their navi-

[1] See this Argument, page 255.

gation on the 30th of April and arrived the same day at its mouth, where it empties into the Uruguay.

On the first of May they went down the stream of this river in search of the Pepiry or Pequiry-Guazú, which they expected to find at a distance of two and a third leagues, but they did not encounter it, although they continued their navigation for a distance of forty-six miles from the mouth of the Uruguay-Pitá where they began the descent of the Uruguay. Reduced to a straight line the distance was about 23 miles; that is to say, it was three times greater than that indicated in the instructions suggested to the Viceroy by the Portuguese Commissioner.[1]

Not having found the Pepiry they went back up stream, supposing that this river might have been the one the mouth of which they passed about ten miles below the bar of the Uruguay-Pitá, and which was the one that figured in the international plan of 1891 under the name of the river of "*Las Antas*," or "*Desmonte*." At the mouth of this new river Dr. Saldanha directed a clearing to be made, and left carved upon an isolated tree in that place the following Latin inscription: "*Post facta resurgens, Pepiry-Guazú.* 1788. *R. F.*" He thus signified that after the reconnoissances made he had arrived at the true Pepiry-Guazú.

A third Boundary line, between the two former ones.

Here we have a third boundary line, between the two already opposed to each other, which only reveals how serious were the uncertainties in the midst of which the Portuguese were proceeding. This river, which was considered by Saldanha as a revelation, was, nevertheless, neither the Pepiry wrongly identified in 1759, nor the true Pepiry or Pequiry-Guazú, the one designated in the "*Mapa de las Cortes*" and the one indicated in the instructions of these Demarcators who were so incapable of any effort.

This river was a third river "Pepiry," "*resurgens*" to suit the convenience of the Portuguese, but destined to keep for only a brief time the wrong name which had been applied to it by the astronomer of that nation. It is now known by the name of "Las Antas," as I have stated, and before that was called "Desmonte," on account of the clearing that Saldanha ordered to be made at its mouth.[2] But this fact also proves

Important conclusion proved by the facts.

[1] The Journals of the Demarcators have been published in the work by Señor Calvo, cited, Vol. 8, page 408.

[2] Studies of the Argentine Demarcator, Don Valentin Virasoro, published in 1892, by the Argentine Geographical Institute.

that the Portuguese Demarcators believed that the false Pepiry of 1759 was not the boundary river, for they sought another river.

The Commissioners Gundin and Saldanha gave an account of the result of their expedition to their respective Commissions, and these directed that they should go back and make a new reconnoisance with special instructions given by each one.

The errors of 1759 in evidence. One of the mistakes made by the Indian in 1759 was already found to be evident, namely his confusion regarding the true river Uruguay-Pitá. The Commissioners Gundin and Saldanha had passed, shortly before arriving at the Apeterebí, the mouth of a river, a southern tributary of the Uruguay, forty-five fathoms in width, which was the same one indicated by the Indian as the Uruguay-Pitá. But when this river was explored in the interior, where it was very well known, the mistake of the guide in 1759 was at once evident.

These corrections were put down by the common agreement of the Spaniards and the Portuguese in the plans of the demarcations of 1791 and of 1891.[1] The instructions of the Viceroy Vertiz, cited by Brazil, are consequently false in their result and inapplicable to the ground.

On the 10th of July, 1788, the Commissioners Gundin and Saldanha started anew from Santo Angelo to extend their survey of the Uruguay, in search of the Pepiry-Guazú, it being agreed that Saldanha with his party should go on in advance as far as the port of Canoas, where he should await his colleague. Four days after Gundin followed, and arriving at that place on the 26th of June, he learned with surprise that Saldanha, embarked in a single canoe, had set forth on his voyage two days before, in order to make a solitary exploration by himself.

The true Pepiry or Pequiry-Guazú of the official Map. The Spanish Geographer Gundin, on his part, went down the Uruguay-Pitá to its mouth, and then navigated the Uruguay up-stream, in search of the true Pepiry or Pequiry-Guazú, and on August 3 discovered it, recognizing it by the entire conformity between the peculiarities of its mouth and the indications given by the two Courts in their Instructions and upon the map which the Demarcators of 1759 carried for their information ; that is to say, a river "*caudaloso*," or of great volume, with a wooded island in front of its mouth, and a reef inside of its bar, and which was to be found up-stream from the Uruguay-Pitá. The river which he found was 110 "*toesas*" or fathoms (215 metres) in width at its mouth ; it had a reef crossing it at 310 "*toesas*"or fathoms from

[1] Maps of the "Argentine Evidence," XVIII Century, Nos. 15 and 17.

its bar, and there was in front of it, in the middle of the Uruguay, a wooded island, which was quite prominent and had an extent of about 850 fathoms in length, and midway a width of about 100 fathoms, and which was located about seventeen miles above the true Uruguay-Pitá. The Portuguese on their part had arrived at the Pepiry of 1759, and on their return to the Uruguay-Pitá (the Port of Canoas) took care to cause the inscription of the Pepiry-Guazú to disappear which they had left at the river of "*Los Antas*," when wandering in their investigations.[1]

The discussion then began between the Commissioners. The Portuguese maintained as the only true ones the rivers Uruguay-Pitá and Pepiry indicated by the Indian in 1759, notwithstanding Gundin and Saldanha had previously recognized, by common consent and without the least hesitation, as the true Uruguay-Pitá the stream which had its sources in the general *Cuchilla* or range confronting that of the Yacuy.

It is unnecessary to dwell upon the details of the double geographical operation now under discussion regarding the two systems of rivers, for they were affirmed on one side and denied on the other. I follow the plan of not considering the geographical question, except when its results confirm or correct doubtful facts. More than this has been a quarrel, almost childish, which has cost time and money, uselessly. For these reasons I have limited myself to putting in evidence the *agreement* arrived at by the engineers of the two nations regarding the exact situation of the rivers delineated upon the "*Mapa de las Cortes*" of 1749. The River San Antonio.

The explorations made on the River Ygnazú gave a result no less surprising for the Portuguese and favorable for Spain and the Argentine Republic, because they in fact proved that the sources of the river Pepiry or Pequiry-Guazú corresponded exactly to those of a river upon the opposite watershed, and agreed with the very terms of the compacts, as well as the instructions of the Demarcators, which called for a river of great volume flowing into the Ygnazú, called the *San Antonio-Guazú*.

The Portuguese Commissioners had proved, as we have seen, that the "*arroyo*" or small stream of 1759 did not fulfil the conditions laid down in the documents which they were endeavoring to locate upon the ground, and the head of the Commission confessed this in a note addressed to the Spanish Commissioners on July 5, 1788. He said: Doubts of the Portuguese Demarcators.

[1] See this Argument, page 265.

... In the same conformity the demarcation of this river Yguazú is to me very difficult, inasmuch as its union with the original sources of the rivers Pepiry-Guazú and San Antonio is not verified, the situation of the former being so doubtful, as there is no person who knows them; on the contrary there were those who said that between the said sources passed a river that had its origin in the fields and settlements of Curitiva, where it is known by the name of the river "Marombas," and which empties into the Paraná with the name of Uruguay, in latitude 25° 53' or a little more.[1]

These words from the chief of the Portuguese Demarcators fully confirm the statements to the same effect expressed on the next page of this Argument. The fact suspected by the Portuguese was exactly true, as was proved by the International Commissioners of 1891.[2] It was besides of vital importance, because it eliminated the river claimed by the Brazilians, leaving as an existing fact, by reason of its hydrographic character and its perfect conformity with the treaties, the river delineated by the Portuguese and Spanish explorers, above the Pepiry or Pequiry-Guazú, on the map that I have presented at page 5.

In another official document of July 8th, of the same year, the chief of the Portuguese Demarcators persisted in doubting that the false Pepiry and the false San Antonio were the rivers of the boundary. He said:

... So far as regards the demarcation of the river Pepiry-Guazú to its headwaters I have encountered no doubt up to the present, but I recognize its identity; and as far as concerns its union with the currents of the rivers San Antonio and Yguazú, you know that the eighth Article in this part is conditional, since it reports the rules established in Article VI, etc., and I do not know how to conjecture the location and manner in which these rivers were put, nor what will be the result of the investigation that must be made of them, without which I consider any determination whatever uncertain, doubtful and precipitate.[3]

---

[1] See this Argument, next page.
[2] The discussion between the Commissioners of Spain and Portugal has been published in the Republic of Uruguay by the Engineer, Don Meliton Gonzalez, in a work which is presented to the Arbitrator among the other volumes, entitled: "*El Límite Oriental del Territorio de Misiones, República Argentina,*" (The Eastern Boundary of the Territory of Misiones, Argentine Republic, by Meliton Gonzalez.) Montevideo, 1882. The matter here quoted will be found on page 212 of the second volume. This impartial work shows the clear justice of the claims of the Argentine Republic in the matter of the boundary.
[3] Correspondence between the Demarcators of Spain and Portugal, published, Gonzalez, Vol II, page 218.

The declaration made by the chief of the Portuguese Demarcators that the boundary described in the eighth Article is conditional proves what I have stated already in this Argument as to its being necessary that this river should correspond to the Pepiry or Pequiry-Guazú in the form required by the legal documents already examined. *Portuguese confession regarding the San Antoni>*

These doubts arise from the suspicion that the headwaters of the San Antonio of 1759 did not correspond with those of the Pepiry, and in the opinion of the chief of the Portuguese Demarcators of 1788 the San Antonio, according to the same treaty, could not be the frontier line, except on condition that its headwaters should correspond with those of the Pepiry or Pequiry-Guazú; that is to say, that its principal sources were the immediate counter-sources, or opposite ones, in respect to the other. No one, according to the said chief of the Portuguese Demarcators, knew, nor had they yet discovered, the sources of the false Pepiry, and it was suspected that between the headwaters of one river and the other crossed the river of Marombas,[1] which took its course from the fields of Curitiva, according to the Indians. It might be noted that in the face of this final negation it is not explained how Brazil could have asserted that the Demarcators of 1759 left the frontier fixed between the sources of the false Pepiry and the false San Antonio. It is seen that the same chief of the Portuguese Commissioners of 1788 already distrusted that wrong location in express terms.[2] It is necessary, said the Portuguese, to previously investigate by means of preliminary surveys before taking the San Antonio as the frontier, and not to proceed in an uncertain, doubtful or precipitate manner; and insisting upon this uncertainty, the Chief of the Demarcators of Portugal also said in an official report, dated December 9, 1788, directed to Commissioner Alvear:—

> The line must follow, according to the conditions stipulated, from the principal source of the river Pepiry or Pequiry-Guazú, by the headwaters of the river San Antonio, to seek the Yguazú, in the form which the treaty methodically specifies, and not inversely.[3]

This Portuguese Chief, because he labored in behalf of reason and justice, worked for Spain. Nothing else, in fact, was ordered by the principal and additional treaties on the question, by the instructions *Double conduct of the Portuguese Commissioners*

[1] Official document of July 5, previously cited. See this Argument, page 268.
[2] Follow the Engineer Virasoro, in the work cited.
[3] Gonzalez, same work.

and the official map, the guide of all that was done and to be done. But when in 1789 the Portuguese Demarcators, Veyga and Cabral, and the Spanish Demarcator Varela y Ulloa arrived at the true system of rivers, geographically and legally considered, the Chief of the Portuguese Demarcators retreated and contradicted himself, thus showing that he considered himself defeated. As a matter of fact, in his report of November 11, 1789, he refers to the fact that on December 20, 1788,[1] he found himself with his Spanish colleague in the Yguazú country, where he supposed that he had found the true Pepiry or Pequiry-Guazú, and was invited by the latter to extend the reconnoissance to a distance of 15 or 20 leagues to the East of the mouth of the false San Antonio upon the Yguazú, in search of another river that would better agree as to location with the true Pepiry or Pequiry Guazú.

Inexplicable contradictions.

Is it possible to explain these contradictions on the part of the chief of the Portuguese Commissioners? Some days before the demarcation along the Yguazú from the mouth of the false San Antonio to the West was disclaimed, because it placed in doubt the fact whether the said San Antonio was really the frontier of the treaty, and in the following year he said quite the contrary, after the proof of the exact character of the "*Mapa de las Cortes.*"[2]

Surely the Portuguese Commissioner did not believe, although he might have conjectured that these headwaters recognized as the countersources of the false San Antonio were no less than those of the river Uruguay, a tributary of the Paraná, that is to say, the same river which the aborigines living in those regions had said was the "Maroubas," which rose in the fields of Curitiva,[3] and yet the Demarcators of 1759 took these headwaters for those of the Pepiry or Pequiry-Guazú.

The fact then remains well settled that it was the chief of the Portuguese Commissioners who indicated and asserted for the first time that the "*arroyo*" or small stream of the San Antonio, wrongly explored in 1759, was not one of the boundary rivers "*caudalosos,*" or of large volume.

Exploration of the true boundary rivers.

The international plan signed by Varela y Ulloa of Spain and by Veyga Cabral of Portugal represents the agreed results of the explorations of the Pepiry or Pequiry-Guazú. The Demarcators, Oyarvide

[1] Gonzalez, book and page cited.
[2] Virasoro, at the place cited.
[3] See this Argument, next pages; demarcation of 1891.

for Spain and Chagas Santos for Portugal, went up to its headwaters in search of the river of the opposite watershed flowing into the Yguazú. I give the general results of this exploration because the Arbitrator should know of them, and it is but just to state that the rivers sought for were found. The Spanish Geographer, Oyarvide, says in his Journal:

... Arrived at the principal source of our river Pequiry,[1] we discussed with the Portuguese Engineer-Geographer the matter of a continuation of the reconnoissance on the other side of the "*cuchilla*" or range of hills, in order to examine whether its headwaters turning to the northward toward the Yguazú might serve as a boundary or dividing line, as frontiers for the true river indicated as the boundary in this part, which is the second point of our instructions, to which he absolutely refused to agree, stating that the order which he had from his Commissioner was only to accompany us in the reconnoissance of this river, which had been concluded in this part, and therefore he would not consider any subject except it related to our return.[2]

The conduct of the Portuguese Geographer was open to reasonable criticism, for he was not only inconsequential in those critical moments, but even inhuman, because Oyarvide, with a few fatigued followers, worn out and with scanty resources, was abandoned in what was then a desert region and at a great distance from the place where the provisions were stored. Only two cases of such censurable conduct happened during the demarcations; that of Chagas Santos abandoning Oyarvide and that of Saldanha deserting Gundín on the Uruguay-Pitá.

Unjustifiable desertion by the Portuguese Geographer.

The Spanish Geographer, however, bravely continued his exploration, discovering the principal source of the San Antonio-Guazú and exploring it until he was certain that it flowed into the Yguazú. On June 17, when he discovered the source of the said river, the San Antonio-Guazú, the Indians came to him saying that they were very tired, that they could not go forward any further, and therefore begged to go back. But Oyarvide, with his strong will, inflexible in the fulfilment of his duty, convinced them that they must go on, and with hopeful words brought them out of the discouragement caused by the unjustifiable retreat of the Portuguese.

Roscio, the chief of the Portuguese Commissioners, then declined to complete the survey of the San Antonio-Guazú, and began to insist

Refusal of the Portuguese to clear up the matter.

[1] Pepiry or Pequiry-Guazú of the "*Mapa de las Cortes.*"
[2] America Latina, Carlos Calvo, Vol. 9, pages 364 and 365.

upon returning to the Paraná in order to proceed with the demarcation which he had before refused to undertake under the pretext of serious doubts. Alvear, the chief of the Spanish Commissioners, insisted upon the survey of the San Antonio-Guazú, asserting the legitimate frontier to be the Pepiry or Pequiry-Guazú, and along that river, in order to proceed in accordance with the fifteenth Article, which prescribed the formation of a map and a provisional report concerning the doubts and their submission, with the corresponding data illustrative thereof, for the decision of the two Courts. The discussion was prolonged, without arriving at any result, from the 26th of November, 1791, the date of the last official communication by the Commissioner Don Diego de Alvear to Col. Roscio, in which he put an end to the controversy and stated that he would give an account of the matter to the Viceroy in order that he might take such action as he thought proper.[1]

Legal deductions from these explorations. Considering the attempt at demarcation of the Treaty of 1777 from a geographical point of view, the result was favorable to Spain on account of the fundamental proofs it furnished in support of the maps and official facts agreed upon by the two Crowns. It will also be shown that these results were not less favorable from a legal point of view; that is to say, when comparing the geographical facts with the treaties to which they refer.

Integrity of the dominions of the two Crowns. The Demarcators should at all times have had the treaties at hand. Article II of the Guaranty Treaty of 1778[2] provided that neither one of the two Crowns should enter upon the territory of the other, but by the boundary claimed by the Portuguese they penetrated into the interior of the dominions of Spain.[3]

Exact boundaries agreed upon. Article III of the same Treaty of 1778 renewed and ratified the boundaries of the Treaty of 1750 in order to guarantee them, as this latter treaty had also guaranteed them. These boundaries were delineated by Portugal in the "*Mapa de las Cortes*," which Spain accepted. Therefore this map, the *basis* and *guide* of the ratified boundaries according to the additional treaty of January, 1751, ought to have been taken to the ground and applied strictly. The Portuguese Demarcators did not do this, and when the Spanish Demarcators insisted upon following these just proceedings the former unjustifiably retired from the field.

[1] Argentine Evidence. Vol. I, page 575.
[2] Argentine Evidence. Vol. I, page 99 and following.
[3] See the remarks on this subject at page 166 and following of this Argument.

The accompanying documents which the Spanish and Portuguese Demarcators exchanged on this point throw a flood of light upon the legal aspect of the intentional errors of the Portuguese Demarcators. It is unnecessary to set forth here all the details of a discussion that was continued during a period of three years. I have presented to the Arbitrator a neutral work, published by an Engineer of the Republic of Uruguay, in which may be found the entire discussion, with all the documents referring to the subject.[1]

I shall, therefore, limit myself to a consideration of the essential documents, in which the question was presented with precision. One of these is the official report of the Spanish Commissioner from Buenos Aires, which was as follows:

Your Excellency: By Article V of the Boundary Treaty of 1750, it was ordered that the dividing line be drawn by the river Pepiry as far as its principal source, and from there by the nearest of those rivers which enter into the Grande de Curitiba, called also the Yguazú, an undertaking which had to be performed in accordance with a map which was sent by orders of the Courts to the Commissioners Don Francisco Arguedas and Don Joseph Fernandez Pinto Alpoym, who were entrusted with the execution of said undertaking.

In this map (which the Portuguese cannot challenge, because it was drawn in Lisbon), the said Pepiry was represented up the stream from the Uruguay-Pitá, and in accordance with this specification the Commissioners sought to find it, believing, by the other reports which had reached them, that it was a river "*caudaloso*," of large volume, and that it had a reef very near its mouth. But the fact is that having reached the first river that flows into the Uruguay through its northern bank after passing Salto Grande, the guide assured them that this was the Pepiry, telling them he had known it by this name since the time he had made an expedition with the Indians of his village to a place which they called La Espía.

The Commissioners, seeing that this river did not agree in any manner with the one represented in the "*Mapa de las Cortes*," continued the navigation of the Uruguay against the stream, with the object of discovering if the information was correct which the guide gave regarding two other rivers which were higher up, and which he said were the Apiterebi and Uruguay-Pitá; and after having observed the situation of both these rivers they reached a fall of one fathom in height, from whose boulders the water descended with such violence that they believed it almost impossible to take the canoes across to the other side, and returned to the

---
[1] See this Argument, page 268.

headquarters of the two parties, where the river indicated by the guide was solemnly recognized as the Pepiry.

As the aforesaid Commissioners acted in this case against the faith due to the "*Mapa de los Cortes,*" which placed the Pepiry against or up the stream from the Uruguay-Pitá, and not down the stream as the river in question was situated, they have left us in their Journal the reasons which they had to act in accordance with the words of the Guide, reasons which in substance can be reduced to only two.

The first was, having believed that as a matter of fact the Uruguay-Pitá was the last river which the Guide had shown them, they inferred that as the Guide had knowledge of this river he must also have knowledge of the one which he called the Pepiry, and which was further down, and the second reason was that they entertained the strong belief that after crossing the fall of one fathom in height it was impossible to find any wide river which, by its situation and other circumstances, could be taken for the Pepiry mentioned in the Treaty.

Although I fully appreciate the work done by the Commissioners of the late demarcation, I cannot refrain from saying that in regard to the subject under discussion they committed a grave error, most prejudicial to the interests of the Spanish Monarchy.

In fact, the last river to which the Guide conducted them, telling them it was the Uruguay-Pitá, is not that river in reality, nor does it spring from the *Cuchilla General* (range of hills) as was then believed, but from a mound which gives waters also to the Iyui-Gnazú, from which mound it flows through hard and stony lands until its junction with the Uruguay at a point eight leagues in a direct line down the stream from the true Uruguay-Pitá, it being also true that from the fall of one fathom in height onward several wide rivers are found in the northern bank of the Uruguay, and one in particular, which is situated up the stream from the already mentioned Uruguay-Pitá, and which has a reef very near its mouth, these being precisely the same signs by which those Commissioners were seeking the Pepiry, so that had they reached this river they would have infallibly recognized it as the Pepiry.

This error having been now discovered, I was forced to correct it in our map, asking my Portuguese colleague to do the same, and to accept as the boundary the "*rio caudaloso,*" or wide and deep river, whose situation, as I have said, is identical with that of the Pepiry represented in the "*Mapa de los Cortes;*" but my colleague has refused to make this correction, under pretext that, by Article VIII of the Preliminary Treaty of 1777, it is ordered that the Dividing Line be drawn by the Pepiry which confronts or can be confronted with the river San Antonio; of all which Your Excellency will be informed by the copies I inclose of the despatches written by me to my Portuguese colleague, and of his respective answers to the same, mine being designated with the numbers I, II, III, and his, with the numbers IV, V, VI.

It would truly be of the greatest advantage for us if the boundary or frontier line should be drawn by this new river, because in that case all the waters of the Uruguay-Pitá would belong to the Crown of Spain;[1] and as the waters more to the East come from Monte Grande, which separates the grass land of these villages from the lands of the Vaqueria belonging to the Portuguese, there would be no difficulty in drawing the dividing line through Monte Grande, which is the only way I see of saving and covering the settlements of the two nations according to the terms ordered in the Preliminary Treaty, as you will see by what I write to Your Excellency in a separate despatch.

God keep Your Excellency for many years. Pueblo de San Juan Bautista, 9th of October of 1789.

JOSEPH VARELA Y ULLOA.

To His Excellency the Marquis de Loreto.[2]

The documents collected in Volume I of the Argentine Evidence, at page 559 *et seq.*,[3] fully prove that the Spaniards not only initiated, but did all that was possible for them to do towards carrying forward the investigations, and that the Portuguese persistently resisted them. The Spanish Commissioner, Varela y Ulloa, said to the Viceroy of Buenos Aires in his note of February 12, 1788, that— *Refusal of the Portuguese to clear up the subject.*

. . . from the opposition manifested by my co-Commissioner to our survey of the said Pepiry-Guazú and from the decisive manner in which he expressed himself on this subject, you will infer that all his thoughts are directed to retarding the demarcation, the truth of which is as clear to me as to yourself.[4]

In another despatch of January 9, 1789, addressed to the chief of the Portuguese Demarcators, he said :

. . . No doubt can be entertained that the late Demarcators acted in this instance against the mind of the two Sovereigns, and against the faith of the map which had been remitted to them by the Courts with orders to act in conformity with the same, whenever it agreed with the topography of the ground.

---

[1] So provided by the Treaty of 1777.
[2] Argentine Evidence, Vol. I, page 577. Group D of Manuscripts, Document No. 11.
[3] Group D of Manuscripts of the same "Argentine Evidence," Letters of Varela y Ulloa and Alvear upon the operations of the Boundary Line.
[4] *Idem*, Vol. I, page 561.

This document merits special attention for the clearness of its evidence. It closes by making to the Portuguese Commissioner the following proposition, as just as it was reasonable:

> ... It being then evident that the river Pepiry represented in the "*Mapa de las Cortes*," is the "*rio caudaloso*," or river of large volume, situated six leagues in a direct line up stream from the Uruguay-Pitá, and also that the demarcation from the mouth of the said Pepiry to the junction of the Yguarey with the Paraná is precisely the same in the treaty of 1750 as in the treaty afterwards made in 1777, I find myself obliged, in virtue of the charge with which I am invested, and in the fulfilment of my duties, to request that Your Excellency recognize this river as the boundary between the dominions of His Catholic Majesty and those of His Majesty the King of Portugal, which recognition I trust to obtain, if Your Excellency should read this note with impartiality and act in the matter with the probity and good faith which has been so much recommended to us.
>
> God keep Your Excellency for many years.
> Pueblo de San Juan Bautista, January 9, 1789.
>
> JOSEPH VARELA Y ULLOA.
>
> To Don Sebastian Xavier da Veiga Cabral da Câmara.

This just and fundamental principle of the Spanish Geographer has been explained and maintained very clearly in the following documents ("Argentine Evidence," Group D of MSS.)

1789. Third Letter of Varela y Ulloa.
1789. Letters of Varela y Ulloa.
1790. Letter of the Viceroy of Buenos Aires.
1794. Letters of Cervino.
1800. Extract from a Memoir of Requena, etc.

These documents, and especially those which were signed by the new Viceroy of Buenos Aires, correct the mistakes of the former Viceroy Vertiz, and re-establish the true and faithful interpretation of the treaties, for which reason they are especially recommended to the attention of the Arbitrator.

Exclusive navigation of the rivers. The claim of Portugal to pass to the Westward of the Line of Demarcation of the Treaty of Tordesillas and divide with Spain its sovereignty over the shores and the navigation of the Rio de la Plata and its great affluents, was one of the principal reasons for the past troubles, according to the language of Article III of the Treaty of 1777.

Spain would lose the only two navigable tributaries of the Uruguay and the largest of all, the Uruguay-Pitá in the East and the Pepiry or Pequiry-Guazú in the West, which is absolutely inconsistent with the spirit of the words used in that solemn compact.

In order that this may be entirely clear let us examine the map of Discoveries, etc.[1] To reach the mouth of the Pepiry or Pequiry-Guazú the boundary traverses the old Spanish Province of Tape, now divided between the Republic of Uruguay and the Brazilian State of Rio Grande, covering the *pueblos*, farms, "*Yerbales*" and pastures according to Article IV of the Treaty of 1777, which directed a line to be drawn so that it—

> ... shall likewise save and cover the Spanish Missions and settlements of said Uruguay, which must remain in their present state in which they belong to the Crown of Spain; ...

The Portuguese pretended to trace a line that starting from Chuy on the Atlantic seeks the mouth of the false Pepiry of 1759, which is the line of red dots marked upon the general map cited. But it should be noted at the same time that this line violated the spirit and text of the prior Article of this Treaty, for it left to Portugal the "*Yerbales*" and pasture fields of the Eastern *Misiones* of the Uruguay, and especially those belonging to the *pueblo* of Santo Angel. This is the dotted line Minister Galvez refers to in the new Instructions of 1782[2] for the Commissioners of Spain, in which he orders them to save these establishments and explains that the word "line" does not mean that it should be a *straight line*, since if it were necessary to make it crooked in order to save the Spanish establishments it should be so traced.

The official maps signed by the Portuguese and Spanish Commissioners who had charge of the demarcation recognize the existence of the "*Vaquerias*" and "*Yerbales*" of Spain in the situation stated, and this acknowledgment makes still more unjust and odious the refusal to protect them by the boundary, honestly applying the treaty. These maps, which are presented to the Arbitrator at the end of this Argument, should be attentively examined. The entire red line marks on the general map of Requena the honest and true limit.

Tracing the line as the Portuguese claimed, the navigation of the Uruguay was not reserved precisely where it was most essential to the

---

[1] See this Argument, at page 27.
[2] See page 258 of this Argument.

Spaniards, as the only highway by which to export the "*Yerba Mate*" (which business is very large down to the present day) from the western or eastern districts of the Uruguay. These regions remained isolated and their industries were condemned to die under the regulations of a foreign customs regime. The general map of South America prepared in 1796 by Don Francisco Requena, of which I present to the Arbitrator an authenticated photograph taken from the original, and also a printed copy, illustrates and represents these facts in a conclusive manner.[1]

The plan of the Portuguese, opposed by the Spaniards, was to apply the treaty separated from its text and from the facts in accordance with it. This plan if carried out would have led to a practical annulment of the treaty and to territorial usurpation, and that was the result of the military acts which occurred between 1801 and 1827. Although Brazil was defeated by the Argentine Republic in that year, this growing country, scarcely yet independent, had neither the population nor the necessary power to impose strictly just conditions upon the powerful country it had conquered, and satisfied itself with compelling it to leave the Rio de la Plata, although allowing it to remain in possession of the usurped territories on the coast of the Atlantic ocean, to the North of the Republic of Uruguay, where its revolutionary Province of Rio Grande is now situated. The very name of this Province confirms the rights of Spain and of the Argentine Republic over it.

Just rule of interpretation. On the other hand, suppose the contrary had happened. Imagine the less favorable case, that the treaty and the instructions of the Demarcators may have been confused and that the facts did not exist or did not appear definitely upon the ground. The rule of interpretation in case of doubt should lean toward Spain, because it was that nation which ceded to Portugal in the Treaty of 1777 the eighth part of the South American continent, as it had already yielded up to it one-fifth of the same by the Treaty of 1750. Portugal and its heirs cannot equitably go further.

I will finally recall the fact which I have already proved in this Argument by the documents which have been collected, that the Map of 1749, on which the boundary was fixed by protocol by both Crowns, was *initiated, proposed and delineated by Portugal*. Spain accepted and signed it under the influence of the Portuguese Queen Doña Barbara. But even under these circumstances the map represents the Pepiry or Pequiry-

[1] See map in the Portfolio of Maps, XVIIIth Century, No. 19.

Guazú as it was claimed by the Spanish Demarcators and as the Argentines maintain it to-day. It was, however, convenient for Portugal not to be bound by its map, so its Boundary Commissioners denied its existence, and the officials of the Archives of Lisbon *could not find it* until 1892, when the Argentine Republic discovered a copy of it in the Archives of the Department of Foreign Affairs of France. Thus matters continued entangled and the spoil which Portugal had attempted to seize seemed secure. But the secret papers presented by the Argentine Republic have illuminated these shadows, and the intrigue appears to have been dissipated at the moment when its designs seemed most sure of success.

The Commissions of Engineers from Brazil and from the Argentine Republic, headed, respectively, by the Baron de Capanema and by Col. José Ignacio Garmendia, began their operations on September 28, 1885, and finished them on September 24, 1891, without any interruption in their harmony. Nothing else could have been expected, under the instructions which the two governments agreed upon and delivered to them as the guide for their work, and the Joint Commission went into the field simply to make a geographical map. The decisions and the results arising therefrom would be determined afterwards by diplomatic negotiations, each party sustaining the pro or con according to its point of view.[1]

International Exploration of Misiones. 1885-1891.

The Journals, Memoirs, and Plans which the officers of the two Commissions prepared with great intelligence and with very full details were of the greatest value for the geography of that region. They are in the Argentine Legation at the disposal of the Arbitrator, as original documents. Their influence has been to advance the diplomatic question, confirming certain vital and definitive facts.[2]

In the meantime the error of the Treaty of 1885 began to be apparent, regarding the admission of the fifth river called "Chopin." The head of the Argentine Commission solicited and obtained an agreement from the two Governments to go on with the reconnoissance until the true river was reached, the San Antonio-Guazú of Oyarvide, considering it as the Eastern boundary of the disputed zone. In the Memoir subscribed by both Commissions in 1891, giving an account to their respective Departments of the termination of their explorations,

Correction of the fundamental error of the Treaty of 1885.

---
[1] See the Memoir of the Department of Foreign Affairs, Argentine Republic, 1892. Argentine Evidence, Vol. I, page 702.
[2] Argentine Evidence, Group D of Manuscripts, No. 21 and following; Vol. I, page 627 and following. Portfolio of Maps, XIX Century, Nos. 29 to 51.

they touched upon only one diplomatic point, that concerning the Chopin. The report said:

> The Argentine commissioners, considering that their work would not be complete without the survey of the *San Antonio Guazú* of Oyarvide or *Yangada*, whose main source at a short distance conforms with that of the *Pequiry-Guazú*, insisted upon demanding the survey of that river, as they supposed it to be the true San Antonio-Guazú, pointed out in the instructions, and not the Chopin, which erroneously takes the place of the former in the treaty of the twenty-eighth day of September, 1885, because this had never been known nor surveyed by Oyarvide, nor is it even mentioned in his Memoir. The Brazilians admitted that the headwaters of the river which Oyarvide named *San Antonio Guazú* were those of the river known in Brazil under the name of "*Yangada*," but they supposed that they could not acquiesce in this demand because no mention was made of this river in the said treaty; neither could they admit that the interpretation of the seventh Article of the Instructions accompanying that treaty, in which the Commissioners were directed to be guided by the work of Oyarvide, would be construed as requiring them to prepare the plan of a river of which Oyarvide only mentioned the sources; all the more then that exploration required as a necessary consequence the exploration of the Yguazú, from the mouth of the Chopin or San Antonio-Guazú to the Yangada or San Antonio-Guazú of Oyarvide. . . . ¹

They feared, like their chief, the Baron de Cotegipe, the results of this exploration, and they would not undertake to proceed with it without an express order from their Government.

> . . . This divergence was brought to the knowledge of the respective Governments in the form of Article XIII of the Instructions. These Governments finding later that the Argentine Commissioners were only reasonable in their demands, provided that the head Commissioners of the two Commissions should proceed with the exploration of that river. . . . ²

Favorable results for the Argentine Republic. Other benefits in regard to details were derived by the Argentine Republic from the skilfulness with which Col. Garmendia and his colleagues directed and carried out the Third International Exploration of Misiones.

Brazil fears a new exploration. Such results were foreseen and feared by eminent diplomats of the

¹ See same reference as in previous note.
² Argentine Evidence, page 634, Memoir of Commissioners. See also Treaty of Arbitration.

Empire. When the Minister of Foreign Affairs of the Argentine Republic, Dr. Irigoyen, proposed in 1876 the previous reconnoissance, the Baron de Cotegipe, in his instructions given to the Minister of Brazil in Uruguay, who conducted with Dr. Irigoyen the negotiation already analyzed, said in the month of July of that year:

> We do not advance a single step, but still find ourselves entangled in the inadmissible idea of a new reconnoissance to be made for the correction of the former ones, and, consequently, subject to the contingencies of renewed claims, already impugned by the Portuguese Demarcators and by ourselves. *The risk attendant upon this new survey will always exist*, no matter what the wording of the Article of the treaty may be, if the line of demarcation is not expressly specified.

The Baron de Cotegipe, the sagacious director of the Cabinet at Rio de Janeiro, had calculated all the disadvantages that would be likely to result to Brazil by the demonstration of the actual truth upon the ground and of the accuracy of the "*Mapa de las Cortes*" of 1749, so he hastened to reject the Argentine proposal of 1876, which had for its object the making of a new international exploration of the disputed Territory. The Argentine project of exploration rejected by Brazil in 1876.

I present to the Arbitrator a Memoir upon this exploration, signed by the Argentine and Brazilian Commissioners, the General Map of the Territory bearing the same signatures, and the partial original maps signed in the same way, which will be found in the Portfolio of Maps of the "Argentine Evidence," XIXth Century, Nos. 29 to 51.[1]

These are international documents, equally binding upon the Argentine Republic and upon Brazil. What they affirm or delineate is law for both nations.

The first questions that were to be determined by the Boundary Commissioners of 1885 were these: *Was the Uruguay-Pitá properly located upon the "Mapa de las Cortes" of 1749 and upon that of the Demarcators of 1777?* Was the exploration of the Demarcators of 1759, which located this river much further to the South, correct? First proof.

The Commissioners of 1885 declare upon the International Map[2] that the Demarcators of 1759, or perhaps more properly the Indian who directed them, made a mistake; and that the Uruguay-Pitá, the river

---

[1] Argentine Evidence, Vol. I, page 627.
[2] Argentine Evidence; Portfolio of Maps, No. 51. The map attached to this Argument at page 5, copied from the former one the location of the Uruguay-Pitá.

which was to be the *basis and guide* of the Demarcation, was the one which was delineated with general correctness upon the "*Mapa de las Cortes*" and upon the map of the Spanish and Portuguese Commissioners in 1777. The "*Mapa de las Cortes*," the *basis* of the boundary treaties which are to be located on the ground is, therefore, officially and definitively declared by Brazil and also by the Argentine Republic to be accurate in this particular, and it is thereby admitted that the Demarcators of 1759 were mistaken.

Second proof. The second question was: The Uruguay-Pitá having been found, does there exist up-stream, or above it, a tributary of the Uruguay which is "*caudaloso*," i. e., of great volume, and which the "*Mapa de las Cortes*" calls Pepiry and the Treaty of 1750 Pepiry or Pequiry? The accompanying International Map also confirmed the work of the Demarcators of 1777 on this point and shows the exploration of this river.

Consequently, it remains officially and definitively proved by Brazil and the Argentine Republic that the Demarcators of 1759 were mistaken when they selected for the boundary an "*arroyo*" or small stream below the Uruguay-Pitá, believing that the river "*caudaloso*," or of great volume, delineated upon the "*Mapa de las Cortes*" did not exist. The "*Mapa de las Cortes*" is, therefore, shown to be accurate in this vital point.

Third proof. Going up the course of the River Pepiry or Pequiry of the "*Mapa de las Cortes*," as far as the high ground that divides the waters between the rivers Uruguay and Yguazú, can there be found the sources near by of any river which is a tributary of the latter and corresponding upon the opposite watershed to those of the Pepiry or Pequiry, and which empties into the Yguazú?[1] The International Map demonstrates that a river in this situation and of this description does in fact exist in conformity with the Map of 1749 and the treaties referring to it, thus confirming the investigations of the Commissioners of 1777. Therefore it is officially and conclusively proved for Brazil and for the Argentine Republic that the river which the boundary must follow at the nearest headwaters corresponding and opposite to the Pepiry or Pequiry-Guazú of the "*Mapa de las Cortes*" does exist in the very position in which it is indicated by that Map and the treaties.

Fourth proof. The Demarcators of 1759, in the official statement of their work done upon the Fifth Day, and those of 1777, looked for the river of the Map of 1749, guided by the following characteristics, given by

[1] Argentine Evidence, Vol. I, Article VIII of the Treaty of 1777.

their Instructions. 1. It must be a "*rio caudaloso*," or river of great volume. 2. It must have a reef near its mouth. 3. It must have an island in the Uruguay in front of this same mouth. These peculiarities are described in Paragraph 132 of the celebrated work entitled—

Historia de las Demarcaciones de Limites en la America, entre los Dominios de España y Portugal; etc. (History of the Demarcations of the Boundaries in America between the Dominions of Spain and Portugal; by Don Vicente Aguilar y Jurado and Don Francisco Requena,- to accompany the General Map prepared by the latter of all the countries through which the Divisory Line passes according to the Boundary Treaty of 1777.)

The preceding statement has also been corroborated in the work of Calvo, Vol. IV, page 126 and following, already presented to the Arbitrator.

Don Felix de Azara, the head of one of the Commissions of Spanish Boundary Demarcators of the Treaty of 1777, and one of the first authorities of his time in regard to South American matters, published a book entitled: Signs of the Pepiry or Pequiry.

Memoirs concerning rural affairs along the Rio de la Plata in 1801, the Demarcation of Boundaries between Brazil and Paraguay at the end of the 18th century and information as to some peculiarities of Spanish South America. Posthumous writings of Don Felix de Azara, Brigadier of the Spanish Marine, and author of works treating of Birds, Quadrupeds and a Description and History of Paraguay and the Rio de la Plata, published by his Nephew, Don Agustin de Azara, etc. Madrid, 1847.[1]

On page 46, speaking of the boundary demarcation in the Territory submitted to the Arbitrator, he says:

The indications of the Pequiry or Pepiry-Guazú are: a river "*caudaloso*" (of great volume) with a *wooded island* in front of its mouth; an "*arrecife*" (reef or ledge) inside of its bar, and it is to be found up-stream from the Uruguay-Pitá.

Another authority accepted as trustworthy by the Portuguese was published by the *Royal Academy of Sciences* of Lisbon in regard to the demarcation of these boundaries. It was entitled:

---
[1] Presented to the Arbitrator among the books of the "Argentine Evidence."

Collection of facts for a History of the Transatlantic Nations which are under Portuguese dominion and their neighbors. Lisbon, 1841.

The Journal of the Demarcators in the explorations of 1759 was published in the seventh volume of that work, which is presented to the Arbitrator among the books of the "Argentine Evidence." That Journal gives the indications of the river Pepiry or Pequiry-Guazú which is sought and states on pages 181, 186 and 187 that said river ought to be navigable, and "*caudaloso*" or of great volume, or at least of considerable size. On page 181 it is stated that an "*arrecife*" (ledge or reef) should be found near its mouth. This is the language:

At this time the said river carried very little water which showed that it would afford very short navigation, and knowing by other information that the Pepiry had a reef or ledge near its mouth, the Commissioners and the Astronomer of Portugal went to reconnoiter it and they found it a half league from there. . . .

On page 188, second line, of the same book, it is said that this stream should have an island in its mouth.

The physical characteristics of the mouth of the river sought for, remain, therefore, officially accepted by the Demarcators in their Journal of 1759. These same characteristics were sought for and delineated by the Argentine-Brazilian Commission, which explored and examined the Territory from 1885 to 1891, and whose international plans accompany this chapter. This question then arises: Did the river delineated in the "*Mapa de las Cortes*" and upheld by the Argentine Republic have those physical characteristics?

The international map of 1891 shows that the river of the "*Mapa de las Cortes*," maintained by the Argentine Republic, is the western tributary of the Uruguay which has the greatest volume of water. In order that the matter may be clearly understood, an engraving is here included of the mouth of the "*arroyo*" or small stream which empties into the Uruguay, and which was mistakenly adopted by the Demarcators of 1759, and also one representing the mouth of the Pepiry or Pequiry-Guazú of the "*Mapa de las Cortes*" and of the treaties, at its junction with the Uruguay. Other original maps showing the junctions of these rivers, signed by the Boundary Commissioners of both nations, are also added.

The simple inspection of these two maps will show to the Arbitrator,

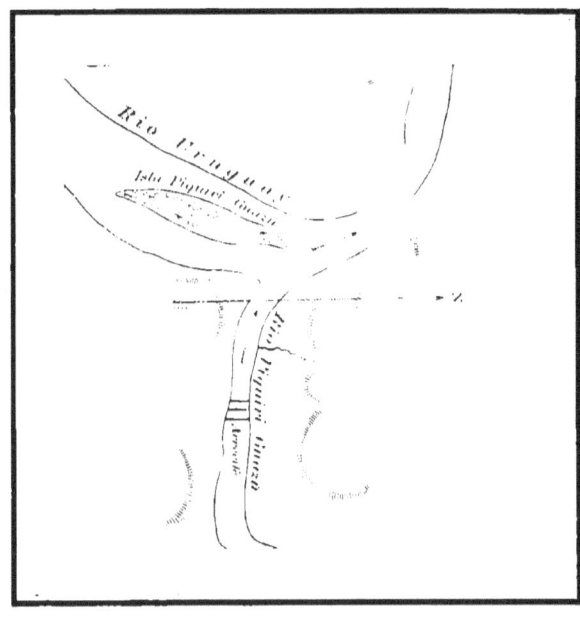

MOUTH of the TRUE RIVER PEQUIRI-GUAZÚ
SCALE 1:50 000

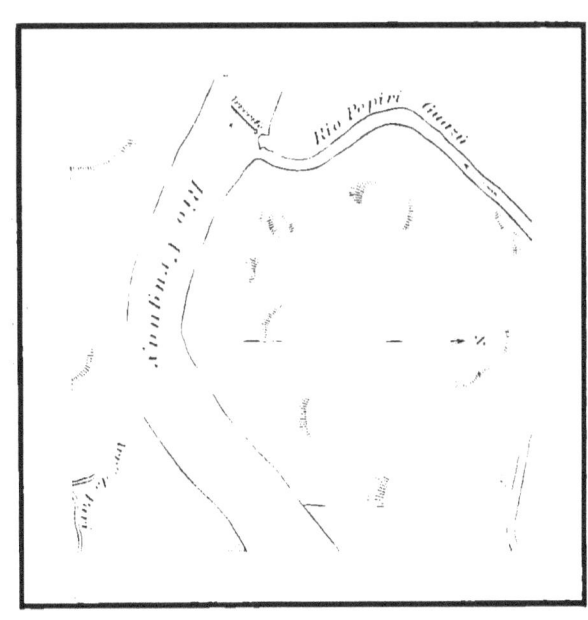

MOUTH of the ERRONEOUS PEPIRI of FIGURE of 1759
SCALE 1:50 000

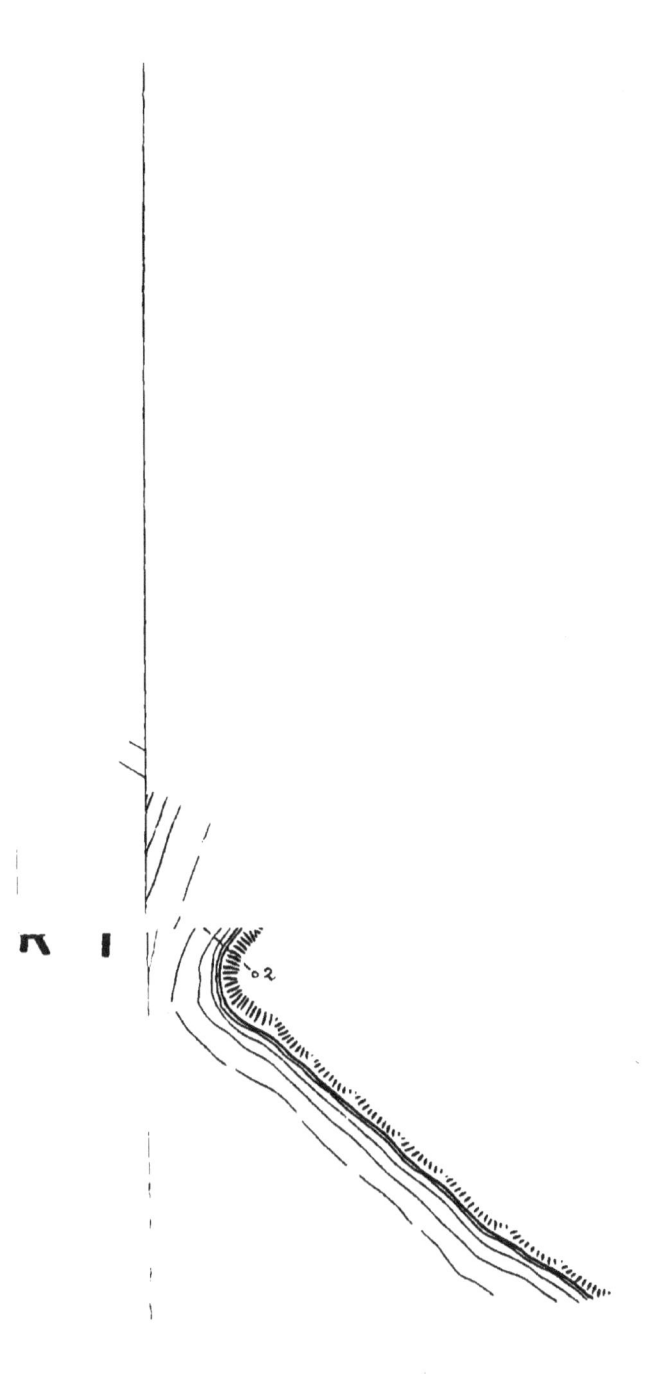

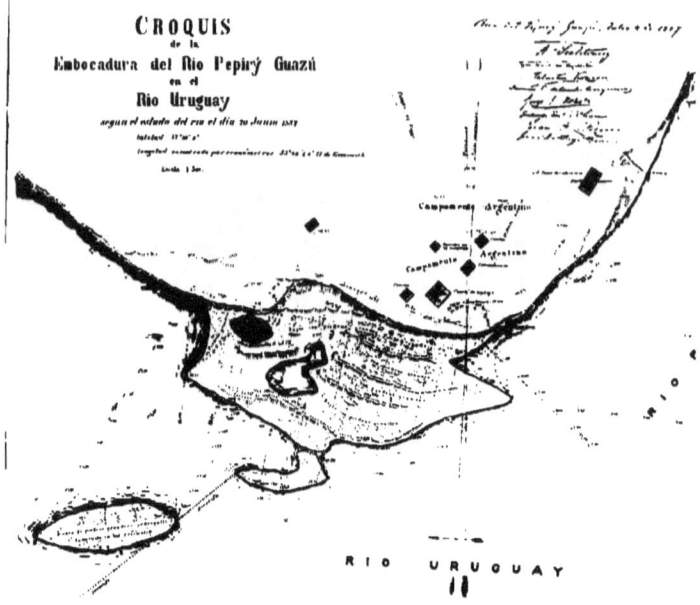

"U"

e Limites
el

PLANO
da
Embocadura do RIO
CHAPECÓ.

Denominado PIQUIRI-GUASSÚ pelos Argentinos

Levantado pela commissão mixta de limites entre o
Imperio do Brasil e a Republica
Argentina

PLANO
de la embocadura del riacuanto
en el Brasil por "CHAPECÓ"
y denominado "PIQUIRI-GUAZÚ"
por los Argentinos

Levantado por la Comision mixta de limites
entre la Republica Argentina y el
Imperio del Brasil

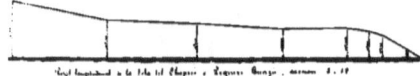

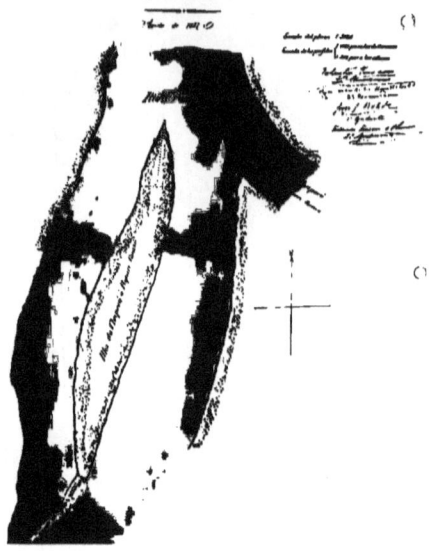

under the official and conclusive declarations of both Brazil and the Argentine Republic, the following facts:

1. That the river of the "*Mapa de las Cortes*" and of the treaties maintained by the latter nation is "*caudaloso*," or of great volume, while the erroneous one selected by the Demarcators of 1759 and maintained by Brazil, is an insignificant "*arroyo*," or small stream.

2. That the river maintained by the Argentine Republic has inside its bar the reef looked for, and which is visible from its mouth, while the river maintained by Brazil does not have such a reef.

3. That there is just opposite the mouth of the river maintained by the Argentine Republic the Island looked for by the Demarcators of 1759 and 1777, (said island having a length of 1,340 metres, according to the International exploration of 1891), while the river maintained by Brazil has no such island.

Some Brazilian writers claim that a small reef situated to the South of the "*arroyo*" or small stream selected in 1759 can be considered as the island sought and found opposite the river of the Map of 1749. But the Demarcators of 1891 state upon their Map and in their International Journal that *below* the mouth of the "*arroyo*" of the Commissioners of 1759 there is a ledge of rock in the Uruguay, only visible when the river is very low. It is impossible, therefore, to mistake this for the large island of the river of great volume mentioned in the treaties.

The Journal of the Brazilian and Argentine Commissioners referring to this point says:

> In the mouth of the river known in Brazil by the name of "*Chapecó*" and which the Argentines call the "*Pequiry-Guazú*," on August 19, 1887, the undersigned Commissioners, charged by the Joint Boundary Commission between the Argentine Republic and the Empire of Brazil with the survey of the rivers Uruguay and Chapecó, or Pequiry-Guazú of the Argentines, having terminated their labors upon the first of the rivers named, from the mouth of the Pequiry-Guazú to this point, where we arrived on the 13th of August, we have been occupied from that day to this date in the preparation of the partial plan of this mouth, and of the Uruguay in front of the same, inclusive of the island which is found in the middle of that river, sounding the mouth and making longitudinal and transverse profiles of the northern part of said island.
>
> The island which is found in the river Uruguay, in the direction of this mouth, has its northern point some metres to the South of

the prolongation of the left bank of the Chapecó or Pequiry-Guazú of the Argentines, considering it in the small portion shown upon the partial plan, but considering the general direction of the river at its last turn the said *point remains in front of the centre of its course*. . . .

To this it should be added that the river Chapecó or Pequiry-Guazú has at a distance of eight hundred metres from its mouth a reef which is visible therefrom and which crosses it from one bank to the other.

Valentin Virasoro, 3rd Commissioner. (Argentine.)
José Candido Gnillobel, 2nd Commissioner. (Brazilian.)

Fifth proof.

The Demarcators of 1777 noticed that the rivers Pepiry and San Antonio, erroneously explored by the Commissioners of 1759, did not have their headwaters either near each other or corresponding to one another on opposite watersheds. The chief of the Portuguese Engineers thought that between their headwaters there passed a third river which originated in Curitiba;[2] and the Commission of Geographers from the two Nations sent to verify this fact found that in fact between their headwaters there was the source of a river that finally emptied into the Paraná and that it had its springs near those of the false San Antonio. They found out, besides, that the sources of the false Pepiry were very far from the two preceding rivers and that therefore they could by no means be made to serve as the boundary according to the terms of Articles V and VIII of the Treaties of 1750 and 1777.[3]

The International Exploration of 1885–1891, made more carefully and with better scientific preparation and means than that of 1777, has proved that between the sources of the Pepiry and the erroneous San Antonio of 1759 *are interposed not one but two rivers* that separate still farther these two watersheds and deprive them of the characteristics required by the treaties. I present herewith to the Arbitrator the International Plan, signed by the Brazilian and Argentine Engineers, which proves this fact, and in which these rivers bear the names of "Capanema" and "Urugua-y."[4] The facsimile of the same is here enclosed. It should be also noted that the river Capanema

---

[1] See the book containing the documents of the Argentine Commission, Second Party. Original in the Argentine Legation, at the disposal of the Arbitrator.
[2] See this Argument, page 268.
[3] See this Argument, page 165.
[4] Argentine Evidence, Portfolio of Maps, Nos. 48 and 49.

Planta
Do
Terreno
Entre
As
Cabeceiras
Dos
Rios
Santo Antonio
E

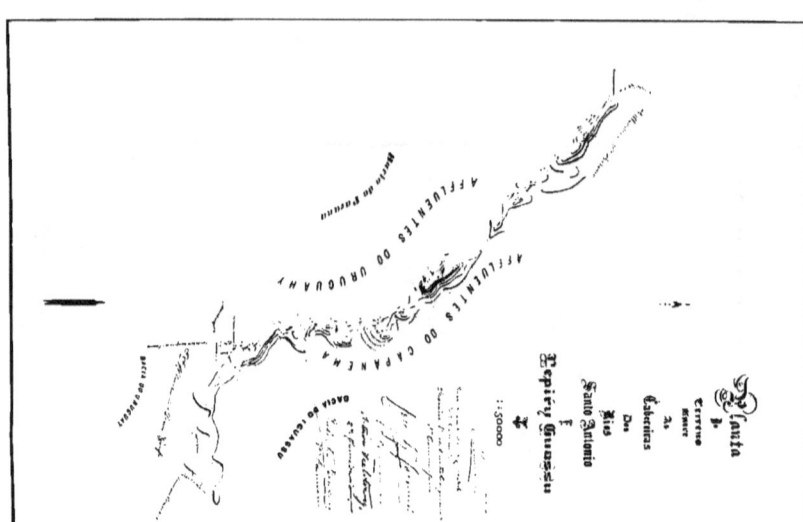

was discovered by this International Exploration, which gave to it the name of the chief of the Brazilian Demarcators.

Brazil and the Argentine Republic have thus officially and definitively established the fact that the rivers Pepiry and San Antonio of 1759 do not have their headwaters either near each other or in the conditions as to correspondence upon opposite watersheds required by the treaties of 1750 and 1777; and that furthermore the only system of rivers that conforms to these requirements, is that of the rivers Pepiry or Pequiry-Guazú and the San Antonio-Guazú, situated to the East of the preceding rivers.

General Dionisio Evangelista Castro Cerqueira, the Third Commissioner of the Brazilian Boundary Commission, engaged in this International Exploration, now accredited as Envoy Extraordinary and Minister Plenipotentiary of Brazil before the Arbitrator in order to defend his country in this matter, accompanied Minister Bocayuva to Montevideo and served as counsellor to him, under the title of chief *ad interim* of that Commission, when the Treaty of 1890 was made.[1] He wrote to the "*Jornal de Commercio*" of Rio de Janeiro, on the 19th of July, 1891, discussing in the following terms the Treaty of Montevideo:

<small>Testimony of one of the Ministers accredited by Brazil before the Arbitrator in this question.</small>

> The Joint Boundary Commission, after the work of my distinguished and esteemed friends, Commissioners Guillobel and Virasoro was ended,[2] declared in official documents *that the true San Antonio-Guazú of the Spanish Geographer Oyarvide is the Yangada and not the Chopin. By the surveys of these distinguished professors it was proven that the nearest river to the Chapecó named by the Spaniards formerly, and by the Argentines to-day, Pequiry-Guazú, and which runs towards the Yguazú, is the Yangada*.[3]
>
> Subsequently, by very full and detailed drawings and surveys made under the immediate direction of the same and of my colleague, Virasoro, and executed by the assistants, Jardin, Rego Barros, Montes and Donsset, and in which we drew curves showing the elevations throughout the zone to demonstrate the *divortia aquarum*, it was demonstrated beyond question that the *Yangada is not only the nearest river to the Chapecó which runs towards the Yguazú, but that it is also its counter-source.*
>
> In like manner as this was proven, from the work carried out with equal carefulness and scrupulous attention on the zone com-

---
[1] See this Argument, page 217.
[2] Guillobel was the Brazilian Commissioner and Virasoro the Argentine Commissioner.
[3] San Antonio-Guazú of the Argentines.

prised between the sources of the *Pepiry-Guazú and the San Antonio*, the conviction was also arrived at that this river [the Chopin] was not the nearest to that which runs towards the *Yguazú* nor its counter-source.[1]

It is important to confirm the affirmations of the Demarcators of the second epoch, according to which the system of the rivers of the Demarcation of 1759, annulled in 1777, did not fulfil the requirements of the instructions. The international surveys from 1885 to 1891 demonstrated that the counter-source of the false San Antonio of 1759 upon the opposite watershed, was not the Pepiry or Pequiry indicated by the Indian, which emptied down stream from the Uruguay-pitá, but a third river, which instead of running like that to mingle its waters with the Uruguay is on the contrary a tributary of the Paraná. The said Minister from Brazil in Washington, General de Castro Cerqueira, explains this clearly in similar terms and in this same discussion, when answering Brazilian writers who attacked him for having accepted, as an honest Demarcator, those facts which it was impossible to efface from the ground. He says:

> The line which divides the waters which descend, on one side toward the river Uruguay and on the opposite side toward the Yguazú, has its terminal point on the western side in the principal spring of the river Pequiry-Guazú.[2] From this point toward the West the divider of the waters is bifurcated in such a way that the northwest branch divides the waters that run to the Yguazú from those that flow into the tributaries of the Paraná, and the southwest branch divides the waters that run into the tributaries of the Paraná from those that flow into the tributaries of the Uruguay.
> *I assert that no one, however wise or learned he may be, can deny the geographical facts.*
> This being so, as the facts show, and the labors of the Boundary Commission prove, *we see the San Antonio rising on the watershed North of the northwest branch and running toward the Yguazú, and on the opposite side, of the same range, with an extension of nearly three leagues towards the Southeast, the numerous sources of the river Uruguai-y, a tributary of the Paraná.* The watershed opposed to that in which the San Antonio rises only gives its waters to the Paraná, *and therefore the counter-source of the San*

---

[1] The rivers San Antonio-Guazú and Pepiry-Guazú of this paragraph are those so called by the Brazilians opposite to the preceding rivers; that is to say, those of the error of 1759. General Cerqueira's letter has been published in the Argentine Memoir of Foreign Affairs. See the "Argentine Evidence," pages 704 and 705.

[2] So called by Brazil; it is the false Pepiry of 1759.

ios

Sanada

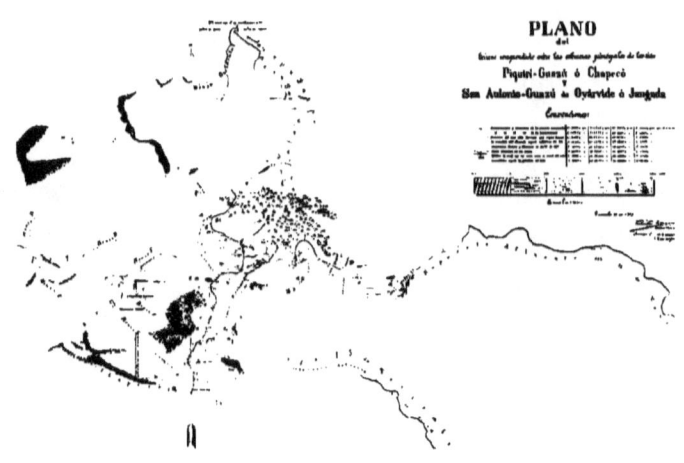

Antonio is the river Urugua-y and not the Pepiry-Guazú, the counter-sources of which are those of another river called the "Capanema," which has springs in common with it and runs down the watershed opposite which is that of the Yguazú, and the river Urugua-y which rises in the opposite watershed and gives its waters to the Paraná.[1]

It is proved by the common authority of the Argentine and Brazilian explorers that the rivers of the system claimed by the latter as the international boundary, or the Western rivers, do not comply with the physical characteristics required for the correspondence of their respective watersheds, or being one the counter-source of the other, as stated in the treaties, the basic map of the Demarcation and the instructions of the two Courts. On the contrary, the international map herewith shows the characteristics of the Eastern system of rivers, according to the treaties, and as they in fact are located upon the ground. Let us refer once more to the Minister of Brazil, General Castro Cerqueira, who says:

> We are discussing now the Yangada (San Antonio-Guazú of Oyarvide) and the Chapecó (the Pepiry-Guazú of the Spaniards), admitting at the same time the definition of Señor Guillobel.
> The line of the watershed between the Uruguay and the Yguazú, which begins in the sources of the Pepiry-Guazú (of 1759) runs with a general course from the West to the East, dividing the waters of the two watersheds, after having separated those that run to the Chopin from those that flow towards and fall into the Chapecó, it passes between the sources of the latter and those of the Yangada, as may be seen in all the maps, in such a way that the different sources of the latter are in front of the others of the Chapecó, there being some that even rise in the same basin. All these springs of the Yangada rise on the watershed of the Yguazú and those of the Chapecó rise on the opposite watershed. *Therefore the Chapecó is the counter-source of the Yangada.*[2]

These are also the facts supported by the Spanish Geographers Alvear, Oyarvide, Azara, Cerviño, Requena and other enlightened defenders of the right of Spain to its boundary by this system of rivers.

[1] See the facsimile of the map showing this fact, page 286.
[2] Which is the one maintained by the Argentines. "Argentine Evidence," Vol. I, page 706.

PART FIFTH.

PRETENDED POSSESSION BY THE EMPIRE OF BRAZIL OF THE TERRITORY IN DISPUTE.

PART FIFTH.

PRETENDED POSSESSION BY THE EMPIRE OF BRAZIL OF THE TERRITORY IN DISPUTE.

I have shown that during the Sixteenth, Seventeenth and Eighteenth centuries Portugal did not occupy the Territory in dispute, nor even its surroundings. The official maps presented, and the most important ones of the Eighteenth century, delineate the Portuguese settlements on the coast of the Ocean. The Spanish-Portuguese Boundary Commission that worked from 1783 to 1800 found and left the Portuguese situated at a great distance from the Territory submitted to the Arbitrator. I affirm, further, that not a single document worthy of confidence can be presented against these Argentine proofs. On the contrary it has been fully demonstrated that ever since the middle of the Sixteenth century this Territory was possessed and settled by Spain. The Demarcators of 1759 and those of 1783 to 1800 found there "*yerbales*" which were cultivated by the inhabitants of the pueblos of Corpus and San Xavier, and all the official documents that refer to those unsuccessful boundary demarcations point to San Xavier and Corpus as the basis of the operations upon the adjacent disputed zone, because they were the pueblos that had jurisdiction over it. Nor can Brazil deny these facts, for they are stated in the instructions and in the reports of the international Boundary Demarcators, signed by both Governments. [Antecedents.]

This state of things lasted until 1845. During the diplomatic negotiations discussed in this Argument referring to the Armistice of Rademaker and the Treaty of Peace with Brazil in 1828,[1] neither Portugal, nor its successor the Empire of Brazil, ever alluded to any possession or pretended to have any whatever. The question between Spain and Portugal about the river Pepiry or Pequiry-Guazú seemed to be forgotten, and the legal and real possession of Spain acknowledged as a fact.

The Paulistas continued during the Nineteenth century the same sort of life which had scandalized Humanity and Portugal itself ever since [Origin of Brazilian claims.]

---

[1] See this Argument, pages 71 to 82, and Argentine Evidence, Vol. I, page 611 *et seq.*

1560. They overran the fields along the frontier, gentlemen of the gallows and the knife, each one exploiting at his own free will the natural wealth of the country, and making a business of smuggling and enslaving the Indians. Tobacco smuggling was their greatest traffic. They carried it from Brazil to the Argentine State of Corrientes or to the Republic of Uruguay, and, introduced across the desert frontiers, it was sold in the Argentine and Uruguayan markets as a national product. In these expeditions the adventurers of San Paulo sometimes passed across the districts adjacent to the Territory in dispute on the East. In 1836 some soldiers came very near its Eastern boundary, when engaged either accidentally or unexpectedly in a fight with wild Indians. The President of the Brazilian State of San Paulo, in the message presented to the Legislature in 1837, said:

> The subjection of the wild Indians is becoming now an absolute necessity, for according to the information given by Major José de Andrada Pereyra in regard to the beauty, extent and fertility of the fields of Palmas that he has just crossed in search of Captain José de Sán Sotomaior, who is a prisoner of the Indians who live wandering across these regions, it is necessary to settle these as soon as possible in the projected colony.

Colony of Palmas, 1838.

Thus arose, in 1838, the Colony of Palmas[1] as a simple halting-place on the road of the Paulistas who travelled between the North of Brazil and the littoral of the Republics of Argentine and Uruguay. It was a mere casual fact, and did not amount to more than a mere form.

The Imperial Government at Rio de Janeiro was ignorant of the existence of Palmas for many years. The local government of San Paulo only supported it on account of rivalries concerning boundaries

Boundary question between the States of Brazil.

with another Brazilian state, that of Santa Catalina. In the pamphlet entitled:

"*Discussao da Questao de Limites entre o Paraná e Santa Catherina ;*" (Discussion of the Boundary Question between Parana and Santa Catalina; by Bento Fernandez de Barros. Published by the Curitiba Literary Club. Rio de Janeiro, 1877.)

which I present to the Arbitrator among the books of the "Argentine Evidence," it is stated [2]—

From 1836 to 1839 many explorers, divided into various groups,

---

[1] See the Map, No. 51, Portfolio of *Argentine Evidence*.
[2] "Argentine Evidence," Vol. II, pamphlet No. 3.

discovered and took possession of the fields of Palmas and of others that they called "*Campos Novos*" or of San Joao. . . .

. . . .
Only after these obstacles had been overcome by great efforts and sacrifices, and after the settlement of Palmas was already flourishing, did the Province of Santa Catalina set up its claims. They were stated by its President Antero, afterwards Baron de Tramandahy, in 1841 and 1844, asking for the territory on the left of the Yguazú, and thereby the fields of Palmas, and other lands in that region which belonged to the Province of San Paulo, but are now included in that of Paraná.

This claim received an energetic answer in the official communication addressed by the President of San Paulo, Manuel de Fonseca Lima e Silva, later Baron de Suruhy, to that of Santa Catalina on the 21st of September, 1844. In this important document, which has already been published, the President of San Paulo stated with great precision the reasons on which he founded the indisputable rights of the Province he administered to the fields of Palmas, saying:

1. *Because they were discovered by the inhabitants* of this Province with the knowledge and by the express order of its Governor.

2. Because prior thereto no other fact can be brought forward in evidence that throws any shadow whatever upon the law that puts the fields of Palmas entirely within the Territory that was adjudicated to the Municipality of Lages, at the time of its first settlement.

The documents of Brazilian origin I have just presented show: <small>Consequences.</small>

1. That the first appearances of the Brazilians in the neighborhood of the Territory in dispute were the casual incursions of the adventurers and scouts of the frontier, from 1838 to 1845.

2. That the National Government of Brazil was ignorant of these events.

3. That when the adventurers settled in Palmas between 1838 and 1845 they found no indication that any other Brazilians had ever been there prior to that time.

4. That the authorities of San Paulo supported the sporadic acts of the adventurers on account of boundary questions under discussion with the State of Santa Catalina, supposing that Palmas was within the territory of Brazil, as the Imperial Government believed up to 1882, as shown by the declarations given at pages 199 to 200 of this Argument.

In none of the official documents concerning these casual settlements <small>Object of the occupation.</small>

in Palmas is there any intimation whatever that they had any international significance, or that the object of the settlement was to strengthen the claims of the Empire over controverted lands. Acts of such gravity could not be done by local governments, and without the knowledge of the general Government.

Significance of these facts. The preceding official Brazilian declarations, as well as those which the Brazilian Minister will present to the Arbitrator as to the origin and existence of the road-station called Palmas, from 1836 to 1877, prove that it never was a national establishment, nor is there any document connected with its foundation which attributes to it a national character, nor any purpose whatever of protecting the frontiers against another nation.

Brazil was ignorant that Palmas was situated on the border of the zone in dispute. The Empire did *not*, as would have been natural, take any part in these movements upon the frontier, for it did not know that they had any influence upon international questions. The truth is, also, that neither the local administrations of San Paulo and Santa Catalina, nor the Imperial Government of Brazil, were aware of the real situation of Palmas as regards the Territory in dispute. They believed it outside of and away from it until 1888. This is proved by the erroneous treaty of 1885. Therefore it is not an act of possession which can with any propriety be invoked under the rules of International Law. In the first place, it was carried out by a State, an internal body of the Empire, without political capacity to perform acts prejudicial to another sovereignty. In the next place, it lacked the primordial element which must attach to a possessory act, the purpose to take possession of that which is considered as its own or not belonging to any one and without a master. Finally, the Imperial Government has declared that its possessions were not upon the disputed Territory.

In this case the first settlers of Palmas were merchants, supported after the fact of settlement by a Province of the Empire, all sincerely believing that they were on the soil of their own country. In fact, until 1888, the Argentine and Brazilian Governments believed that the eastern boundary of the Territory in dispute was the river Chopin on the side towards the Yguazú.[1] Such was the ignorance as to the interior geography of *Misiones*, which since 1750 had only been explored in its fluvial outlines.

The boundary question did not exist. On the other hand from 1800 to 1857 there was no question raised as to the boundaries between the Argentine Republic and Brazil.

[1] See the Treaty of 1885, in which this was declared, and that of the Arbitration in which the error was corrected.

Once independent these two countries did not bear in mind the differences between Spain and Portugal about the river Pepiry or Pequiry-Guazú, and neither the discussions nor the treaties of the time permit any presumption that there was any uncertainty as to their frontiers.

More than a half century of forgetfulness by Brazil and the peaceful possession of the Territory by Spain and the Argentine Republic from 1516 to 1893, confirmed the rights of the latter. Neither Portugal nor Brazil granted any authority to the aggressions of the Paulistas upon the dominions of Spain, but on the contrary they eloquently condemned them, and the Brazilian writers who now invoke these crimes as an evidence of international dominion commit a great error.

In 1847 Brazil oppressed the Republic of Uruguay, a feeble and weak nation, in order to compel a settlement of its boundary questions. The boundaries were traced in Article III of the Treaty of 1777 with entire clearness, but Brazil wished to advance its frontier much farther South, taking away half of the territory of that Republic by the right of force. The full Council of State of the Empire, called to meet in consultation by the Emperor, issued a document of the greatest importance in favor of the Argentine Republic. The language used by the Council was as follows:

_{Brazil excludes from its possessions the Territory submitted to the Arbitrator, 1847.}

> The several Departments met in Council of State declare the following: 1. That the Treaty of October 1, 1777, which established the said boundaries, was never fully executed. 2. That during the war which followed in 1801 between the Crowns of Spain and Portugal the Portuguese conquered the territory between the "*Cochilha Geral*" and the Uruguay, and from the Quarahim to the place where the river Peperi-Guassú empties into the Uruguay. . . .

This precious document proves overwhelmingly that the possessory rights claimed by Portugal in the Rio de la Plata, as a result of conquests made during the war of 1801 (rights which as a matter of fact did not in reality exist), had as their object the territory on the *East of the Uruguay, as far as the Pepiry-Guazú*. This of course excludes the Territory now submitted to Arbitration from the claims set up by Brazil in 1847.[1]

It should be noted that Brazil, in 1884, maintained that the conquests of Portugal in 1801 included the Territory now in controversy, but this assertion was corrected by the solemn official document put forth by the Empire which is cited above.

[1] Collection of Treaties of Brazil, Pinto, presented, Vol. III, page 305.

First discussion between the two countries The first discussion in regard to their boundaries and the first allusion to the difficulties of 1750 and 1777 between the Argentine Republic and Brazil took place, as has been shown, in 1856, when Minister Paranhos demanded the final arrangement of the pending demarcation. It is very noteworthy that in the Memoir with which he opened this negotiation the Brazilian Minister made no allusion to Palmas, nor did he make any mention whatever of the existence of Brazilian colonies within the Territory in dispute.¹ In reality they did not exist. The action of San Paulo was confined to Palmas and the nearest districts, and the general belief was that Palmas was situated outside of the area embraced by the question of 1759 and 1789. So matters continued, the Argentine Republic possessing by inheritance from Spain the Territory in controversy, and asserting its rights by the law relative to the Treaty of 1857.

Brazilian road through Misiones, 1863 The President of the State of San Paulo in the Message of 1885, already quoted, adds:

> In 1862, by the Order of May 8, the Government ordered a road to be opened from Palmas to Corrientes. The charge of this work was entrusted to Manuel Marcondes de Sá, who made the surveys. He left the "*fazenda*" or farm of Captain Hermogenes, situated in Palmas on the edge of the woods; from there he went to Campo Eré, separated from Palmas by a forest, the entrance to which is very difficult, and it is 12 leagues long. From the extremity of the Campo he began to explore the region most convenient for a road, and was fortunate to find on the high ground between the Yguazú and the Upper Uruguay an admirable plain of hard soil in a direction East and West. The large swamps that exist a little beyond Campo Eré were left on one side. . . .
>
> *There are at Campo Eré the ruins of a strange building; and it is evident that men worked there at some very remote period.* The ruins form a square a thousand feet in extent, the walls having been built of unburned bricks, but one can yet clearly see the entrance and the remains of a paved road that runs towards the West. The interior presents a surface nearly flat, but in the middle there rises a construction, the base of which is 150 feet in diameter, and it is 20 feet in height. *The version that history naturally gives of the ruins is that they are the remains of a Spanish fort, situated on their boundary line, but the history of the Republic does not give the least information as to this fort.*

Offensive and defensive attitude of the Argentine Government, 1863. The news that Brazilian employés from Palmas had really entered the Territory in dispute reached Buenos Aires shortly afterwards; and

¹ See the Memoir referred to in the Argentine Evidence, Vol. II, pamphlet 1, page 49.

the Argentine Government immediately ordered the following defensive and offensive steps to be taken: 1. That a protest be addressed to the Brazilian Government for this violation of Argentine territory. 2. That the Government of the State of Corrientes, which administered the affairs of *Misiones*, be ordered to make investigations as to the advances that had taken place. 3. That the army of the Argentine Republic be prepared for service.

The Minister of Foreign Affairs of the Argentine Republic sent to the Government of the Empire the protest to which he refers in the Memoir presented to Congress in 1863. Argentine protest.

The following is the text of the protest referred to, which was published in the Memoir of the Minister of Foreign Affairs for 1863, page 56:[1]

DEPARTMENT OF FOREIGN AFFAIRS,
BUENOS AIRES, *February* 13, 1863.

The undersigned, Minister of Foreign Affairs, has received instructions from His Excellency the President of the Republic, to address himself to the Government of His Majesty the Emperor of Brazil, declaring that the determination of the boundary line which must be drawn in accordance with existing treaties not having been made between the Argentine Republic and Brazil, the Argentine Government cannot authorize by remaining silent, acts of possession of Argentine territory, or of any territory that may belong to the Argentine Republic after the final determination of the boundary line. The undersigned is in consequence compelled to express to the Government of His Majesty the Emperor of Brazil, the propriety of making no alterations whatsoever regarding the possession of the lands in question, as such alterations, not being based upon any legitimate right, can only serve to produce similar acts of possession on the part of the Argentine Government, a result which this Government desires by all means to avoid.

The Government of the undersigned is in possession of authentic information regarding acts of occupation of Argentine territory which the Government of His Majesty the Emperor claims, and in virtue of this information said Government has thought it necessary to take this measure in defence of its rights.

. . . .

At the same time that the Argentine Government ordered the necessary investigations to be made as to the Brazilian advances upon the zone in question, it obtained from the Government of Corrientes the Effective possession of the disputed Territory.

[1] Argentine Evidence, Vol. 1, page 479. MSS. Group G. No. 12.

reports already referred to, and also the following from the Argentine Vice-Consul at Uruguayana, a Brazilian town on the Uruguay River:

Ever since 1857 "*Yerba*" or native tea has been raised in the Corrientes *Misiones*, and the managers engaged in this business, with very limited resources, cut a road for mules from near San Xavier to the first "*Yerbal*" at Tabay, without being in any way helped by any government, . . . so the development of the "*Yerba*" trade in the Corrientes *Misiones* has been very slow; nevertheless, last year in this "*Yerbal*" of Tabay, there was prepared from 12 to 14 thousand *arrobas*. The amount will be greater this year, for a great many persons have come over from the Brazilian *Yerbales* on the left bank of the Uruguay, for the *Yerbales* on that side have become exhausted and ruined by excessive gathering and for want of a proper care in trimming the branches of the tree. A factory for the preparation of *Yerba* has also been established, with the object of exporting the *Yerba* by the river Uruguay, avoiding overland freightage, and because the *Yerba* tree is of a better kind (Bompland found 18 different varieties of this tree), as also on account of the existence of virgin *Yerbales* in the corner which the *River Pepiry or Pequiry-Guazú forms with the Uruguay, on the right bank of both rivers, and half a league from the water's edge.*

This establishment sought the license of the Government of Corrientes in 1860, and it is only lately and after overcoming a thousand difficulties that the managers have been able to make their first expedition, descending the river on the boat "*Progreso*" as far as Restauracion with nearly four thousand *arrobas* of "*Yerba Mate*," a part of which was sent to Buenos Aires. . . .

. . . Your Excellency will perceive not only the private but the public interest which must be felt in this establishment in the Argentine Republic, because being established under the protection of the Government it implies the moral and practical right thereto, as also the refusal to acknowledge the claims which the Government of Brazil pretends to have over the Territory on which it is located; and yet it is nevertheless to be regretted that the Government of Corrientes should have imposed on this *Yerba* a police tax of two gold dollars for each *arroba*, under the pretext of paying for police protection which does not exist, thus throttling an enterprise that should rather be aided, not only because it would stimulate industry in these remote regions but also because the recognition of these facts is very important so far as the territorial rights of the Argentine Republic are concerned. The Manager has presented a claim to the Governor of the Province of Corrientes and hopes to be exonerated from the payment of this exorbitant tax.

This document, dated at Uruguayana November 16, 1862, and signed by the Vice-Consul of the Argentine Republic, Don C. Kasten, forms part of an official paper of the Department of Foreign Affairs of the Argentine Republic, which has been deposited in the Argentine Legation under my charge in Washington, at the disposal of the Arbitrator. This report, which agrees with the other documents referred to in this Argument, proves that at the time Brazil claims to have opened a road from Palmas to Corrientes the Argentine settlements in the Territory in question extended as far as its eastern boundary, that is to say, as far as the Pepiry or Pequiry-Guazú of the "*Mapa de las Cortes*," and were subject to the payment of Argentine taxes.

Having taken the preceding steps the Minister of Foreign Affairs of the Argentine Republic sent to his colleague of the War and Navy Department the following note, desiring him to prepare the Nation for a campaign:

<small>Argentine military preparations.</small>

(Private.)

BUENOS AIRES, *February* 18, 1863.
To H. E. the Minister of War and Marine, Brigadier General Juan Andres Gelly y Obes.

SIR: The Government of Brazil has persisted for a long time in the purpose of enlarging its territories, taking that which belongs to the Argentine Republic.

Leaving out of the question the boundaries that belong to Brazil on the left bank of the Uruguay, and those which must be separately considered as connected with those of the Republic of Uruguay and Brazil, and limiting ourselves to those that are located between the left bank of the Uruguay and the Rio Grande de Curitiba, the dividing line established by virtue of the treaties in force has been passed for a long distance by Brazilian settlements recently established.

By the third Article of the Treaty of October 1, 1777, it was provided that the navigation of the rivers La Plata and Uruguay and the lands of their two banks, northern and southern, should belong absolutely to the Crown of Spain and its subjects, to the place where the river Pequiry or Pepiry-Guazú empties into the same Uruguay on its western bank, extending the possessions of Spain on the said northern bank as far as the dividing line which will be formed beginning by the part toward the Sea in the small stream of Chuy.

It was said in the Treaty of January 13, 1750, that the dividing line in this portion of it would proceed from the mouth of the Ybicuy by the waters of the Uruguay until arriving at those of the river Pepiry or Pequiry which empties into the Uruguay on its western bank, and would continue up the stream of the Pepiry to its principal source, from which it would proceed by the highest ground to the principal source of the nearest river which emptied into the Grande de Curitiba, or Yguazú, by the waters of the said river nearest to the Pepiry and afterwards by those of the Yguazú to where the latter empties into the Paraná upon its eastern bank.

The Demarcators intrusted with the execution of the Treaty of 1750 had doubts as to the designation of these boundaries, but they made the Demarcation guided by the statements of an Indian, notwithstanding they were not in conformity with the instructions given by the common agreement of the Governments of Spain and Portugal.

But as all this was annulled by the Treaty of 1777 it cannot be invoked for any purpose.

In the Eighth Article of that Treaty, amplifying the matter contained in the third Article, the provisions of the fifth Article of the Treaty of 1750 are repeated, with some further explanations. It says that the belongings of the two Crowns having been indicated as far as the place where the river Pepiry or Pequiry-Guazú enters the Uruguay the high contracting parties agreed that the dividing line should follow up the stream of the said Pepiry to its principal origin or source, and from there go by the higest land, under the rules given in the sixth Article, until the headwaters of the San Antonio were met, which empty into the Grande de Curitiba, the other name of which is the Yguazú, and following this down until it falls into the Paraná on its Eastern bank.

The Demarcators charged with carrying out this line found some difficulties in the way. The question was to know which were the rivers Pequiry and San Antonio mentioned.

The Portuguese Demarcator asserted that they were those marked on the plan annulled by the Treaty of 1777; but that never had any value on account of the manner in which this plan was prepared in opposition to the instructions given in virtue of the Treaty of 1750. There was, then, no reason to invoke this plan, and the reasons of the Spanish Demarcator were irresistible. The instructions given for the execution of the Treaty of 1750 said :

The signs of the Pequiry or Pepiry-Guazú are a "*rio caudaloso,*" or river of large volume, with a wooded island in front of its mouth, and a reef inside of its bar ; and these to be found above the Uruguay-Pitá.

Given these indications of the Pepiry-Guazú the San Antonio was designated, which was the one that had its headwaters the nearest and inclined to the Yguazú.

The Spanish Demarcators found the true rivers Pequiry and

San Antonio, but the Portuguese Demarcator was not willing to agree that the tracing of the line should be made.

From that time the question continued pending until the Government of Brazil undertook to legitimize its claims, securing their recognition in a treaty with the Government of the Paraná, the line traced by the Demarcators of 1759 violating the instructions and the treaty of 1750 which was annulled by that of 1777, the Portugese Demarcator capriciously refusing the true demarcation which that treaty established.

Fortunately the Treaty between Brazil and the Government of the Paraná, of December 14, 1857, was not carried out, and things remained in the situation in which they were left by the Treaty of 1777.

Taking for the boundary between Brazil and the Republic the true rivers San Antonio and Pepiry-Guazú, the Argentine territory is extended by fifteen hundred square leagues, which Brazil intended to appropriate to itself. In fact it had given the names of these rivers to others which were small and insignificant, and by this means expected to advance its line and secure this extension. It has built forts on either side of the Uruguay, placing one on the right bank and to the left of a small river which it called the Pepiry. This act appears to have been done in virtue of the Treaty of Paraná, which the Government does not recognize, and at the same time it occupied islands which were evidently Argentine.

It has been necessary to address the Imperial Government, asking that the status of the disputed Territory since 1777 be not changed and that there should be no acts of occupation which although void would compel the Government to take other action.

Therefore, in defence of this immense national Territory it is necessary to take the measures which are indispensable. For this purpose I forward to your Excellency the statement of the facts for the action which the Government desires to take to guarantee our frontier and the dominion of our islands.

God keep you for many years.

RUFINO DE ELISALDE.

By this time Brazil was deeply complicated in the internal struggles going on in the Republic of Uruguay, and shortly afterwards the Empire invaded with an army the territory of that Republic and, allied to some of the local parties, made war upon its Government. This circumstance without doubt decided the Empire to clear up for the moment the Argentine side of its horizon. So it sent a Plenipotentiary to Buenos Aires to explain matters. The Minister of Foreign Affairs of the Argentine Republic informed the National Congress of the fact in his Memoir of 1864, in the following terms: *Complications of Brazil in the Rio de la Plata. Arrangement of the Argentine question.*

Afterwards, Don José Felipe Pereyra Leal was accredited Minister Resident, who contributed very efficaciously on his part towards cementing the bonds of friendship that unite us to the Government of the Emperor of Brazil and to the dissipation of the reasons for distrust by which peace might be compromised.[1]

General political revolution. The Imperial Government was engaged in the war with Uruguay when the Republic of Paraguay, which had been converted into a military camp by the Dictator Lopez, with one hundred thousand excellent troops, perfectly armed, and with the most powerful squadron of the Rio de La Plata, also took part in the war against Brazil, and in accord with the party that governed the Republic of Uruguay. Then a general conflagration broke out in that extremity of South America, and the Argentine Republic, situated between the belligerents, took great pains to preserve the strictest neutrality. But Brazil needed the alliance of the Argentine Republic, and this fact explains why, in the critical period through which the Empire was passing, it would have preferred the co-operation of the Argentine Republic to its small pretensions to territorial extension.

The alliance of Brazil and the Republics of Argentine and Uruguay against the military giant of Paraguay was, in fact, arranged at the beginning of 1865.[2] The final solution of the boundary question was therefore postponed. The Argentine Congress was informed of this by the Minister of Foreign Affairs in his Memoir for 1865 (page 8):

> The Republic had *important* business to discuss with the Imperial Government and sent a mission to this effect. But these matters were postponed on account of the questions with the Republic of Uruguay.[3]

Abandonment of the Road across Misiones. The road from Palmas to Corrientes, which had led to the matters discussed, was abandoned for the time. Some of the monuments left on this road were later invoked as indications of Brazilian possession of the Territory submitted to the Arbitrator. The chief of the Argentine Demarcators of 1885–1891 sought for an explanation of these marks from the chief of the Brazilian Demarcators, who answered categorically that there were no such possessory acts. His language is as follows:

---
[1] Memoir of 1864, page 5, Archives of the Argentine Legation in Washington and Library of the Department of State.
[2] This treaty has been presented to the Arbitrator in this Argument.
[3] Argentine Legation, Washington.

There is absolutely nothing in the case you mention of marks with Brazilian arms in the *Campina do America*, for they also exist in San Pedro, a place which received its name from Brazilian officials more than twenty years ago, when there was a commission charged with examining the means of communication with this side at the beginning of the war with Paraguay, and have nothing to do with boundaries.[1]

In 1865 the Argentine Government, already allied to the Empire of Brazil, denied the Government of Paraguay the permission to cross the Territory of *Misiones* with its armies, and this was the *Casus belli* that brought upon the Argentine Republic the general war of 1865–1870. But on the other hand it authorized its Brazilian ally to lead troops against Paraguay across this Territory, and these troops came over the road of Palmas that was first opened in 1863. The refusal of the Argentine Government to permit Paraguay to attack Brazil by going across the Territory in dispute is contained in a state paper of universal celebrity, officially published in the Memoir of the Department of Foreign Affairs of the Argentine Republic for 1865, page 167 and following. This work is at the Argentine Legation in Washington at the disposal of the Arbitrator.

The Government of Paraguay on this solemn occasion addressed to the Argentine Republic a note dated January 14, 1865, which has been published in the above-cited Memoir. In it the following language was used:

Argentine dominion recognized by Paraguay.

> Without prejudging the policy your Government may deem proper to follow in the present war between Brazil and Paraguay, respecting the convictions leading to it, the Government of the undersigned does not presume this policy is of such a nature as to prevent your Government granting this act of just reciprocity, allowing the transit of the army of this Republic to the Brazilian Province of Rio Grande do Sul under the conditions proposed. And as the pressing circumstances demand the immediate solution of this friendly proposition, the bearer of this note, Dr. Don Luis Caminos, is charged to receive and bring back the answer that your Excellency's Government may see fit to give to this communication.

The *Misiones* were interposed between Paraguay and the Brazilian province of Rio Grande, and after its request had been refused Paraguay marched across that territory and occupied that of Rio Grande. These facts which I have narrated are undoubtedly fully corroborated

---

[1] Argentine Evidence, Vol. III, document No. VII.

by documents in the State Department of the United States, for its agents in Buenos Aires, Paraguay and Rio de Janeiro must have sent detailed reports acknowledging and affirming the dominion of the Argentine Republic over *Misiones* down to 1865.

The official declaration by the President of San Paulo, made in his Message for 1865, just cited, is not less interesting for the Argentine cause, where he recalls the fact that in Campo Eré, in the Territory submitted to Arbitration, there exist the ruins of a Spanish village. This is the *pueblo* indicated on the Maps of 1612 and of 1667, which exploited the "*Yerbales*" under the jurisdiction of San Xavier and Corpus (see page 86 of this Argument) and also the pueblo which the Spanish Minister of State, Don José Galvez, ordered the Demarcators of the Treaty of 1777 to cover with the frontier line (see this Argument, page 258). Thus we have once more proved the traditional possession of Spain.

It seems scarcely worth while to dwell upon the error of the explorers who, according to the same Brazilian Message, discovered the Campo of Palmas, for there was no such discovery, and the fact that the Argentine Republic exercised no authority in that particular place in 1836 cannot prejudice its Sovereignty. There should be applied to this case the official doctrine of Brazil, declared by the Visconde de Porto Seguro and by the Visconde de Uruguay against France.[1]

Argentine Dictatorship. It is also proper to recall the fact that from 1833 to 1862 the Argentine Republic suffered from a sort of national disintegration, primarily induced by the dictatorship of Rozas from 1833 to 1852, and after that date by the separation of the State of Buenos Aires and the resulting civil war, so that the first measures conservative of the Territory of *Misiones* were taken in 1863, immediately after the country had been organized under the Presidency of General Mitre.

In the Memoir of the Minister of Foreign Affairs of the Argentine Republic, presented to the National Congress in September, 1892, the claims set up by Brazil to the disputed Territory were discussed. That country had permitted the understanding that the Empire possessed it, but its diplomacy, disappointed at the rejection of the negotiations in which the whole extent of that Territory had been claimed by it, as has been shown, solemnly confessed that it lacked the possession invoked, and in 1879 prepared to attempt to secure by Parliamentary efforts what it had failed to obtain by other means. This was the origin of the governmental measures which the Empire adopted in

[1] See this Argument, pages 180 and 20.

1879 and in 1880, directing the settlement of colonies of the frontiers of the Province of Paraná and upon the disputed zone. It proceeded cautiously, under the pretext of explorations, in order to see what effect would be thereby produced upon the Government and the people of the Argentine Republic. These acts were begun at first along the Imperial frontier, although the decrees authorizing them referred to the occupation of the Territory in controversy.

In an official note, dated October 17, 1880, Señor Dominguez,[1] the Argentine Minister in Rio de Janeiro, wrote to his home Government, as follows:

> When these colonies are established there will be a sort of cordon of military colonies garrisoning the frontier to which the Government of Brazil claims to have a right and to be in possession. I take the liberty of reminding your Excellency that I have reported to the Government the progress of these settlements for the past two years, in my notes 222, 226, 290 and 291.[2]

In the early part of 1881, when the founders of these military colonies had already entered on the lands in controversy, Señor Dominguez held a conference with the Minister of Foreign Relations of the Empire, and advised the Argentine Government of the result of his action as follows:

> Señor Pedro Luis arrived in this city on the sixth, and came to see me on the same day, but did not touch upon the matter. On the following day we met twice and he then spontaneously stated that he wished to inform me of what had happened as to the military colonies which were ordered to be established upon our frontier on the rivers Chapecó and Chopin. He assured me that he knew nothing about it when the Department of War resolved to send thither Captains Borman and Dantas to found those military colonies; *that as soon as he knew it, he declared to the Minister of War that that measure was inconvenient; that it was a matter which concerned his Department and not that of War, and that orders were immediately given that those officers should leave the frontier.* We then exchanged declarations of our best wishes for the maintenance of good friendship between the two countries, and the Minister closed, saying *that he hoped some means would be found to settle the boundary question without hurting in the least the feelings of either nation.*

[1] Señor Dominguez was for some years the Argentine Minister in the United States and now in England, and is universally esteemed for his probity, his serious character and his wide information.

[2] These communications are collected in the "Argentine Evidence," Vol. I, page 611.

I then declared that the withdrawal of those two colonies seemed to me very convenient, and that *when this was done*, I also believed that the termination of the question in an amicable way would not be difficult.

The Emperor, on his part, had wished to dissipate the alarm of Señor Dominguez by speaking to him personally. The Argentine Minister said in the same note:

On the third inst. I had a private conversation with the Emperor, during which, after asking me for news from my country as usual, he spoke to me of our boundary question. *It is necessary, he said to me, that we arrange this question, because it is convenient for all and there is no difficulty in it.* I replied that the Argentine Government was very desirous of settling it, and His Majesty, after adding some words which proved his sincere desire to arrive at this result, closed by saying that the Minister of Foreign Relations would very soon speak to me about this matter.[1]

Señor Dominguez had proceeded very effectively. The establishment of the colonies was not only suspended but categorically disapproved by the Imperial Government. But afterwards the politicians of the Empire, believing that the Argentine Cabinet would not maintain its position, on account of the civil war going on in that country, resolved to have the troops sent back to the frontier, and after encouraging the colonies of Chopin, Chapeu and Palmas which had penetrated into the Territory in controversy, upon the high lands separating the valleys of the Paraná and the Ygnazú, thinking that they occupied their own territory, they established their colonists at Santa Ana and Campo Eré in 1881. This is clearly proved by the Brazilian documents presented to the Arbitrator.

New official confession that Brazil did not possess Misiones.

Such an audacious movement was, nevertheless, a grave error on the part of the diplomacy of the Empire, which very materially prejudiced Brazil in the diplomatic discussion carried on concerning this subject, for it proved incontestably that it never had been in possession of the Territory, which possession was the only title offered by its statesmen, since the Emperor had declared in 1857, through the illustrious Señor Paranhos in his Memoir to the Argentine Confederation, that the Empire lacked any written right to claim the *Misiones*.[2]

Furthermore, these recent usurpations and aggressions could not in

---

[1] See "Argentine Evidence," Vol. I, page 673.
[2] "Argentine Evidence," Vol. I, page 649.

any way benefit the claims of Brazil, because they were made in violation of the *statu quo* which both governments always observed under the Treaty of 1777 and that of 1778, and also because, having been protested against in proper time by Señor Dominguez, they were thereupon categorically disapproved of by the Imperial Government, and, finally, because, in the Zeballos-Bocayuva Treaty, Brazil recognized the Argentine sovereignty over the towns which were furthest within the disputed Territory, such as Campo Eré.

The Argentine Republic at once took the necessary measures to keep and reinforce its rights and possession in the Territory menaced by Brazilian action, and, resolving to carry the arms and laws of the nation into the country of *Misiones*, passed the law confirmatory of our possession on December 20, 1881. Though national from its very origin, the Territory of Misiones had been attached to the local jurisdiction of the Province of Corrientes during the long period of administrative disorganization which was caused in the Republic by the Civil War, and that law reincorporated the Territory under the national jurisdiction, erecting it into a Government with boundaries corresponding to those of the Treaty made by the Courts in 1777. The decree of March 16, 1882, organized the new Government, affirmed our rights to the boundaries claimed and established the capital at Corpus, an old mission which was thereafter to be called "Ciudad San Martin."[1]

Argentine measures to defend its rights in Misiones.

The official statements made on behalf of the Imperial Government in regard to the Territory of *Misiones* have already been commented upon in this Argument, and attention is particularly called to the publications made in May, 1882, in the "*Diario Oficial*,"[2] which are of great importance to the case of the Argentine Republic. The results of the reports asked for by the Brazilian Cabinet showed that the Military Colonies were outside of the Territory in question, and said:

Brazil declares it has not occupied the Territory in dispute.

> The foundation of our military colonies cannot be the subject of any claim, *because those colonies are situated outside of that Territory*, as shown by the Memoir presented by Councillor Doria to the General Assembly.

Although the colony of Campo-Eré was advanced into the centre of that Territory, it was thus officially disavowed by the explicit language cited, and its existence, verified by the Joint Commission presided over by General Garmendia and by the Baron de Capanema, indicates an occupation without any legal force, which would inure at the

---
[1] See this Argument, page 94.
[2] See this Argument, page 199 and Argentine Evidence, Vol. III, Document No. III.

right time to the proper sovereignty. The Zeballos-Bocayuva Treaty vindicated again the fact that it belonged to the Argentine Republic.

<small>Brazil proposes an arrangement of the boundary.</small> After the conferences held by the Plenipotentiary Dominguez with the Emperor and with his Minister of Foreign Relations, the Brazilian Plenipotentiary in Buenos Aires, the Baron de Aranjo Gondim, received instructions to propose an arrangement of the question.

On June 2, 1882, the Baron de Aranjo Gondim officially stated to the Department that "desiring to avoid complications and maintain the friendly relations that happily exist between the two countries," he was charged with proposing to the Argentine Government the opening of negotiations " for a definitive adjustment of the boundary question." This was fully answered on the 10th by the Minister of Foreign Affairs, who after referring to the clandestine occupation of a portion of the Territory in controversy by officials of the Imperial army, notwithstanding the categorical denial by Minister Souza to Señor Dominguez, and stating that all the attempts at an arrangement had fallen through on account of the policy of postponement pursued by the Baron de Cotegipe, declared that the Argentine Government had always been and was then disposed to reopen negotiations, in order to terminate without further delay a question which ought not to be continued any longer between the two countries. He concluded by saying:

> Therefore, if, as I suppose, Your Excellency is authorized and provided with the necessary instructions to treat the matter, I take pleasure in stating to you, in compliance with those I have received from the President, that we can begin the negotiations, and I hope they may be effective.

No reply was made to this until the 19th of July, when among other statements the Baron de Aranjo Gondim added a very important declaration, frank and precise in its terms, which in effect repudiated any authorization of the foundation of colonies or military garrisons, as his Sovereign and the head of his Cabinet had already done. He said:

> Passing to another point, permit me to assure Your Excellency that the information is not correct that the military colonies exist and are increasing, notwithstanding the declaration made to Señor Dominguez. *The colonies are founded upon the left bank of the river Chapecó and on the right of the Chopin, that is, in territory recognized as Brazilian, outside of that which is in controversy between the two countries.*[1]

---

[1] "Argentine Evidence," Vol. I, page 199.

The Argentine title does not refer to the Chopin, the fifth river wrongly introduced into the discussion, but to the Yangada or the San Antonio-Guazú of Oyarvide, located more to the East than the former. But notwithstanding this the proposition of the Brazilian Government clearly indicates a disapproval of the foundations undertaken within the area bounded by the four rivers of the dispute.

It has been demonstrated in this Argument (page 203) that both Brazil and the Argentine Government thought that the eastern boundary of the Territory in question, towards the Yguazú, was the River Chopin, and they so declared in the compact of 1885.[1] It has also been made evident that on perceiving this error both Governments, at the time their respective engineers together explored this Territory, corrected the mistake, transferring the boundary yet further to the East, from the river Chopin to the river San Antonio-Guazú of Oyarvide, but improperly called Yangada for a short time past by the Brazilians.[2] So that the Territory submitted to Arbitration extends as far as the aforesaid Eastern boundary on the watershed of the Yguazú.[3] The Brazilian villages found in 1885 by the international Demarcators between the watersheds of the eastern Rivers, the San Antonio-Guazú and Pepiry-Guazú, the accidental settlement of which in 1840 and in 1881 I have above narrated, did not import an act of dominion over Argentine territory, for the ignorance of both governments concerning the region through which the eastern boundary of the lands in question extended explains why Brazil considered these camps and fields as its property and as located outside of the disputed area. When in 1879 and in 1880 Brazil decreed the military occupation of the eastern banks of the rivers Chopin and Pepiry-Guazú, or Chapecó, as modern Brazilians call it, they did so under the impression that it was an occupation of a territory not in question, and this was solemnly declared by the Empire in its Official Journal and to the Argentine Government, which protested against this advance on account of its possible general consequences, both in the conferences and the note that have been cited. The international explorations of 1885–1891 having clearly proved the error of the position taken by Brazil, their settlements and colonies are left without any international effect and have no legal value whatever.

The acts and declarations of Brazil.

Error invalidates judicial acts.

---

[1] "Argentine Evidence," Vol. I, page 203.
[2] See this Argument, page 204. Argentine Evidence, Vol. III, Document No. VIII.
[3] Argentine Evidence, Vol. I, page 634.

Campo Eré, which was founded in 1881[1] in the Territory in dispute, was occupied by peasants of all nationalities, who were there as simple occupiers of wild lands. If any individual exercised authority in the name of Brazil he also obeyed the Argentine laws, for every time the Argentine forest inspectors arrived there[2] the sparse inhabitants who were scattered in those forests obeyed his authority.

But whatever may have been the nature of those settlements occupied by Brazilians on the disputed lands, the prior declarations of the Imperial Government and the Zeballos-Bocayuva treaty, as moral precedents, reduce them to mere private acts, without any character of international possession. At the same time the plan presented at page 94 of this Argument and the laws and decrees of 1881 and 1882 concerning the federalization of *Misiones* prove that the Argentine Government strengthened its dominions by definitive acts, while Brazil declared on the contrary that its acts had no bearing or effect upon this Territory, as they were entirely outside of it.

The Brazilian Demarcators recognize the Argentine possession. The demarcation of 1885 to 1891 also gave the important result that the Argentine possession was recognized in an official note addressed by the chief of the Brazilian Commission to the chief of the Argentine Commission. The text of this communication will be found copied in Vol. III of the "Argentine Evidence" (Document No. VI), and the original is at the disposition of the Arbitrator in the Argentine Legation.

When the Brazilian Commission crossed the river Yangada it was reported to them in several places that a public official of the Argentine Government was going about that region in search of a landmark cut on stone by the Commissioners of the last century. But later on the same official, known as Gustavo Niederlein, asserted that the territory should be bounded by the Yangada, and the impression upon the inhabitants was still greater when it was learned that a certain Argentine official was opening a road and preparing a plan of a river which was said to be the source of the Yangada and which was situated outside of the territory to which the treaty refers, bounded by the Chopin and by the Chapecó.

Here in Palmas I found the population impressed, not only with what was said as to the sovereignty of the Territory but also by acts which seemed preparations for taking possession, such as

---
[1] See page 307 of this Argument.
[2] I have shown at page 98 *et seq.* of this Argument the alarm raised in the Brazilian Congress by these acts of Argentine jurisdiction.

the enrollment of the inhabitants and their properties, the fact that Niederlein had addressed himself to a notary requesting the registry of lands, and an Argentine officer copying one by one the names of individuals qualified as national guards, etc. This impression was so strong and had so taken root in the minds of the people that the members of the Municipal Council came in a body to welcome the Brazilian Commission, and their speaker, Lieut. Colonel Alberto Marquez de Almeida, in his speech gave expression to the feeling of uncertainty in which they were in regard to the future of the municipality, and their desire to know to which country they would belong. I answered that by the treaty the Commission was only to proceed to survey the territory in dispute and under the instructions it could not discuss the question of law, and therefore could give them no light on that subject, but could only assure the members of the Council that the Government was animated by the most sincere desire to decide this old question according to the strictest principles of right and that all would be treated with entire justice. When questioning the reasons for the sort of speech with which we had been received I learned that on repeated occasions Argentine officials had said that the territory in dispute undoubtedly belonged to their nation, for this merely depended upon retracing the true San Antonio which ran farther to the East.

I insisted that the Commissioners not having been charged with the scientific work, nor qualified or authorized to formulate a decision, no value could be given to the opinions of auxiliaries of the Commission. Later I was informed that Major Tolosa said that the city would soon be Argentine and this was repeated to me several times. I gave no importance to it, and do not even remember who said it to me.

But even if the Empire and the Republic of Brazil had not both solemnly repudiated these acts that compromised the honesty of their international conduct, and disavowed all responsibility therefor, they would be invalid by the express text of the permanent Treaty of 1777 and its correlative of 1778, which declared perpetual the reciprocal guarantees of the possessions of the two monarchies in America, and by which they bound themselves not to settle the lands of either of the two sovereigns in case of doubts as to boundaries. See Articles XIX and XX of the Treaty of 1777, and Articles II and III of the Treaty of 1778. This is the *statu quo*. The treaties and the occupation.

The Argentine possessions are not in the same situation. The Argentine Republic does not claim, like the agents of the Provincial Government of San Paulo, to have discovered this territory in modern times, vacant and desert, but it continued the occupation begun by Spain in the sixteenth century and consequently, by remaining within the lines of its traditional possessions, West of the red line of the "*Mapa de las Cortes*" of 1749, it respected the treaties and only used that to which it had a perfect right.

SUMMARY OF THE ARGENTINE ARGUMENTS.

I.

Spain discovered and settled the Territory submitted to the Arbitrator and maintained its possession thereof against the aggressions of Portugal, sometimes peacefully and sometimes by force of arms, from the time of the Discovery until 1810. (This Argument from page 17 to 67, and from page 105 to 121.)

II.

The Argentine Republic has succeeded to Spain in its possession and in its territorial rights. (This Argument from page 68 to 104.)

III.

These rights are contained in the Treaty of 1777, which expressly ratified and made valid a portion of the Treaty of 1750 in which the boundaries are set forth. Brazil has not only accepted this fact but actually asserted it. (This Argument, from page 169 to 172.)

IV.

The boundaries of the Treaty of 1750 were traced upon an official map, the "*Mapa de las Cortes*," ordered to be prepared in 1749 by Portugal and accepted by Spain in 1751. This map, authenticated by a protocol written upon it, and signed by the Plenipotentiaries of Spain and Portugal, now presented to the Arbitrator, delineates the disputed boundary in the location claimed for it by the Argentine Republic. (This Argument, pages 137 to 153.)

V.

According to the doctrine universally accepted, boundary treaties are permanent and war does not invalidate them. This has been maintained by Presidents John Quincy Adams and Buchanan in the United States, and it is so laid down in the treatise of Wharton. (This Argument, page 183.) The documents presented in the " Argentine Evidence" (Vol. I, pages 419 to 436,) show that from 1804 to 1806 the Governments of Spain and Portugal were occupied in preparing a final boundary treaty upon the basis of the Treaty of 1777, which they considered valid. These documents also prove that Portugal declared in 1802 that the conquests made in South America in the war of 1801 had no effect in virtue of the Treaty of Badajoz, which confirms the statements made in this Argument (page 183) and destroys all effect of the assertion made on behalf of Brazil that that war annulled the treaty, and that Portugal took lands of Spain in South America, for the King of Portugal returned these dominions to Spain.

VI.

The Treaty of 1777 and the "*Mapa de las Cortes*" are the rules accepted by all the Spanish Republics of South America for the determination of the boundary questions between themselves and between them and Brazil. (This Argument, page 177 *et seq.*)

VII.

The Empire of Brazil acknowledged the validity of the treaties between Spain and Portugal in its boundary disputes with the Argentine Republic, with New Granada and with Venezuela. Brazil also proposed that the same rule of law should govern, with some restrictions, in the settlement of its frontiers with Colombia. In the case of New Granada the Empire of Brazil expressly accepted the validity of the "*Mapa de las Cortes*" of 1749. The treaties of 1750 and 1777, and the "*Mapa de las Cortes*" incorporated in them, are the fundamental rules for the determination of this boundary question. (This Argument, page 145.)

There is circulated in Europe a book officially inspired by Brazil and in the preparation of which the Baron de Rio Branco assisted, who is commissioned by that country to defend its claims in this Arbitration. That official book "*Le Brésil*," says on page 3 that the boundary with Bolivia was determined by the treaty of March 27, 1867, "*en prenant à peu près pour base le traité de Saint Ildefonso* (1777)." On the same page it also adds:

> The frontier of Colombia is not settled; it is the beginning of the western frontier. There is on the North and South of the Equator, in the basins of the rivers Negro and Japura, a territory

comprising more than 250,000 square kilometers, which is claimed by both countries (Brazil and Colombia) and to some portions of which Venezuela, Ecuador and Peru also lay claim. On June 25, 1853, Brazil proposed to Colombia a treaty by which it offered certain concessions relative to the boundaries determined by the treaties of Madrid and San Ildefonso, but which were not accepted.

Colombia maintains the full application of the Treaty of 1777 and could not therefore accept the reservations referred to, but these citations show that Brazil recognized in the case of Bolivia, as in those of New Granada and Colombia, the validity of the Treaty of 1777.

VIII.

The boundary demarcation of 1759, annulled by the Treaty of 1761, was void from the beginning from inherent defects, since the Portuguese and Spanish Commissioners declared that they had deviated from the "*Mapa de las Cortes*" and from their Instructions, because they did not find upon the ground the rivers with the characteristics required by those documents. (This Argument, page 230 *et seq.*)

IX.

The international explorations ordered by the treaties of 1777 and of 1885 prove the errors of the Demarcators of 1759, since these explorations found the rivers in the places in which they were delineated by the "*Mapa de las Cortes*" of 1749, and having the characteristics attributed to them by the Instructions. (This Argument, page 250 *et seq.* and in the print page of the results of the Demarcation of 1891.)

X.

The Argentine Republic has possessed and still possesses the Territory up to the river drawn on the Map of 1749, and Brazil has acknowledged this, inviting the Argentine Government in 1882 to make an arrangement *in virtue of* said occupation. (This Argument, page 68 *et seq.* and page 103.)

XI.

The Argentine Republic has respected the *statu quo* of the Treaty of 1763 [Argentine Evidence, Vol. I, page 83, and Treaty of 1777,

Article 19] and has never advanced a step towards Brazil, while that country has persistently advanced its frontiers upon the territories of weaker nations on the Rio de la Plata, the Paraguay and the Uruguay, leaving the territory now under discussion like a wedge almost surrounded by these advances. This irregularity of the frontier is consequently the direct result and the natural fruit of the political aggressions of the Empire of Brazil, and it can have no bearing upon this Arbitration.

XII.

The colonies founded by Brazil in the Territory submitted to the Arbitrator were established by mistake, because neither the Argentine Republic nor Brazil knew the true position of the boundaries of this Territory. (This Argument, pages 203 to 204.)

XIII.

Brazil solemnly declared upon different occasions that it had not attempted to take possession of the Territory in dispute, that the colonies against which the Argentine Republic had protested in 1863 and in 1881 were located outside of this Territory, and that it is not favored by the *uti possidetis*. (See this Argument, page 199; and see also Argentine Evidence, Vol. III, Documents Nos. VI, VII, VIII.)

XIV.

The ignorance of both the Argentine and Brazilian governments in regard to the location of the rivers forming the eastern boundary of the Territory in controversy was clearly shown in the Treaty of 1885, which designated the river Chopin as the frontier on the East. According to this boundary the Brazilian colonies against which the Argentine Government protested appeared to be wholly or partially within the Territory of Brazil. (This Argument, page 203.)

XV.

The international exploration, however, carried out by virtue of the Treaty of 1885, showed the error of the two Governments regarding the eastern boundary of the Territory in dispute, which should run along the river San Antonio-Guazú of Oyarvide, that is to say the river to the eastward of the Chopim. (This Argument, page 204.)

XVI.

The mistake being perceived, both Governments declared that the Territory in dispute really extended as far as the said river San Antonio-Guazú of Oyarvide, and it was so stated in the Treaty of Arbitration of 1889. The Brazilian colonies in consequence were brought within the Territory in dispute. (This Argument, page 204, and Argentine Evidence, Vol. III, Document No. VIII.)

XVII.

This fact, proved by an official international exploration in 1889, cannot be invoked by Brazil as a basis for the application of the doctrine of *uti possidetis*. The universal doctrine, sustained by American writers and stated by Marshall, Upshur, and Wharton, is that "Discovery gave title to the Government by whose subjects or by whose authority it was made against all other European Governments, which title might be consummated by possession." (Wharton, Int. Law, sec. 2.) Spain discovered and possessed the Territory now submitted to the Arbitrator. The Argentine Republic continued that possession, and has maintained it up to the present time. The doctrine of *uti possidetis* therefore unquestionably favors that country.

XVIII.

The acts of possession of the Brazilians were without any purpose to take or assert possession of a disputed territory left without any one to care for it, but were under the supposition that they were upon their own territory, not questioned by the Argentine Republic. Such occupation by mistake of points upon the Territory submitted to the Arbitrator, taken in connection with the protests of the Argentine Republic and the declarations of Brazil of its lack of any intention to occupy Argentine territory, or question it, entirely take away from these acts all legal or international character. Argentine sovereignty cannot, therefore, be in any way prejudiced by them. (This Argument, page 199 *et seq.*)

SUMMARY OF THE BRAZILIAN ARGUMENTS AND THEIR BRIEF REFUTATION.

I.

"The Treaty of January 13, 1750, determined that each one of the contracting parties should hold what they then possessed, and tracing the frontier by the Pepiry or Pequiry and by the nearest river which flowed into the Yguazú, that which lay to the East of those two rivers was recognized as belonging to the Portuguese Government."

That is what the Argentine Government maintains. The discussion is as to which stream is the Pepiry or Pequiry. The "*Mapa de las Cortes*" fixes in the most clear and unquestionable manner as the boundary for the possession of the two Crowns the river by that name which empties into the Uruguay *above* the Uruguay-Pitá, in accord with the text of the Treaty of 1750. So that this allegation by Brazil is in support of the Argentine Argument.

II.

"The Demarcation of 1759 and 1760 was made in a regular manner and in entire conformity with the Treaty of 1750, with the Instructions sent for its execution, with the local traditions and with the map prepared and published by the Jesuits in 1722 and 1726."

It has been shown in this Argument that these conclusions are entirely incorrect and that these Demarcations were annulled by the two Crowns. (Page 160.) The only map prepared was that known as the "*Mapa de las Cortes*."

III.

"All the territory situated to the eastward of the rivers Pepiry-Guazú and San Antonio was, consequently, recognized as belonging to Portugal."

That is an error. The Demarcation which was ended in 1759 and 1761 was annulled, the Sovereigns of Spain and Portugal ordering the marks and other boundary signs to be destroyed, and declaring anew in absolute force the Treaty of Tordesillas. There was not, therefore, such a recognition of the sovereignty of Portugal over the Territory in dispute. (This Argument, page 160.)

IV.

"The Treaty of February 12, 1761, annulled that of 1750, but it could not invalidate the fact of the Portuguese possession, which did not arise therefrom, because it was prior to it, and the existence of which was recognized in the same. This fact is a subsisting one."

This sophistical conclusion is answered above. The Treaty of Tordesillas was a written law, recognized by the King of Portugal and ratified by the Treaty of 1761 concluded with Spain. In accordance with the provisions of that treaty thus ratified in express terms Spain possessed the disputed Territory in law and in fact. (This Argument, pages 17 to 67 and pages 105 to 121.) No possession can be invoked against the written title of a Sovereign who preserves and defends his rights, as Spain did in the Treaty of 1761, with the agreement of Portugal.

V.

"The Treaty of 1750 was not annulled because there was any error in the Demarcation made between the Uruguay and the Yguazú, neither for the reason that the two contracting parties changed their ideas as to their respective possessions or their agreement in regard to the direction of the frontier line. It was annulled on the part of Spain on account of the Colony of Sacramento, which the Portuguese never gave up, and by reason of the opposition of the Jesuits, who did not wish to abandon the Misiones ceded to Portugal."

Whatever may have been the cause of the nullity, it was declared by both Crowns. I have shown, nevertheless, in this Argument (page 228 *et seq.*) that the Demarcation of 1759, made in consequence of the Treaty of 1750, did have inherent vices which made it void. The Argument is, besides, ill-founded, because there was a great territorial difference between the Treaty of 1750 and that of 1777. By the former Portugal took the Eastern Misiones of Uruguay (now the Brazilian State of Rio Grande do Sul), while by the latter Spain preserved its vast possessions.

VI.

"The fact of a possession prior to 1750 existing, and there being no error in the Demarcation, any new adjustment which may be made should naturally agree with this, as a practical expression of the right of Portugal."

It is impossible dispassionately and without some preconceived purpose in view to maintain that the Demarcation of 1759 was not erroneous and badly executed, when scientifically and legally examined. But if Brazil admits that demarcation, which was a result, it must also admit its cause, the "*Mapa de las Cortes,*" which proves the error in that work.

VII.

"And on that, in fact, was founded the Treaty of October 1, 1777, reproducing the frontier of 1750, and respecting the possession then recognized; and, giving to the rivers which formed it the names placed by the respective Demarcators, it sanctioned the Demarcation by this fact."

This argument is favorable to the Argentine Republic. Brazil admits that the Treaty of 1777 reproduced the boundaries of the Treaty of 1750. It accepts the validity of both treaties. Consequently it accepts the application to the case of the "Mapa de las Cortes." The possessions that each of the Sovereigns desired to preserve, according to these boundaries and to the language of the treaties, were separated in that map by a red line. This follows the river Pepiry or Pequiry-Guazú maintained by the Argentine Republic. Consequently Brazil accepted that possession and recognized it as being that of Spain by the Treaty of 1750, confirmed by that of 1777, and as that of the Argentine Republic since its independence.

VIII.

"The intention of the two Courts in this respect was manifested in the Instructions sent for the execution of the Treaty of 1777 by the Government of Spain, by the Viceroy of the United Provinces of the Rio de la Plata and by the principal Spanish Commissioner to his subordinate."

The Viceroy of Buenos Aires, recently arrived at his post from Europe, was led into error by a Portuguese Demarcator. His instructions, instead of confirming the mistaken work of 1759 in the field, gave a third frontier between the rivers of that void Demarcation and those of the "*Mapa de las Cortes.*" The King of Spain refused to authorize this new entanglement, and the negotiator of the Treaty of 1777 was by a royal order charged in 1782 to prepare other instructions in which the text of the treaty was explained and judicial rules were given which were obligatory upon the Demarcators. The documents and commentaries at page 258 of this Argument prove this. In those instructions it was ordered that the line should be so traced as to save the pueblos, farms, and even the pasture fields of the Spaniards. The Territory submitted to the Arbitrator had groves of yerba trees, which were cultivated and put to commercial uses by the Spaniards of Corpus and San Xavier. The people of the latter place navigated the river Pepiry or Pequiry-Guazú. (See this Argument, page 232, "Argentine Evidence," Vol. I, page 527.)

IX.

"All that, therefore, by the Spanish Commissioners was done, who were appointed by virtue of the Treaty of 1777, showing that the frontier ran along the course of two rivers distinct from those designated in the treaty and entirely unknown, was void."

This is a violent and erroneous statement. The Demarcators of the Treaty of 1777 complied conscientiously with their duty in seeking the true river of the map of 1749, incorporated in the Treaty of 1750, and in that of 1777 by the express ratification which it made of the two preceding documents. Furthermore, the fifteenth Article of the Treaty of 1777 directed that in case of doubts a detailed study and examination should be made of the ground, accompanied by the maps, in order that the two Courts might definitely settle the matter. This was done by the Spanish and Portuguese Demarcators of 1783 to 1791, and far from being invalid their proceedings were perfectly legal, because they honestly applied the treaty.

X.

"And although the Spanish Government received and supported the idea of its Commissioners, desiring a substitution for the frontier clearly and solemnly adjusted, yet before this could be carried out it would be indispensable to secure the agreement of Portugal. It did not have that consent. Consequently the frontier stipulated in 1750 and confirmed in 1777, subsisted until the treaty of the latter date was annulled by the effect of the war of 1801."

The Argentine Republic takes the position that the frontier agreed upon in the treaties of 1750 and of 1777 now exists and is the boundary of its possessions. The Treaty of Badajoz put an end to the war of 1801. That war did not invalidate or annul the permanent treaties, according to the doctrine universally accepted and which is set forth in this Argument. The Treaty of Badajoz, far from modifying the boundaries agreed upon in 1750 and 1777 in South America, confirmed them in its third Article in an explicit manner, for Portugal being dominated by Spain the latter modified its boundaries then existing in Europe, adjudging in its own favor the town of Olivencia. In America and in Asia its boundaries remained intact, and the King of Portugal ordered his officials who had occupied dominions of Spain to evacuate them immediately and give them up to the Spanish officials. This is fully proved by the documents of the "Argentine Evidence," Vol. I, pages 419 to 435. If there had been any modifications or changes which invalidated boundaries theretofore agreed upon in solemn compacts the fact would have been stated in the Treaty of Badajoz, as in the case of Olivencia. Furthermore, it is a new contradiction by Brazil, which accepts the acts prior to 1801 which favor it and declares void those adverse to it.

XI.

"This annulment continued in consequence of the following facts:

The War of 1808.

The transfer of the Crown of Spain to Napoleon I and shortly afterwards to his brother.

The independence of the United Provinces of the Rio de la Plata, without previously renewing the Treaty of 1777 or making any other in its place.

The recognition of the independence of these Provinces on the part of Portugal without also any renewal of the same treaty or making any other suitable to the new circumstances.

The independence of Brazil proclaimed while the question of boundaries was still unsettled between Portugal and the said Provinces."

The documents presented regarding the events subsequent to 1801 and down to 1828 in the valley of the Rio de la Plata prove that Portugal recognized the boundaries in the treaties until the independence of Brazil in 1822. The Argentine Republic, emancipated in 1810, and Brazil, emancipated in 1822, cannot claim any other territories upon the map of the World than those which belonged to the Crowns from which they inherited them. These boundaries were those of the Portuguese map of 1749, approved in 1751 by both Courts, and incorporated into the treaties of 1750 and 1777. (This Argument, page 419 et seq.)

XII.

"The annulment of the Treaty of 1777 being therefore proved, as it is, upon which the Argentine Government bases its claim, the question then is determined by the *uti possidetis*, as a fact anterior to the Treaty of 1750, in which it was recognized and respected."

This may be answered by reference to paragraphs 7, 8, 9, 10 and 11 above. The Treaty of 1777 has been accepted by Brazil in this and other cases as the ratification of the treaty of 1750. (This Argument, page 170 et seq.) The Treaty of 1750 gave in the "*Mapa de las Cortes*" the boundaries of these possessions, and according thereto the Territory in dispute belongs to Spain and to the Argentine Republic.

XIII.

"The Argentine Government, morally obligated by the Treaty of 1857, cannot reject the *uti possidetis* as the basis of the right of Brazil, not only because it assented to the provisions of this treaty, but also because it officially recognized it by means of the declaration made by its Minister of Foreign Affairs in the explanations that he gave in the Chamber of Deputies when they discussed the said treaty of the Paraná."

The Treaty of 1857 does not morally obligate any one except Brazil. I have shown how the Argentine Congress rejected the Treaty in the form in which it had been negotiated by the Executive. The Congress substituted for it another, in which it declared that the boundary between the two countries ran along the course of the *eastern rivers*, by the rivers delineated in the "*Mapa de las Cortes*," and which this Argument defends. The legislative sanction, therefore, which was given to the treaty was against the claim of Brazil, and its Plenipotentiaries accepted it, yielding to the necessity of conciliating other interests. It was necessary to induce the Argentine Republic to make another treaty providing for the return of fugitive slaves, and this was a matter of vital importance for Brazilian industries. The Brazilian diplomats, Bocayuva and Lisbon, have demonstrated, as has been shown in this Argument [page 184 *et seq.*], that Brazil cannot invoke without prejudice to itself the Treaty of 1857. It has, furthermore, been examined in detail in the Memoir of the Minister of Foreign Relations of the Argentine Republic presented to the Arbitrator in Volume I of the "Argentine Evidence," page 643, and Vol. III, Doc. No. V.

XIV.

"Consequently the frontier between the Uruguay and the Yguazú runs, according to the Demarcation of 1759 and 1760, by the rivers Pepiry-Guazú and San Antonio (of Brazil)."

This is an unfounded affirmation. The Demarcators of 1759 were mistaken and their action is for that reason void. This invalidity was, moreover, declared in the Treaty of 1761. So that this boundary does not exist, nor has it ever existed in fact.

The argument is, however, indirectly favorable to the cause of the Argentine Republic. If Brazil claims that the Demarcation of 1759 was properly made and that it is valid, why refuse to recognize the validity of the treaty by virtue of which said Demarcation was carried out; that is to say, its legal foundation? If the effect is recognized then its cause must be acknowledged, and consequently the "*Mapa de las Cortes*," which was really the treaty itself reduced to a graphic form. The Treaty of 1750 was ratified and made valid so far as regards these boundaries by that concluded in 1777. At the same time Brazil admits that there is a law which applies to the case. That law favors the cause of the Argentine Republic.[1]

XV.

The "*Mapa de las Cortes*" is the map of South America published in 1775 by the chief cosmographer of the King of Spain, Don Juan de la Cruz Cano y Olmedilla.

This argument has been made by the chief of the Commissioners of Brazil engaged in the International Exploration of 1885-1891, the

---

[1] These fourteen arguments were presented to the Argentine Government in 1882 in the document entitled: "Contra-Memorandum," presented to the Arbitrator in Vol. II of the "Argentine Evidence," No. 6; and they were also published in the Memoir of the Minister of Foreign Affairs of the Empire of Brazil, for the year 1886, pages 25 *et seq.*, which is also presented to the Arbitrator. But other arguments have been also made in favor of the Brazilian cause which will be stated and explained.

Baron de Capanema, already referred to. It is another erroneous assertion. Olmedilla never was, as is known from public documents, the chief cosmographer of Spain. Nor was he ever a geographer, nor a traveller. He never went away from Madrid except to France, where he studied map-drawing. He was merely an artist, an engraver. His principal known works are beautiful engravings representing the costumes and apparel worn in Spain. This has been clearly shown and proved in an official publication made by the Argentine Government, which is presented to the Arbitrator, with the request that it be considered a part of this Argument upon this point, entitled "Arbitration on Misiones," printed in English. Two separate copies accompany the same.

Olmedilla, who was not a scientific man, delineated wrongly the situation of the river Pepiry or Pequiry-Guazú, because he could not have had before him the "*Mapa de las Cortes,*" that being a secret document, but the Spanish Government, perceiving the fact, ordered the plates of the map to be mutilated and withdrew it from sale.

XVI.

Brazil invokes in its favor numerous maps of Argentine origin in which the boundary is traced along the western rivers.

These maps have no value, although in some cases they bear the signatures of employees of the Argentine Government. This has been declared by the Argentine Government to that of Brazil in the Memorandum of January 30, 1883, presented to the Arbitrator ("Argentine Evidence," Vol. II, pamphlet No. 4, page 78) as follows:

All these publications, even when, as in some cases, they have been subsidized or aided by the Government, were edited under the direction and responsibility of their authors, who, more or less interested in this great question, have been led into errors which cannot be considered as in any way compromising the rights of the Republic.

This same assertion, that the Argentine Republic did not have official maps, was repeated in the Memoir of the Minister of Foreign Relations of that country in 1892 (Argentine Evidence, Vol. I, page 683) as follows:

To put an end to the frequent citations of maps, edited in the Argentine Republic or representing it, made by some diplomats as arguments against the rights and claims of the same, I will say that the National Government has emphatically declared that no official maps exist.

But it is not surprising that the authors of such maps should make mistakes when the two Governments fell into errors also and signed treaties which were inaccurate in their geographical terms, as in the case of that made in 1885, afterwards corrected upon the ground and by the provisions of the Arbitration Treaty of 1889, when the river *Chopin* was accepted as the Northeast boundary of the Territory instead of the *Yangada* or San Antonio-Guazú of Oyarvide. Brazil itself has officially declared its ignorance of the geography of *Misiones* in the "Contra Memorandum" presented (Argentine Evidence, Vol. II) and in the Memoir of the Minister of Foreign Affairs of 1886, before cited, page 29, in the following language:

> Considering that neither the rivers in question nor the zone in dispute included by them were ever at any time explored by Brazilians and Argentines with the purpose of verifying the surveys made by the Portuguese and Spanish in the preceding century.

The errors of the maps, therefore, can have no force as an argument either in law or in fact, since it is shown that the geographical facts were unknown, and neither government can determine these grave questions by private or theoretical surveys. Furthermore, the Argentine Republic denies that the maps in question have any authority, whatever may be the official title of the authors, used as a mere recommendation to give commercial value to their work. Some of the maps were dedicated to Argentine Presidents and other high personages by mere courtesy and without any action by them concerning such publications.

XVII.

Brazil claims that maps made by the Jesuits prior to 1749 can be substituted for the "*Mapa de las Cortes.*"

Some of these maps are anonymous and theoretical, made in Rome for the Company of Jesus for the administrative purposes of the order, that is to say merely in order to know the situation of its colonies without regard to political considerations. I present to the Arbitrator a complete study of these maps in the book "Arbitration on Misiones," cited in this Chapter, and also refer to the discussion of this subject in this book at pages 65 to 85. From the analysis of these maps cited by Brazil it appears that the greater part are favorable to the Argentine Republic, for they delineate the river Pepiry or Pequiry above the Uruguay-Pitá.

I present to the Arbitrator as a further proof of this argument, in the Portfolio of Maps of the "Argentine Evidence" the following maps, some of which bear an international character. They are cited with corresponding numbers, in the Portfolio of Maps.

No. 1. 1612. General Map of South America, by Rui Diaz de Guzman. (The original is preserved in the General Archives of the Indies, Seville.)

XVII Century.

Upon this map, which includes the country lying between Latitude 1° and 53° South, the river Pepiry is delineated as the most important tributary of the Uruguay, and a Pueblo of Spaniards and Indians near its headwaters.

No. 2. 1656. Map of Paraguay, Chile, etc., by the Geographer, N. Samson d'Abbeville.

This map delineates the Territory in dispute within the possessions of Spain, and the great distance from this Territory submitted to the Arbitrator to the Portuguese should be noted. This map is one of the respected authorities of that epoch.

No. 3. 1667. Map of Paraguay, or the Province of the Rio de la Plata, with adjacent regions. Tucuman et Sancta Cruz de la Sierra. Amsterdam. Gulielmus Blaeuw exundit.

The Original of this map dated in 1630 forms part of the large Atlas of Blaeuw, published in 1667. The preceding observation is also applicable to this map.

No. 4. 1667. *Paraquaria vulgo Paraguay cum adjacentibus*, by P. Vicentio Carrafa. Amsterdam. Joannes Blaeuw.

This map, by the most celebrated and respectable author of his time, is found in the Library of Congress, Washington, D. C. It delineates the Pepiry or Pequiry as the most important tributary of the Uruguay, confirming the official map of 1612. The river Pepiry or Pequiry has the same geographical position and direction as given to it by the

"*Mapa de las Cortes*" of 1749, confirmed by the international explorations of 1790 and 1891. [See the engraving herewith.]

XVIII Century.   No. 5.   1703.   Map of Paraguay, Chile, etc., by the Geographer Guillaume de L'Isle, of the Royal Academy of Sciences.

This map shows the Spanish Possessions and the Portuguese advances into the Government of the Rio de la Plata, always, however, leaving the Territory now in dispute very far from the Portuguese frontier and within the dominions of Spain.

No. 6.   1719.   Map of Paraguay, Chile, the Straits of Magellan, etc. Anonymous.

This shows the Spanish Possessions in the Provinces of Guayra and Uruguay and the advances of the Portuguese on the Littoral. The Territory now in dispute remains in the same situation, favorable to the Argentine Republic, as in the preceding map.

No. 7.   1733.   *Typus Geographicus Chile, Paraguay, Fretti Magallanici*, etc., by P. Alfonsos d'Ovalle.

Like the maps of 1703 and 1719, it indicates the Spanish Possessions and the advances of the Portuguese. The Territory now in question remains very distant from the Portuguese frontier and under the dominion of Spain.

No. 8.   1749.   Map of the *Misiones* of the Company of Jesus, on the rivers, etc., by Padre Joseph Quiroga.

In this map the red line which marks the boundary of the Misiones on the East includes the territory within one degree of longitude up the stream of the Uruguay above the point of the junction of that river and the Uruguay-Mini, and passes by the headwaters of the Ygnazú. Carrying the boundary to the East of the sources of the Ygnazú, as it is traced by Padre Quiroga, who was a high official of the Jesuits and settled in their possessions in the Misiones of the zone now in question, would result in giving the Spaniards the right to claim lands to the eastward of this river Pepiry or Pequiry.

No. 9.   1749.   Map of the Confines of Brazil, with the Lands of the Crown of Spain in South America. Taken from the Archives of the Minister of Foreign Affairs, Paris.

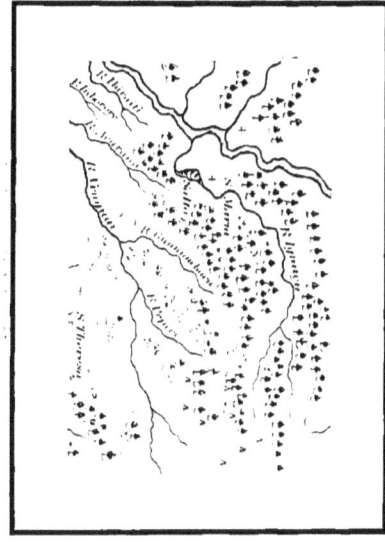

This is a copy of the "*Mapa de las Cortes*," an integral part of the Treaty of 1750, and was to serve as the base and guide for the Demarcators.

No. 10. 1749. Apocryphal Copy of the same map above.

This is the map found inserted in the Portuguese collection of Treaties, by Borges de Castro. Its differences with the true "*Mapa de las Cortes*" have already been referred to in this Argument, page 139.

No. 11. 1751. Map of the Confines of Brazil with the Lands of Spain in South America. Archives of Lisbon, "*Mapa de las Cortes.*"

No. 12. 1751. Photographic copy of the True "*Mapa de las Cortes*," which served for making the Treaty of 1750, existing in the Archives of the Minister of State, Madrid.

This map has on its back the Protocol with which the negotiators of the Treaty of 1750 authorized it. It is the copy of that map which was preserved in the Archives of Spain.

No. 13. 1752. Map of the Confines of Brazil with the Lands of the Crown of Spain in South America.

The original of this map exists in Lisbon, in the possession of the Conde de Verdigueira, as stated in the note at the foot of page 215, Vol. I, "Argentine Evidence," and this Argument page 154.

No. 14. 1762. Map of Paraguay, Chilo, Magellan Land, etc. By S. Robert de Vangondy, etc.

No. 15. 1787. "*Plano Corografico*" of the reconnoissances connected with the demarcation of Article 8 of the Preliminary Treaty of Boundaries, of October 11, 1777, carried out by the second Spanish and Portuguese subdivisions, in order to remove the doubts which had arisen between the respective Commissioners.

The photographic copy presented was taken from the original in the Archives of the Department of State in Madrid. This map of 1777 delineates the river Pepiry or Pequiry-Guazú in the same location as the maps of 1612, 1667 and 1749, presented.

No. 16. 1788. Photographic Copy, reduced size, of the Map of Varela y Ulloa and of Veiga Cabral de Camara, taken from the original in the Archives of the Department of State at Madrid.

No. 17. 1788. Photographic Copy of a portion of the preceding map which shows the river Uruguay.

No. 18. 1791. Map of Oyarvide.

No. 19. 1796. Photographic copy, reduced size, of the map of the Lieut.-Gen. Francisco Requena, taken from the original in the Archives of the Department of State at Madrid.

No. 20. 1796. Copy of a portion of the preceding map.

Nos. 21, 22, 23. 1796. Facsimiles of three maps from the Atlas of Feliz de Azara, showing the basin of the Paraná, that of the Paraguay, and a special chart relating to the question of boundaries with Brazil.

XIX Century.

No. 24. 1802. Autograph plan, by Cabrer, of the Territory in dispute.

No. 25. 1853. Spherical chart of the Argentine Confederation and the Republics of Uruguay, Paraguay, made in 1802, by José Maria Cabrer, and published in Paris in 1853.

No. 26. 1863. Map of the Republic of Paraguay. Dedicated and presented to his Majesty, Napoleon I, Emperor of the French by the Count Lucien de Brayer, Consul of France in Paraguay.

No. 27. 1877. Official map of the Province of Corrientes.

This is the map cited in this Argument, page 91.

No. 28. 1887. General map of the Argentine Republic, published by the eminent Peruvian geographer, Don Mariano Felipe Paz Soldan.

This map contains the departmental divisions of the *Territory of Misiones*.

No. 29. 1887. Joint Boundary Commission. General plan of the mouth of the river Pepiry-Guazú (of 1759) in the river Uruguay. Scale 1 : 2,000.

No. 30. 1887. Joint Boundary Commission. Partial plan of the mouth of the river Pepiry of 1759. Scale 1 : 500.

This plan signed by the Argentine and Brazilian Commissioners shows that there was no island but only a bank of stones somewhat below the mouth of that river.

No. 31. 1887. Joint Boundary Commission. Profiles of the mouth of the river Pepiry.

No. 32. 1887. Joint Boundary Commission. First Partial Plan of the river Uruguay. Scale 1 : 50,000.

No. 33. 1887. Joint Boundary Commission. Second Partial Plan of the river Uruguay. Scale 1 : 50,000.

This plan shows the mouth of the river Pepiry-Guazú, with the wooded island in front and the reef within its mouth.

No. 34. 1887. Joint Boundary Commission. Plan of the mouth of the river Pepiry-Guazú or Chapecó, with the longitudinal and transverse profiles of the island of the Pequiry-Guazú. Scale 1 : 5,000.

No. 35. 1887. Joint Boundary Commission. Partial plan of the upper part of the river Pequiry-Guazú. Scale 1 : 50,000.

No. 36. 1887. Partial plan of the lower part of the river Pequiry-Guazú. Scale 1 : 50,000.

No. 37. 1887. Joint Boundary Commission. Copy of the plans of the rivers Pequiry-Guazú and Chopin, made by assistants of the Brazilian Commission.

No. 38. 1887. Joint Boundary Commission. Plan of the Headwaters of the river known in Brazil as the "Chopin." Scale 1 : 20,000.

No. 39. 1887. Joint Boundary Commission. Plan of the rivers Pequiry-Guazú and San Antonio-Guazú of Oyarvide. Scale 1 : 10,000.

No. 40. 1887–8. Joint Boundary Commission. Partial plan of the line dividing the waters of the rivers Chopin, Pequiry-Guazú and San Antonio-Guazú of Oyarvide. Scale 1 : 20,000.

No. 41. 1889. Joint Boundary Commission. Plan of the lands included between the principal headwaters of the rivers Pequiry-Guazú or Chapecó and the San Antonio-Guazú de Oyarvide or Yangada. Scale 1 : 10,000.

No. 42. 1889. Joint Boundary Commission. Plan of the mouth of the river San Antonio-Guazú of Oyarvide or Yangada. Scale 1 : 5,000.

No. 43. 1887. Joint Boundary Commission. First partial plan of the river Chopin. Scale 1 : 50,000.

No. 44. 1887. Joint Boundary Commission. Second partial plan of the river Chopin. Scale 1 : 50,000.

No. 45. 1887. Joint Boundary Commission. First partial plan of the river Y-Guazú. Scale 1 : 50,000.

No. 46. 1887. Joint Boundary Commission. Second partial plan of the river Y-Guazú. Scale 1 : 50,000.

No. 47. 1888. Joint Boundary Commission. The river Pepiry-Guazú or Pepiry of 1759. Scale 1 : 50,000.

No. 48. 1888. Joint Boundary Commission. Plan of the lands between the headwaters of the river San Antonio of 1759 and the river Pequiry of 1759. Scale 1 : 50,000.

No. 49. 1888. Joint Boundary Commission. Sketch of the headwaters of the Pequiry-Guazú (Pepiry of 1759) and the San Antonio (of 1759), showing the division of the waters and the highest lands.

No. 50. 1888. Joint Boundary Commission. River San Antonio of 1759. Scale 1 : 50,000.

No. 51. 1889. Joint Boundary Commission. General plan of the Territory in dispute between the Argentine Republic and Brazil. Scale 1 : 250,000. Signed by the Commissioners of the two countries.

No. 52. 1893. Official plan of the grants of land made by the Argentine Government within the Territory in dispute.

By a review of these maps and plans the Arbitrator will notice that the official maps, French, Peruvian, Paraguayan, Uruguayan, English and Jesuit, all show that the claims of the Argentine Republic are well founded. They bear universal testimony to the justice of the Argentine cause.

Respectfully submitted.

ESTANISLAO S. ZEBALLOS,
Envoy Extraordinary and Minister Plenipotentiary
of the Argentine Republic

JOSIAH QUINCY,
of Counsel.

WASHINGTON, D. C., *February 10, 1894.*

INDEX TO THE ARGENTINE ARGUMENT.

PART FIRST.

Page.
Importance of this International Dispute. Geographical View of the Disputed Territory, . . . 5

PART SECOND.

1. Possession and Jurisdiction of Spain in the Territory submitted to the Arbitrator. 1500–1810, . . 17
Recognition of the Sovereignty of Spain by Brazil, . . 62
2. Possession and Jurisdiction of the Argentine Republic in the Territory submitted to the Arbitrator. 1810–1893, 68

PART THIRD.

Aggressions of the Portuguese on the Territory of Spain. 1596 1810, . . 107

PART FOURTH.—THE PUBLIC LAW OF THE CASE.

1. Treaties between Spain and Portugal. 1493–1777, . . 125
2. Treaties between the Argentine Republic and Brazil. 1810 1890, ... 177
The Demarcations. 1753 to 1791. 1885 to 1891, 226

PART FIFTH.

Pretended Possession by the Empire of Brazil of the Territory in Dispute, ... 293
Summary of the Argentine Arguments, . . . 315
Summary of the Brazilian Arguments and their Brief Refutation, 320
List of Maps, . . . 329